ESSENTIAL
WORLD HISTORY

Henry Brun

AMSCO

A MSCO SCHOOL PUBLICATIONS, INC.

315 Hudson Street, New York, N.Y. 10013

Contributing Author, Document-Based Questions: Margaret Franson

REVIEWERS:
Christine V. Paynton, Loma Vista Adult Center/Mt. Diablo Adult Education, California

Teresa Prober, Instructor, Adult High School Program, Fayetteville Technical College, Fayetteville, North Carolina; former teacher, Flora Mcdonald Academy, Red Springs, North Carolina

Paul Tremel, Director, Adult High School, Seminole Community College, Sanford, Florida

Composition: *Publishing Synthesis, Ltd.*

New Maps, Timelines, Charts: *Hadel Studio*

Cover design: *Meghan J. Shupe.* *Photo of Dover Castle, Dover, England, from Picturequest/Brand X*

Interior design: *Merrill Haber*

Photo Research: *Tobi Zausner*

Literary Permissions: *Angela Calk*

Research Assistance: *Wilfredo Morales*
          Ilana Petraru

Please visit our Web site at:
www.amscopub.com

When ordering this book, please specify: **R 021 P**
or ESSENTIAL WORLD HISTORY

ISBN-10: 1-56765-636-6
ISBN-13: 978-1-56765-636-6

NYC Item 56765-636-5

Printed in the United States of America

1   2   3   4   5   6   7   8   9   11   10   09   08   07   06

PREFACE

Essential World History is designed to provide students with a readable and enjoyable discovery of the development of civilizations and cultures in Asia, Africa, Europe, the Middle East, and the Americas. From the first efforts of early humans to use fire and make weapons and tools to the creation of the Internet by modern humans, the many ways in which people have responded to their environments are described. As these human experiences are revealed, students will learn the cause and effect relationships that underlie the rise and fall of nations, kingdoms, and empires and the coming of wars and revolutions. Students will read about the great achievements of our human race and the forces that threaten us with destruction.

Through this study of historic events, personalities, and forces, students will discover the patterns of human experience that have shaped the present and may illuminate the future.

Essential World History contains the following features:

- **Content Richness.** World regions and the civilizations that developed in them are comprehensively covered. Contemporary crises and dangers are traced from their historic origins. World leaders and key figures are presented in their historical contexts.

- **Standards Based.** The text has been developed in conformity to the curricular and assessment requirements common to several states.

- **Test Preparation.** To assist students to develop the skills required for standardized and nonstandardized examinations, a wide range of question and exercise types appear within and at the conclusion of each chapter in the form of Chapter Reviews. Multiple-choice questions; map, chart, and graph interpretation exercises; chronology exercises; and document-based questions (DBQs) are strategically placed throughout the book.

- **Illustrations.** Photographs, drawings, posters, cartoons, and maps illuminate and clarify important topics and serve to help students develop their interpretive skills.

- **Reference Section.** Regional maps, a glossary, Internet links, and an index, all located in the back of the book, will provide students help in understanding the material in the rest of the book.

CONTENTS

MAPS

Early Cultures and Civilizations

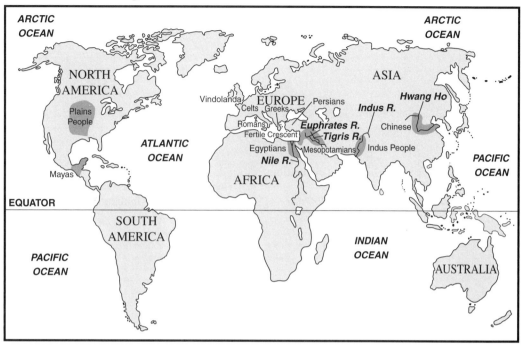

B.C. and A.D.

The system of dating events that we now use was invented by a Christian monk in the year 532. To him, the most important year was the one in which he thought Christ had been born. He called this year "A.D. 1." The initials "A.D." stand for the Latin phrase *anno Domini,* which means "in the year of our Lord." The monk said that all dates since the birth of Christ should be written with the initials "A.D." Thus, for example, a historian might write that Christianity was made the official religion of the Roman Empire in A.D. 395. This event occurred 394 years after the year A.D. 1.

Dates for events before the birth of Christ should, according to the monk, be written with the initials "B.C." These initials mean "before Christ." Thus, the year before A.D. 1 was 1 B.C. The year before that was 2 B.C., and so on. In discussing dates that occurred before A.D. 1, the higher the number, the earlier the date. Today, writers often drop the initials "A.D." but never "B.C." If there are no initials accompanying dates, we assume that writers are referring to events since the birth of Christ.

In some cultures and countries today, it is more common to use "B.C.E." instead of "B.C." and "C.E." instead of "A.D." "B.C.E." stands for "before the Common Era," while "C.E." stands for "Common Era."

"Here's another one . . . 'Single male into hunting and making arrows seeks female with gathering skills.'"

UNIT I

AN INTRODUCTION TO WORLD HISTORY

CHAPTER 1
Studying Cultures and Civilizations

Social scientists' task is to study the world and its cultures and civilizations. They seek to determine how these began and developed, what they were like in the past, what they are like at present, and what they might be like in the future. Among the social scientists' tools are the disciplines of history, geography, economics, and political science. Allied to these disciplines are archeology, anthropology, and sociology. How social scientists use these tools to discover and explore the world will be described in this chapter.

HISTORY

History is the story of humanity's growth and development, its passage through time. History is found in the written records of the past. These records tell us about humanity's achievements and failures, and more simply, what people have said, thought, and done as they developed their many cultures and civilizations. We study history in order to understand better how our own society and other societies came to be what they are.

Historians must be skilled at investigation and analysis. Take, for example, Dr. Robin Birley, an archeologist and historian. Dr. Birley has spent decades excavating a Roman fortification in northern Britain. The Romans built Vindolanda in the first century A.D. and occupied it until about the year 400. In 1972, Dr. Birley began finding the remains of writing tablets. On these wooden panels, the Romans had written personal letters, reports about the strength and condition of their garrison (military post), and accounts of food and supplies. Dr. Birley and his assistants were able to read the Latin script by photographing the tablets with infrared film. They then had to interpret this cursive script, which is a forerunner of our modern handwriting.

By 2003, approximately 1,900 writing tablets had been unearthed. For Dr. Birley and other historians, they create a picture of life on the northern frontier of the Roman Empire nearly 2,000 years ago. Historians in many countries can now draw conclusions about how these ancient Romans lived and worked. Although scholars may disagree and interpret Dr. Birley's findings differently, their knowledge of the Roman Empire and its people has been increased. As time goes on, improvements in technology and investigative techniques will provide more information. Newer and different conclusions about the Roman Empire will be reached. In other words, historical interpretations vary from one period to another.

The tablets discovered by Dr. Birley are original writings of the ancient Romans, or *primary sources* of information. Historians use such primary sources to help them write their interpretations and views of the past. For example, in 1997, Anthony Birley, Dr. Birley's brother, published a biography of the Roman emperor Hadrian. This book, written by a modern historian rather than by an ancient Roman, is a *secondary source* of information. Historians often use combinations of primary and secondary sources to reach conclusions or interpretations that are published in reports, articles, books, and textbooks.

In addition to written records, historians use oral histories. In many societies of the past, and a few in the modern world, history was memorized and transmitted by word of mouth from one generation to another. Certain skilled persons were trained to do this. In West Africa, these oral historians were known as *griots*. In Western Europe, they were known as bards or *skalds*.

Whether oral or written, the basic function of history is to help us better understand the past and present, and possibly, to glimpse the future.

TIME FRAMES AND PERIODIZATION

In the year A.D.1324, King Mansa Musa made a pilgrimage to the holy city of Mecca. A dedicated Muslim, Mansa Musa ruled the great West African empire of Mali. For generations, the king's long journey was well remembered. He was accompanied by 60,000 people. His caravan carried 24,000 pounds of gold loaded on 80 camels. In addition, 500 servants carried about six pounds of gold each. Few kings of the Middle Ages (A.D. 500–1500) could display such wealth.

1. Time Frames.   During the Middle Ages, three great empires—Ghana, Mali, and Songhai—flourished in West Africa. Great things were also happening in other parts of the world in this *time frame* or *period*. Germanic kingdoms replaced the Roman Empire. The Byzantine Empire dominated Asia Minor (Turkey), the Balkan region of southeastern Europe, North Africa, and much of the Middle East. The power of Europe's Christian rulers was threatened by the armies of Islam. They swept out of Arabia to create a Muslim Empire in the lands taken from the Byzantines and others. The Mayas, builders of great cities in Central America, were conquered by the Toltecs. During the same period, the Aztecs of central Mexico put together a great empire. Significant change also came to East Asia: Muslims conquered India, and Mongols took control of China.

It is important to understand that the exciting Middle Ages, or medieval period, is only one of the many time frames into which historians divide human history. During the Classical Age (500 B.C.–A.D. 500), for example, many civilizations contributed to the development of humankind. Two of these—the Roman Empire in Europe and the Han Empire in China—developed political, economic, and cultural systems that greatly influenced other parts of the world.

Classical Age

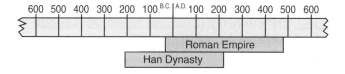

2. Periodization.   This is a tool used by historians to help us understand how the cultures and civilizations that existed during the same time frame interacted. It is also a means of expanding our knowledge of any period by examining important developments in different regions.

It is exciting to learn the details of Mansa Musa's fabulous pilgrimage to Mecca in 1324. We can appreciate this event better if we discover more about the period in which the journey was made. What was happening elsewhere in Africa and other parts of the world? How and why do historians distinguish one historical period from another? Usually, there are great themes or patterns of political, cultural, and economic development and change occurring in a particular period. This theme or pattern makes the period different from others. For example, the Stone Age (500,000 to 5,000 years ago) is divided into the Paleolithic (500,000 to 10,000 years ago), the Mesolithic (10,000 to 8,000 years ago), and the Neolithic (8,000 to 5,000 years ago) periods.

During each of these periods, people responded to their environments is particular ways. The greatest change came during the Neolithic period, or New Stone Age. It was then that people learned to grow their food, instead of hunting or gathering it. The beginning of agriculture made possible the first towns and villages. Some of them became the first cities. Every period of time has patterns of development. Often, perhaps usually, they are seen only when historians look back at the events of the period.

CONFLICTING INTERPRETATIONS

Historians and archeologists often disagree about the conclusions to be drawn from the interpretation of evidence.

1. Evidence of Rome's Founding? In May 2005, Dr. Andrea Carandini, one of Italy's most famous archeologists, discovered a palace buried beneath the ruins of the Roman Forum. Dr. Carandini stated his belief that the palace belonged to the first king of ancient Rome, whose name might have been Romulus. According to legend, the city of Rome was founded by twin brothers—Romulus and Remus—around 750 B.C.

Other scholars were skeptical. They claimed that Dr. Carandini lacked sufficient proof that the palace is linked to the founding of Rome. Some cited problems of interpretation of evidence that would take 20 to 30 years to be properly analyzed.

2. A Mother Culture of Mesoamerica? Archeologists also disagree over the question of how much influence the Olmecs, a 3,000-year-old civilization of Mexico and Central America, had in the shaping of other Mesoamerican civilizations. Some scholars regard the Olmecs as the creators of the first civilization in the region and the "mother culture" of other Mesoamerican cultures that later arose in the region. Others disagree, claiming that the Olmecs and neighboring groups all shared ideas about religion, art, and political structure.

In February 2005, Dr. Jeffrey Blomster of George Washington University issued a report describing his investigation of evidence related to the distribution through Central America of Olmec pottery. Dr. Blomster stated that the evidence proved the Olmecs were spreading their culture throughout the region. He claimed that the appearance of Olmec-made pottery in so many Mesoamerican locations indicated that the Olmecs had developed the dominant culture of the region. Other Mesoamericans imitated Olmec style and form, he said.

This conclusion was challenged by other scientists. They claimed that although Olmec accomplishments were remarkable, other cultures in the area were also making important contributions to the development of Mesoamerican civilization. To these scientists, the Olmecs were a "sister culture" of surrounding cultures that independently developed styles similar to those of the Olmecs.

The historian's task is to formulate theories and conclusions that can be supported by the weight of evidence.

ANTHROPOLOGY

The study of how humans have developed biologically and culturally is pursued in two related areas of scientific research—*physical anthropology* and *cultural anthropology*.

1. Physical Anthropology.   A 2004 study of a fossil thighbone has shown that a type of prehuman may have been able to walk upright on two legs as early as 6 million years ago. A team of researchers led by anthropologist Robert Eckhardt of Pennsylvania State University analyzed CAT scans of a fragment of the left femur of *Orrorin tugenensis*. The remains of this chimpanzee-size creature were discovered in Kenya in 2000. According to Dr. Eckhardt, the CAT scans reveal that the internal structure of the bone is considerably closer to that of an upright, two-legged human than to the leg bone of a chimpanzee. Although the anthropologists do not know what *Orrorin* looked like, Dr. Eckhardt believes that gradual development of structural changes to the leg bones of this type of prehistoric creature would have been accompanied by behavioral changes. He and his team regard this analysis as solid evidence for *bipedalism* (walking on two legs) dating to 6 million years ago. This analysis strengthens the belief of some scientists that *Orrorin* is an ancestor of modern humans. Other anthropologists, however, point to features like *Orrorin*'s teeth, which are more apelike, as evidence that the species may be more closely related to the chimpanzees.

Dr. Eckhardt and other scientists who study the physical characteristics of early peoples are physical anthropologists.

2. Cultural Anthropology. Anthropologist Paul Sillitoe of Durham University, England, has done extensive fieldwork in Papua New Guinea. In 1983, he researched the use of stone tools by the highland people of the Mount Hagan region. New Guinea is a large island north of Australia. It is the last place on Earth where substantial populations still depend on stone tools. Until the 1930's, the Mount Hagan region was believed to be uninhabited. Then gold prospectors and government officers discovered more than a million people living there. Dense settlements of thatched houses and vegetable cultivations were found along valley sides. Their owners were using stone tools and agricultural methods extending back over 9,000 years. Their ancestors, along with the peoples of ancient Mesopotamia (Iraq)

Chinese archeologists find partially preserved bodies of people from as long ago as 4,000 years in Xinjiang Province, China.

and Mesoamerica (Central America), were among the first humans to practice farming.

Sillitoe's research enabled him to discover that the stone ax blades used by the New Guinea highlanders were very similar to those used during the Stone Age in Europe. The ax blades were made by hand—a slow, laborious process—from stones taken from local quarries and streambeds. Stone axes were regarded by the New Guinea highlanders as wealth. They were traded throughout the region and presented as gifts at social events such as marriage, birth, and death. They were also used as compensation to settle disputes.

This cultural anthropological study led to a better understanding of a sophisticated technology that has long been extinct elsewhere in the world.

SOCIOLOGY

The study of the formation of human societies and social organizations, their structure, and the interaction and behavior of people in organized groups is called *sociology*.

David Émile Durkheim (1858–1917), a French scholar, was one of the founders of sociology. He created one of the first scientific approaches to the study of social life in modern societies.

In his 1893 work *The Division of Labor in Society*, Durkheim examined the ways social order was maintained in different types of societies. He focused on the division of labor and how it differed between traditional (e.g., agricultural) societies and modern (industrial) societies. Durkheim argued that in traditional societies everyone does more or less the same type of work and has many things in common. Well-regulated behavior helps to hold the society together. Subsistence farmers, for example, live in communities that are self-sufficient and knit together by a common heritage and common work. In modern societies, however, the highly complex division of labor results in a different kind of solidarity. Different specializations in employment and social roles create dependencies that tie people to one another. People must rely on others to provide most of the goods (food, clothing, etc.) and services (transportation, communication, medical treatment, etc.) that they need. Workers earn money to pay for these needed goods and services.

Durkheim also theorized that the increasing division of labor makes modern society more complex. For some people, social interactions become more confusing, leading to an eventual

American sociologist Gao Shan *(left)* talks to the press in 2001 after a private meeting with U.S. Representative Shelia Jackson Lee of Texas *(right)*. Gao Shan had been arrested while working in China, was held in prison there for five months, and then was released.

breakdown in the standards and rules that regulate their behavior. For such people, society becomes more impersonal. They feel rootless and unrelated to society. Durkheim called this state *anomie*. People in a state of anomie are likely to engage in negative or destructive types of behavior, especially suicide.

Durkheim believed that people have a degree of attachment to their social groups (religious group, fellow workers, team, club, etc.). He called this *social integration*. Abnormally low levels of social integration can disorganize society. To prevent this from happening, he proposed the formation of professional groups to encourage solidarity among adults.

In books such as *Elementary Forms of the Religious Life* (1912), Durkheim examined the role of religion and mythology in shaping the worldviews and personalities of people in certain non-Western societies.

Through his pioneering work in sociology, Émile Durkheim gave social scientists another set of tools to use in their study of the human experience.

GEOGRAPHY: THE PHYSICAL ENVIRONMENT

People's lives have always been shaped by their physical surroundings. Rivers, lakes, oceans, forests, deserts, mountains, and other natural features affect how and where people live and work. These natural surroundings are their *environment*.

Other factors, such as climate and soil, are important parts of this environment. They too affect the ways in which people live and work. Geography is the study of physical environments and how people live in these environments. The following examples will help make clear the relationship between people's lives and their environments.

Many thousands of years ago, during a time called the Ice Age, the northern part of the world was covered with snow, ice, and dense forests. The air was cold and the ground was hard. People had to struggle to survive in this harsh environment. They spent almost all of their time and energy hunting animals and gathering roots and berries. These hunters and gatherers were wanderers. They did not settle on the land or farm it.

People living in the southern part of the world had an easier way of life. These early people lived in the great river valleys of Southwest Asia (the Middle East), India, and China. The warm climate and fertile soil were good for farming. The people used the water from great rivers such as the Tigris, Euphrates, Nile, Indus, and Hwang Ho to grow crops and raise animals. They used the clay from the riverbanks to make building bricks for shelter. Settlements arose. Villages grew into towns and cities.

The relationship between environment and society is one of the essential elements of geography. Location is another. Understanding the physical layout of the world, especially its division into regions, is an important tool for understanding the world. The absolute location of each region, as determined by latitude and longitude, can enable us to find any place on a globe or map.

The physical and human systems found in each region are also parts of the study of geography. Atmospheric, geological, and biological forces produce landforms, climate, and animal and vegetable life. Human systems include the populations in each region and their cultural, economic, and political systems.

The study of geography enables us to use these interrelated elements to learn about the world by viewing it both physically and culturally.

ECONOMICS

Economics has been called the study of how people satisfy their wants and needs. One of the basic facts of economic life is *scarcity*—there is not enough of everything to satisfy all our wants and needs. Economics is also the study of supply and demand. Economics tells us how the people in a society obtain *goods and services*. Everything we use or produce in our lives may be regarded as either a good or a service. Goods, such as food and clothing, and services, such as education and medical care, are demanded by consumers and provided by producers. Our basic demands, or needs, are for food, shelter, clothing, and security. Beyond these needs, we may require or want a variety of other goods and services, ranging from education to vacations to entertainment. Goods and services that are in short supply or that are scarce or difficult to produce will be more expensive than ones that are abundant or easily produced.

The quantity and quality of the goods and services that we obtain and use depend on our income. Most income comes as payment for the work that we do. Surplus income—the money remaining after we purchase goods and services—can be deposited in a savings bank or invested in securities. Stocks, bonds, mutual funds, and other financial instruments are shares in businesses. By purchasing these shares, we earn additional income in the form of dividends, interest payments, and profits from the sale of securities.

1. The Role of Government in the Economy.   Just as every person must make economic decisions about the kind of employment to seek and what to do with the income earned from this work, government too must engage in economic decision making. Because the operation of a nation's economy is so important to the well-being of its people, a government must periodically regulate the nation's economy. In the United States, for example, the Federal Reserve Board raises interest rates for borrowing money when it wishes to encourage people to save rather than invest their excess income. The board takes this action to prevent *inflation*, which is a rapid increase in the prices of goods and services. This was done in late 2004, when a series of small interest rate increases was begun.

Another form of economic decision making by a government is to seek to increase or decrease the value of its currency (money) against the value of the currency of other nations. A government takes such action to make it easier for its citizens to do business with the citizens of other nations. In January 2004, the trade deficit of the United States had climbed to a record $43.1 billion. Imports from China flooded U.S. markets, while American exports were hurt by declining demand in Europe and other parts of the world. In response, the U.S. Treasury Department allowed the dollar to weaken against European and Asian currencies throughout 2004. The weakened dollar made U.S. goods and services less expensive to foreign buyers. This encouraged U.S. exports.

Individuals, businesses, and governments must apply critical-thinking skills in order to make informed and well-reasoned economic decisions. They must gather information and think carefully about alternative courses of action.

2. Types of Economic Systems.   Different types of economic systems are in operation throughout the world. In *traditional economies*, people are concerned mainly with obtaining food, clothing, shelter, and other necessities. They usually rely on farming, herding, hunting, or fishing to satisfy their needs. They produce only as much as they need to survive, with few if any surpluses. In contrast, *command economies* operate at the will of the government. The government controls industry and agriculture and decides what goods will be produced, how those goods will be made, and the prices that consumers will have to pay for them. The government of a command economy also sets the standard of living for its people, deciding how much workers will enjoy privileges such as comfortable housing and luxury products. China, which has been ruled by the Communist Party since 1949, was for many years an example of a command economy. This changed dramatically in the late 20th and early 21st centuries as China's leaders allowed more private ownership of businesses and foreign investment.

In contrast, *market economies* operate in response to the laws of supply and demand and to market forces such as the scarcity of goods and resources. Motivated by the desire to earn profits, individuals and business make the decisions about what products will be made, bought, and sold. The United States has a market economy. The New York Stock Exchange and the giant shopping malls throughout the country are the best-known symbols of America's market economy.

The world economy changed dramatically by the 21st century. The process of *globalization*—the reduction of barriers to the movement of goods and services, workers, and money among nations—has led to increased economic interdependence. Powerful multinational corporations conduct business operations in many countries. Regional organizations and agreements, such as the European Union (EU) and the North American Free Trade Agreement (NAFTA), have been created to increase trade and economic cooperation among member nations. The EU includes a central European bank, a parliament, and a single European currency. By 2002, the euro had been adopted by 12 nations. In China and elsewhere in Asia, and in Latin America, the growth of market economies resulted in more purchasing power and a higher standard of living for millions of people. The World Bank, the

Soviet collective farm, 1963. Residents view posters calling for increased production of milk and other agricultural products.

International Monetary Fund (IMF), and the World Trade Organization (WTO) regulate the global economy, respond to crises, and provide money for economic development. The world's most powerful industrial nations have formed the Group of Eight (G-8). Their top leaders meet annually to coordinate policies and keep the global economy healthy.

Economists study the policies of these organizations, as well as economic activities such as banking, taxation, labor, trade, and government regulation. The effects of globalization on people and nations have become very important to economists.

POLITICAL SCIENCE

People developed laws and customs about how to live with one another and with other groups. These laws and customs became the roots of government. Political scientists study the different forms of government and the ways citizens relate to them.

1. Types of Governments.   The physical environment affected how people were governed. In Southwest Asia, India, and China, people living in the river valleys sailed the rivers and built the roads needed to trade goods and ideas with one another. These rivers and roads also made it possible for strong rulers to bring many people and large areas of land under their control.

Kingdoms arose, which in time grew into mighty empires. The pharaohs of Egypt, the rulers of India, and the emperors of China governed great kingdoms and empires because even their outer boundaries could be reached by soldiers and administrators.

In Europe, a different physical environment produced different kinds of government. In Greece, for example, communities were separated by rugged hills and mountains. Good soil for farming was limited. The few fertile patches were scattered. An uneven coastline, cut by bays and inlets, further divided the land. People living in a small farming or fishing village were isolated from other villages.

Small groups of warriors in hilltop forts defended the villages against enemies. Local rulers controlled only the small areas within easy reach of those forts. Thus, the Greeks developed independent city-states instead of great kingdoms.

At first, these city-states were *monarchies*—they were ruled by kings. In time, some of the Greeks wanted the citizens to have more political power. A new form of government, called *democracy*—rule by the people—was developed. Among the Greeks, however, it was a limited form of democracy. Noncitizens, slaves, and women were not allowed to participate.

Nevertheless, both monarchy and democracy have endured as forms of government practiced by many nations and peoples. In modern times, most kings and queens are the rulers of *limited*, or *constitutional, monarchies*. Real political power has been given to elected lawmaking bodies and government officials. The practice of democracy has been expanded to provide all citizens with basic rights and freedoms and the opportunity to participate in the political life of their countries. The United Kingdom is an example

Greek city-state.

of a modern constitutional monarchy. Queen Elizabeth II is the hereditary monarch and head of state. As such, she is the symbol of Britain's history and tradition. However, the elected prime minister is the head of the government, while laws are made by an elected Parliament.

Beyond the constitutional monarchies are the *republics*. The Romans invented the republican form of government when they abandoned the monarchy. (In Latin, *res publica* means "rule by the people.") Instead of kings, the Romans elected consuls and magistrates to govern them. Their laws were made by a senate of wealthy landowners and an assembly of ordinary citizens.

Originally democratic, the Roman republic eventually became a *dictatorship*. It was ruled at first by alliances of political leaders, and then by emperors, who held power by military force. Other nations have also had republican forms of government but have operated as dictatorships, giving few if any political rights to their citizens. In modern times, the Union of Soviet Socialist Republics (1922–1991), the People's Republic of Korea (North Korea), and the Socialist Republic of Vietnam have been nations with republican forms of government but with authoritarian modes of leadership. The United States and many other nations around the world, however, are republics that are also democracies.

Certain political philosophies have explicitly rejected democracy. Fascism in Italy (1922–1943), Nazism in Germany (1933–1945), and communism in the former Soviet Union and present-day China and North Korea have all demanded loyalty to a particular political party and its leaders. Such dictatorships have been called *totalitarian* because their leaders have maintained their power by attempting to wield total control of their nations and citizens.

2. Political Rights.   Citizens of totalitarian nations and other dictatorships have few political rights. They are required to subordinate their needs to those of their governments. Among the many responsibilities imposed on these citizens are unquestioning loyalty and obedience to their government and its leaders. Following orders and performing service to the state are what is expected of them.

In contrast, the citizens of democracies expect their governments to guarantee and protect basic personal freedoms such as speech, press, religion, and assembly, and always to act in the best interest of their citizens. Democratic governments are elected by voting citizens to promote and protect their well-being. In addition to rights, the citizens of democracies have responsibilities. Chief among them is the responsibility to be educated about political, economic, and legal matters so that they can make informed decisions about public issues and candidates for office. The more we understand about the political systems with which we live, the more critically we can evaluate them and the better we can determine how to improve the governments that protect our lives, property, and rights.

CULTURE AND CIVILIZATION

Customs, beliefs, family life, housing, and other human activities are affected by the physical environment.

The Native Americans who lived on the Great Plains of North America developed a *culture*, or way of life, suited to the open grasslands. The buffalo herds that wandered across the grasslands provided the Plains people with food, clothing, and shelter. Since they had to follow the herds from place to place, they developed a portable home called a *tepee*. It was made of buffalo skins wrapped around long poles. The tepee could easily be taken down and set up again in another location.

The horse was the major form of transportation. It gave hunters the speed to run down and kill buffalo. Besides speed, the horse had the power and endurance to carry or drag household goods over long distances.

The Plains people did not believe in private ownership of land. Instead, they believed that the plains over which they traveled belonged to everyone. Their wandering life did not encourage large groups to settle in one place and unite under one government. Most people lived in small groups. Their leaders, or chiefs, were men who were usually the most successful hunters and warriors. Medicine men were also important. They were believed to have magical powers that would aid the hunters.

The physical environment of the Maya people of southern Mexico and Central America was quite different from that of the Plains people. Maya farmers cleared small plots of land out of the rain forest. In the hot, humid climate, they grew mainly corn and other crops. As a result, the Mayas developed a settled farming culture that differed from the wandering way of life of the Plains people.

In time, the Mayas built great cities made of stone. More than a thousand years before Columbus sailed to America, they had developed a great civilization.

Ruled by chiefs and priests, the Mayas built pyramids similar to those found in Egypt. Temples to the Maya gods sat atop these pyramids. Like other advanced peoples, the Mayas developed a

Pyramid in the Maya city of Tikal
(Guatemala).

system of writing. They devised a calendar to set dates for planting crops. To make trade easier, they built stone-paved roads connecting their cities. The Mayas carried on a widespread trade with other parts of Mexico and Central America. Contacts with other cultures brought the Mayas new goods and ideas.

The borrowing by one culture of attractive elements from another culture is known as *cultural diffusion*. In the late 1990's, the people of France began to adopt the American practice of celebrating Halloween. To many, this was another example of the diffusion of American culture. For several decades, the French people had been using many borrowed American words and expressions instead of native French ones. And American fast-food chains were an established fact in French life. Did French culture require protection from American influence? For many French people, celebrating Halloween was more a matter of gaining economic profits by adopting American products and business methods than of abandoning their own culture.

The people of the past faced similar challenges. They succeeded very well in adapting to their environment and then used it to improve their lives. Keep these ideas in mind as you begin Chapter 2, "The Prehistoric Period."

Chapter Review

 ESSAY QUESTIONS

1. List the disciplines used by social scientists to study the world and its cultures and civilizations.

2. Select *one* discipline and explain how it helps us to understand the world and its people.

3. Describe the work of Dr. Robin Birley by answering the following questions:
    a. To which social science discipline(s) does Dr. Birley belong?
    b. What is the purpose of Dr. Birley's work?
    c. What has Dr. Birley discovered or concluded from the evidence available to him?
    d. What do you find most interesting about Dr. Birley's work? Explain your answer.

Chapter 2
The Prehistoric Period

APPEARANCE OF MODERN HUMANS

1. Presapiens. Between 1994 and early 2005, paleontologists working in Ethiopia discovered the bones and teeth of a primitive predecessor of modern humans (*homo sapiens sapiens*). *Ardipithecus ramidus* was probably less than four feet tall, walked upright on two feet, and ate a plant-based diet. It lived approximately 4.5 million years ago and was one of the oldest presapiens.

In the millions of years before humans appeared in East Africa, between 100,000 and 200,000 years ago, several other types of presapiens lived. Around 2.5 million years ago, *Homo habilis* began to make stone tools. Another species, *Homo erectus*, appeared in Africa 1.8 million years ago. It had a skeletal structure similar to that of modern humans, hunted animals, learned the use of fire, and may have had limited language skills.

2. Neanderthals. The best-known presapiens were the *Neanderthals*, who lived in parts of Europe, Asia, and Africa from about 250,000 years ago to about 28,000 years ago. These strongly built people hunted woolly mammoths, giant cave bears, and other large animals that lived during the *Ice Age*.

The Ice Age began about 1,500,000 years ago and ended about 10,000 years ago. While it lasted, much of the northern portions of the Earth were covered with thick sheets of ice, called *glaciers*, which slowly moved south from the Arctic regions. Because of the cold climate during the Ice Age, food was scarce and only the strong survived.

When the Ice Age ended and the climate warmed, the large fur-bearing animals hunted by Neanderthals died out. Shortly after, the Neanderthals also disappeared, for the Ice Age animals had been their main source of food. Scientists think that the Neanderthals may not have had the ability to learn how to find new sources of food.

3. Cro-Magnons. The *Cro-Magnon people* were early humans who lived in Africa, Europe, and Asia at the same time as the Neanderthals. They appeared around 50,000 years ago. Since they

Mammoth drawn by a Cro-Magnon artist
in a cave at Font-de-Gaume, France.

evolved further, developing skills and belief systems more complex than those of the Neanderthals, scientists have called them *Homo sapiens* (knowledgeable people). They did not evolve into *Homo sapiens sapiens*, or modern humans.

The Cro-Magnon people used a variety of tools and weapons. They were skilled craftspeople, who often decorated their products with patterns or carved them into the shape of animals. Using bone, antler, and ivory, they made harpoons and other weapons. These materials were also used to make needles with which hides could be sewn into comfortable, better-fitting clothes.

The Cro-Magnon people buried their dead in a way that showed a belief in an afterlife. Cro-Magnon skeletons have been excavated wearing the remains of fine clothes, necklaces, and bracelets. Tools and carved figurines lay at their sides. Anthropologists believe that these objects, or grave goods, were to be used by the dead in another world.

The paintings and carvings of the Cro-Magnons are regarded as evidence that they believed in magic. Painting images of animals on the walls of their caves may have been an attempt to make hunting successful. Carved figures of pregnant women may have represented the life-giving power of nature.

4. Modern Humans. The Cro-Magnons were close in physical appearance and mental ability to *modern humans*, who appeared around 37,000 years ago, while the Cro-Magnons still hunted and gathered. The Cro-Magnons, however, eventually disappeared. Modern humans continued to evolve and develop because they had greater ability to adapt to changes in their environment.

Like the presapiens and humans who died out, modern humans became hunters and gatherers and developed languages, organizational skills, religious and magical beliefs, and art forms. These are the main components of *culture*. Eventually, modern humans would build civilizations.

ESSAY QUESTIONS

1. Identify *two* types of presapiens.

2. Describe *two* accomplishments of presapiens that were important to human development.

3. Identify *one* type of early human.

4. State the difference between *Homo sapiens* and *Homo sapiens sapiens*.

5. Explain why modern humans survived and evolved, while presapiens and early humans died out.

A Family of Anthropologists

Anthropologists are scientists who study human beings—their physical characteristics, origins, cultures, and *artifacts* (objects made by humans). In 1959, anthropologists Louis and Mary Leakey, a husband-and-wife team from Kenya, made important discoveries at Olduvai Gorge, in Tanzania, Africa. Mary Leakey uncovered the bone fossils of an early presapien, later called *East African Man*. He was estimated to have lived 1.76 million years ago. The Leakeys decided that he was not a direct ancestor of modern people. They believed that another presapien whose bones they had found, *Homo habilis*, was one of our direct ancestors. Even though both presapiens had lived at the same time, *Homo habilis* was more like modern humans than was *East African Man*. Their discoveries convinced the Leakeys that human development began in Africa. Louis Leakey died in 1972. His work was continued by Mary and their son, Richard. In 1978, Mary Leakey discovered the footprints of presapiens who had lived 3.7 million years ago in Tanzania. In 1984, Richard Leakey made another startling find. Near Lake Rudolf in Kenya, he uncovered the first complete skeleton of *Homo erectus*. This presapien had lived 1.6 million years ago. As a result of the Leakeys' work, we know more about the appearance of early presapiens.

How did the Leakeys increase our knowledge of early peoples?

STONE AGE PEOPLES

The discovery and use of fire gave early people warmth against the cold, light against the dark, and the means to cook food. When our early ancestors learned to chip the hard stone called *flint* to make the first tools and weapons, they took another great step toward improving their lives.

1. The Old Stone Age. Also called the *Paleolithic Age,* this era lasted from about 500,000 to 10,000 years ago. Presapiens, early humans, and modern humans originated in Africa and *migrated* into Europe, Asia, and the Americas. These Paleolithic peoples were hunter-gatherers, moving from place to place in search of sources of food and suitable shelter, such as caves. They traveled in small groups, staying in one place only as long as the plants and animals there could supply them with food and clothing. Paleolithic hunter-gatherers followed set routes, moving from campsite to campsite over a large territory. They often changed their travel patterns because the number of people in their group had increased. It was difficult to find an environment that would support a large group indefinitely. Therefore, from time to time, a few couples would split off and form a new group, which would then stake out its own territory.

Toward the end of the Paleolithic Age, the climate of the Northern Hemisphere became warmer and wetter. Much of the desert between Central Africa and North Africa, now known as the Sahara, changed to grasslands. This made it easier for early hunter-gatherers to move into North Africa and from there into the Middle East and Europe.

Paleolithic people learned to work flint into sharp points for tools and weapons. They also learned the organization and team-work necessary to hunt large animals.

Climate changes affected the environment in which early hunter-gatherers lived. Modern humans (*Homo sapiens sapiens*) were more adaptable to change than were other Paleolithic people. They learned to create new kinds of tools, shelters, and hunting techniques. This helped modern humans to survive the environmental changes that eventually destroyed presapiens and early humans.

2. The Middle Stone Age. Human technology advanced rapidly during this era, also called the *Mesolithic Age,* which lasted from 10,000 to 8,000 years ago. As the last Ice Age came to an end, the climate became warmer. The glaciers and forests that covered the northern portions of the Earth began to disappear. The large animals that had thrived in the extreme cold died off. The animals that took their place were smaller. To get enough food, hunter-gatherer bands had to hunt more frequently, and with greater skill and organization.

As the environment changed, people invented new tools and weapons to help them adapt to the new conditions. One important invention was the *microlith.* It was a small, triangular-shaped blade of stone used for knives and spears. Because of its small but

Old Stone Age Sites in Western Europe

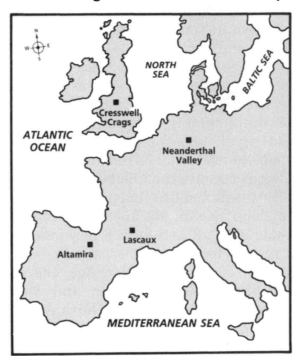

1. Which of the Stone Age sites shown on the map was separated by the sea from the other sites?
    a. Altamira
    b. Neanderthal Valley
    c. Creswell Crags
    d. Lascaux

2. Describe the lifestyle of Paleolithic people.

---

sharp edge, the microlith blade could pierce an animal's hide better than earlier stone weapons. Another useful invention was the bow and arrow. The points of arrows were also made of microliths. Better weapons enabled early people to hunt more efficiently. This increased their food supply.

Other inventions during the Middle Stone Age included the fishhook, the fishnet, and boats made from hollowed logs. They enabled people living near rivers, lakes, and the sea to catch more fish. The first pottery, made of sun-baked clay, was used to store food and water.

3. The New Stone Age. This period lasted from about 8,000 to 5,000 years ago. During these years, the lives of early people were

Farmers harvesting grain they planted as seeds. Permanent villages arose as farming became a way of life.

changed in so many ways by so many new ideas and inventions that scientists give the name *Neolithic Revolution* to this period. ("Neolithic" is the special scientific term for New Stone Age. "Revolution" means a period of great change.)

a. *Growth of agriculture.* The greatest change was in the way people obtained food. Early people had always been hunters and gatherers, or *nomads*. They followed the seasonal movements of animals to hunt and looked for plants, nuts, berries, roots, and other wild foods to gather. These activities made them wanderers with no permanent homes.

Gradually, people learned that plants grow from seeds. They began to put seeds in the ground to grow food. They became farmers. As farmers, they could settle in one place and build permanent homes. People no longer had to move from place to place to find food. At the same time, people realized that by taming sheep, cattle, goats, pigs, and other animals, they could increase their supply of meat and clothing. They became herdkeepers as well as farmers.

Agriculture (farming and the raising of animals) began around 11,000 B.C. in the Middle East, possibly in southern Turkey. The change from the hunter-gatherer way of life to farming took place all over the world in roughly the same time period. Agriculture allowed people to produce surplus food, which could be stored for future use. This meant that some people did not have to farm. They could become soldiers, traders, or craft workers. They developed more diversified societies.

Technology advanced even further as people developed new tools and skills. A hoe was invented to prepare the ground for planting seeds. To harvest the grain, farmers used a curved, bladed tool called a sickle. Farm households needed storage containers. People learned to make pots by shaping clay on a potter's wheel. They learned to spin animal hairs (such as sheep's wool) and plant fibers into thread and weave the thread into cloth. A milling stone was invented to grind grain into flour. Where rain was scarce, *irrigation* was developed to bring water to fields where crops grew.

b. *Growth of towns.* As time went on, some farming communities grew into towns. One of the earliest was Catal Huyuk, in central Turkey. Its people built their houses around 9,000 years ago. Not all farmers lived in settled communities. Some were members of *pastoral* societies, groups that moved from place to place herding animals.

c. *Creation of governments.* The leaders of farming communities and towns developed the earliest forms of government. Those who became powerful enough to rule others were often the wealthy people who owned more land and livestock than others.

d. *Creation of religions.* As people tried to persuade the spirits of nature to help the growth of their crops and herds, religious ceremonies became more elaborate. Men and women who were most skilled at conducting prayers, ceremonies, and magical practices became the first *priests* and *priestesses*.

e. *Age of Metals.* During the late New Stone Age, people learned that tools and weapons made of metal were better than

A toolmaker hammers a bronze sword into shape. Metal tools and weapons were a great improvement over those made of stone.

those made of stone. At first, early metalworkers hammered copper into the shapes of spearheads, arrow points, knives, or any other tool they needed. After a while, they discovered that mixing melted copper and tin produces an even harder metal called *bronze*. Finally, people learned how to use iron. The *Age of Metals* began about 5,000 years ago.

 MATCHING EXERCISE

Match each term in Column A with its description in Column B.

Column A	Column B
1. Neolithic Revolution	*a.* Better tools and weapons are made.
2. spinning and weaving	*b.* Priests and priestesses conduct ceremonies.
3. irrigation	*c.* Farming begins.
4. religion	*d.* River water is brought to crops.
5. Age of Metals	*e.* Better clothing, blankets, and tents are made.

4. The Beginning of History.   Toward the end of the New Stone Age, people made one of the greatest inventions of all time. They created a way to put their thoughts into a permanent form by inventing a system of writing. Scientists believe that the Sumerians in the Middle East were the first people to set down symbols for words and sounds.

The use of writing marks the end of the *prehistoric period* and the beginning of the *historic period*. After people learned to write, they left records of their lives and created literature. Scholars today can read these records and learn what happened thousands of years ago. Without written records, scholars and scientists can only guess at how people lived and what they thought.

 SENTENCE COMPLETION

Complete the following sentences:

1. Written language was an important invention because —.

2. The difference between the prehistoric period and the historic period is —.

3. During the Middle Stone Age, technological improvements included —.

CHRONOLOGY

Timelines help us know when events happened. By looking at a timeline, we can easily see whether a particular event occurred before or after or at the same time as another event. Use the information on Timeline A and Timeline B below to answer the following questions:

1. According to Timeline A, during which years did the Old Stone Age take place?

2. When was the earliest point in time that modern humans appeared?

3. Identify the *two* groups of early hunter-gatherers who appeared by 50,000 B.C.

4. Which group existed longer—Neanderthals or Cro-Magnons?

5. After the Old Stone Age ended, what had happened to Neanderthals, Cro-Magnons, and modern humans?

6. List the Stone Ages shown on Timeline B.

7. State the time span of the Middle Stone Age.

Timeline A

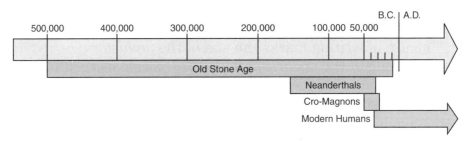

Timeline B

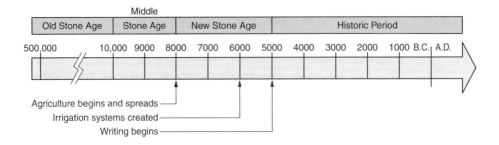

8. Identify some important accomplishments of modern humans during the New Stone Age.

Chapter Review

▶ **MULTIPLE-CHOICE**

Choose the item that best completes each statement.

1. Presapiens first walked the Earth approximately (a) 5 million years ago (b) 3 million years ago (c) one million years ago (d) 100,000 years ago.

2. The Ice Age began about (a) 5 million years ago (b) 3 million years ago (c) 1.5 million years ago (d) 500,000 years ago.

3. The earliest human ancestors first appeared in (a) Europe (b) Asia (c) Africa (d) North America.

4. A presapien type who lived around 2.5 million years ago was (a) *Homo habilis* (b) *Homo erectus* (c) Neanderthal (d) Cro-Magnon.

5. During the Ice Age, much of the northern portions of the Earth were covered by (a) swamps and marshes (b) glaciers and thick forests (c) grasslands (d) humid rain forests.

6. The type of early ancestor closest in appearance and ability to modern humans was (a) *Homo erectus* (b) Neanderthal (c) *Homo habilis* (d) Cro-Magnon.

7. The term *Homo sapiens sapiens* refers to (a) presapiens (b) humans (c) modern humans (d) nonhumans.

8. Neanderthals can best be described as (a) Paleolithic hunters (b) Mesolithic fishers (c) Neolithic farmers (d) pastoral herders.

9. Cro-Magnon craftspeople were able to (a) make tools and weapons of bone and ivory (b) sew fine clothes (c) paint animals' images on cave walls (d) do all of these.

10. Scientists who study human cultures and physical appearances are called (a) archeologists (b) naturalists (c) paleontologists (d) anthropologists.

11. The microlith was an important invention of the (a) Ice Age (b) Paleolithic Age (c) Mesolithic Age (d) Neolithic Age.

12. The transition from a hunter-gatherer lifestyle to agricultural and pastoral pursuits was called the (a) Neolithic Revolution (b) Mesolithic Transition (c) Paleolithic Exchange (d) none of these.

13. Among the technological advances that increased food supplies was (a) cloth making (b) irrigation (c) the potter's wheel (d) house building.

14. The making of tools and weapons of copper, bronze, and iron began the (a) Paleolithic Age (b) Mesolithic Age (c) Neolithic Age (d) Age of Metals.

15. The historic period began when people invented a system of (a) hunting and gathering (b) writing (c) pastoralism (d) agriculture.

 MATCHING EXERCISE

Match each item in Column A with its description in Column B.

Column A	Column B
1. *Ardipithecus ramidus*	a. uncovered presapien fossil remains
	b. early farming town
2. *Homo sapiens*	c. one of oldest presapiens
3. Cro-Magnon	d. "knowledgeable people"
4. Louis and Mary Leakey	e. painted on caves
5. Catal Huyuk	

 ESSAY QUESTIONS

1. Discuss the differences among presapiens, early humans, and modern humans.

2. Trace human growth and development through the three stages of the Stone Age.

3. Describe the impact of environmental changes on prehistoric peoples.

4. List the factors that led to technological advances in prehistoric times.

5. Explain why towns, diversified societies, religions, and the first governments appeared during the New Stone Age.

UNIT II

THE ANCIENT WORLD

Civilization resulted from the development of agriculture, the increase in population that agriculture brought about, and the need to solve problems presented by the environment. Some of the world's first civilizations arose near rivers. The Mesopotamian, Egyptian, Indus Valley, and Yellow River peoples organized under strong governments. In order to grow enough crops to feed large populations, they needed the direction of capable and powerful leaders to construct and maintain canals that brought river water to their fields. They also needed the rulers' soldiers to protect their crops and fields in return for the payment of taxes.

Civilization has been defined as the culture of cities. Culture involves the way people live and work, their language, religion, art, music, values, and customs.

CHAPTER 3
The First Civilizations

Many important early civilizations developed in the Middle East in what is called the *Fertile Crescent*. This large arc of land starts at the eastern end of the Mediterranean Sea and curves northeastward and then south, ending at the Persian Gulf. The first major civilization that we know about, the Sumerian civilization, started in the eastern half of the Fertile Crescent. This region was known as Mesopotamia. Most of Mesopotamia lay between the Tigris and Euphrates rivers in what is now Iraq.

A second important civilization began along the Nile River in Egypt. This Egyptian civilization grew and prospered for more than 2,500 years. It was one of the most splendid in all history.

Beyond the Middle East, a third civilization, that of the Celts, began in what is now Europe. The Celts were farmers, herders, warriors, artists, and traders. As they came into contact with other peoples, the Celts exchanged ideas and customs. The Celts greatly influenced the early civilizations in Western and Northern Europe.

PEOPLES OF THE FERTILE CRESCENT

Advanced civilizations have existed in the Middle East for about 6,000 years. Some of them created great *empires* (groups of different lands and peoples under one ruler). Other cultures were smaller or weaker but are remembered because their ideas and ways of life greatly influenced the history of the world.

1. The Sumerians. The first people to develop an advanced civilization in Mesopotamia were the Sumerians. About 4000 B.C., they settled in the fertile land where the Tigris and Euphrates rivers flow into the Persian Gulf. This part of Mesopotamia was called Lower Mesopotamia.

    a. *City-states.* The Sumerians built *city-states*. A city-state included a city and the farms and villages around it. The Sumerians regarded each city-state as the property of a god. The city-state was ruled by a priest-king who represented the god.

    b. *Irrigation system.* Not much rain falls during the year in Mesopotamia. Sumerian farmers created an irrigation system to water their crops, especially during the dry season. The farmers dug ditches to bring water from the rivers to the fields. The flow of water was regulated by dams and gates.

    c. *Writing.* The Sumerians invented the first system of writing. Called *cuneiform*, it consisted of wedge-shaped marks. The marks were pressed into clay tablets with a stylus, or pointed stick. The Sumerian written language contained more than 700 symbols. Each symbol stood for a name of something, an idea, or a sound. The cuneiform system of writing was later used by other peoples of Mesopotamia.

    d. *Engineering feats.* The Sumerians were the first people to use wheeled vehicles for transportation. They also invented the arch, a curved structure built to support weight over an opening in a building. The temples in which the Sumerians worshipped their gods were the largest and tallest buildings in the city-states. These *ziggurats*, as the temples were called, were towers with many levels.

The Ancient World: First Civilizations

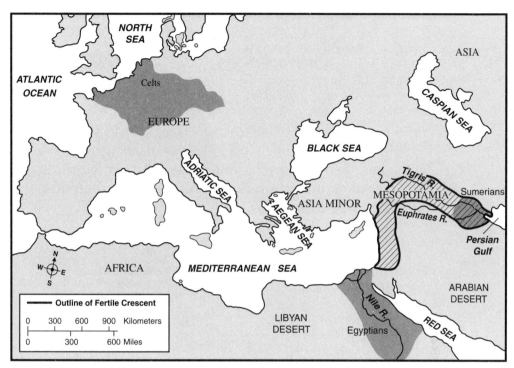

1. Locate Celts, Egyptians, and Sumerians on the map. For each, identify a nearby river or other body of water.

2. Name the region in which the Sumerians lived.

3. Why do you think early civilizations often developed near rivers or other bodies of water?

---

e. *Religion and literature.* Religion played a very important part in the life of the Sumerians. They believed that everything that happened was the will of the gods and could not be changed. Much Sumerian literature describes their religious beliefs. Other literary works, such as the poem *Gilgamesh*, tell about the adventures of heroic individuals. Part of *Gilgamesh* is the story of a great flood that nearly destroyed the world. (It is similar to the account of Noah and his ark in the Old Testament of the Bible.)

Throughout most of their history, the Sumerian city-states fought against one another. About 2360 B.C., a strong leader named Sargon forced the city-states to unite under his rule. Sargon's rule lasted for about 55 years. After his death, foreign

Decoder of Cuneiform

The Sumerians invented cuneiform, the first system of writing. In modern times, no one could read cuneiform until the secret of its meaning was unlocked, or decoded. This was done by Sir Henry Rawlinson, a 19th-century British army officer and scholar.

In 1833, Major Rawlinson was sent to Iran. When not occupied with his military duties, he pursued his interest in Iran's ancient past. He became determined to translate the cuneiform writings carved on the wall of a 1,700-foot cliff at Bisitun. The only way Rawlinson could do this was by dangling from a rope 500 feet above the ground. After two years of work, he was able to decode the first two paragraphs of the writings.

In 1846, after more than 10 years of work, Rawlinson succeeded in translating the Persian and Mesopotamian forms of cuneiform. Historians had gained a valuable tool for investigating ancient Middle Eastern civilizations.

Sir Henry Rawlinson.

Why do you think historians regard Sir Henry Rawlinson as a pioneer?

invasions and new wars among the city-states caused the downfall of Sumerian civilization.

2. The Babylonian Empire. Around 2300 B.C., invaders from what is now Syria conquered the city-states of Lower Mesopotamia. A king named Hammurabi (ruled 1792–1750 B.C.) became the greatest ruler of this new empire. He made the city of Babylon his capital and called his empire Babylonia.

a. *Law code.* Hammurabi was known for his wisdom and justice. He developed one of the first written law codes in the world. Hammurabi's Code had nearly 300 laws. It provided rules for settling problems that arose in the everyday lives of the Babylonians. These laws were designed to prevent the strong from oppressing the weak. For example, the code outlined the rules and punishments for dishonest business practices and nonpayment of debts. It also regulated the fees of doctors and protected the right of women to own certain types of property.

The Babylonian Empire, 2300 B.C.

EXPLAIN: For both trade and agriculture, the Babylonian Empire was well located.

The code substituted legal penalties for personal revenge in dealing with crimes. In many cases, however, the required punishments were severe, such as cutting off a hand or putting out an eye.

Long after the end of the Babylonian Empire, Hammurabi's Code continued to influence the development of other legal systems.

b. *Scientific advances.* The Babylonians made many other contributions to the development of a high level of civilization in Mesopotamia. Their *astronomers*, scholars who studied the stars and planets, developed a lunar calendar. (*Lunar* means that it was based on the phases of the moon.) The calendar provided for a 12-month year, a 7-day week, and a 24-hour day. Babylonian scholars created a system of arithmetic based on the number 60. They gave us the 60-minute hour and the 360-degree circle.

The rulers who followed Hammurabi could not hold the empire together. In time, mountain tribes from the north and east conquered the Babylonians.

The many different groups that formed states in the Tigris-Euphrates Valley adopted the Sumerian culture. Consequently, all the civilizations that formed in the area can be referred to as Mesopotamian.

3. The Hittites.   From Asia Minor, the greater part of the area known today as Turkey, the Hittites invaded Mesopotamia. They conquered Syria and Babylonia shortly after 1600 B.C. The Hittites had a great advantage over the other peoples of the Fertile Crescent. Most civilizations made their tools and weapons of bronze. The Hittites had learned to refine iron ore into weapons. Iron ore was more readily available than the metals that go into making bronze. More important, iron weapons were harder and stronger than bronze ones. This advantage enabled the Hittites to challenge Egypt for control of the Fertile Crescent. A long struggle took place between the two powers.

Until the fall of their empire, around 1200 B.C., the Hittites kept their iron-making skills a secret. Eventually, other people learned how to make iron tools and weapons.

The Hittites developed a system of laws that required the payment of damages for crimes or wrongdoing. The idea of paying fines is regarded as an improvement over the harsh punishments in Hammurabi's Code.

4. The Phoenicians.   The long struggle between the Egyptians and the Hittites weakened both empires. This offered opportunities for less powerful Fertile Crescent peoples to become more important in the Middle East.

a.   *Trade network.*   The Phoenicians settled on the eastern shore of the Mediterranean Sea in what is now Lebanon. They became merchants and sea traders. Their ships sailed all over the Mediterranean Sea and to some areas along the Atlantic Ocean. Phoenician trading colonies were set up in many lands. The greatest of these colonies was Carthage in North Africa.

From distant places, goods were brought to Sidon and Tyre, two trading cities in Phoenicia. Phoenician merchants took the ideas and knowledge of the advanced civilizations of the Middle East to other lands. By 1100 B.C., the Phoenicians were the most important merchants in the lands bordering the Mediterranean Sea.

Phoenician trading ships carried goods such as cloth, dyes, and timber.

b. *Alphabet.* To keep better business records, the Phoenicians developed an advanced system of writing. Their *alphabet* used 22 symbols to represent sounds. This way of writing was more efficient than the cuneiform system used by the Sumerians. Eventually, the Greeks adopted and refined the Phoenician alphabet. It became the basis of the alphabet we use today.

5. The Hebrews. The people of ancient Israel, the Hebrews, never built a large empire. But their religious and moral ideas changed the world. The Hebrews, also called Jews, were the first people to believe in one God. This belief is called *monotheism*. It gradually replaced *polytheism*, the belief in many gods held by other peoples of the ancient world. Hebrew teachings about justice and the principles of right and wrong, combined with their belief in monotheism, gave rise to Judaism. It became one of the major religions of the world. Eventually, Jewish teachings influenced the development of two other major religions, Christianity and Islam.

Much of the history of the Hebrews is written in the Old Testament of the Bible. The Hebrews were originally tribes of

The Hebrew Kingdom, 1000–925 B.C.

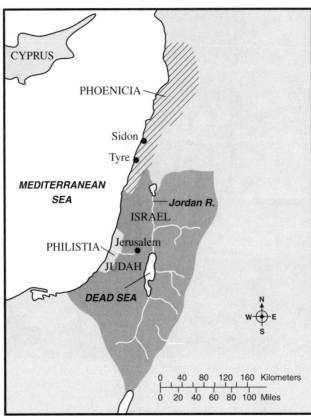

1. Identify the country that bordered the Hebrew Kingdom on the northwest.

2. What names were used to designate the northern and southern portions of the Hebrew Kingdom?

3. Locate Philistia in relation to the Hebrew Kingdom and the Mediterranean Sea.

4. What were *two* bodies of water located inside the Hebrew Kingdom?

---

wandering herders from Mesopotamia. They were brought to Israel, also called Canaan, by Abraham. During a time of famine, some Hebrews moved to Egypt, where they were made slaves. After a long period of captivity, the Hebrews were freed and led back to Israel by Moses. The Bible states that during the journey, God came to Moses on Mount Sinai and gave him the Ten Commandments, a code of moral behavior.

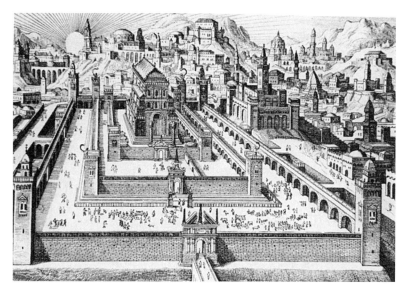

The Temple of Solomon in Jerusalem, as an artist in 1650 imagined it.

From about 1200 to 600 B.C., the Hebrews developed an advanced civilization. Around 1025, the tribes united under Saul, their first king. Saul led the fight against the Philistines, a neighboring people, for control of Israel. He was followed on the throne by David. This great king built the city of Jerusalem and made it his capital.

The Hebrew kingdom reached its peak of strength and wealth under David's son, Solomon. During his rule, from about 975 to 935 B.C., Solomon made alliances with other kings, sent ships to trade in distant lands, and beautified Jerusalem. He built a great temple in Jerusalem. Its beauty amazed those who saw it. The Temple of Solomon became the center of Jewish religious life.

After Solomon's death, his kingdom split into two parts. Civil wars weakened the Hebrew kingdoms. Many different peoples conquered the Jews. In time (63 B.C.), Israel became part of the Roman Empire. To punish the Jews for their constant rebellions, the Romans destroyed Jerusalem and scattered many of the Jews to different parts of the world (about A.D. 135). Israel did not become an independent nation again until A.D. 1948.

6. The Assyrians.   The rise of the Assyrian Empire in northern Mesopotamia influenced most of the Fertile Crescent from about 1100 to 650 B.C. The Assyrians were excellent soldiers. Their skilled cavalry and iron weapons enabled them to conquer a large part of the Middle East. Babylonia, Israel, Phoenicia, Syria, Egypt, and much of Asia Minor all became part of the Assyrian empire.

The Assyrians were known for their cruelty. They ruled their enormous empire by a combination of efficient administration and terror. Those who opposed the Assyrians were killed or harshly punished. Conquered peoples were heavily taxed.

In spite of their harsh ways, Assyrians contributed a great deal to the growth of civilization. Perhaps their most important accomplishment was the fine library built by Assurbanipal, the last of the great Assyrian kings. Located in his capital of Nineveh, this library of many thousands of clay tablets preserved the knowledge of the advanced culture of the Babylonians.

Dislike of Assyrian rule was strong. Chaldeans from Mesopotamia and Medes from Persia joined forces to make war on Assyria. They captured Nineveh and destroyed Assyrian power in 612 B.C.

7. The New Babylonian Empire. The Chaldeans of Babylonia became the next conquerors of the Fertile Crescent. King Nebuchadnezzar (ruled 605–561 B.C.) rebuilt the city of Babylon. The Hanging Gardens, a pyramid structure with steps, became one of the wonders of the ancient world. The Chaldeans also became known for the cruelty of their rule. Their conquest of Phoenicia and Israel resulted in the imprisonment of many Hebrews. The Hebrew captives were marched to Babylon and made slaves.

The Chaldeans became expert *astrologers*. They worked out detailed tables of the movements of the stars and planets. They also invented the signs of the zodiac. They believed that this knowledge helped them to predict future events. The Chaldeans' study of the stars and planets was important to development of the science of astronomy.

After the death of Nebuchadnezzar in 561 B.C., the Chaldean Empire began to decline. It was conquered by Cyrus the Great of Persia in 539 B.C.

8. The Persians. The Persians were the ancestors of many of the people of present-day Iran. Both the Persians and the Medes lived in the region east of Mesopotamia. The capital city of the Medes was Ecbatana. Until 550 B.C., the Persians were ruled by the Medes.

a. *Persian rule.* Cyrus the Great, a Persian general, led his troops to victory over the Medes and captured Ecbatana in 550 B.C. This action began a long series of conquests of the Fertile Crescent

The Persian Empire, 500 B.C.

and the lands beyond. By the time Cyrus died in 529, Persian rule extended from the Aegean Sea to the borders of India. The Persians conquered Egypt in 525 B.C. and took control of parts of southeastern Europe. This made the Persian Empire the largest and most powerful one in the Middle East.

The Persians showed great skill in government. Unlike the Assyrians and Chaldeans, the Persians respected the religions, languages, and customs of their subject peoples. Persian kings provided efficient government and allowed much freedom of thought to the many different peoples in their empire.

The empire was divided into provinces. Each was ruled by a governor, or *satrap*. Inspectors, called "the Eyes and Ears of the King," traveled to each province and reported to the king on the behavior of his governors. Well-constructed roads connected the various sections of the empire and made rapid communications possible. The roads also helped traders move their goods easily. All provinces paid taxes, but the taxes were not high. As a result, there were few revolts against Persian rule.

b. *Religious beliefs.* Persian religious beliefs had a strong influence on the government of the empire and its treatment

Cyrus the Great conquered Babylon in 539 B.C. Cyrus allowed the Hebrews held captive there to return to Israel.

of its subjects. In the early 600's B.C., Zoroastrianism arose from the preachings of Zoroaster, a religious philosopher. He taught that there was one god, Ahura Mazda, who represented the forces of good. Ahura Mazda was engaged in an eternal struggle with Ahriman, who represented the forces of evil. Humans had to choose which side to support. Eventually, Ahura Mazda would triumph and judge the actions of all people. Those who were good would be rewarded in heaven. Those who were evil would be punished in hell. Persian kings believed that Ahura Mazda would help them if they ruled with justice and fairness.

The Persian Empire controlled the Middle East for more than 200 years. In the 4th century B.C., the Persians were conquered by a Greek and Macedonian army led by Alexander the Great.

 ESSAY QUESTIONS

1. Explain how environment influenced the rise of the world's first civilizations.

2. Identify the region known as the Fertile Crescent and list the civilizations that developed there.

3. Compare and contrast the achievements of *two* Mesopotamian civilizations.

4. State the reasons why you AGREE or DISAGREE with each of the following statements:
    a. Military invasions and conquests did not affect the rise and fall of civilizations in the Fertile Crescent.

b. Both polytheism and monotheism were important to the people of the Fertile Crescent.

5.   Describe the development of writing in the Fertile Crescent.

 MATCHING EXERCISE

Match each term or name in Column A with its description in Column B.

Column A	Column B
1. cuneiform	*a*. the Chaldean king who made Babylon into one of the wonders of the ancient world
2. ziggurat	
3. Sargon	
4. Hammurabi	*b*. a tower of many levels built by the Sumerians
5. Judaism	
6. monotheism	*c*. the major religion created by the Hebrews
7. polytheism	
8. Solomon	*d*. a belief in many gods
9. Nebuchadnezzar	*e*. the Persian leader who conquered most of the Middle East by 529 B.C.
10. Cyrus the Great	
	f. the writing system developed by the Sumerians
	g. the Babylonian king who developed an early law code
	h. the Hebrew king who built a great temple in Jerusalem
	i. the king who united the Sumerian city-state about 2360 B.C.
	j. a belief in one god

ANCIENT EGYPT

Favorable geographic conditions enabled the Egyptians to develop one of the world's first advanced civilizations. Since the Old Stone Age, people have been living along the Nile River, which flows through northeast Africa, from its source in the highlands of Ethiopia to the Mediterranean Sea. Each summer the Nile overflows, depositing rich soil on the fields around it. This fertility and a warm climate encouraged the development of agriculture and settled communities. The surrounding deserts kept most attackers away. Sufficient food supplies and security from enemies gave the Egyptians the time and energy to develop their unique culture.

1. Egypt Unites. The Nile River provided the Egyptians with easy means of transportation and communication. Therefore, the villages along the Nile had frequent contact and exchange of products and ideas. As their populations increased, the Egyptian villages merged into cities. The cities grew into two kingdoms— Upper Egypt in the south and Lower Egypt in the north, near the Nile Delta.

Local rulers slowly gained control over larger areas. About 3000 B.C., a ruler named Menes united Upper and Lower Egypt into one kingdom. Menes set up his capital at Memphis and established Egypt's first *dynasty*. Dynasties are a succession of rulers from the same family. The last dynasty to rule Egypt was the 30th, which ended around 343 B.C.

2. The Pharaohs. The rulers of Egypt were called *pharaohs*. They had absolute, or total, power over everyone and everything in Egypt. They owned all property, they made all decisions, and they were worshipped as gods. At their direction, great temples were built and huge statues were created. Many of these structures still stand. The pharaohs made Egypt prosperous by promoting trade with other peoples. Egyptian ships sailed to faraway places to find new products and new sources of wealth.

The pharaohs also maintained powerful armies to protect Egypt from its enemies. Some pharaohs wanted to gain control over more land. During the Empire Period of Egyptian history (1580–1150 B.C.), the armies of the pharaohs conquered Syria, Israel, Phoenicia, and other neighboring lands. The rulers of the defeated areas paid tribute (taxes) to the pharaohs in the form of gold, silver, jewels, and food. Many of the conquered peoples became slaves in Egypt.

Two of the most important pharaohs were Thutmose III and Ramses II. Thutmose III, a military genius, ruled from 1483 to 1450 B.C. He led his armies to many victories. Ramses II ruled from 1304 to 1237 B.C. Under him, Egypt's empire reached its greatest size.

Although pharaohs were usually men, some were women. The most famous of Egypt's female pharaohs was Hatshepsut. She greatly increased Egypt's trade and artistic development during her rule from 1472 to 1458 B.C.

3. Religious Beliefs and Practices. The Egyptians worshipped many gods. Re, the sun god, was the god of the living. Osiris was

The Egyptian Empire, 1450 B.C.

1. Name the *two* regions into which ancient Egypt was divided.

2. Locate the Nile Delta and identify two cities near it.

3. Name the *three* deserts and *two* large bodies of water that surround Egypt.

4. Why do you think the Greek historian Herodotus called Egypt "the gift of the Nile"?

the god of the underworld, or the realm of the dead. He represented the forces of good. His wicked brother, Set, led the forces of evil. In the endless struggle against evil, Osiris was aided by his wife, Isis. Her magic was the source of life and fertility. Their son, Horus, was associated with light, heaven, and all things good and beautiful. Horus aided his father's struggle. The story of Isis was linked to the annual flooding of the Nile. When Osiris was killed by Set, the goddess used her magic to restore life to Osiris just as the Nile restores life to Egypt.

The Egyptians believed that each person's soul, or *ka*, could live on after death. It would be judged by Osiris according to the good and evil done by the person in life. The soul would live only if the body was preserved to look as it did in life. To

Hatshepsut, the First Woman Pharaoh

It was not usual for women to rule in the great civilizations of the ancient Middle East. Yet from 1472 to 1458 B.C., a queen named Hatshepsut ruled Egypt. For approximately 14 years, this strong-willed woman assumed all the titles and power of a pharaoh and governed Egypt with skill and efficiency.

As was the custom among Egypt's royalty, Hatshepsut was married to her brother, Thutmose II. He ruled for only eight years before he died. In addition to his queen, Hatshepsut, he left behind Thutmose III, his son by another woman. Since the boy was too young to rule, Hatshepsut took control of the government. After a time, she had herself crowned as pharaoh. She thus became the first woman pharaoh in the history of Egypt.

Hatshepsut expanded Egypt's trade with other peoples and began a program of constructing temples and other public buildings. The arts were encouraged. Egypt's trading and military strength grew. Riches flowed into the country from other lands in the Middle East and Africa.

Hatshepsut's power slowly declined. Her stepson, Thutmose III, took control of the army. Military victories made him popular with the people. Late in Hatshepsut's reign, Thutmose III became equal in power and position to Hatshepsut. Soon after, Hatshepsut died. It is not known if she died naturally or was killed.

What was remarkable about Hatshepsut's career?

preserve the body, Egyptian priests developed the art of *mummification*. This is the process of treating a body with herbs and oils and then wrapping it tightly in narrow strips of linen cloth before placing it in a sealed coffin. So great was the skill of the priests that many mummies are still whole even though thousands of years have gone by.

4. The Pyramids. To house their mummies, the pharaohs built huge tombs in the shape of pyramids. Each of these enormous stone structures took thousands of workers many years to complete. Rooms in the pyramids were filled with all the objects the

The Great Sphinx of Giza is said to be a likeness of Khafre, pharaoh of the 4th Dynasty. His pyramid is in the background.

dead pharaoh would need in his or her life after death. Painted on the walls of the rooms were scenes showing the pharaoh's family life and his or her accomplishments.

Modern scholars have learned much about life in ancient Egypt by studying the interior of the pyramids. One of the most informative tombs was that of the pharaoh Tutankhamen. He ruled from about 1361 to 1351 B.C. Tutankhamen's tomb was discovered by a scholar named Howard Carter in A.D. 1922. Opening the tomb enabled scholars to see just what kinds of things were buried with a pharaoh.

5. The Power of the Priests.   Egypt was a land of many gods, temples, and rituals. For centuries, the several priesthoods (especially that of the god Amon-Re) held great power over the lives and beliefs of the people. The priests taught that they would ensure the fertility of people, land, and animals through the proper performance of religious hymns and ceremonies.

Pharaoh Amenhotep IV, also known as Akhenaton, ruled from 1379 to 1362 B.C. He introduced the worship of a single god, the new sun god Aton. This movement toward monotheism was strongly opposed by the priests, who feared the loss of their traditional power. Although the royal family and some nobles turned to Aton, the more conservative people of the villages and countryside continued to worship the old gods, whose anger they feared. The priests made sure that Pharaoh Akhenaton's teachings did not survive his death.

6. Technical and Scientific Achievements. The Egyptians excelled at architecture, designing large stone temples as well as pyramids. Their engineers directed the building of these structures, as well as dams and irrigation canals to improve agriculture.

Accomplished Egyptian artists carved massive statues and covered the walls of temples and tombs with colorful paintings and carvings. They also created delicate jewelry and many types of pottery.

Egyptian scribes invented *hieroglyphics*, a system of writing that used pictures and symbols to express sounds, words, and ideas. From the *papyrus* plant, they created a type of paper on which they wrote in ink their history, scientific knowledge, and government records. The scribes created libraries in which to house their papyrus scrolls. The Rosetta Stone, discovered by a French soldier in 1799, enabled scholars to translate hieroglyphics. The stone bears the same inscription in Greek letters and Egyptian hieroglyphics.

Around 4200 B.C., Egyptian astronomers invented a calendar that divided the year into 12 months of 30 days each. Five feast days, or holidays, were added to the end of the year to make 365 days.

In pursuit of land surveys and construction projects, Egyptian mathematicians developed a system of geometry and an arithmetic system based on the number 10. Egyptian doctors performed complicated surgery and used drugs to lesson pain.

7. Egypt's Decline. Wars at home and in foreign lands weakened the Egyptian Empire. The Assyrians conquered Egypt around 667 B.C. They were followed by the Persians, Greeks, Romans, and others. Not until the 20th century did Egypt again become an independent nation.

SENTENCE COMPLETION

From the list that follows, select the name or term that best completes each sentence.

Menes	ka	hieroglyphics
dynasty	mummification	papyrus
pharaoh	pyramids	calendar
Hatshepsut		

1. The Egyptian system of writing that contains pictures and symbols is called —.

2. A — of Egypt had absolute power and was worshipped as a god.

3. The Egyptians believed that a person's — would live on after death.

4. About 3000 B.C., — united Upper and Lower Egypt.

5. The Egyptian — divided the year into 12 months and 365 days.

6. Pharaohs built huge tombs in the shape of —.

7. — preserved bodies so that a person's soul could live on after death.

8. Egyptian literature was written on rolls of —.

9. A succession of rulers from one family is called a —.

10. The best-known female pharaoh was —.

 EXPOSITORY WRITING

1. In a short paragraph, explain why the goddess Isis was so important to the Egyptians.

2. Write a paragraph comparing the Sumerian, Phoenician, and Egyptian writing systems.

THE CELTS OF EUROPE

In the ancient world, no people lived in as many lands or affected the early development of as many nations as did the Celts. They spread out through Central and Western Europe and the British Isles. From 700 B.C. to A.D. 100, Celtic civilizations grew in what are today Britain, Ireland, Spain, France, Germany, Switzerland, Austria, Hungary, and the Czech Republic.

1. Way of Life.   The Celts spoke similar languages and had similar ways of life. But they were divided into tribes ruled by kings and, sometimes, by queens. Tribes living in the same geographic area often fought one another. The leaders of the tribes were warriors who seemed to take great pleasure in fighting. Most Celts, however, were peaceful, hardworking farmers and herders.

Social standing in the tribes depended on the number of cattle a man or woman possessed. Women were equal to men and could speak and vote in tribal councils. They also had the right to carry weapons and to fight in tribal wars. Although the Celts kept

Celtic Migrations, 500 B.C.

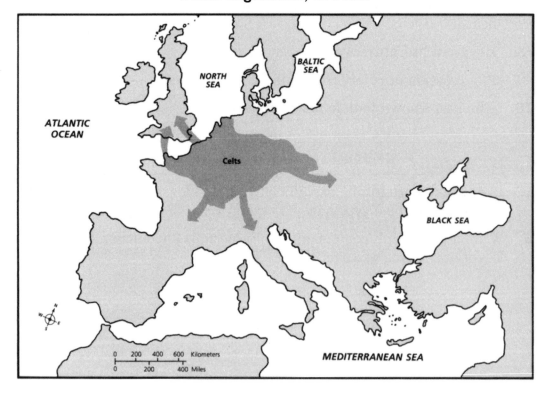

slaves, they had a deep respect for individual rights. Celtic law was based on the belief that people were responsible to one another rather than to a central government or nation. Wrongdoing was regarded as a violation of private rights. A person who had harmed another was required, as punishment, to give something of value to the injured person's family.

The Celts built no great cities. Instead, they lived in towns and villages, usually located on hilltops. The Celts fortified, or protected, the villages by surrounding them with deep ditches and high walls.

2. The Shaping of Europe. The Celts bought the knowledge of ironwork to much of Europe. They used iron plows to prepare the ground for planting and iron scythes to cut grain. These tools and others influenced the type of farming carried on in Europe for centuries.

The roads the Celts built helped the people of Europe to move from place to place more easily. Some roads were covered with timber and stone. The Celts transported their goods in four-wheeled carts and drove two-wheeled chariots.

The Celts were skilled in the arts and crafts. They decorated their weapons, chariots, and jewelry with gold, silver, enamel, and precious stones. Their clothes were made of brightly colored wool.

The Celts had no written language. Their priests and learned men, both called *druids*, could read and write Latin, Greek, and

This Celtic sculpture of a wild boar is made of bronze. It was discovered in France.

other languages. But Celtic history and stories were remembered in oral form. Celts composed long, exciting poems about the great events in their lives and the deeds of their heroes. These poems were memorized and recited by specially trained men called *bards*. Celtic oral literature influenced the development of European written literature. Love of adventure and heroism and an appreciation of humor were among the values handed down to writers of later times.

3. Celts and Romans.   By A.D. 100, most of Western Europe had been conquered by the Roman Empire. The Gauls, as the Romans called the Celts, came under Roman rule. The Romans ended the tribal wars. They gave the Celts Roman law, the Latin language, and the opportunity to trade with distant lands. High-ranking Celtic officials represented their people in the Roman government. Celtic warriors gave up fighting or joined the Roman armies. As the Roman and Celtic cultures gradually blended, a new culture arose. The foundation of European civilization was being established.

Today, the Celtic heritage can be seen most strongly in Ireland, Scotland, and Wales. In these countries, as well as in Cornwall (in southern England) and in Brittany (in northern France), Celtic languages are still spoken by some people.

 DEFINITIONS

Explain the meaning of each of the following terms:

    a. tribe

    b. fortified village

    c. scythe

    d. druid

    e. bard

 ESSAY QUESTION

In a short paragraph, tell why the Celts, who did not create a great empire, are important in history.

Chapter Review

> **MULTIPLE-CHOICE**

Choose the word or expression that best completes each statement.

1. Cuneiform writing, ziggurats, and the arch were inventions of the (a) Sumerians (b) Celts (c) Hittites (d) Egyptians.

2. An important invention of the Babylonians was (a) mummification of the dead (b) iron tools and weapons (c) a system of arithmetic based on the number 60 (d) fortified hilltop villages.

3. The Ten Commandments and the Old Testament were handed down to us by the (a) Hebrews (b) Phoenicians (c) Persians (d) Egyptians.

4. Two civilizations known for their cruelty to subject peoples were the (a) Hebrews and Phoenicians (b) Assyrians and Chaldeans (c) Sumerians and Persians (d) Egyptians and Celts.

5. The largest empire of the ancient Middle East was the (a) Hebrew (b) Egyptian (c) Babylonian (d) Persian.

6. Egypt has always depended on water from the (a) Jordan River (b) Nile River (c) Euphrates River (d) Tigris River.

7. The ruler who united Egypt was (a) Solomon (b) Thutmose III (c) Ramses II (d) Menes.

8. During its period of decline, Egypt was conquered by the (a) Celts and Hittites (b) Hebrews, Phoenicians, and Medes (c) Assyrians, Persians, Greeks, and Romans (d) Sumerians and Chaldeans.

9. The Celts spread their civilization into what is now (a) Egypt and Babylonia (b) Israel and Lebanon (c) Britain, France, Spain, and Germany (d) Hungary and Poland.

10. The foundation of European civilization was established by the blending of the cultures of the (a) Celts and Egyptians (b) Celts and Babylonians (c) Celts and Romans (d) Celts and Persians.

IDENTIFICATIONS

For each name listed, write responses to questions 1 and 2.

Menes	Hammurabi	Nebuchadnezzar
Tutankhamen	Moses	Cyrus the Great
Akhenaton	Solomon	Zoroaster

1. What was happening at the time that this person lived?

2. Why was this person important?

TIMELINE QUESTIONS

Look at the timeline below. Use the information on the timeline to answer the following questions:

1. Which civilization shown lasted for the longest time?

2. Which *two* civilizations started at about the same time?

3. Name *five* pharaohs who ruled during the time of the Hittites.

4. Which civilization shown lasted for the shortest time?

5. Which civilization shown lasted into the A.D. period?

Timeline

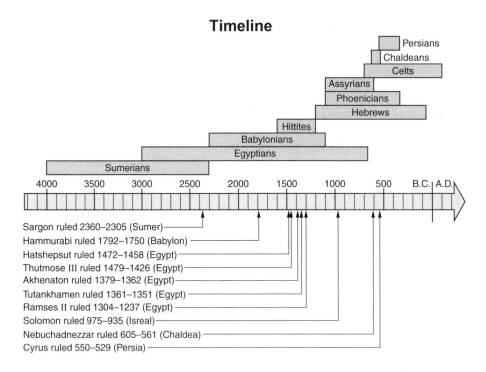

Connections: The First Civilizations

The Middle East has been called the "cradle of civilization." The reason is that many important early civilizations developed in this region. The achievements of these civilizations contributed greatly to the growth of our modern world. Yet historians tell us that in ancient Europe, long before the rise of Middle Eastern civilizations, people had been building great tombs and temples of stone. Many of these *megaliths*, as they are called, are older than the pyramids and ziggurats of the Middle East. It is clear that some prehistoric European peoples had great architectural and engineering skills. Could there have been more than one "cradle of civilization"?

1. Select the statement that best describes the passage above.
    a. Prehistoric Europeans were more advanced than the people of the Middle East.
    b. The people of the Middle East learned to build pyramids and ziggurats from prehistoric Europeans.
    c. People in different regions of the world develop similar knowledge and skills even without much direct contact with one another.
2. Explain the meaning of the following title of an article written about the megalith builders of prehistoric Europe:

ANCIENT EUROPE IS OLDER THAN WE THOUGHT

Stonehenge, a group of megaliths found on Salisbury Plain, England, possibly dates back to the New Stone Age.

DOCUMENT-BASED QUESTION

This question is based on the accompanying documents (1–3). It will improve your ability to work with historical documents.

Historical Context:

One of the characteristics of a civilization is some form of government. In the first civilizations, people's lives were regulated by laws made by rulers. Often, rulers claimed that these laws came from a divine source, or a god.

Task:

Using information from the documents and your knowledge of world history, answer the questions that follow each document. Your answers to each question will help you write the document-based essay.

Document 1. Excerpt from the Code of Hammurabi, a listing of 282 laws compiled by the Babylonian king Hammurabi during his reign, 1792–1750 B.C.

> 196. If a man put out the eye of another man, his eye shall be put out.
> 197. If he break another man's bone, his bone shall be broken.
> 198. If he put out the eye of a freed man, or break the bone of a freed man, he shall pay one gold mina.
> 199. If he put out the eye of a man's slave, or break the bone of a man's slave, he shall pay one-half of its value.

> **Source:** "Hammurabi's Code of Laws," translated by L.W. King, 1910. Found at http://eawc.evansville.edu/anthology/hammurabi.htm

Based on this document, how does the social status of the victim affect the punishment for the crime?

Document 2. Excerpt from the *New American Standard Version Bible,* Exodus 20, listing six of the Ten Commandments that, according to Jewish tradition, God revealed to Moses.

> 5. Honor your father and your mother, that your days may be prolonged in the land which the LORD your God gives you.
> 6. You shall not murder.
> 7. You shall not commit adultery.
> 8. You shall not steal.
> 9. You shall not bear false witness against your neighbor.
> 10. You shall not covet [desire] your neighbor's house; you shall not covet your neighbor's wife or his male servant or his female servant or his ox or his donkey or anything that belongs to your neighbor.

Based on this document, what might be the purpose of commandments Five through Ten?

Document 3. Excerpt from *The Precepts of Ptah-hotep* (c. 2200 B.C.), which gives instructions from a father (an Egyptian official) to his son.

> If you have, as leader, to decide on the conduct of a great number of men, seek the most perfect manner of doing [it] so that

your own conduct may be without reproach. Justice is great, invariable, and assured; it has not been disturbed since the age of Ptah [the father of the gods]. To throw obstacles in the way of the laws is to open the way before [to] violence.

> **Source:** Horne, Charles F. *The Sacred Books and Early Literature of the East.* Vol. II. New York: Parke, Austin, & Lipscomb, 1917, p. 62. Available at http://fordham.edu/halsall/ancient/ptahhotep.html

Based on this document, why is it important for both leaders *and* people in a society to obey laws?

DOCUMENT-BASED ESSAY

Using information from the documents and your knowledge of world history, write an essay in which you:

- Discuss the role that law played in the first civilizations.
- Describe the types of human behavior covered by these early rules and laws.
- Explain how law improved the quality of life in the first civilizations.

Chapter 4
Asian Civilizations

The Middle East and North Africa were not the only areas to develop major early civilizations. Important civilizations also existed farther east. As in Mesopotamia and Egypt, the eastern settlements grew up along rivers. One developed in the Indus River Valley on the Indian subcontinent. (The subcontinent now includes the countries of India, Pakistan, Bangladesh, Bhutan, and Nepal.) Another arose in the Hwang Ho (Yellow River) Valley in China. As civilizations spread in India and China, rulers built great empires. *Philosophers* created religious and moral guides for living that still influence millions of people. The early civilizations of Asia also produced great art, scientific discoveries, and technological advances.

EARLY CIVILIZATIONS IN INDIA

The Indus River Valley civilization flourished from around 2500 to 1500 B.C. in what is now Pakistan and western India. The floods of the Indus River brought water and rich soil to the area, as did the Nile floods to Egypt. The Indus floods, however, were less regular and sometimes more violent than those of the Nile. To protect their crops, the people of the Indus Valley dug irrigation ditches and built flood barriers. Productive agriculture led to a population increase and the rise of a rich civilization.

1. Early Cities. The people of the Indus Valley built several large cities and many villages. Mohenjo-Daro and Harappa were two of the major cities. They contained large public buildings, homes, and shops, all built of brick. The wide, straight streets were paved. Sewers under the streets carried off waste and water. Many of the homes had indoor bathrooms.

    a. *Economic life.* Farming was the main activity of the Indus Valley people. They also traded with the people of the Middle East. Skilled workers in the Indus Valley cities made bronze tools, gold and silver jewelry, and fine pottery.

    b. *Religious and cultural life.* Not much is known about the life and thoughts of the Indus people. Present-day scholars have

Early Asian Civilizations

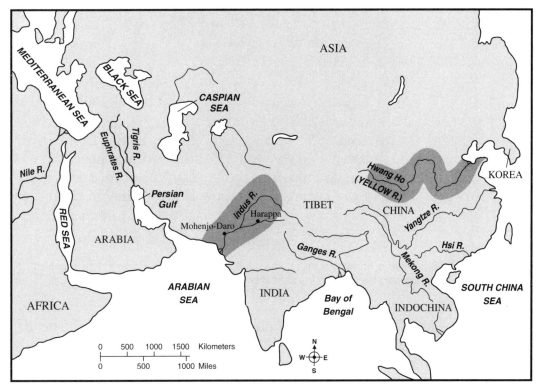

Indicate whether each of the following statements is *true* (**T**) or *false* (**F**).

1. Indian civilization began in the Nile River Valley.

2. Harappa and Mohenjo-Daro were centers of civilization in the Indus River Valley.

3. Merchants in the cities of the Tigris and Euphrates river valleys could send ships into the Arabian Sea through the Persian Gulf.

4. Chinese farmers benefited from the Ganges River.

5. The people of Indochina used water from the Mekong River to grow their crops.

---

not yet been able to read the Indus writing. It is thought that the Indus people had an organized religion. Also, it is thought that they worshipped a goddess whom they believed helped women have children and helped make crops grow.

Scholars disagree about what caused the end of the Indus civilization around 1500 B.C. Possibly the Indus River changed its course and flooded the farmland. Possibly some disease killed most

This seal, or stamp, shows a water buffalo and some Indus writing on it. The seal was found by archeologists in the ruins of Mohenjo-Daro.

of the people—the name Mohenjo-Daro means "place of the dead." Without written sources of information, researchers must study stone beads, handicrafts, and other surviving physical evidence to develop a more detailed picture of this civilization. It remains the least known of the four major ancient urban cultures, which also include Egypt, Mesopotamia, and China.

2. The Aryans. About 1500 B.C., groups of warriors and herders from Central Asia, called Aryans, started invading the Indus Valley. Dravidians, survivors of the Indus civilization, opposed the Aryans. In time, the Aryans conquered the northern section of India. The Dravidians retreated to the south. Aryan warriors settled on farms, built villages, and founded great cities.

    a. *Caste system.* An important feature of the Aryan way of life was the *caste system*. It divided people into four major groups called castes and set up strict rules for living. A person was born into a caste and could not leave it, except in rare cases. A person in one caste could not eat with anyone in another caste or marry a person from another caste. Certain types of jobs were reserved for a particular caste. Members of other castes could not do this work.

    The highest caste was the Brahmin. It included priests and scholars. Warriors and government officials made up the second caste, the Kshatriya. The third was the Vaisya, which included landowning farmers, merchants, and craft workers. Laborers belonged to the Sudra group. The caste system continued to exist in India until the mid-20th century A.D.

Those people who performed the least respected jobs were called *pariahs*, or untouchables. They were not included in the caste system and were not allowed to associate with caste members.

   b. *Cultural developments.*   The Aryans spoke a language called Sanskrit. They developed a system of writing and set down their religious stories and songs in books known as *Vedas*. (Veda means "knowledge.") One of the important parts of the Vedas is the Rig-Veda. It consists of some 1,000 songs of praise to the many gods the Aryans worshipped.

   Another important collection of religious writing is the *Upanishads*. It includes discussions on the meaning of life and the nature of the universe.

3. Hinduism.   Two of the world's great religions developed in India—Hinduism and Buddhism. Hinduism is the older of the two faiths. It reflects Aryan beliefs and practices as described in the Vedas. Some basic Hindu ideas are set forth in the Upanishads.

   The most important of the gods honored by Hindus is Brahma, the world soul. He is thought to be the source and creator of all life. Complete peace and happiness, according to the Hindus, will come to a person when the person's soul is united with Brahma. Before this can happen, a soul must be purified.

   Hindus believe that purification comes about through *reincarnation*, the rebirth of the soul. When a person dies, his or her soul is reborn in another person or in an animal. The form the soul takes depends on the kind of life a person has led. The good or bad deeds one performs influence the future life of one's soul. This law of cause and effect is called *karma*.

4. Buddhism.   The second great religion that developed in India is Buddhism. It grew out of the teachings of Siddhartha Gautama, who lived between 563 and 483 B.C. Gautama, an Indian prince, gave up a comfortable family life to search for meaning in life. He tried to find out why there was so much suffering in the world. After years of wandering and thinking, Gautama believed that he had found the answer to his question. He then became known as "Buddha," the "Enlightened One."

   Buddha taught that one must live a life based on good conduct, serious thinking, and a willingness to give up pleasures of the

As Buddhism spread throughout Asia, the likeness of Buddha was adapted to resemble the people living in a particular area. Shown is a Buddha from Japan carved from wood.

body. By following these teachings, one can avoid reincarnation and enter *nirvana*. Nirvana is a condition that will give one's soul perfect peace.

Buddhism became a strong religion, especially in China, Japan, and other parts of Asia.

The Enlightened One

In 532 B.C., an Indian prince named Siddhartha Gautama left his family and life of luxury to find the reasons for life and death. During his search for truth, Gautama practiced the mental and physical disciplines of yoga. He tried fasting and self-sacrifice to better control his mind and body.

Gautama endured this hard life for six years. Then, one day, enlightenment came. Gautama felt that he understood the true meaning of life. He became the "Enlightened One," or "Buddha," and spent the rest of his life teaching the Way of Life.

The teachings of Gautama Buddha require people to know the Four Noble Truths and to follow the Middle Way. These are the Four Noble Truths:

1. All human life is filled with pain and sorrow.

2. Pain and sorrow is caused by the desire for pleasure and possessions.

3. By giving up all desires, a person may be free from pain. The soul then reaches nirvana. Nirvana means perfect peace.

4. Nirvana may be reached by following the Middle Way.

The Middle Way is to follow the Eightfold Path, eight guides to good conduct, good thoughts, and good speech. Buddha taught people to be unselfish and to deal kindly and honestly with one another.

Gautama's teachings are called Buddhism. Belief in Buddhism has spread throughout the world. Today, millions of people are Buddhists.

Why was Gautama called the "Enlightened One"?

5. The Empire of the Mauryas.   Starting about 321 B.C., an Indian conqueror named Chandragupta Maurya gained control over northern India. He began the Mauryan Dynasty.

Chandragupta's grandson, Asoka, expanded the Mauryan Empire to include almost all of India. After a particularly bloody battle, Asoka gave up the idea and practice of war and became a Buddhist. At his direction, monks spread the teachings of Buddha to other parts of Asia, the Middle East, and North Africa.

Asoka had rules of conduct for his people carved on stone pillars, which were set up throughout the empire so that everyone could see them. Justice, charity, and nonviolence were among his teachings. After Asoka's death in 236 B.C., the Mauryan Empire declined.

The Mauryan Empire, 250 B.C.

1. Identify *two* large geographic areas of India controlled by the Mauryan Empire.

2. Explain how rivers may have both aided and hindered the expansion of the Mauryan Empire.

6. The Gupta Empire.   About 500 years after the Mauryas, another powerful dynasty, the Gupta, ruled over much of India. The Guptas ruled from about A.D. 320 to 535.

Under the Gupta emperors, India entered a golden age of peace, prosperity, and cultural achievement. Indian mathematicians invented the decimal-based number system we use today. The work of Gupta writers and artists became well known outside of India. Their work later influenced the literature and art of the Middle East and Europe. Southeast Asia wholeheartedly accepted the culture of the Gupta Empire.

In the 400's, Huns from Central Asia invaded India. They caused the downfall of the Guptas. After the mid-500's, India experienced many centuries of weak government and foreign invasions.

The Gupta Empire, A.D. 400

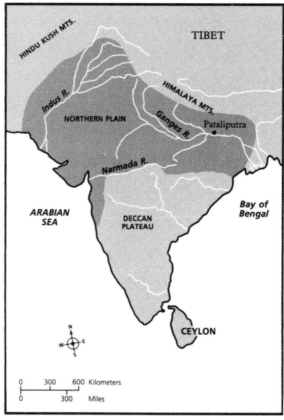

PROVE or DISPROVE: Irrigation was not a problem for the farmers of the Gupta Empire.

TRUE OR FALSE

Indicate whether each of the following statements is *true* (**T**) or *false* (**F**).

1. The first cities on the Indian subcontinent were built in the Ganges River Valley.

2. Mohenjo-Daro and Harappa were built of brick and had paved streets and sewers.

3. The people of the Indus civilization probably worshipped a goddess.

4. Scholars agree that the Indus civilization ended as the result of a great fire.

5. Mohenjo-Daro means "place of the dead."

DEFINITIONS

Explain the meaning of each of the following terms:

a. Aryans
b. Dravidians
c. caste system
d. Brahmins
e. untouchables
f. Sanskrit
g. Vedas
h. Upanishads

MATCHING EXERCISE

Match each name or term in Column A with its definition or description in Column B.

Column A	Column B
1. Hinduism	a. the "Enlightened One"
2. Brahma	b. the state of perfect peace
3. reincarnation	c. the oldest of India's great religions
4. Siddhartha Gautama	d. the most important Hindu god
5. nirvana	e. rebirth of the soul

MAKING CORRECTIONS

Reread "5. The Empire of the Mauryas," on page 61, and "6. The Gupta Empire," on page 62. Find out what is wrong with each of the following statements. Then rewrite each one as a correct statement.

1. Starting about 321 B.C, an Indian conqueror named Chandragupta Maurya gained control over southern India and began the Gupta Dynasty.

2. Asoka became a Hindu and then sent Hindu priests to spread their teaching in Europe and North America.

3. Rules of conduct for Asoka's subjects were hidden so that no one could see them.

4. Under the Gupta emperors, India entered a dark age of poverty and cultural decline.

5. Southeast Asia rejected the culture of the Gupta Empire.

THE CULTURE OF EARLY CHINA

One of the world's most advanced civilizations arose in the river valleys of China. This civilization was shaped by the contributions of its ruling dynasties and by the teachings of its great thinkers. As time passed, the Chinese came to consider their civilization to be the most highly developed in the world.

1. The Hwang Ho.   The earliest Chinese civilization began in the valley of the Hwang Ho, or Yellow River, between 3000 and 2500 B.C. Other early Chinese civilizations developed in the fertile valleys of the Yangtze and Hsi rivers.

The rich soil and abundant water in the Hwang Ho Valley aided the growing of crops. The farmers raised, in particular, two types of grains—millet and wheat. To protect their fields from frequent flooding, the Hwang Ho farmers built *dikes*. These earth mounds kept the river within its banks. The farmers also dug irrigation canals to carry river water to their fields in dry weather. One of the reasons for the rise of government in the Hwang Ho Valley was the need for an organized way of regulating the dike and canal systems.

Hwang Ho farmers planting rice. In the foreground are canals that carry water from the river to the fields.

2. The Shang Dynasty. About 1750 B.C., the first of the Shang rulers came to power in the Hwang Ho Valley. The Shang Dynasty ruled northern China for about 700 years. Tools and weapons made of bronze gave the Shang power and wealth.

 a. *Achievements.* In this period, people developed a written language. At first they scratched picture symbols on pieces of animal bone. Then Shang writers developed *calligraphy*, a way of drawing characters, or symbols, to express words and ideas. They used 2,000 such characters. The characters were written with a brush and ink, on strips of silk, bamboo, or paper.

 Rapid advances in technology took place during the Shang period. Improved methods of casting bronze enabled Chinese craftspeople to produce highly decorated containers. Artisans learned to use kaolin, a fine white clay, for making pottery. They developed unique shapes and glazes for their pottery. The Shang also learned to raise silkworms, to spin thread from the cocoons, and to weave silk cloth.

 The Shang built large palaces, government buildings, and religious shrines. (The shrines were places where the Chinese worshipped their ancestors.) The tombs of Shang kings and nobles were magnificently furnished. Beautiful ornaments of stone, jade, and bone, as well as bronze containers and wooden chariots, have been found in the tombs.

The Shang Civilization, 1500 B.C.

EXPLAIN: Loyang was the center of the Shang civilization.

---

b. *Militarism.* The Shang conquered approximately 1,800 city-states in northern China. The Hwang Ho Valley had to be defended from attacks by less advanced people living outside it. Superior Shang military forces, equipped with war chariots and bronze weapons, kept the valley safe. As time went on, however, the Shang rulers became less able to continue the constant fighting. About 1028 B.C., people called the Chou joined with other tribes in western China. The Chou and their allies overthrew the Shang.

3. The Chou Dynasty.   Chou rule lasted about 800 years, from 1028 to 256 B.C. During this time, important advances were made. Many cities and towns grew up. The number of skilled craftspeople and merchants increased. Money in the form of small coins began to be used. People could pay for goods with money instead of bartering. Trade expanded and made the dynasty prosperous.

a. *Political theories.* Under the Chou, the Chinese developed the idea that their rulers were gods. They called the king the "Son of Heaven." But the people believed that the king would have

This bronze container, in the shape of a rhinoceros, was used in Shang religious ceremonies.

the support of the other gods only as long as he ruled justly. If he was unjust and lost the favor of the gods, the people had the right to overthrow him. This principle of *revolution* was put into action many times during China's long history.

b. *The arts and philosophy.*   Art, literature, philosophy, and scholarship also received encouragement during the Chou period. The Chinese system of writing became highly refined. The forms of the characters used today have changed very little over 3,000 years.

For centuries, the Chinese have followed the teachings of their great philosophers. Philosophers are people who seek wisdom and truth and think about the principles that should guide a person's life. One of the greatest Chinese philosophers was Confucius, who lived between 551 and 479 B.C. He is, perhaps, the most honored person in Chinese history.

Confucius taught that the ideal way of life could be achieved through self-control and proper conduct. Respect shown by children for their parents, pupils for their teachers, and citizens for their rulers are examples of proper conduct. Confucius also taught respect for ancestors. People, he said, should live by this rule: "Do not do to others what you do not want them to do to you." The pupils of Confucius wrote down many of his ideas and put them into books such as the *Analects*. Confucianism is regarded by some as a religion and by others as a code of behavior.

Much of Confucius's work was devoted to preserving the literature of China. He lived in a troubled time, made violent by conflicts between kings and nobles. His fear of the destruction or loss of the works of philosophers who had lived before him made Confucius gather earlier writings into a work called the *Five Classics.*

Respect for tradition and the ways of the past was an important part of Confucian teaching. It caused the Chinese to dislike sharp changes in their way of life. This attitude had a strong effect on Chinese society for centuries.

Taoism is another Chinese religion. It arose from the teachings of Lao-tzu, a philosopher who lived at the same time as Confucius. Lao-tzu urged people to live simply and in harmony with nature in order to learn the true meaning of life. People should take no action to change what happens to them. Lao-tzu taught his followers to be humble and kind, even when insulted or injured by others. Those who follow the Way, or the Tao, will find inner peace, he said.

Despite many similarities between Taoism and Confucianism, there was one important difference. Confucius stressed the importance of good government. Lao-tzu thought that people were better off with as little government as possible.

Confucius and Lao-tzu lived at the same time as Siddhartha Gautama. The religions that arose from the teachings of these men have influenced the thinking of people in Asia and throughout much of the world for more than 2,000 years.

c. *Era of Warring States.* Power struggles between the Chou kings and their nobles weakened the kings. Rulers of states often fought one another. The last 200 years of Chou rule are called the "Era of Warring States." Finally, the ruler of the Ch'in, the strongest of the warring states, overthrew the Chou king in 256 B.C. The Ch'in ruler took control of China by forcing the other nobles to accept him as king in 221. From this new dynasty, Ch'in, China got its name.

 ESSAY QUESTION

What would cause the Chinese to feel that they had a right to start a revolution?

MATCHING EXERCISE

Match each term in Column A with its description in Column B.

Column A	Column B
1. *Analects*	*a.* power struggles between kings and nobles
2. *Five Classics*	*b.* writings of philosophers who lived before Confucius
3. Taoism	*c.* the teachings of Lao-tzu
4. Era of Warring States	*d.* a book containing the ideas of Confucius
5. Ch'in Dynasty	*e.* replaced the Chou Dynasty

4. The Ch'in Dynasty. The rule of the Ch'in was brief but important. The best known Ch'in ruler was Shih Huang Ti, which means "First Emperor." A strong and determined leader, he built his kingdom into an empire by extending his control southward to the Hsi River. Uniform laws, standardized currency, and new roads unified China into a single country. The emperor destroyed the power of the warring nobles. He appointed officials to rule the 36 states, or provinces. These actions strengthened the central government of China. The basic form of government set up by Shih Huang Ti remained unchanged until the 20th century A.D.

The wandering tribes living on the plains to the north of China threatened the Ch'in Dynasty. To protect his people, Shih Huang Ti completed the Great Wall of China. This huge structure, which still stands today, extends across 1,500 miles of northern China. From the watchtowers and forts along the Great Wall, Chinese soldiers were able to keep Mongols, Huns, and other enemies out of the empire.

Shih Huang Ti disliked scholars who praised the Chou Dynasty and criticized his rule as being cruel and harsh. To stop criticism of his government, he jailed philosophers and teachers and burned Confucian books.

Shih Huang Ti died in 210 B.C. This ended the Ch'in Dynasty. A power struggle among the generals of the Ch'in army was won by Liu Pang. He established the Han Dynasty, the next to rule China.

5. The Han Dynasty. This dynasty lasted from 206 B.C. until A.D. 220. Throughout these years, Han emperors increased the size of China by conquering new lands. Eventually, the Han

The Ch'in Dynasty, 220 B.C.

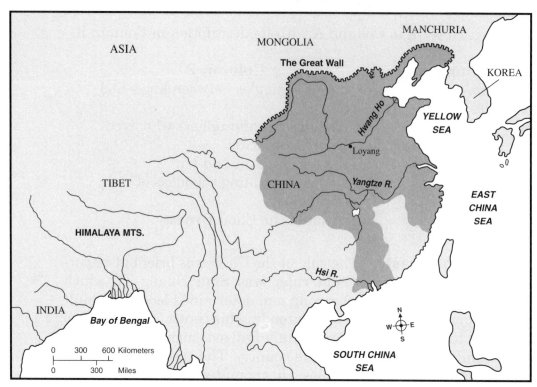

Indicate whether each of the following statements is *true* (**T**) or *false* (**F**).

1. The Ch'in ruled areas of China that were between the Great Wall and the Hsi River.

2. Mongolia and Manchuria were ruled by the Ch'in.

3. Loyang was a Yangtze River port.

4. The Great Wall protected the Ch'in lands from the Indians and Tibetans.

---

controlled one of the largest and wealthiest empires in the ancient world.

  a. *Civil service.* The Han ruled their empire with the help of appointed officials who were paid salaries to perform certain duties. To fill these government jobs, public examinations were held. The men who scored the highest on the tests received the appointments. The examinations tested a candidate's knowledge of law, mathematics and, in particular, the writings of Confucius. The best students from colleges throughout the empire took the

The Builder of the Great Wall

The Great Wall is 20 to 50 feet high and 15 to 25 feet thick.

A huge wall extends across 1,500 miles of northern China. It was built by order of Shih Huang Ti.

Turkish nomads, called Huns, lived on the plains northwest of China. Their fierce horsemen often swept down on Chinese towns and villages, killing and robbing. Shih Huang Ti realized that his new empire would not last long if he did not find a way to protect China from its northern enemies.

To keep the Huns out, the emperor decided to connect smaller walls built in different places into one "Great Wall." At first, most of the workers building the wall were convicts. However, convict labor alone was not enough to finish the wall. Perhaps one-third of all Chinese men were forced to help build the wall.

A wide road and many watchtowers were built along the top of the Great Wall. Large numbers of Chinese soldiers were stationed at different points on the wall.

Once the northern border was safe, Shih Huang Ti conquered large por-tions of southern China. The emperor was determined to unify China under his rule. He destroyed the power of those nobles who opposed him. He forced many nobles to move to his cap-ital city so that he could control them. Citizens were ordered to turn in their weapons to the government. Only sol-diers were permitted to be armed.

The emperor built roads to improve trade and communication. Law was standardized, or made the same, throughout China. Money, weights, and measures were also standardized. This made the buying and selling of goods and services easier.

Other advances were made. The Chinese system of writing was simpli-fied and improved. Many scientific works were written during this period.

Shih Huang Ti died in 210 B.C. For the next thousand years, the emperors of China continued Shih Huang Ti's policy of unifying China under one royal government.

1. How did the Great Wall help Shih Huang Ti enlarge and unify the Chinese Empire?
2. Indicate whether each of the following statements is *true* (**T**) or *false* (**F**):
    a. Shih Huang Ti was a democratic leader.
    b. After Shih Huang Ti's death, all of his policies were abandoned.

The Han Dynasty, A.D. 220

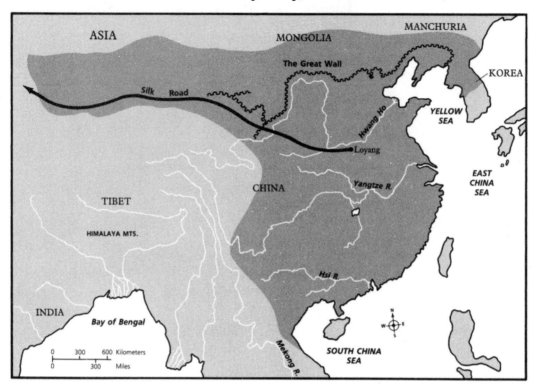

Choose the item that best completes each sentence or answers each question.

1. In which general direction is India from Manchuria?
   (*a*) northeast (*b*) southwest (*c*) south (*d*) north

2. In which general direction is China from India?
   (*a*) northeast (*b*) southeast (*c*) northwest (*d*) southwest

3. The Silk Road linked China to countries to the
   (*a*) east (*b*) north (*c*) south (*d*) west.

4. The Great Wall protected China from invaders from the
   (*a*) east (*b*) west (*c*) north (*d*) south.

5. The northernmost river in China shown is the (*a*) Yangtze
   (*b*) Hwang Ho (*c*) Hsi (*d*) Mekong.

---

examinations after training in an imperial school in the Han capital.

Thousands of able officials entered the Han civil service as a result of this examination system. Even young men from very poor families could take the test. The system provided a degree of

Trade caravans on the Silk Road, the great highway of Central Asia.

equality of opportunity that was rare in the ancient world. It remained in use under each dynasty that followed the Han.

A weakness of the civil service examination system was the emphasis placed on the learning of old classics rather than new ideas. As a result, most government officials resisted change. This led to problems for China in later years.

b. *Cultural exchange.* The Han extended their empire into Southeast Asia and to the borders of Persia and India. This brought the Chinese into contact with other civilizations and led to the exchange of knowledge with different peoples. Along the Silk Road, which ran from China through Central Asia to the Middle East, Chinese traders met Western merchants.

In A.D. 105, the Chinese invented paper. The world's first dictionary was written during the Han Dynasty.

Contact with India led to the introduction of Buddhism into China. Large numbers of *peasants* (small farmers) were attracted to this religion. As Buddhism spread, religious centers called *monasteries* were built throughout China. Monks taught and meditated within the monastery walls. Wealthier believers gave gifts of tax-free land to the monasteries. In later times, the religion of many Chinese became a blend of Buddhist and Taoist teachings.

As the years passed, Han rulers became weaker. They found it difficult to prevent revolts by the peasants and the rise of local rulers called warlords. In time, the warlords caused the dynasty to fall. The next several hundred years were a time of great unrest.

This neighing and pawing horse was found in a tomb of the T'ang Dynasty period.

6. The T'ang Dynasty.   The next important dynasty to rule China was the T'ang. It lasted from A.D. 618 to 907. Under the T'angs, China entered a golden age of cultural and political achievement. The rulers restored a strong central government. They increased the size of the empire by adding Korea and Tibet. Expanded trade brought more wealth to China.

   a. *Cultural contributions.*   T'ang painters and sculptors developed new forms and styles of expression. Scholars wrote more encyclopedias and histories than ever before. The writing of poetry flourished. One of China's greatest poets, Li Po, wrote in the 700's. The invention of printing made possible the production of more books. As a result, literature became available to greater numbers of people.

   b. *Wu Chao.*   A remarkable person who lived during this period was the Empress Wu Chao, the wife of Emperor Kao-Tsung. During a long illness, the emperor asked his wife to help rule the empire. Empress Wu encouraged agriculture and silk production. She commissioned scholars and artists to work for her.

   In A.D. 690, after the death of her husband, Wu Chao began governing China on her own. She was the only woman to do so. Many government officials disapproved of Wu because she was a woman. More people turned against her when she established civil service examinations for women. In 705, those who opposed Wu forced her to turn over the throne to her son. She died soon after.

In A.D. 907, the T'ang Dynasty came to an end. The emperors had lost power to provincial governors during a long period of decline. When the provinces declared themselves to be independent states, China became weak and disunited. As the empire began to break up, foreign invaders conquered and ruled China.

ESSAY QUESTION

The period of T'ang rule in China is called a "golden age." List *one* political and *two* cultural developments that explain why the period was "golden."

SENTENCE COMPLETION

Complete each the following statements:

1. Chinese civilization was shaped by the contributions of —.

2. The earliest Chinese civilization began in —.

3. Other early Chinese civilizations developed in the —.

4. Shang artisans learned to use kaolin —.

5. Under the Chou Dynasty, the Chinese developed the idea that —.

6. The basic form of government established by Shih Huang Ti remained —.

7. A strength of the Han civil service examination system was —.

8. Under the T'ang Dynasty, the size of the empire was —.

CHRONOLOGY

For each of the following dynasty names, state the dates of its rule. Then rearrange the names in their proper chronological order (1–5).

a. Ch'in   *d.* T'ang
b. Han   *e.* Chou
c. Shang

DEFINITIONS

Explain the importance of each of the following:

a. Hwang Ho
b. calligraphy
c. revolution
d. Great Wall
e. Silk Road

Chapter Review

▶ **MULTIPLE-CHOICE**

Choose the item that best completes each sentence.

1. Two cities of the Indus River Valley civilization were (*a*) Hwang Ho and Yangtze (*b*) Mohenjo-Daro and Harappa (*c*) Vaisya and Sudra (*d*) Loyang and Hsi.

2. The Aryans who invaded the Indus Valley introduced (*a*) the caste system (*b*) farming (*c*) the wheel (*d*) bronze weapons.

3. An important part of Hinduism is the belief that the soul is purified through (*a*) prayer (*b*) reincarnation (*c*) ritual (*d*) study.

4. The belief that the soul can enter a state of perfect peace, called nirvana, is part of the teachings of (*a*) Taoism (*b*) Confucianism (*c*) Buddhism (*d*) Shintoism.

5. Two great dynasties to rule over India were the (*a*) Shang and Chou (*b*) Han and Manchu (*c*) Ch'in and T'ang (*d*) Maurya and Gupta.

6. The earliest Chinese civilization developed in the valley of the (*a*) Hwang Ho (*b*) Indus River (*c*) Silk Road (*d*) Hsi.

7. Chinese government developed because of the need to regulate (*a*) bronze tools and weapons (*b*) dikes and canals (*c*) civil service examinations (*d*) philosophical teaching.

8. The Chinese method of writing developed under the (*a*) Chou Dynasty (*b*) T'ang Dynasty (*c*) Shang Dynasty (*d*) priests.

9. The "Son of Heaven" was a title given by the Chinese to their (*a*) kings (*b*) scholars (*c*) philosophers (*d*) priests.

10. The writings of Confucius were collected in a book called (*a*) *Rig-Veda* (*b*) *Sagas* (*c*) *Upanishads* (*d*) *Analects*.

 ESSAY QUESTION

Explain how each of the following contributed to the development of civilization in ancient Asia.

Buddha   Confucius   Shih Huang Ti
Asoka   Lao-tzu   Wu Chao

 CHRONOLOGY

Use the information on the timeline below to answer the following questions.

Timeline

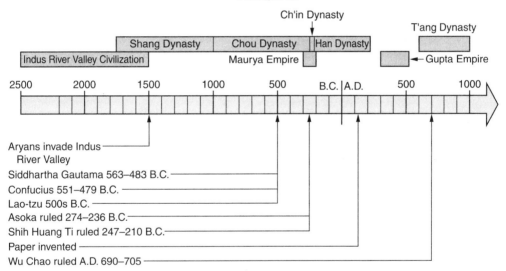

1. Which civilization is the oldest?

2. Which Indian empire overlaps three Chinese dynasties?

3. In which dynasty did the founder of Taoism live?

4. Which civilization, empire, or dynasty lasted for the longest period?

5. Which dynasty overlaps both B.C. and A.D. dates?

Connections: The Invaders

While warriors of the Shang dynasty were taking control of the Hwang Ho Valley, waves of invaders began to smash into what is now Europe. These invaders, called Indo-Europeans, swept out of western Asia in search of land and riches. The Indo-Europeans, like the Shang warriors, were fierce fighters who used bronze weapons and often fought on horseback and in chariots.

The Indo-Europeans spread their language and culture throughout Europe. Greeks, Romans, Celts, Slavs, and Scandinavians were all descendants of Indo-Europeans. Groups of Indo-Europeans, the Aryans, invaded India, where they pushed the Dravidians and other peoples south.

During this period, between 2000 and 1500 B.C., the Chinese began to form dynasties while the Indo-Europeans generally remained divided into small kingdoms and city-states. Nevertheless, conquest by strong rulers occurred in both Europe and China. Beginning with the Shang, Chinese rulers eventually built their holdings into a great empire. In time, the same thing was done by the Greek and Roman descendants of the Indo-Europeans.

1. List differences between and similarities of the Indo-Europeans and the Chinese.

2. Identify the changes brought by the Indo-Europeans to the areas they invaded.

DOCUMENT-BASED QUESTION

This question is based on the accompanying documents (1–5). It will improve your ability to work with historical documents.

Historical Context:

Early Asian civilizations developed in what are now the Indus River Valley of India and the Hwang Ho (Yellow River) Valley in China. Like the early civilizations of the Middle East and North Africa, they created religions and codes of behavior. Hinduism and Buddhism arose in India; Confucianism and Taoism, in China.

Task:

Using information from the documents and your knowledge of world history, answer the questions that follow each document. Your answers to each question will help you write the document-based essay.

Document 1. Excerpt from *The Laws of Manu*, a text sacred to Hindus dating from the 1st or 2nd century A.D.:

Action which springs from the mind, from speech, and from the body produces either good or evil results.

Coveting the property of others, thinking in one's heart of what is undesirable and following false doctrines are the three kinds of sinful mental action.

Abusing others, speaking untruth, detracting from the merits of all men, and talking idly shall be the four kinds of evil verbal action.

Taking what has not been given, injuring creatures without the sanction of the law . . . are . . . kinds of wicked bodily action.

In consequence of many sins committed with his body, a man becomes in the next birth something inanimate; in consequence of sins committed by speech, [he becomes] a bird, or a beast; and in consequence of mental sins, he is reborn in a low caste.

> **Source**: G. Buhler, *The Laws of Manu*. Oxford, England: Clarendon Press, 1886.

According to this document, what kinds of actions are considered evil and what are their consequences?

Document 2. Excerpt from one of the Buddha's best-known teachings, "The First Sermon of the Buddha," 6th century B.C.:

This, monks, is the Noble Truth concerning the Origin of Suffering: verily it originates in that craving . . . that seeks satisfaction now here, now there; that is to say, craving for pleasures.

This, monks, is the Noble Truth, the Path which leads to the Cessation of Suffering: the laying aside of, the giving up, the being free from . . . this craving.

This, monks, is this . . . Noble Eightfold Path, that is to say, right views, right intent, right speech, right conduct, right means of livelihood, right endeavor, right mindfulness, and right meditation.

> **Source:** *Buddhism: A Religion of Infinite Compassion*, edited and translated by Clarence H. Hamilton. New York: The Liberal Arts Press, 1951, pp. 28–29, 32.

According to this document, what does the Buddha believe causes suffering and how can it be ended?

Document 3.   Study the illustration on page 60.

What does it tell us about the importance of Buddhism to the Japanese people?

Document 4.   Excerpt from the *Tao Te Ching*, the collected teachings of the Chinese Taoist philosopher Lao-tzu, 6th century B.C.:

> *Verse 9*
> Fill your bowl to the brim
> and it will spill.
> Keep sharpening your knife
> and it will blunt.
> Chase after money and security
> and your heart will never unclench.
> Care about people's approval
> and you will be their prisoner.
> Do your work, then step back.
> The only path to serenity.
>
> *Verse 37*
> When there is no desire,
> All things are at peace.

> **Source:** *Tao Te Ching by Lao Tzu, A New English Version*, translated by Stephen Mitchell. New York: Harper Collins, 1988.

According to this document, what types of behavior does Lao-tzu believe a person should avoid and what would result if these behaviors were avoided?

Document 5.   Excerpt from *Analects*, a record of the sayings of the Chinese philosopher Confucius (551–479 B.C.) compiled by his students:

> Confucius said, "Lead the people by means of government measures and regulate them with laws and punishments, and they will avoid wrongdoing but will have no sense of honor and shame. Lead them with virtue and regulate them by the rules of propriety, and they will have a sense of shame and, moreover, set themselves right." (*Analects* 2:3)

Confucius said, "If a ruler sets himself right, he will be followed without his command. If he does not set himself right, even his commands will not be obeyed." (*Analects* 13:6)

Source: *The Analects of Confucius,* translated by Arthur Waley. George Allen & Unwin, 1958.

According to this document, what behavior does Confucius say a ruler should follow to be effective?

DOCUMENT-BASED ESSAY

Using information from the above documents and your knowledge of world history, write an essay in which you:

- Discuss shared codes of behavior of the four religions and philosophies.
- Explain how the behaviors suggested are important to a civilized society.

Chapter 5
The Glory of Greek Civilization

In the area of the Aegean Sea, a number of people developed complex civilizations. Some of these civilizations were on large islands. Others were on the coast of Asia Minor and the peninsula of Europe now called Greece. The Greeks created the first advanced civilization on the European mainland. This civilization reached its height in Athens between about 500 and 300 B.C. The standards the Greeks set for art, literature, learning, and government still influence our way of life.

THREE AEGEAN CIVILIZATIONS

Between about 2000 and 1100 B.C., three major civilizations prospered in the area of the Aegean Sea.

The Minoans on the island of Crete, just south of Greece, created magnificent cities and a rich culture.

On the mainland and islands of Greece, the Hellenes built fortified cities and established kingdoms. They were aggressive and warlike; they were also a seafaring people who founded colonies and trading posts throughout the Aegean lands.

On the coast of Asia Minor, the Trojans built the great city of Troy. Its location enabled the Trojans to control the trade routes between the Aegean Sea and the Black Sea.

1. The Wealth of Minos. From about 1700 to about 1400 B.C., the civilization of Crete was the most important one in the Aegean world. The term Minoan comes from the name Minos, a legendary king of Crete. Some historians give the name Minos to all the rulers of Crete.

a. *Trading power.* Crete had poor soil and good harbors. As a result, the Minoans became seafaring merchants whose great wealth came from trade. Minoan ships carried goods throughout the Aegean and Mediterranean seas. People in other lands greatly desired products from Crete: gold and silver, jewelry, swords, and ivory carvings.

The Minoans did not feel the need for a large army. Instead, the king built a powerful navy that kept the seas free from pirates.

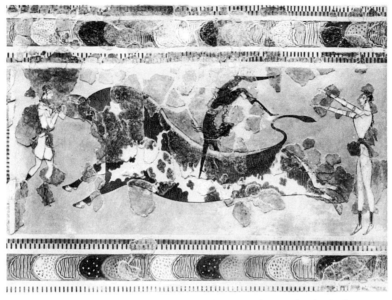

This wall painting shows an athlete leaping over the back of a bull.

The navy protected Minoan settlements along the shores of the Mediterranean. It also collected payments due the king from conquered people.

 b. *Complex culture.* The Minoans made beautiful clay vases, bronze daggers decorated with enamel, gold cups, and other luxury goods. Their palaces and the homes of their wealthier citizens were decorated with wall paintings. The Minoans also enjoyed efficient plumbing systems with drains and tiled pipes.

 Among the sports practiced by Minoan athletes were boxing and the dangerous pursuit of leaping over bulls.

 The Minoans regarded the bull as an animal sacred to the Earth Mother goddess. They worshipped the goddess as the source of life and fertility.

 The most impressive city on Crete was Knossos. The king lived in Knossos in a huge palace. It contained hundreds of richly decorated and furnished rooms, which faced large, open courtyards.

2. The Fall of the Minoans. It is not known what caused the decline of Minoan civilization. Some historians believe that Hellenes invaded Crete sometime between 1450 and 1350 B.C. Others think that the eruption of a volcano on a nearby island destroyed the cities of Crete. It is known that by 1400 B.C. the Hellenes on mainland Greece had opened direct trading with Egypt and Syria. Such trade would not have been possible if the Minoan navy had still controlled the seas.

Of Legends, Kings, and Heroes

The ancient Greeks gave to the world a rich body of *legends*. Legends are stories about heroes and the great deeds they performed. Legends are generally believed to have some basis in fact, but they cannot be proved.

One such legendary hero was Theseus, king of Athens, in the days when the Minoans of Crete were at the peak of their power.

When he was a boy, Theseus was captured by the Minoans and taken to Crete. There, he and other Greek boys and girls were trained as dancers and acrobats. On religious festival days, they performed the sacred bull dance in which the dancers had to leap over the horns of a charging bull. If the dancers survived, a greater horror awaited them. One by one, they were led to a monster called the Minotaur, who ate them. The Minotaur was part man and part bull. He lived in a *labyrinth*, a twisting maze, under the royal palace of Knossos. Theseus entered the labyrinth, killed the Minotaur, and escaped from Crete.

Today, the legend of Theseus the king has been brought to life by the novelist Mary Renault. Renault presents Theseus to us in two brilliant books—*The King Must Die* and *The Bull from the Sea*. Theseus's many adventures and brave deeds described in Greek legend are woven into a story that is told by the king himself. Readers enter the Aegean world as it was around the time of the Trojan War. The wealth and power of Crete and the dangerous lives of Greek warriors and seafarers are skillfully re-created. While Theseus may not have existed, the civilization dramatized by Renault is quite real.

1. Why should people interested in Greek history read the novels of Mary Renault?

2. Why did the Minoans perform bull dances?

By 1350 B.C., Knossos no longer existed as a great city. The Hellenes had become the great power in the Aegean world.

Much of what we know about the Minoan civilization is the result of the work of Sir Arthur Evans, a British *archeologist*. Evans began to dig up the ruins of Knossos in the early 20th century A.D. Since then, other archeologists, many of them from Greece, have increased our knowledge of Minoan cities.

3. The Trojan Wars.   After the fall of Crete, the Hellenes of Greece turned their drive for power elsewhere. They expanded their trade northward into the Black Sea region and into Asia Minor. As time passed, the Hellenes came into conflict with the city-state of Troy. The Trojans controlled the entrance to the Black Sea. Hellenic ships were forced to pay tolls to the Trojans. Between 1200 and 1180 B.C., two Trojan Wars were fought.

a. *Homer's tales.*   Centuries afterward, a Greek poet named Homer created a long poem about the wars. It is called the *Iliad*,

According to the Roman poet Virgil, Troy was conquered by the Greeks after the Trojans took in a huge wooden horse left outside the city's walls. Greeks, hidden in the horse, crept out at night and opened the city gates for the rest of their army.

and it is thought to be based on oral, or spoken, poetry carried down by tradition through many years. In the poem, Homer describes the mighty deeds of legendary heroes. He says nothing about commercial rivalry as a cause of the Trojan Wars.

According to Homer, the Trojan Wars started after Paris, a son of the king of Troy, kidnapped Helen, the beautiful wife of a Greek king. An army of Greek heroes, including Achilles and Odysseus, sailed to Troy to rescue Helen. The great battle between Achilles and Hector, prince of Troy, in which Hector is killed, is a high point of the poem. The Greeks finally defeated the Trojans and destroyed Troy.

Whether these events took place or not, the *Iliad* is a tale of high adventure. It is also a rich source of information about the warfare, customs, and religious practices of the Greeks. The poem emphasizes the early Greek appreciation of courage and individual effort.

Homer created another long poem, the *Odyssey*, about the adventures of Odysseus on his long journey home after the fall of Troy. Today, Homer's two poems are regarded as great works of literature.

b. *Archeological discoveries.* Our knowledge of Troy is based on the work of Heinrich Schliemann. This German

This jar shows the Aegean peoples' feeling for the sea. An octopus, fish, and other sea life are depicted on this 3,000-year-old jar.

archeologist discovered and dug up the ruins of Troy in the late A.D. 1800's. He proved that the city of Troy as described by Homer had really existed.

4. The Decline of the Aegean Peoples.   Following the destruction of Troy, the Greek cities fought one another. The constant warfare weakened them. In time, invaders from the north, called Dorians, conquered the Hellenes. The newcomers used iron swords and spears. The brittle bronze blades of the Greeks proved to be of little use against such weapons.

The Dorians did not have a high level of civilization. As a result, the way of life of the Aegean peoples declined after about 1200 B.C. Several centuries passed before the Greek city-states rose to new heights of achievement.

 DEFINITIONS

Explain the meaning of each of the following terms.

  a. Minos
  b. Knossos
  c. labyrinth

  d. bull dance
  e. Minotaur

TRUE OR FALSE

Indicate which of the following statements are *true* (**T**) and which are *false* (**F**).

1.   The *Iliad* is a long poem about the Trojan Wars.

2. According to Homer, the Trojan Wars began when a beautiful woman named Helen was kidnapped by the son of a Trojan king.

3. The *Odyssey* describes the adventures of Achilles during his journey home after the fall of Troy.

4. Historians believe that everything in Homer's poems is completely true.

5. The *Iliad* and The *Odyssey* are considered to be minor works of literature.

WRITING EXERCISE

In a short paragraph, describe the decline of the Hellenes.

TIMELINE QUESTIONS

Use the information from the timeline below to answer the questions that follow:

TIMELINE: AEGEAN CIVILIZATIONS

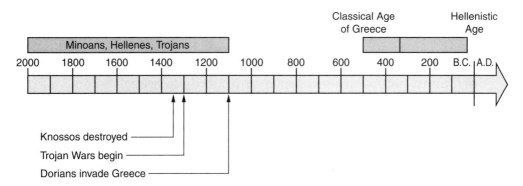

1. How many years are shown for the Minoan, Hellenic, and Trojan civilizations?

2. When did the Dorians invade Greece?

3. How many years passed between the Dorian invasion of Greece and the beginning of the Classical Age of Greece?

4. Arrange the following events and ages in chronological order (1–5).
     Hellenistic Age
     Knossos destroyed
     Classical Age of Greece
     Dorians invade Greece
     Trojan Wars begin

THE ACCOMPLISHMENTS OF ATHENS

Greek civilization reached its highest point of development in the *Classical Age*, which began around 500 B.C. During this period, Greeks excelled in the arts and sciences and in the creation of new forms of government. Divided by rugged mountain ranges, the Greeks did not develop political unity. Even though they shared a common language, culture, and religion, they did not become a nation. Instead, the Greeks created *poli*, or city-states, which remained divided and independent of one another.

Each city-state (*polis*) was governed as its citizens thought best. A city-state ruled by a king was called a *monarchy*. One ruled by nobles was called an *aristocracy*. A polis run by wealthy merchants and landowners was called an *oligarchy*.

The city-state of Athens chose men of ability from all classes of society to govern it. Most of its free male citizens could vote and hold public office. Such a system of government was called a *democracy*, which means rule by the people. Athens led Greece in the practice of democracy and in the encouragement of art and learning. It became the most famous and honored Greek city-state.

1. Athenian Democracy.   Athens had tried other forms of government before it developed into a democracy. Solon, a man famous for his wisdom, greatly aided the growth of democracy. He improved Athenian government in the 570's. One of his laws allowed all free male citizens, even the poorest, to vote in the Assembly, the lawmaking body of Athens. By the 5th century, most male citizens of Athens could participate firsthand in making major decisions. Such a government was called a *direct democracy*.

a.   *Training citizens.*   An Athenian male began preparing for his role in the city's democratic government at the age of 18. At that time, he took a public pledge to defend Athens and its gods. After two years of military training, he entered active military service. This active service was considered to be a citizen's most important obligation.

When a young Athenian finished his service in the military, he had the right to speak and vote in the Assembly. After the age of 30, he might be chosen to serve in the Council of 500, which supervised the army, the navy, and the financial affairs of Athens.

A citizen might also be chosen to serve as one of the 6,000 jury-men of Athens. They heard legal cases and handed down verdicts. There were no judges or lawyers.

Finally, a citizen of Athens might be elected to serve as one of the Ten Generals who led the armed forces of Athens. Such an honor had a drawback. If a general lost a battle, he would be tried by jury and either exiled or executed.

b. *Limits to democracy.* Athenian democracy did not extend to everyone. Athenian women had no political or legal rights. Neither did slaves, who were usually prisoners of war. Also excluded from participation in the government were residents who were not born in Athens and, therefore, were not citizens. As a result, Athens was ruled by a minority, not a majority, of its residents.

 ESSAY QUESTION

Compare Athenian democracy with modern American democracy. Focus on:

1. Lawmaking bodies
2. Court system
3. Voting rights

2. Learning in Athens. An Athenian boy was given an education so that he could serve his city well. He learned grammar by reciting the works of Homer and other great poets. To further develop his appreciation of the arts, he was taught to sing and to play a musical instrument. In addition, he studied geometry, astronomy, geography, and public speaking. Because the Greeks believed in training the body as well as the mind, a boy also took athletic instruction. He participated in the sports of wrestling, swimming, running, and throwing the javelin and discus. A male slave supervised a boy's activities throughout the day.

Athenian girls were taught to be good wives and mothers. They learned weaving, household management, and the care of children. After marriage, between the ages of 14 and 16, a woman lived under the supervision of her husband and rarely left her home.

3. Athenian Culture. Most Greek cities encouraged the development of the arts and the sciences. But the devotion of Athens to learning made it the most creative city in Greece. Talented people from throughout the Greek world came to Athens to learn. The best artists, architects, and sculptors worked there. They beautified the city with their creations. Dramatists wrote plays that are still performed today. Philosophers, mathematicians, and scientists opened schools and taught pupils from all over the Greek world.

a. *The great minds of Athens.*   Socrates (470–399 B.C.) was considered to be the wisest philosopher in Athens. He earned his living as a stonecutter and accepted no pay from those he agreed to teach. By constantly asking questions, he forced his pupils to think about the meaning of ideas such as virtue, courage, good, and evil. He taught people to search for the truth about themselves. Socrates questioned everything and everyone, including the actions of Athens's leaders. In time, he angered those in authority. Socrates was tried and convicted of corrupting youth. When he refused to accept exile, he was condemned to die by drinking poison.

Plato (427–347 B.C.) was the most famous pupil of Socrates. Plato wrote about many basic ideas of life in works called *dialogues*. He established a school, called the Academy, in which he taught philosophy, science, and mathematics. Plato asked his pupils to think about such questions as "What is good?" "What is true?" "What is beautiful?" One of Plato's main concerns was to

Socrates: philosopher and teacher.

The Theater of Dionysus in Athens was one of many open-air theaters where plays by Aeschylus, Sophocles, and others were performed.

set up an ideal form of government. He described this government in *The Republic*, his most famous written work.

Aristotle (384–322 B.C.) studied under Plato. In time, Aristotle opened his own school, the Lyceum. There he wrote hundreds of essays about the results of his research in logic, politics, and science. Much of his scientific work was in botany and biology. Aristotle taught the value of practicing the "Golden Mean," which meant doing all things in moderation by avoiding extremes, or excesses.

b. *Dramatists.* Aeschylus (525–456 B.C.), Sophocles (496–405 B.C.), and Euripides (484–406 B.C.) wrote plays called tragedies. Their works dealt with serious themes, such as war, death, justice, and the relationships between gods and ordinary people. Aristophanes (about 448–385 B.C.) wrote comedies to make people laugh. His plays made fun of politicians, philosophers, and other dramatists.

c. *Historians.* Herodotus (484–425 B.C.) and Thucydides (about 471–400 B.C.) became famous as historians. They may have been first to write about what actually happened and the first to do research to check their facts. Herodotus wrote about the wars between the Greeks and Persians. Thucydides described the Peloponnesian War, the long civil war in which the Greek city-states fought one another.

IDENTIFICATIONS

For each of the following persons, list one of his contributions to the culture of Athens:

a. Socrates   *e.* Aristophanes
b. Plato   *f.* Herodotus
c. Aristotle   *g.* Thucydides
d. Aeschylus

 ## SENTENCE COMPLETION

From the list that follows, select the term that best completes each sentence.

polis   direct democracy
monarchy   Assembly
aristocracy   Council of 500
democracy   Ten Generals

1. A city-state ruled by nobles was called a(n) —.

2. A city-state ruled by a king was called a(n) —.

3. The — led the armed forces of Athens.

4. The — made the laws of Athens.

5. A system of government in which citizens can vote and hold office is called a(n) —.

6. The — supervised the army, the navy, and the financial affairs of Athens.

7. If citizens personally participate in making public decisions, the government is called a(n) —.

8. The Greek term for a city-state was —.

 ## ESSAY QUESTIONS

1. Explain why Socrates was condemned to die.

2. Describe Plato's work as a philosopher and teacher.

3. State a main idea of Aristotle's teaching.

4. Explain how the plays of Aeschylus, Sophocles, and Euripides differed from those of Aristophanes.

5. Identify the works of Herodotus and Thucydides.

SPARTA: THE MILITARY STATE

Sparta was the second important city-state in Greece. Unlike Athenians, Spartans cared little about democracy or the arts. Many of them limited their interests to military matters. Once Spartan government and society became fully organized around 600 B.C., the Spartans did not want to make any more changes in their way of life. They ignored the ideas of other Greeks and limited their contact with other city-states. Sparta became the strongest military power in Greece.

1. Spartan Government.   The Spartans elected two kings every nine years. A council of elders (28 men over the age of 60) and an assembly of free Spartans over the age of 30 advised the kings. Real power, however, was in the hands of a committee of five *ephors* elected every year by the assembly. The ephors closely watched the actions of the kings, controlled the education of

A Spartan horseman in
bronze, from about 550 B.C.

children, and supervised the slaves. They also tried to make sure that all citizens lived up to the standards set by the government. In Sparta, the life of the individual served the needs of the state.

2. The Spartan Way of Life.   Every Spartan male was a professional soldier. He spent his childhood training for military service and most of his adult life in the army. All Spartan boys, from the age of seven, lived away from home in military training camps. They were taught to be patriotic, courageous, and physically tough. Spartans expressed themselves in as few words as possible. They endured pain and hardship without complaint. They showed respect for their elders.

Spartan men were required to marry at the age of 30 in order to produce children. But they continued to live in military barracks. Spartan men had no home life until the age of 60, when they were finally discharged from military service.

Spartan women received no formal education. Instead, they were physically conditioned to be healthy mothers. They had more freedom than the women of any other Greek city-state, and their legal rights were equal to those of men.

Spartan citizens were not allowed to participate in trade or manufacturing. Noncitizens carried on these activities for the Spartans. Although Spartans owned the farms, non-Spartan slaves, called *helots*, did the work. Sparta remained mainly agricultural. It did not develop industry but engaged in limited trade.

Spartan life was harsh. Other Greeks had no desire to live that way. But they admired Spartan discipline and the willingness of the Spartans to live by their own rules and standards.

 ESSAY QUESTIONS

1. Compare Athens and Sparta with regard to government, cultural activities, and lifestyle.

2. Explain why you would prefer to have been an Athenian or a Spartan.

THE PERSIAN AND PELOPONNESIAN WARS

During the 5th century B.C., the Greek city-states twice defeated attempts by the mighty Persian Empire to conquer them. To fight

The Greek World, 500 B.C.

the Persians, the Greeks temporarily united under the leadership of Athens. Following their victory over the Persians, the city-states began to fight one another. These struggles led to disaster for all of Greece.

1. Conflict With Persia. By 522 B.C., the Persian Empire controlled all of the Middle East. It included many Greek cities in Asia Minor. When these cities rebelled against Persia in 499, Athens sent ships to help them. This action angered Darius, the king of Persia. He decided to conquer Greece and punish Athens. To meet the Persian threat, Athens and Sparta formed an alliance.

a. *Greek victory at Marathon.*   In 490 B.C., the outnumbered Athenian army defeated the Persians at Marathon. (A runner was sent 25 miles from Marathon to Athens to report the victory. Today that run is honored whenever marathon races are held.) The Athenian victory at Marathon forced Darius to withdraw from Greece.

b. *Greek setback.*   In 480 B.C., Xerxes, the son of Darius, attacked Greece. The Persian king's forces, numbered in the thousands, overwhelmed a few hundred Spartans and their allies heroically defending the mountain pass of Thermopylae. Then the Persians captured Athens and set fire to it.

c. *More Greek victories.*   The Athenians fought back at sea and defeated the Persian fleet in a great naval battle at Salamis. After more Greek land and sea victories during the next year, the defeated Persians left for home. The Greek victories saved the freedom of the city-states and the democratic governments adopted by Athens and some of the other poli. To prevent further attacks by Persia, Athens organized the city-states into a loose alliance called the Delian League. With the Persian threat removed, the Greeks were able to continue building their rich civilization.

2. The Age of Pericles.   Following the Persian Wars, Athens entered a period of glory and power. During this time, an outstanding man named Pericles led Athens. He made the city beautiful by encouraging the construction of fine temples and other buildings. The Parthenon, which still stands, was the most important of the buildings. It honored Athena, the main goddess of Athens. Pericles also wrote new laws that made the government even more democratic. His interest in learning attracted talented scholars and artists to Athens. The Age of Pericles, which lasted from 460 to 429 B.C., is regarded as the period when Greek culture reached its highest level. It is also called the Golden Age of Greece.

3. The Peloponnesian War.   Athens tried to use the Delian League to build an empire. City-states in the league were forced to pay taxes and give land to Athens. Led by Sparta, the other city-states rebelled.

From 431 to 404 B.C., Sparta and Athens fought a long and destructive war to determine which city-state would control the Peloponnesian peninsula (southern Greece). Eventually, Sparta, with help from Persia, defeated Athens and its allies.

Sparta become the leader of Greece and put an end to democratic government in Athens and other city-states. But Sparta had been too

This is a reconstruction of the Parthenon, which was originally erected in 437 B.C.

weakened by war to hold power for long. In 371 B.C., the city-state of Thebes, aided by Persian money, defeated Sparta. The other city-states refused to accept Theban leadership. More wars broke out.

While the Greek city-states were destroying themselves, the kingdom of Macedonia was building its power to the north of Greece. In 338 B.C., King Philip II conquered Greece. He then united the city-states by force. Greece and Macedonia became one kingdom.

 MATCHING EXERCISE

Find the name in Column B that best matches the description in Column A.

Column A	Column B
1. It included all of the Middle East.	*a.* Persian Empire
2. He decided to conquer Greece after the Greek city states in Asia Minor rebelled against Persia.	*b.* Darius *c.* Xerxes *d.* Marathon
3. It was the place at which the Athenians defeated a large Persian force.	*e.* Thermopylae *f.* Salamis *g.* Delian League
4. This mountain pass was defended by the Spartans against the Persians.	
5. He led the Persians who captured and set fire to Athens.	
6. It was the site of a great naval battle between the Athenians and Persians.	
7. The Athenians organized a loose alliance of city-states.	

Alcibiades

The Athenians landing in the harbor of Syracuse.

In 416 B.C., the city-state of Athens prepared to attack Syracuse, a city in Sicily and an ally of Sparta. This was but one more battle in the long Peloponnesian War (431–404 B.C.) between Athens and Sparta.

The leader of the Athenian expedition was supposed to be a young general named Alcibiades. He was the nephew of Pericles and a friend of Socrates. Alcibiades was handsome, talented, and courageous. He was easily Athens's most popular military commander. Athenians felt sure of a victorious campaign.

On the eve of sailing for Sicily, a strange event occurred. Throughout Athens, statues of the god Hermes were defaced or destroyed. The citizens of Athens were outraged. The political enemies of Alcibiades accused him of the crime. Word quickly spread that Alcibiades and his friends had ruined the statues while on a drunken rampage through the city streets. With public anger at a peak, Alcibiades did not dare stand trial. He fled Athens. Sparta welcomed him. Alcibiades persuaded the Spartans to send troops to Syracuse to help fight the Athenians.

The Athenians were led by an incompetent general named Nicias. The Athenians laid siege to Syracuse and were about to enclose the city entirely when the Spartan force arrived and saved the city. The Athenians then attempted to leave but were trapped and defeated by the Syracusans. Most of the Athenian army was either killed or captured.

After the Athenian disaster at Syracuse, Alcibiades served both the Spartans and the Persians against the Athenians. However, after several years, the forgiving Athenians once again placed Alcibiades in command of their armed forces. After a few victories over the Spartans, the Athenian navy was defeated in 406 B.C. Alcibiades again lost favor and fled. Athens suffered more defeats. The once-proud city-state was finally conquered by Sparta in 405. That same year, Alcibiades, once Athens's favorite, was killed by his enemies.

Why was the ruination of Alcibiades's career bad for Athens?

The Peloponnesian War

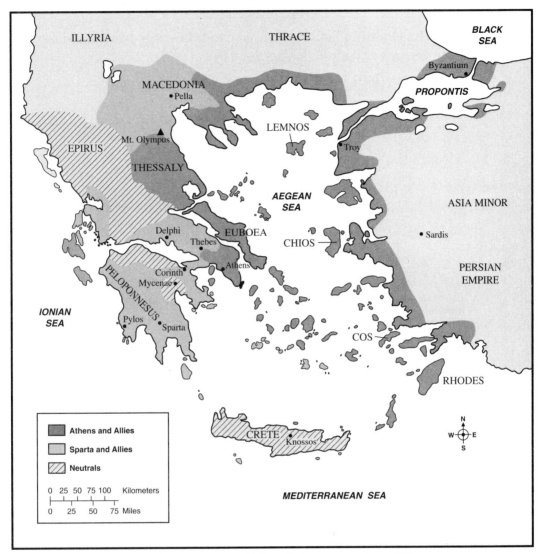

1. **PROVE or DISPROVE:** "The Peloponnesian War was a small-scale conflict that had little impact on the Greek city-states."

2. Identify *two* allies of Athens, *two* allies of Sparta, and *two* neutral countries.

TIMELINE EXERCISE

Using the timeline below, arrange the following events and periods in the proper chronological order (1–7).

TIMELINE: CLASSICAL AGE OF GREECE

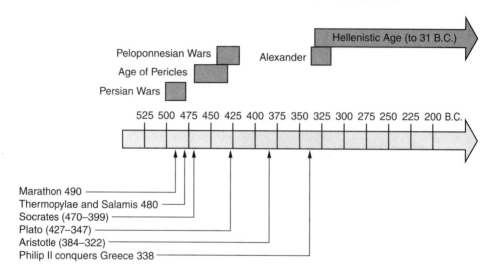

Battle of Salamis
Birth of Socrates
Age of Pericles
Revolt of Greek cities in Asia Minor against Persia
Battle of Thermopylae
Battle of Marathon
Conquest of Greece by Philip of Macedonia

THE RISE OF MACEDONIA AND THE HELLENISTIC AGE

Shortly after he had conquered Greece, Philip II of Macedonia was murdered. His son, Alexander, became king. Alexander led Macedonia and Greece into a new era called the *Hellenistic Age*. It was marked by great political and cultural change.

1. The Macedonians.   Macedonia was a mountainous country north of Greece. Most of its people were rugged herders and farmers. Few Macedonians had as great an interest in learning as did the Greeks. During his years as king, Philip II stopped the

Alexander the Great.

Macedonians from killing one another in blood feuds and clan wars. He unified his people into a nation. Philip created a powerful army, which he trained and disciplined thoroughly. He taught the Macedonians to fight in large, heavily armed formations called *phalanxes*. As a result, Macedonia became a strong military power that other nations feared.

Philip admired the advanced culture of the Greeks. He brought Aristotle to Macedonia to give his son, Alexander, a Greek education. The Greeks, Philip believed, would never unite except under his rule. After he conquered them at the Battle of Chaeronea (338 B.C.), he organized the city-states into the Hellenic League. Only Sparta was not a member. Philip allowed the city-states to govern themselves as long as they gave him military support.

Philip's great dream was to conquer the Persian Empire. His death prevented him from carrying out his plans. But Alexander made Philip's dream come true.

2. The Hellenistic Age. In 334 B.C., Alexander started his conquest of the Persian Empire. While accomplishing this goal, he took over Egypt. Then he moved across the Middle East to the Indus River Valley. In 324, he turned back into Persia. Alexander the Great now ruled over a great empire.

   a. *Hellenistic culture.* Whenever Alexander's soldiers marched, they founded cities. One of them, Alexandria in Egypt, became the most important city of the empire. It developed into a major center of learning and trade. The Greeks and Macedonians

Alexander's Empire, 323 B.C.

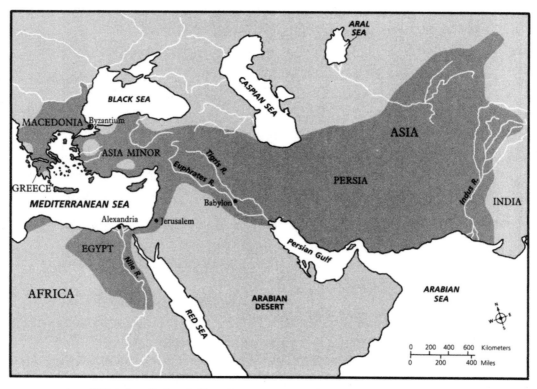

1. Which of the following were included in Alexander's empire?
    a. Macedonia and Greece
    b. Egypt
    c. Asia Minor and Persia
    d. all of the above

2. **EXPLAIN:** Alexander planned a "world state" in which the best of many cultures would blend.

---

who settled in the cities of the empire were encouraged to marry Persians, Egyptians, Syrians, and others of the native populations. Such marriages brought about the gradual blending of the Hellenic, or Greek, culture of the West with the Eastern cultures of the Middle East. The resulting Hellenistic culture combined the best ideas and achievements of East and West.

As trade increased in Alexander's empire, the Hellenistic cities grew wealthy. Elaborate temples, government buildings, and theaters turned these cities into places of beauty as well as centers of learning and art. From all over the civilized world, scholars, artists, scientists, and merchants came to the great Hellenistic cities.

b. *Alexander dies.* Alexander's dream of conquering and ruling the known world ended with his death in 323 B.C., at the age of 33. None of his followers had enough power to continue the campaigns into new areas or to hold the empire together. It was divided among Alexander's strongest generals, who made themselves kings of Macedonia, Syria, and Egypt. The Greek city-states became independent once again.

Despite the breakup of Alexander's empire, the culture of the Hellenistic cities continued to develop. Hellenistic art and science became highly advanced. Greek was the major language of the lands around the eastern Mediterranean Sea. By 200 B.C., however, another civilization, the Roman, was gaining in power and influence. As the Roman civilization spread to the east, Hellenistic ideas and achievements were absorbed into the Roman way of life.

3. The Greek Heritage.   Greek ways and ideas, particularly those of Athens, still affect our lives. For example, today's Olympic Games originated with the early Hellenes. They used the athletic contests as a means of honoring their gods, whom they believed lived on Mt. Olympus. The first recorded Olympic Games occurred in 776 B.C. The Greeks dated their history by the Olympic Games, which were held every four years.

Greek drama, which influenced the development of the modern theater, is performed today. Greek architecture is seen in every city of the Western world. Philosophy, geometry, physics, and many other subjects taught in schools today originated with the Greeks. An important idea we got from the Greeks is the relationship between a sound mind and a healthy body.

Perhaps the Greeks' greatest gift to us is the idea of democracy. This concept of government has shaped the political development of the United States and many other nations. From the Greek practice of democracy arises our belief in freedom and in the worth of the individual.

Chapter Review

MULTIPLE-CHOICE

Choose the item that best completes each sentence.

1. Three important Aegean civilizations in the period from 2000 to 1100 B.C. were the (*a*) Syrian, Persian, and Egyptian (*b*) Hebrew, Indus, and Chinese (*c*) Macedonian, Spartan, and Theban (*d*) Minoan, Hellenic, and Trojan.

2. The greatest city of Crete was (*a*) Knossos (*b*) Troy (*c*) Athens (*d*) Sparta.

3. According to legend, the Minotaur was a (*a*) poem (*b*) Minoan king (*c*) river (*d*) monster.

4. The Hellenes opened direct trade with Egypt and Syria by (*a*) 200 B.C. (*b*) 1700 B.C. (*c*) 1400 B.C. (*d*) 2000 B.C.

5. Much of what we know about ancient Crete is the result of the work of (*a*) Sir Arthur Evans (*b*) Heinrich Schliemann (*c*) Homer (*d*) Theseus.

6. The *Iliad* and the *Odyssey* were written by (*a*) Sir Arthur Evans (*b*) King Philip II (*c*) Homer (*d*) Aristotle.

7. The *Iliad* describes the (*a*) Trojan Wars (*b*) Persian Wars (*c*) Peloponnesian War (*d*) Macedonian Wars.

8. The *Odyssey* is the story of the (*a*) kidnapping of Helen (*b*) journey of Odysseus (*c*) courage of Achilles (*d*) death of Socrates.

9. The Dorians conquered the (*a*) Minoans (*b*) Trojans (*c*) Hellenes (*d*) Persians.

10. The Dorians used weapons made of (*a*) iron (*b*) bronze (*c*) stone (*d*) copper.

THEMATIC WRITING

Write a paragraph about each of the following themes:

1. The growth of democracy in Athens

2. The participation of Athenian citizens in their government

3. The differences between Athenian democracy and American democracy

4. The differences between Athens and Sparta

✍ ESSAY QUESTIONS

1. Explain how the Persian Wars temporarily united the Greeks.

2. State the causes and results of the Peloponnesian War.

3. Describe the career of Alexander the Great and explain how he changed the Middle East.

4. Compare the Hellenic and Hellenistic civilizations.

5. Discuss the Greek heritage and the ways it enriched and influenced the modern world.

Connections: Two Cultures Meet

Zoroaster, a Persian religious leader.

While the Greeks were building their civilization, their long-time enemies, the Persians, were developing a rich civilization of their own. The Persians and their allies, the Medes, overthrew the cruel Assyrian Empire in 612 B.C. At that time, the Persians and Medes held all of what is now Iran and the northern Tigris-Euphrates Valley.

In 550 B.C., the King of Persia, Cyrus the Great, united the Persians and the Medes. He then conquered the peoples of the Fertile Crescent and Asia Minor. In time, Persian kings extended the empire from India to Egypt. Even though they failed to conquer Greece, the great kings of Persia ruled the mightiest empire of the ancient world.

A great cultural contribution of the Persians was Zoroastrianism—the religious teaching of Zoroaster. Zoroaster's ideas about an eternal struggle between good and evil strongly influenced the lives of the Persians. Persians were taught that they could contribute to their own salvation by doing good works and avoiding wickedness. Persian beliefs in people choosing between good and evil and then facing final judgment are similar to the ideas found among the Hebrews and, later, among the Christians.

Alexander the Great and his army of Greeks and Macedonians conquered the Persian Empire in 331 B.C. It was Alexander's dream to blend the Greek and Persian cultures. Persian customs and beliefs were adopted by the Greeks. The beauty of Persian cities, such as Persepolis, was noted by the Greek artists, architects, and engineers who accompanied Alexander. In turn, the Persians were much influenced by the art, learning, and language of the Greeks. This blending of the Greek and Persian cultures resulted in a new, rich Hellenistic civilization.

1. Identify the correct statements:
   a. The Persians failed to conquer the other peoples of the Fertile Crescent.
   b. Persian civilization influenced the Greeks.
   c. Zoroaster was a great military leader.
   d. The Persian Empire included what is now Iran.
   e. Egypt conquered the Persians and the Greeks.

2. Explain why you AGREE or DISAGREE with each of the following statements:
   a. Zoroastrianism influenced Judaism and Christianity.
   b. Cyrus the Great and Alexander the Great had little impact on the Middle East.

DOCUMENT-BASED QUESTION

This question is based on the accompanying documents (1–5). It will improve your ability to work with historical documents.

Historical Context:

Early complex civilizations developed around the Aegean Sea. The first advanced civilization on the mainland of Europe was created by the Greeks. It reached its height in Athens between 500 and 300 B.C. The influence of Greeks on Western culture continues today, especially their creation of the form of government called democracy, or rule by the people.

Task:

Using information from the documents and your knowledge of world history, answer the questions that follow each document. Your answers to each question will help you write the document-based essay.

Document 1. Excerpt from the "Funeral Oration" by Pericles, honoring the Athenian soldiers who died in the Peloponnesian

War. Reported by the Greek historian Thucydides (471–400 B.C.) in his *History of the Peloponnesian War*:

> Let me say that our system of government does not copy the institutions of our neighbours. It is more the case of our being a model to others, than our imitating anyone else. Our constitution is called a democracy because power is in the hands not of a minority but of the whole people. When it is a question of settling private disputes, everyone is equal before the law; when it is a question of putting one person before another in positions of public responsibility, what counts is not membership of a particular class, but the actual ability which the man possesses. . . . Here each individual is interested not only in his own affairs but in the affairs of the state as well.
>
> **Source**: Thucydides, *The History of the Peloponnesian War*, translated by Charles Forster Smith. London: Penguin Books, 1972, pp. 145, 147.

According to this document, what ideas characterize a democracy?

Document 2. Excerpt from *Plutarch's Lives* by the Greek writer Plutarch, discussing the life and achievements of Lycurgus, considered the founder of the military system of government of Sparta:

> The training of the Spartan youth continued till their manhood. No one was permitted to live according to his own pleasure, but they lived in the city as if in a camp, with fixed public duties, thinking themselves to belong, not to themselves, but to their country.
>
> [Lycurgus] trained his countrymen neither to wish nor to understand how to live as private men, but, like bees, to be parts of the commonwealth, and gather round their chief, forgetting themselves in their enthusiastic patriotism, and utterly devoted to their country.
>
> **Source**: *Plutarch's Lives*, translated by Aubrey Stewart and George Long. London: G. Bell & Sons, 1914, Vol. I, pp. 90–92.

According to this document, what was the relationship between the Spartan people and their country?

Document 3. Study the illustration on page 93.

What does the statue show us is a major interest of Spartan society?

Document 4.   Excerpt from Aristotle's *Politics* (about 340 B.C.), in which he discusses the purposes of government:

> First, let us consider what is the purpose of a state. . . . We have already said, in the first part of this treatise, . . . that man is by nature a political animal. And therefore, men, even when they do not require one another's help, desire to live together . . . [and] are also brought together by their common interests. This [well-being] is certainly the chief end, both of individuals and of states. And also for the sake of mere life, . . . mankind meet together and maintain the political community.

> **Source**: *The Politics of Aristotle*, translated by Benjamin Jowett. NY: Colonial Press, 1900.

According to this document, what does Aristotle believe are the reasons that people form political communities?

Document 5.   Study the map on page 102.

To what continents did Alexander spread Hellenistic culture?

DOCUMENT-BASED ESSAY

Using information from the above documents and your knowledge of world history, write an essay in which you:

- Compare the governments of Athens and Sparta and the relationship of the people to their governments.
- Discuss what values are most important in a democratic society.

Chapter 6
The World of Rome

During the Classical Age in Greece, a group of people called the Latins were gaining power in what is now Italy. From their capital city of Rome, they gradually moved outward to establish a great empire in Europe, Africa, and the Middle East. The Latins, or Romans, also created a distinctive way of life and form of government. Their ideas continue to influence us today.

THE CITY OF ROME

According to legend, two brothers named Romulus and Remus built the city of Rome. It is located in the center of the west coast of the Italian peninsula. The early people of Italy believed the brothers to be the sons of Mars, the god of war. After being raised in the wilderness by a wolf, Romulus and Remus looked for a special place to start a city. They chose the spot where they saw seven vultures fly seven times around seven hills. While building their city, the brothers fought. Romulus killed Remus and became the first king of the city that bears his name—Rome.

1. Early Rome. Whether Romulus and Remus ever lived is not known. It is a fact, however, that the Latins, an Indo-European people, settled on several hills near the Tiber River between 1000 and 800 B.C. They were attracted by a warm climate, fertile land, and the river. As their farming villages grew in size, more Latins and people from other tribes in central Italy joined them. By 500 B.C., the villages united to become the city-state of Rome.

Living north of Rome were a people called Etruscans. They had an advanced civilization and greatly influenced Rome. Not much is known about the Etruscans because scholars have not been able to decipher their writing. What is known comes from the household articles and paintings found in their tombs. The early Romans benefited not only from the advanced Etruscan civilization but also from trade and cultural contacts with the Greek cities of southern Italy and Sicily.

   a. *Social classes.*   In time, the Romans divided into two classes of citizens. Those whose families first settled Rome and who held the best lands were called *patricians*. All the other

ANCIENT ITALY, 500 B.C.

1. **EXPLAIN**: The Latin tribes were able to benefit from contact with the advanced peoples living nearby.

2. **EXPLAIN**: Geography determined the site on which the Latins built Rome.

---

citizens were called *plebeians*. They were the working class—craftspersons, farmers, and merchants. As Rome became more prosperous, the interests of the patricians and plebeians became different. Tension rose between the two classes.

    b. *Expansion in Italy.* From 340 to 270 B.C., Rome fought a series of wars that enabled it to conquer most of Italy. This was made possible by Rome's well-trained and disciplined armies of citizen soldiers. These legions brought other Latins and Samnites, Etruscans, and Greeks under Roman control.

    Rome's military conquests were also aided by the geography of the Italian peninsula. Running north and south through Italy, the Apennine Mountains did not prevent Roman troop movements or the building of roads and bridges that connected all of Italy with Rome.

Some of the conquered Italian peoples were given Roman citizenship. Others became military allies of Rome.

2. The Roman Republic. From 616 to 509 B.C., Etruscan kings ruled Rome. After winning their freedom from the Etruscans, the Romans did not want any more kings. They organized a more democratic type of government in which elected officials held power and made the laws. This government was called a *republic*.

a. *Aspects of government.* At first, only patricians could hold public office in Rome. But the plebeians kept demanding more rights for themselves. Finally, in 287 B.C., the plebeians won equal rights as citizens. As members of the Assembly of Tribes and the Assembly of Centuries, they voted on issues and passed laws.

During the period of the Roman Republic, the highest officials were the *consuls*. The assemblies elected two each year. The consuls enforced the laws, ensured that the city was properly administered, and commanded the army in time of war.

Officials called *magistrates* assisted the consuls. The Assembly of Centuries elected the magistrates, who had special titles and duties. *Quaestors* handled such matters as counting the number of people in the city and determining the value of property for tax purposes. *Aediles*, officials like mayors, kept order and took care of public buildings. *Praetors*, or judges, presided over trials in the courts.

In times of emergency, when quick decisions were needed, the consuls sometimes chose one man to rule. Called a *dictator*, he could serve for no more than six months. The government followed the dictator's decisions without question.

The government body called the Senate had the most power. The consuls appointed the 300 members of the Senate for life terms. Originally, only patricians could be senators. Later, plebeians too could hold this office. The Senate proposed laws, handled foreign affairs, and controlled public finances.

To protect their rights, plebeians in the Assembly of Tribes elected ten men called *tribunes*. These powerful men could *veto* decisions of the consuls and the Senate.

Political organization was one of the Romans' greatest talents. In more recent times, the organization of the Roman Republic served as a model for the governments of many nations, including the United States.

b. *Decline of the Republic.* The Roman Republic functioned efficiently for nearly 500 years. The Republic broke down during the civil wars that occurred between the patricians and plebeians. A number of changes caused these conflicts. Some of these changes came from the growth of an empire. As new wealth poured into Rome, the patricians became richer. The plebeians, however, did not always share in this wealth. As their farms were absorbed by an increasing number of large agricultural estates, many plebeians were forced off their lands and became unemployed. Rising tensions led to violence.

3. Roman Law. Another Roman contribution to the world was the development of a body of laws, a legal code. The Romans had great respect for the law. They insisted that all citizens be treated fairly. To make sure that everyone would know the laws, the laws were written on 12 tables, or tablets. About 450 B.C., the Romans set up the tables in a public place. Children had to memorize the laws on the Twelve Tables.

As the empire grew, laws had to be created to govern people who were not Roman citizens. These new laws were added to the original Roman laws on the Twelve Tables. When making legal decisions, government officials took into consideration the laws and customs of the conquered peoples. This practice incorporated the ideas of other peoples into Roman law.

Romans studying and discussing the laws on the Twelve Tables.

The Romans developed the practice of keeping records of the legal decisions of judges throughout the empire. When these recorded decisions were used to decide new cases, Roman law became international.

Roman ideas about law continue to influence the legal codes of countries today. The influence is especially strong in European countries along the Mediterranean Sea and in Latin America.

In the United States, several principles of Roman law are a significant part of our idea of justice:

1. All citizens are equal under the law.

2. A person is believed to be innocent until proved guilty.

3. A person has the right to know who is accusing him or her of wrongdoing.

4. A person should not be punished for what he or she thinks.

4. The Expansion of Rome.   As conflicts with neighboring peoples became frequent, the Romans became skilled soldiers. All male citizens between the ages of 17 and 46 could be called into the army. As Rome turned to the conquest of other lands, the army and its commanders became more important in public affairs.

Between 343 and 290 B.C., Rome fought several wars with its neighbors. As a result, most of Italy came under Rome's control. Roman officials, supported by Roman legions, governed the defeated territories. Latin, the language of the Romans, became familiar to the conquered peoples. Roads were built to link the territories to Rome. A Roman navy, founded to defend new colonies, soon became a powerful force in the Mediterranean.

a. *Punic Wars.*   Rome's greatest enemy was Carthage, a city-state founded by Phoenicians in North Africa. Rome and Carthage competed for the control of trade in western areas bordering the Mediterranean Sea. This competition resulted in three destructive wars. Called the Punic Wars (Punic means "Phoenician"), they took place between 264 and 146 B.C.

In the second war, Carthaginian forces led by a great general named Hannibal invaded the Italian peninsula. Hannibal badly damaged the Roman army before it forced him to retreat. A Roman general named Scipio finally defeated Hannibal in North Africa. The third and last war ended with the destruction of Carthage.

Victory in the Punic Wars left Rome in control of what are now Spain, Sicily, Sardinia, and Corsica and of the coast of North

Rome, Carthage, and the Hellenistic Kingdoms, 270 B.C

Complete each of the following sentences:

1. Carthage was a great city in —.

2. Egypt was a — kingdom.

3. Rome and Carthage faced each other across the — Sea.

4. Southern Spain was controlled by —.

Africa. The Romans rebuilt Carthage and used it as a naval base and commercial port.

b. *Other wars.* By 64 B.C., Rome had conquered almost all the lands around the Mediterranean Sea, including Macedonia, Greece, Syria, and Asia Minor. These lands became Roman provinces and were ruled and taxed by Roman governors.

The person mainly responsible for the conquest and reorganization of the eastern Mediterranean lands was Pompey. He was one of the most powerful Roman generals and political leaders during the years from 78 to 48 B.C.

In the 50's B.C., the Romans decided to bring under their rule the peoples north of Italy. From 58 to 51, the armies of Julius Caesar invaded Gaul (present-day France). Caesar's victories

Two Generals

The growth of Rome's power brought it into conflict with Carthage, a powerful city-state in North Africa. Three Punic Wars (264–146 B.C.) resulted. At the end, Rome won and ruled the central and western Mediterranean. A highlight of these wars was the conflict between two brilliant generals.

In 216 B.C., at Cannae in southern Italy, Hannibal of Carthage faced a Roman army twice the size of his own. When the Romans attacked, the center of the Carthaginian army retreated, drawing the Romans into a trap. Hannibal's troops on the left and right sides of the center outflanked the Romans and crushed them. In just a few hours, over 50,000 Roman soldiers died.

The battle of Cannae was only one of Hannibal's amazing achievements. The year before Cannae, Hannibal and his army had marched 9,000 miles from Spain to Italy. They had crossed the Pyrenees, France, and the Alps into northern Italy. Hannibal had begun the journey with 90,000 infantry, 12,000 cavalry, and 37 war elephants (the ele-phant was the "tank" of the ancient world). But only two-thirds of his troops had survived the cold and snowy trip over the Alps.

After Cannae, Hannibal remained in Italy for 14 years, attacking the Romans at every opportunity. The Roman armies sent against him were no match for him. After losing several battles, the Romans retreated to walled cities. Hannibal continued to attack, but without siege weapons, such as battering rams and large catapults, he could not capture the well-defended cities. The city of Rome successfully resisted Hannibal's forces.

In the meantime, while Hannibal was kept at bay in Italy, a Roman general named Publius Scipio was defeating Carthaginian armies in Spain. After gaining control of Spain, Scipio decided to turn the tables on Carthage. In 204 B.C., Scipio invaded North Africa, the site of Carthage itself.

Hannibal was forced to leave Italy in 203 B.C. Carthage was in danger. The armies of Rome and Carthage met at

Hannibal and his army crossing the Rhone River on their way to Italy.

Zama, near Carthage, in 202. Scipio, using many of the tactics created by Hannibal, completely defeated the Carthaginians. After the battle, Hannibal's first and only defeat, Carthage surrendered.

Publius Scipio was named Scipio Africanus in honor of his victory at Zama. Scipio was a fair-minded and cultured man as well as a brilliant general. His peace terms were generous. Carthage was allowed to govern itself and Hannibal remained in power. The mercy Scipio showed Hannibal and Carthage was bitterly condemned by many Roman leaders. They wanted both Hannibal and Carthage destroyed.

In 199 B.C., Scipio was elected to the office of censor, an official who supervised the census and public morals. In 184, his enemies accused him of bribery. Scipio Africanus retired from public life and died soon after.

Hannibal, forced to flee from Carthage, was hounded by Rome for years. Unable to find a safe haven, Hannibal ended his own life in 184 B.C.

Why was Scipio's defeat of Hannibal very important to the Romans?

extended the Roman empire into Western Europe. In time, much of present-day Britain, Germany, Austria, Switzerland, Rumania, and Bulgaria became part of the empire.

5. The Decline of the Roman Republic. The growth of the empire brought great changes to Rome. As slaves and riches from the conquered areas poured into Rome, the wealthy patricians became even wealthier. They gained more land and more power.

An increase in trade in the growing empire led to the rise of a new middle class of businesspeople called *equestrians*. As these people became more prosperous, they demanded a greater share of privileges from the government.

a. *Revolt of the plebeians.* Plebeians did not generally benefit from the new wealth coming into Rome. The increased use of slave labor caused widespread unemployment among the plebeians.

Plebeians who owned and worked small farms could not compete with the expanding number of *latifundia*. These were the large estates owned by patricians and worked by slaves. The latifundia produced more crops more cheaply than the plebeian farmers could. The plebeians often could not earn enough from the sale of their crops to pay their taxes. As a result, many plebeians were forced to sell their lands to patricians and equestrians.

Without work or land, large numbers of plebeians moved to the cities and became part of an unemployed mob. They lived on gov-

Rome After the Punic Wars, 133 B.C.

I. Match each area in Column A with a description in Column B.

Column A

1. Spain, Carthage, Greece
2. Gaul
3. Germania
4. Alexandria, Jerusalem, Babylon
5. Sardinia, Sicily

Column B

a. not controlled by Rome or the Hellenistic kingdoms
b. Roman-controlled islands
c. crossed by Hannibal during his invasion of Italy (218–203 B.C.)
d. Roman territories
e. Hellenistic cities

II. **PROVE or DISPROVE**: After the Punic Wars, Rome controlled much of the western Mediterranean region.

---

ernment handouts of grain. To keep the plebeians from rioting, the government entertained them with public games. The crowds particularly liked chariot races and armed combats. In the combats, men called gladiators fought each other, sometimes to the death.

In political affairs, many plebeians had nothing left but their votes. These they often sold to the politicians who paid or promised the most. The plebeians' economic problems and their loss of political power led to a long period of civil wars. Ambitious generals and political leaders claimed to be defenders of the plebeians. The pro-plebeian generals led troops against the armies of the patricians and other wealthy men who controlled the Senate. As Romans fought Romans for control of the government, many died and much property was destroyed. Among the bloodiest of the civil wars was the conflict between Marius, a pro-plebeian general, and Sulla, the senatorial leader, that began in 88 B.C. Thousands were killed before Sulla temporarily restored the power of the Senate, making himself dictator.

b. *Rise of dictators.* Most Roman citizens seemed to be willing to trade representative government for peace and security. More and more often they turned to dictators. Dictatorships became more permanent. The six-month limit for a dictatorship was no longer observed. Abuses of power occurred frequently. During the civil wars, these political and military leaders ruled by force. They kept the peace by killing their enemies or exiling them to faraway places.

One of the most famous of the military leaders was Julius Caesar. His rise to power marked the beginning of the end of the Roman Republic.

6. The Rise and Fall of Julius Caesar.
Caesar believed that the government of the Roman Republic would not be able to rule the empire effectively. He may have been the first Roman leader to be aware of this problem. As a politician, Caesar had become popular with the plebeians by acting as a champion of their rights. Caesar achieved power in 60 B.C. by joining forces with Marcus Licinius Crassus, the richest man in Rome, and Gaius Magnus Pompey, the successful and popular general. The three men used Crassus's money, Pompey's military power, and the plebeians' votes delivered to Caesar to gain control of the government. Known as the First Triumvirate, Crassus, Pompey, and Caesar had enough power to rule the Roman world and to end the civil wars. The triumvirate ruled from 60 to 53 B.C.

a. *Consolidating power.* Caesar's military campaign in Gaul (present-day France) gave him command of an army. After the death of Crassus in 53 B.C., Caesar fought with Pompey for control of the Roman government. Civil wars began again. As Caesar and his army marched into Italy, Pompey went to Greece to organize his forces in the eastern Mediterranean. In the great battles that followed, Caesar defeated the armies of Pompey in Italy and Greece. Pompey fled to Egypt, where he was killed. Caesar then defeated Pompiian forces in Spain and North Africa.

Julius Caesar.

In 46 B.C., Julius Caesar became sole ruler of the Roman Empire. He was a very capable dictator. He made the army and the government more efficient. The size of the Senate was increased to make it better represent the provinces. Citizenship was extended to more people in the provinces. Caesar improved the tax system and introduced a more accurate calendar. More jobs were created; he reduced by more than half the number of people receiving free grain.

b. *Envy of Caesar.* Although Caesar had all the power of a king or an emperor, he did not have the title. He knew that the Roman people would accept a dictator but not a king. (Romans had been opposed to kings since the time of the Etruscan rulers.) While achieving his successes, Caesar had made many enemies who resented his power. In 44 B.C., a group led by Marcus Brutus murdered Julius Caesar. Brutus and his friends claimed that they had acted to prevent Caesar from crowning himself king.

The anger of the Roman people at Caesar's death forced the murderers to flee to the provinces. Control of Rome fell to Marc Antony, a friend of Caesar's. A new civil war began as Antony's armies marched against the forces of Brutus and his supporters.

DEFINITIONS

Explain the meaning of each of the following terms:

a. Senate
b. Patricians
c. Plebeians
d. Etruscans
e. Republic

 MATCHING EXERCISE

Match each term in Column A with its meaning in Column B.

Column A	Column B
1. Twelve Tables	a. government bodies to which plebeians could be elected
2. consuls	
3. magistrates	b. a conflict between two groups of citizens in the same country
4. assemblies	
5. tribunes	c. the early Roman legal code
6. dictators	d. ten officials who had the power to stop consul and Senate actions
7. equestrians	
8. latifundia	e. group of three men who ruled Rome from 60 to 53 B.C.
9. First Triumvirate	
10. civil war	f. the two highest officials in Rome
	g. Roman middle class of businesspeople
	h. large patrician estates worked by slaves
	i. government officials who assisted the consuls
	j. men who ruled alone and whose decisions were not questioned

 ESSAY QUESTIONS

Explain why you AGREE or DISAGREE with each statement.

1. The growth of the Roman Empire made the plebeians wealthy and the equestrians and patricians poor.

2. Small farms could not compete with the increasing number of latifundia.

3. The breakdown of the Roman Republic was partly caused by civil wars.

4. Julius Caesar was murdered because he made himself king of Rome in 46 B.C.

PAX ROMANA IN THE ROMAN EMPIRE

In the civil war that followed the death of Julius Caesar, Octavian, the grandnephew and adopted son of Julius Caesar, joined forces with Marc Antony. Together they defeated the forces of the murderers of Caesar. Octavian and Anthony ruled the Roman world until disagreements over Antony's alliance with Cleopatra, Queen of Egypt, brought on still another civil war. In the sea battle of Actium in 31 B.C., Octavian's ships defeated the fleet of Antony and Cleopatra. To avoid capture by Octavian, Antony and Cleopatra committed suicide.

Octavian took complete control of the government and became Rome's first emperor. He ruled from 27 B.C. to A.D. 14. The Senate gave Octavian the title of Augustus. Under Augustus, the empire entered a period of peace, security, and accomplishment in many fields. For the next 200 years, the Roman Empire enjoyed what is called the *Pax Romana* (Roman Peace).

1. A Golden Age.   With the civil wars finally ended, the Roman Empire expanded and became more prosperous. Roman merchants traded with the Han Empire in China, with the Parthian Empire in the Middle East, and with India.

  a. *Greek influence.*   The Roman conquest of Greece and the Middle East brought the Romans into contact with the Hellenistic civilization. The Romans admired the Greeks and learned from them. As a result, Roman architecture, sculpture, drama, and literature improved. Greek, rather than Latin, became the language of many educated Romans. The blending of art forms, languages, and ideas produced the rich Greco-Roman culture.

The portraits of Marc Antony (left) and Cleopatra on Roman coins.

The Roman Empire, A.D. 120

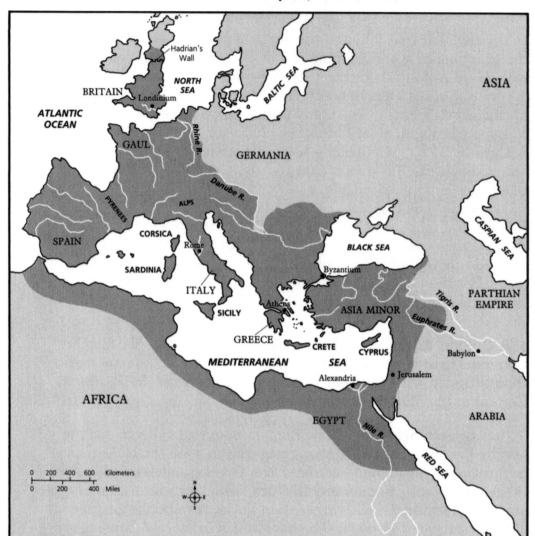

Use the information on the map to complete or answer the following:

1. What rivers formed part of the northern boundary of the Roman Empire?

2. Name the province that was protected by Hadrian's Wall.

3. Name *two* rivers in the eastern part of the Roman Empire.

4. Name the southernmost province of the Roman Empire.

5. What empire lay east of the Roman Empire?

b. *New construction.* Roman engineers improved life in the empire by building roads, dams, drainage systems, and aqueducts. (Aqueducts carried water to cities through pipes.) Many of the roads that the Roman engineers built are still in use.

The public baths were an important part of Roman life. These huge buildings contained steam rooms, gymnasiums, hot and cold pools, and libraries. Large numbers of people attended events in the Colosseum in Rome, an arena in which gladiators fought. Another impressive structure in Rome was the Circus Maximus, where chariot races were held.

Wherever Roman armies went, new cities and towns were built. As a result, Roman architectural styles spread throughout Europe, North Africa, and the Middle East.

2. The Emperors. During the period of the *Pax Romana*, both good and bad emperors ruled the empire.

a. *Bad emperors.* One of the worst was Caligula (ruled A.D. 37–41), a madman who insisted that he was a god. After he had committed many murders and other crimes, a group of military officers and senators killed him.

Nero (ruled A.D. 54–68) murdered his mother and his wife. He was suspected of causing the great fire that destroyed half of Rome

Paving stones

Drainage ditch

Curbstones

Gravel and concrete

Stone slabs　　　　Crushed stone and rubble

The building of the Appian Way. Some sections of the road are in use today.

in 64. Nero placed the blame for the fire on a religious group called the Christians. He ordered Christians to be burned to death or sent to the arena to be killed by wild animals. When some of Nero's troops revolted and marched on Rome, he killed himself.

Nero's death in A.D. 69 ended the rule of the Julio-Claudian emperors. After a year of renewed civil war (the Year of the Four Emperors), during which ambitious candidates replaced one another in rapid succession, the Flavian emperors came to the throne. Vespasian and his son, Titus, defeated a Jewish revolt in the province called Palestine and destroyed the city of Jerusalem. They then did much to restore the financial and political stability of the empire. Domitian, the last of the Flavians, struggled with financial problems and an uprising in Germany (Germania).

b.   *Good emperors.* A line of capable emperors, called the Antonines, ruled in the 2nd century A.D. Trajan (ruled A.D. 98–117) expanded the borders of the empire to their greatest limits. Hadrian (ruled A.D. 117–138) greatly admired Greek culture. He spent much of his rule traveling through the empire to supervise the strengthening of frontier defenses and the building of public works. To mark the northwestern limit of the empire, Hadrian ordered the building of a wall across northern England. Regarded as a great feat of military engineering, Hadrian's Wall was a complex system of forts, signal towers, outposts, supply bases, and a great defensive ditch. The completion of this project signaled a major change in imperial policy from expansion and conquest to consolidation. The limits of the empire had been set.

Marcus Aurelius (ruled A.D. 161–180) was one of the best emperors. He was a soldier, writer, and philosopher who had to spend much of his time fighting enemies who attacked Rome's borders. Nevertheless, he wrote a famous book titled *Meditations*. In the hope of saving the lives of Roman soldiers, he allowed some German tribes to settle on Roman lands. Marcus Aurelius died during a plague that swept through the empire and killed one-fourth of the Roman population.

Marcus Aurelius's son, Commodus (ruled A.D. 180–192), became the next emperor. This young man's rule proved to be a disaster. He preferred fighting in the arena as a gladiator to solving the many problems of the empire. Eventually, he was strangled while taking a bath.

The death of Commodus ended the *Pax Romana*. Military leaders now openly took over the government. Other peoples became powerful enough to challenge the Romans. Economic and political problems increased and gradually weakened the Roman Empire.

Constantine, the first Christian emperor of Rome.

c. *A divided empire.* In an attempt to strengthen the empire, Diocletian (ruled A.D. 284–305) divided the empire into two parts, eastern and western. Diocletian, who held most of the governing power himself, ruled from his eastern capital in Asia Minor. The co-emperor ruled from Milan in northern Italy, which was better located than Rome to defend the empire's northern border. The city of Rome no longer served as the capital of the Roman Empire.

In 306, Constantine was named emperor. In 324, he reunited the empire and ruled alone until his death in 337. About 330, he moved the capital of the empire to Byzantium, which he renamed Constantinople.

After 395, the empire was permanently divided. The western part became weaker and poorer. The eastern part grew stronger, wealthier, and increasingly Greek in language and culture.

     SENTENCE COMPLETION

Complete each of the following sentences:

1. In the battle of Actium in 31 B.C., Octavian —.

2. Under Augustus, the empire —.

3. For the next 200 years, the Roman Empire —.

4. The blending of Greek and Roman art forms, language, and ideas —.

5. In the second century, the Antonine emperors —.

THE RISE OF CHRISTIANITY

In A.D. 30, the Roman governor in Palestine (present-day Israel) ordered the death of a Jewish religious leader named Jesus, also called Christ. Afterward, the followers of Jesus spread his ideas throughout the Roman Empire and beyond. In this way, an entirely new religion called Christianity developed. It became one of the great religions of the world.

1. The Beginning of Christianity.   Not much is known about the early life of Jesus. It is believed that he was born in Bethlehem in Palestine during the rule of Augustus. While a youth, Jesus lived in Nazareth and was taught the Jewish faith. He worked as a carpenter. Then, when he was about 30, he began to travel about, teaching anyone who would listen to his ideas about religion.

Jesus told the people that God loved everyone. He urged people to act toward one another with kindness: Do to others as they would want others to do to them. (This idea is called the Golden Rule.) If people act properly toward one another and do God's will, Jesus said, they will enter the kingdom of heaven when they die.

This 16th-century Flemish painting shows Jesus being led away to be crucified. Pontius Pilate is washing his hands.

According to the Old Testament of the Bible, God planned to send a *messiah* to make the world a better place. Many people believed that Jesus was the messiah, or Christ, the son of God.

To help him teach people, Jesus chose 12 men to travel with him. These men were called *apostles*, or disciples. The Roman government was told that Jesus and his apostles were dangerous. They might lead a revolt against the authority of Rome. Pontius Pilate, the Roman governor of Palestine, ordered the execution of Jesus. Soldiers from the Roman garrison in Jerusalem crucified him. This was a common way to kill criminals at the time.

A few days after Jesus had died on the cross and been buried, the disciples claimed that they had seen him and had talked with him. They believed that Jesus was indeed the son of God and had risen from the dead, or been *resurrected*. The belief in the resurrection of Jesus became an important part of Christian thought.

The disciples hurried to spread the news of the resurrection of Jesus to the Jews. They tried to persuade people to believe in Jesus as the son of God who would save the world from evil.

2. The Growth of Christianity. One of the most important Christian *missionaries*—those who spread the teachings of Jesus—was Paul. He had been born a Jew and was a Roman citizen. As a grown man, he accepted the teachings of Jesus and became a Christian. Paul traveled throughout the eastern part of the Roman Empire to tell others about the teachings of Jesus. He urged all people, Jews and non-Jews (called Gentiles), to become Christians. The Christian religion attracted more and more followers.

In time, Roman authorities became concerned about the increasing numbers of people who would not worship the Roman gods. The Roman government began to persecute the Christians to make them give up their beliefs. Despite the efforts of the Roman government to stamp out Christianity, the new religion continued to grow.

In A.D. 313, Emperor Constantine issued the Edict of Milan. This order made Christianity equal to all other religions in the Roman Empire. Constantine is considered to be the Roman Empire's first Christian emperor because he officially became a Christian just before he died. By 395, under Emperor Theodosius, Christianity had become the official state religion of the Roman Empire.

CRITICAL THINKING

PROVE or DISPROVE: The spread of Christianity was due as much to Roman emperors as to Jewish missionaries.

DEFINITIONS

Write a sentence of your own to explain the meaning of each of the following terms:

a. Christianity   *d.* resurrection
b. apostle   *e.* missionary
c. crucifixion

PARAGRAPH COMPLETION

From the list that follows, select the term or terms that best completes each sentences in the paragraph:

state religion   emperor   Christianity
Theodosius   Roman Empire   Constantine
Edict of Milan

In A.D. 313, Emperor _(1)_ issued the _(2)_. This order made _(3)_ equal to all other religions in the _(4)_. Constantine became Rome's first Christian _(5)_. By A.D. 395, under Emperor _(6)_, Christianity had become the official _(7)_ of the Roman Empire.

THE FALL OF ROME

After the *Pax Romana* had ended around A.D. 190, the problems of the Roman Empire deepened. Although the empire lasted for another 300 years, its military, economic, and political systems became weaker. Outside forces and new ideas brought changes. The empire could not control these forces and lost power.

1. The Breakdown of the Roman World.   The peace and security of the empire depended greatly on the Roman legions. These professional soldiers defended the borders, maintained order within the empire, built roads, and collected taxes. In the later years of the empire, an increasing number of Romans did not wish to serve. To get soldiers, the government had to rely upon *conscription*, forcing men to serve. The conscripts often resented military service. Some deserted. Also, non-Romans were hired. These were mainly Germans living on the borders of the empire. In time, the legions became more German than Roman. Such hired soldiers, called *mercenaries*, served and fought primarily for pay. They had no loyalty to the Roman Empire.

The mercenary soldiers did not do a very good job of defending the borders or of keeping order within the empire. Weak emperors and ambitious generals used the legions to fight one another for control of the empire. This led to new civil wars. Barbarian tribes from areas north and east of the empire moved into the Roman territory. Criminal gangs disrupted life in cities. This unrest led to a breakdown of law and order. In the countryside, the owners of large agricultural estates formed their own *militias*, or small private armies.

The lack of law and order caused an economic breakdown. As merchants became unable to move their goods safely along the roads of the empire, trade fell off. Less money circulated. Farmers and landowners could not pay their taxes and had to abandon their lands. Slaves ran away from the estates. All these developments meant that less food was produced.

The legions often murdered the emperors they did not like and chose new rulers. To keep their soldiers happy, the emperors gave them large amounts of money. However, the coins were made of cheap metals. They contained very little gold or silver. As a result, Roman money became almost worthless.

Diseases and a falling birth rate reduced the population of the Romans during the years of unrest. Adding to the problems was widespread unemployment in the cities. People abandoned the cities to seek a better life in the countryside. People lost hope in their ability to solve the empire's problems.

2. The Invaders.   From the 3rd to the 5th century, large groups of German tribes moved into the rich farmlands of the western portion of the Roman Empire. From long contact with the empire, they had developed an admiration for Roman civilization. Some had become Christians. Others wanted to seize Roman wealth.

During the winter of A.D. 406, the Rhine River froze. Thousands of Germans poured into the empire. In 410, and again in 455, the city of Rome was attacked and looted.

a. *The Huns.* German pressure on the empire's frontiers increased as a result of the Hun invasions of Western Europe in the 4th and 5th centuries. The Huns were fierce horsemen from Central Asia who terrorized much of Europe and drove many German tribes into the Roman Empire. Led by their king, Attila, the Huns built their own empire in Eastern Europe. The Hun advance westward was stopped by a combined Roman-German force commanded by a Roman general named Aetius, at the *Battle of Chalons* in A.D. 451.

b. *Odoacer.* After the death of Attila in 453, the Hun Empire broke up. The German tribes then regained control of Europe and what was left of the Roman world there. The official end of the empire came in A.D. 476, when a German general named Odoacer forced the last Roman emperor to give up his throne. Odoacer made himself king of Italy.

For most of Europe, the Classical Age was over. In the Hellenistic cities of Asia Minor and the Middle East, however, the Eastern Roman Empire continued. This Byzantine Empire, as it came to be called, lasted for several centuries. As a result, very different cultures developed in the East and the West after the fall of Rome.

The Roman Empire and the Invaders, A.D. 400

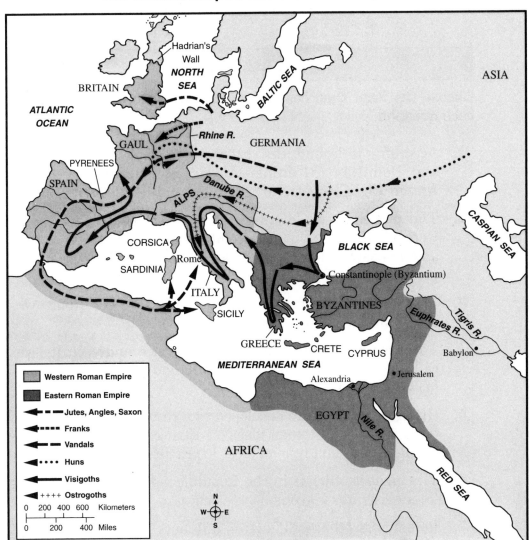

Use the information on the map to complete the following:

1. List the invaders that moved through each area.
    - *a.* Britain   *d.* Italy
    - *b.* Gaul   *e.* North Africa
    - *c.* Spain

2. Name two parts of the Roman Empire where most of the invasions occurred.

Chapter Review

▶	**MULTIPLE-CHOICE**

Choose the item that best completes each sentence or answers each question.

1. According to legend, the city of Rome was built by (*a*) Titus and Domitian (*b*) Julius Caesar and Octavian (*c*) Marc Antony and Cleopatra (*d*) Romulus and Remus.

2. The plebeians could influence the actions of the Roman Republic through the (*a*) assemblies and tribunes (*b*) consuls and magistrates (*c*) Senate and dictator (*d*) generals and priests.

3. The most successful of the early dictators of Rome was (*a*) Hannibal (*b*) Pompey (*c*) Julius Caesar (*d*) Odoacer.

4. The Roman Empire's 200 years of peace and security was called the (*a*) latifundia (*b*) *Pax Romana* (*c*) Circus Maximus (*d*) Colosseum.

5. Greco-Roman culture developed as a result of the blending of (*a*) German and Roman ideas (*b*) Etruscan and Roman ideas (*c*) Hellenistic and Roman ideas (*d*) Etruscan and Greek ideas.

6. The highest officials in the Republic were the (*a*) quaestors (*b*) magistrates (*c*) consuls (*d*) legates.

7. Roman ideas that still have an influence in the United States and Europe concern (*a*) law and justice (*b*) military activities (*c*) trade and agriculture (*d*) agricultural technology.

8. The proper order of these events is as follows: (*a*) death of Julius Caesar, birth of Jesus, rule of Marcus Aurelius (*b*) birth of Jesus, death of Julius Caesar, rule of Marcus Aurelius (*c*) rule of Marcus Aurelius, birth of Jesus, death of Julius Caesar (*d*) rule of Commodus, death of Julius Caesar, birth of Jesus.

9. The permanent division of the Roman Empire into eastern and western sections took place in (*a*) A.D. 476 (*b*) A.D. 395 (*c*) A.D. 192 (*d*) A.D. 3.

10. Which statement is true? (*a*) Paul tried to persuade Pontius Pilate not to kill Jesus. (*b*) Paul traveled with the German

invaders to spread Christianity. (*c*) Paul preached Christianity in the eastern part of the Roman Empire (*d*) Attila converted the Romans to Christianity.

TIMELINE QUESTIONS

Look at the timeline below. Use the information on the timeline to answer the following questions.

1. Which event occurred first? Second? Third?
   Punic Wars
   barbarian invasions
   rule by Etruscan kings

2. Name *two* major events that occurred during the period of the Roman Republic.

3. During what period of Roman rule was Jesus born?

4. About how many centuries were there between the founding and the fall of Rome?

5. Did the division of the empire occur before, after, or during the *Pax Romana*?

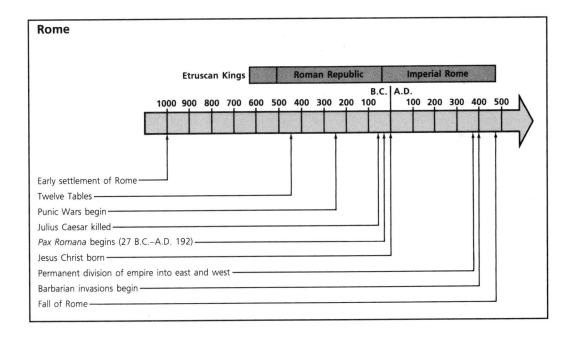

TABLE COMPLETION

Compare government in ancient Rome with modern American government by completing the table below on a separate sheet of paper.

Branches of Government

	Legislative (makes laws)	Executive (enforces laws)	Judicial (judges and interprets)
Rome			
United States	Congress: Senate and House of Representatives	President and cabinet	Supreme Court and federal courts

THEMATIC WRITING

Write a paragraph or two about *each* of the following themes:

1. The rise of the Roman Republic

2. Greco-Roman culture

3. The end of Roman democracy

4. Christianity and the Roman Empire

5. Germans, Huns, and the fall of the western Roman Empire

DOCUMENT-BASED QUESTION

This question is based on the accompanying documents (1–4). It will improve your ability to work with historical documents.

Historical Context:

The organization of the Roman Republic became a model for the governments of the United States and other democratic nations. However, under the rule of emperors, Roman democracy was abandoned even though the form and structure of the Republic were retained.

Task:

Using information from the documents and your knowledge of world history, answer the questions that follow each document.

Connections: The New Romans

Twenty-first-century Americans have sometimes been called the "new Romans." In making the comparison, some historians have said that Americans, like the ancient Romans, had been ruled by kings but then organized themselves into a republic. Rome had its Twelve Tables of Law. The United States has its Constitution. Roman laws were made by a Senate. The United States also has a Senate. Romans elected tribunes, consuls, praetors, and aediles to run their government. Americans elect the same kinds of officials but call them representatives, governors, judges, and mayors.

American presidents have power and prestige similar to that of the Roman emperors. The military and political power of the United States influences world affairs just as the power of the Roman Empire once did.

Other comparisons between the "new" and the "old" Romans can be made. In the areas listed, state ways in which modern Americans are similar to ancient Romans.

Romans	Americans
1. Entertainment (Colosseum, Circus Maximus)	
2. Urban problems	
3. Plebeians and patricians	

Your answers to each question will help you write the document-based essay.

Document 1.   Extract from the Roman historian Polybius, who lived from 200 to 118 B.C.:

> As for the Roman [Republic's] constitution, it has three elements, each of them possessing sovereign powers: [Consuls, Senate, and Assemblies of Tribes and Centuries]. Their respective share of power in the whole state has been regulated with such a scrupulous regard to equality and balance. . . . The result . . . is a union sufficiently firm for all emergencies, and a constitution than which it is impossible to find a better. For whenever any danger from without compels them to unite and work together, the strength which is developed by the State is so extraordinary, that everything required is unfailingly carried out.

Source: *The Histories of Polybius*, Vol. 1., translated from the text of F. Hultsch by Evelyn S. Shuckburg. London: Macmillan and Co., 1889.

Based on this document, what are two reasons why Polybius admired the government of the Roman Republic?

Document 2. Study the illustration on page 107.

What does it tell us about the rule of law under the Roman Republic?

Document 3. From Roman historian Cornelius Tacitus, who lived from A.D. 57 to 120:

> Augustus won over the soldiers with gifts, the populace with cheap grain, and all men with the sweet of repose [peace], and so grew greater by degrees, while he concentrated in [gave to] himself the functions of the Senate, the magistrates and the laws. He was wholly unopposed, for the boldest spirits [men] had fallen in battle . . . , while the remaining nobles . . . were raised the higher by wealth and promotion, so that . . . they preferred the safety of the present to the dangerous past. How few were left who had lived under the Republic. Thus the State had been revolutionized, . . . stripped of elements of equality.
>
> **Source:** Tacitus, "The Transition From Republic to Principate," Annals, 1.2–4, translated by Alfred Church and William Brodribb. NY: Macmillan and Co., 1891.

According to this document, in what ways did Augustus replace democracy with dictatorship?

Document 4. Extract from a history of Rome by the Greek historian Dio Cassius (A.D. 155–235), who was giving advice to the current Roman emperor:

> If you feel any concern at all for your country, . . . reorganize the government and regulate it. . . . Put an end to the insolence of the populace and place the management of public affairs in the hands of yourself and the other best citizens.
>
> You should yourself, in consultation with the best men, enact all the appropriate laws, without the possibility of any opposition . . . from the masses. You and your counselors should conduct the wars according to your own wishes, all other citizens rendering instant obedience to your commands. . . . Whatever business is done would be managed in the right way instead of being referred to the popular assembly. . . . We should be happy in the enjoyment of blessings which are vouchsafed to us, instead of being embroiled [trapped] in hazardous wars abroad or in unholy civil strife. For these are the evils found in every democracy.
>
> **Source:** Dio Cassius: *Volume VI*, Loeb Classical Library Volume 83, translated by Earnest Cary. Cambridge, MA: Harvard University Press, 1917.

According to this document, why was Dio Cassius warning the emperor about democracy?

DOCUMENT-BASED ESSAY

Using information from the above documents and your knowledge of world history, write an essay in which you:

- Discuss the democratic features of the government of the Roman Republic.
- Explain how democracy ended under the Roman Empire.

UNIT III

NEW PATTERNS OF CIVILIZATION

CHAPTER 7
The Middle Ages

Historians label the years between A.D. 500 and 1500 in Europe the Middle Ages, or the Medieval Period. This period of 1,000 years came between the decline of the western Roman Empire and the beginning of what is known as the Modern Age (1500 to the present). This era has been further divided into the Early Middle Ages (500 to 1000), a period of heavy migrations of warring peoples across Europe, and the Later Middle Ages (1000 to 1500), when religious and political conflicts contrasted with artistic and technological achievement.

During the Medieval Period, Western Europe became increasingly German in language and culture. Much of Eastern Europe was ruled by the mighty Byzantine Empire, in which Greek language and culture was foremost. While the Middle East and North Africa experienced the rise of Islam and the growth of a Muslim empire, Europeans were terrorized by raiders and colonizers from Scandinavia.

THE RISE OF GERMAN EUROPE

After the western Roman Empire fell in A.D. 476, Germanic tribes transformed the provinces it ruled into a collection of kingdoms. During the early part of the Middle Ages, the Germanic kings struggled with one another for more power and land. Local wars broke out, causing loss of life and disruption to farming and trade. Bandits lurked in areas where law and order had broken down.

Roads were no longer maintained, and communities had less interaction. People began to speak dialects, or different forms of Latin and German. Latin dialects developed into French, Italian, Spanish, Portuguese, and Romanian (the Romance languages).

a. *The Frankish Kingdom.* One of the strongest German tribes in Western Europe was the Franks. They occupied much of what is now France. A powerful Frankish kingdom was created late in the 5th century by a strong king named Clovis, who defeated Frankish rivals and conquered other Germanic tribes in Gaul. Clovis converted the Franks to Roman Catholicism. This enabled him to gain the support of the pope.

Clovis's descendants were weak kings. Control of the Frankish kingdom passed into the hands of strong nobles. These officials were known as *Mayors of the Palace.*

The Frankish kingdom dominated Western Europe in the 8th and 9th centuries. Strong leadership was provided by members of the Carolingian family.

b. *The Carolingians.* Charles Martel, as Mayor of the Palace, defeated invading Arabs, who had crossed the Pyrenees Mountains from Spain, at the Battle of Tours in 732. This battle prevented Muslims from penetrating farther into Christian Europe.

Martel's son, Pepin, became Mayor of the Palace in 741. With the pope's approval, he made himself king of the Franks in 751. Pepin drove the Lombards, a Germanic people, out of central Italy and gave their lands to the pope. The Donation of Pepin gave the Catholic Church control of portions of central Italy (the *Papal States*) for more than 1,000 years.

1. The Empire of Charlemagne. The greatest Frankish king was Charlemagne, who ruled from 771 to 814. (His name means Charles the Great.)

Charlemagne fought other German tribes to gain power over them. Most of the tribes were converted to Christianity. He eventually ruled over an area that included what are now France, Germany, Austria, and Switzerland. He also controlled northern Italy and northeastern Spain.

a. *Holy Roman emperor.* The pope, Leo III, was grateful to Charlemagne for increasing the number of Christians in Europe. When a local uprising forced the pope to flee from Rome in 799, Charlemagne marched to Rome and defeated the pope's enemies. He then put the church leader back into office. In appreciation,

Charlemagne.

Leo III crowned Charlemagne Holy Roman emperor in 800. This honor meant that Charlemagne was considered to be the Christian successor to the emperors of Rome.

One of Charlemagne's great contributions to civilization in Europe was his encouragement of learning. Although he spoke Latin and understood Greek, he could not read or write. (Few people of that time had these skills.) To further education in his kingdom, he set up a school in Aachen for his family and other children of ability. The school attracted scholars from many lands and became a model for other schools. Alcuin, a famous English scholar, was recruited to administer the school.

b. *Decline of the empire.* Charlemagne's empire did not last after his death. His son was not a good ruler. Charlemagne's grandsons could not rule the lands together. They went to war against one another. In the mid-800's, a formal agreement divided Charlemagne's empire into three kingdoms. The western one eventually became France. The eastern kingdom in time became Germany. The middle kingdom was fought over for centuries and became part of several present-day countries, including Austria and Italy. Later, the title of Holy Roman Emperor was used by many German kings. But most of those who held the title had little real power. Charlemagne's successors were unable to protect Western Europe from new invasions.

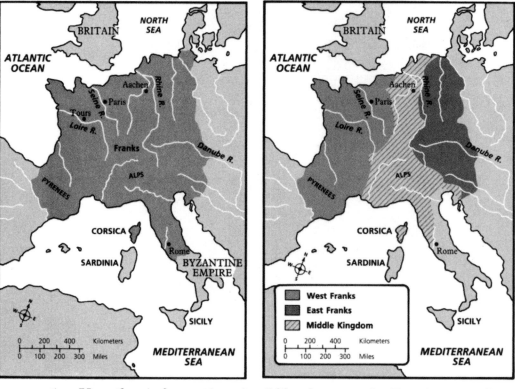

Charlemagne's Empire, 814

Frankish Kingdoms, 843

1. Use the information in "Charlemagne's Empire, 814" to answer the following:
   a. Name *three* rivers that were entirely within the boundary of Charlemagne's empire.
   b. What is the distance in miles between Aachen and Rome?
   c. Name the island that was part of the empire.
   d. Name the empire that controlled southern Italy and Sicily.

2. Use the information on "Frankish Kingdoms, 843" to answer the following:
   a. Name the kingdom that had the Pyrenees within its borders.
   b. What city shown on the map was located in the Middle Kingdom?
   c. Corsica was part of what kingdom?

2. Germanic Tribes in Britain.   While some Germanic tribes were invading the Roman Empire in Italy, others were invading Britain. Tribes known as Angles, Saxons, and Jutes met with fierce resistance from the Romano-British (the Celts). According to some accounts, a Celtic military leader named Arthur defeated the Germanic tribes in many battles. Around 500, Arthur led his cavalry to a great victory over the Germans, or Anglo-Saxons, in a battle fought at a place called Mount Badon. The Germans did not advance any farther in Britain for many years. (Even to this day, storytellers write about the adventures of King Arthur and his knights.)

About 550, the Angles and Saxons (Anglo-Saxons) attacked again and conquered the Celts. Many of the Celts fled to Ireland, Wales, and Scotland. Others merged their culture with that of the Anglo-Saxons. The Angles and Saxons divided the rest of Britain into many kingdoms, which fought one another for years. By 700, they began to cooperate with one another and turn southern Britain into the nation known as England.

About 600, Christian missionaries were sent to England to teach the people about Christianity. The most influential was Augustine, a monk, who began his conversions in the kingdom of Kent in southeastern England. Within a short time, most of the English had accepted this religion. The Christian Church became an important force in shaping the culture of England.

Alfred, a great Anglo-Saxon king, ruled from 871 to 899. At his command, the laws of his people were written down. To encourage learning, he set up a school that taught both English and Latin. Alfred himself translated books from other languages into English.

3. New Invaders From the North.   Starting in the late 700's, fierce raiders from northern Europe attacked settlements along the coasts of England and France. The raiders, called Northmen or Norse, became better known as Vikings. They came from the present-day countries of Norway, Sweden, and Denmark.

The Vikings sailed into the Mediterranean and raided southern France. They moved up rivers to loot cities such as Paris and London. Scotland and Ireland also felt the blows of the Viking warriors. Some Vikings crossed the North Atlantic to settle in Greenland and Iceland. A few reached the coast of North America, probably in the area of Newfoundland, now part of Canada.

a. *Danelaw.*   In 878, King Alfred kept the Vikings from overrunning England. The invaders agreed to stay in northeastern

Viking Raids, 800–900

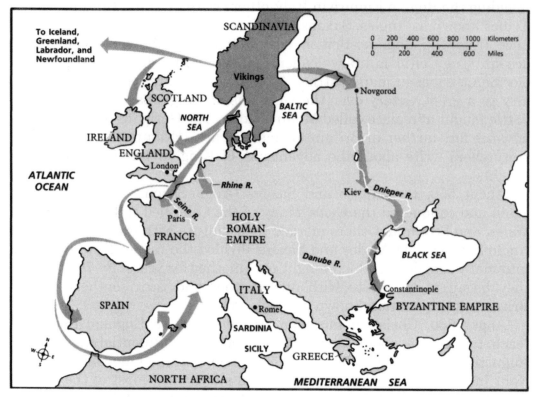

1. Indicate whether each of the following statements is *true* (**T**) or *false* (**F**).
   a. Vikings came from Scandinavia.
   b. Viking raids affected only countries around the North Sea.
   c. The Vikings traveled from Novgorod to Constantinople.
   d. France and Spain were untouched by Viking raids.
   e. Vikings made use of rivers to reach their targets.

2. **EXPLAIN:** The Vikings were great sailors. They voyaged to many lands.

England in an area that came to be called the Danelaw. They soon became farmers, merchants, and traders. Most of them also became Christians.

   b. *Norman invasion.* To stop the terrible raids in France, a Frankish king in 911 gave a Norse chief part of the northwestern section of the country. This area is still known as Normandy. Vikings settled there and learned the ways of the Franks. In 1066, a Norman duke, William, and his army sailed to England and

The Conqueror

On October 14, 1066, two armies faced each other near the port of Hastings, England.

One army was led by William, Duke of Normandy. His army of Normans had invaded England from France. William's purpose was to claim the English throne. Descended from Norse Vikings, William was a skilled and ruthless military commander. He led a veteran army of infantry, archers, crossbowmen, and cavalry.

Opposing William was the newly crowned king of England, Harold II. Harold and his English followers were Anglo-Saxons. Their ancestors were German invaders who had colonized England after the Roman Empire had collapsed. Harold was wise, brave, and a strong ruler. Yet he and his troops were at a disadvantage. They had just made a forced march to Hastings following a major battle and victory against Norse invaders in northern England. The English were tired. In addition, they were outnumbered and on foot. They had neither cavalry nor archers to support them.

In spite of these disadvantages, the English fought fiercely. At first, the Norman cavalry was unable to break through the Anglo-Saxon shield wall. Then the battle turned in William's favor when the English were tricked into breaking ranks to pursue fleeing Normans. The Norman knights on horseback were then able to turn and ride down the English on foot. Harold continued to fight until he was killed. So ended the long Anglo-Saxon reign in England.

Following the Battle of Hastings, William the Conqueror seized London. On Christmas Day, 1066, William was crowned king of England. Norman barons took the best English lands. Norman bishops took control of the Church in England. For the Anglo-Saxons, Norman rule brought new laws, heavy taxes, and a long period of misery as a conquered people.

How did the Battle of Hastings affect the history of England?

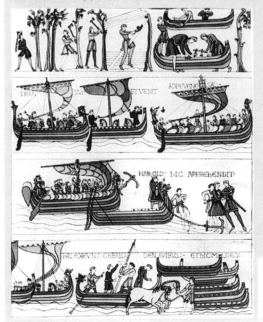

William the Conqueror prepares to invade England. This image is part of the Bayeux Tapestry, which illustrates the Norman conquest of England.

A Viking ship dug up in Norway. By custom, Viking chiefs were often buried in their ships. A carved headpost (*right*) found in another buried Viking ship.

defeated the Anglo-Saxon king. William the Conqueror introduced the Norman language, laws, and government into England. He drew England more closely into European affairs.

After 1066, the Vikings stopped their raids. Many had settled in new places and became farmers, traders, and craft workers. However, from Hungary a Central Asian people called Magyars attacked parts of Germany, Italy, and France. Southern France and Italy also were raided, but by Arabs from Spain and North Africa.

CRITICAL THINKING

1. Explain why you AGREE or DISAGREE with each of the following statements:
   a. Charlemagne had the support of the pope.
   b. Charlemagne's empire lasted for a long time after his death.
   c. Christian missionaries had little success in England.
   d. The Viking raids lasted about 200 years.
   e. Medieval Europeans feared the Vikings.

2. In what ways were Clovis, Alfred, and Charlemagne similar?

FEUDALISM AND THE MANORIAL SYSTEM

After Charlemagne's empire broke apart, the people of Europe had no strong central government to look to for protection or help. Land was the main source of wealth. Large landholders had the most authority because, in many instances, land took the place of money. People were often paid for their services in land. The land-holders needed people to protect the land and to farm it. Two systems came into being to meet the need to defend and farm the land. They both provided political, social, economic, and military organization to Europe.

1. Feudalism.   In order to protect the property they already had and to acquire more, large landholders needed people to fight for them. The landholders, or *lords*, granted land to an individual in return for the promise to defend the lord. The fighting man, or *knight*, became the *vassal* of the lord. The land given to the vassal was a *fief*, or *feud*.

   a.   *Vassals.*   The vassal owed his master a certain number of days of military service each year. He had to give money to the lord

William the Conqueror grants the lands of an Anglo-Saxon noble to a Norman vassal.

when the master's oldest daughter married. A payment was also required when the lord's oldest son became a knight. In addition, vassals had to entertain the lord and members of his household when the master inspected their lands. If a lord was captured by an enemy, vassals had to contribute money or goods to free him.

In return for these services, the lord provided money and soldiers for the common defense. Roads and villages were maintained by the lord.

The lord also acted as a judge to decide disputes among his vassals. If a case was particularly complicated, he might call on certain vassals to give advice.

Vassals could have vassals of their own. They had the right to divide their land and give parts of it to men who promised loyal service in return.

All lords were men. During the Middle Ages, the wife of a lord was called a lady. A lady rarely held property in her own name. As a result, most women did not have the means to create vassals.

b. *Decline of feudalism.* Feudalism in Western Europe lasted for about 400 years, from the 800's to the 1200's. The relationship between lord and vassal changed when business and trade became more prosperous. Money was then easier to obtain. Lords could hire men to fight and pay them with money instead of land.

Changes in methods of warfare also helped end feudalism. Knights in heavy armor on horseback no longer scattered lightly armed infantry, or soldiers on foot. The introduction of the crossbow, the powerful longbow, and armor-piercing arrows made the hand-to-hand combat of the knights obsolete. Bowmen, or archers, as they were also called, were expensive to hire. Only kings and wealthy nobles could afford to do so. As royal armies increased in size and strength, the authority of kings grew and feudalism declined.

Feudalism was also weakened by the Crusades (1095–1291). For 200 years, Western European kings fought a series of religious wars against the Muslim Empire. The purpose was to recover Jerusalem and the Holy Land (present-day Israel) for Christianity. These wars stimulated a desire for Middle Eastern goods and an increase in trade. Towns and cities grew and expanded, giving kings new taxes and revenues. This increased their power and made kings less dependent upon their nobles. Also, serfs who ran away to the towns could find new ways to earn a living and were no longer bound to the land and their feudal lords.

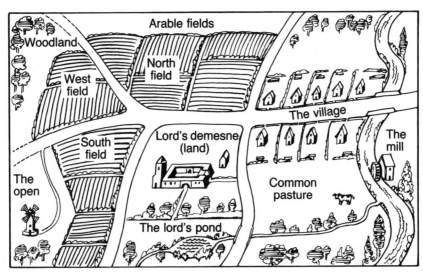

A medieval manor.

From the 14th to the 17th century, strong national governments arose in Europe. Decreased in number and power by the Crusades and other wars, the nobles were forced to submit to the authority of kings.

2. The Manorial System.   The relationship of the lord to the peasants who worked on his land is called the manorial system.

  a.   *Castles.*   The lord lived in the *manor*, a large house or castle, near the center of his lands. (The word "manor" also referred to the whole estate.) The peasants lived in small houses or huts close to the castle. Fields, orchards, and forests surrounded the buildings.

During the Middle Ages, wars never seemed to stop, and raiders might attack at any time. The castle was designed to give people protection. Thick walls enclosed the castle. In front of the walls might be a water-filled ditch called a *moat*. To get over the moat, one had to cross a drawbridge that was lowered from inside the castle. In times of danger, peasants took shelter within the castle walls.

  b.   *Serfs.*   Peasants who worked in the lord's fields were called *serfs*. They belonged to the land. When the ownership of the manor changed hands, serfs stayed on the land.

Serfs had to spend most of their time working in the lord's fields and taking care of his animals. They could use some of the land to raise food for themselves. (Only a few peasants owned their own land.) Serfs had few rights or freedoms. For instance, they could not marry or leave the manor without permission from the lord. Nor could they advance to higher social positions. Their lives were filled with hard work and poverty.

c. *Manor life.* Manors were largely self-sufficient. Most needs of the inhabitants were provided for without help from the outside. The serfs grew food for everyone. Each family took care of its own medical problems. Tools, weapons, clothing, furniture, and most else required by the peasants and the lord's family were made on the manor. There were few places where goods could be bought, and factories did not exist. Only a few items (such as salt for preserving food and iron for making tools and weapons) had to be brought to the manor from the outside world.

At times, the wealthy lord of a manor presented a *tournament*, or contest between knights, for the entertainment of all—nobles, knights, and serfs. Using lances, swords, and battle-axes, knights fought each other, sometimes to the death. Visiting entertainers, such as actors, singers, jugglers, and wrestlers, also helped to brighten the serfs' hard lives.

Many serfs spent their entire lives on the manor. Such isolation kept people ignorant of what was happening in other places. They had few chances to exchange ideas or learn new ways.

 MATCHING EXERCISE

Match each term in Column A with its meaning in Column B.

Column A	Column B
1. lord	*a.* land given to a vassal
2. vassal	*b.* water-filled ditch
3. tournament	*c.* large landholder
4. fief	*d.* able to take care of one's needs
5. knight	without help from others
6. lady	*e.* the wife of a lord
7. manor	*f.* large house or castle
8. moat	*g.* person who promised to fight in
9. serf	return for a gift of land
10. self-sufficient	*h.* one who belonged to the land and
	had few rights or freedoms
	i. man who fought on horseback
	j. contest between knights

ESSAY QUESTIONS

1. Explain why life on a feudal manor would or would not appeal to you.

2. Describe the organization given to Europe by the feudal and manorial systems.

3. State *three* developments that weakened feudalism.

THE ROMAN CATHOLIC CHURCH

After Christianity was made the official religion of the Roman Empire, the Church became known as the Roman Catholic Church. (The phrase means the universal church of Rome.) The organization of the Church gave the pope in Rome much power. He was aided by cardinals and bishops, who supervised the work of the priests. In the Middle Ages, every manor and every town had a church. Each church had a priest to conduct religious services.

Church officials served as advisers to lords and kings. The Church conducted schools and provided places for travelers to stay. In many areas of Europe, the Church was the only form of government. It kept law and learning alive in Europe.

1. The Power of the Church.   During the Middle Ages, a time of great unrest and uncertainty, the Church provided a place of refuge and hope. Christians believed that one who lived a good life and who followed the rules set down by God and the Church would be rewarded by a happy life in heaven. A person who did something wrong could usually undo the wrong by begging forgiveness from God and by performing good deeds.

To make sure that the Church would have the final word in disputes, Church leaders set up their own courts. In these courts, wrongdoers were tried and judged under *canon law*. Under this law of the Church, those who disagreed with the teachings of the Church could be convicted of *heresy*. Heresy was regarded as a terrible crime. A common punishment for it was *excommunication*. An excommunicated person was barred from all churches and from the salvation of the soul offered by the Church. This meant that the person would not go to heaven.

The Church might use another form of punishment against a lord or king. The pope could place a nation or fief under an *interdict.* This punishment banned all church services in an area. Such a situation often made the people fearful and angry. They would demand that their ruler give in to the will of the pope so that religious services could be held.

2. The Church and Learning. During the Middle Ages, few people knew how to read and write. Church officials generally had both skills. People who needed to have something written—a letter, a marriage agreement—would go to a priest or other church official for help. In addition to their religious duties, many church officials served as secretaries, advisers, and teachers.

    a. *Universities.* The Church encouraged the development of the first universities in Europe. These centers of learning trained young men to become officials of the church. Universities also prepared students for other careers. At the university in Salerno, Italy, founded in the 800's, a student could study medicine. The school in Bologna, also in Italy and founded in 1088, specialized in law. Among the universities established in the 1100's and 1200's that still exist are the University of Paris in France and the universities at Oxford and Cambridge in England.

Oxford University was founded by the Church to train new religious leaders.

b. *Scholars.* Most of the great thinkers of the Middle Ages were men of the Church. One famous scholar was Thomas Aquinas, who lived from 1225 to 1274. He wrote about faith and reason and the need for both in order to understand God.

Roger Bacon, a Catholic friar in England in the 1200's, is considered to be the founder of experimental science. He conducted experiments and research to learn about the natural world. One of his studies led him to predict the coming of the airplane, a 20th-century development.

3. The Church and Art. Most art of the Middle Ages served the Church. Works of art made the insides of churches beautiful. Music that was sung or played reminded people of God. Churchmen known as monks decorated the pages of the Bibles they copied. (Since there were no printing presses at that time, all copies of books had to be written and illustrated by hand.) Among the most beautiful of the decorated Bibles is the *Book of Kells*, created by monks in Ireland.

The most impressive buildings of the Middle Ages were the great churches in the cities and towns. Everything in these buildings was done to help the worshippers feel the presence of God. Two major styles of churches were built.

One style, the Romanesque, was the main type of church put up between 1000 and 1150. These churches had thick stone walls, very small windows, and rounded arches.

About 1150 to 1300, a second style, the Gothic, came into being. These churches had thinner stone walls, high ceilings, large windows filled with stained (colored) glass, pointed arches, and tall towers. Many windows pictured events from stories in the Bible.

4. Church Organization and Structure. Under feudalism, the Western European countries had weak central governments. The Roman Catholic Church was the only source of international authority and organization

a. *Church personnel.* To exercise power throughout Western Europe, the Church adopted the organization of the Roman Empire. The supreme leader of the Roman Catholic Church is the *pope*, who lives in the Vatican in Rome. Since the 11th century, each pope has been elected for life by the College of Cardinals.

The *cardinals* are the next highest-ranking Church officials. Each cardinal has authority over a region containing many religious districts, or *dioceses*. Each diocese is led by a *bishop*. Larger districts, called *archdioceses*, are under the authority of *archbishops*.

Priests provide leadership and guidance to churches and local communities called *parishes*.

Monks and *friars* are members of religious orders. They often live in monasteries and are governed by strict rules. Three such monastic orders were founded during the Middle Ages—the Benedictines (6th century), the Franciscans (13th century), and the Dominicans (13th century).

Women who enter religious life are called nuns. They often live in *convents*.

b. *Division in the Church.* Differences over Church language, rituals, and beliefs caused a split in European religious affairs. In 1054, the Roman Catholic Church, led by the pope, split from the Greek Orthodox Church led by the *patriarch*, or bishop of Constantinople. This division has lasted to the present day. The Greek Orthodox Church later split into a number of Eastern Orthodox churches.

Notre Dame Cathedral, Paris: The pointed arches at the base of this building, the "rose" (circular) stained-glass window above, and the tall towers are hallmarks of the Gothic style of architecture. How does this style differ from the Romanesque style?

SENTENCE CORRECTIONS

Reread "1. The Power of the Church," on pages 151–152, to find out what is wrong with each of the following statements. Then rewrite each as a correct statement.

1. The Church offered little to the people during the safe, peaceful period of the Middle Ages.

2. A person in the Middle Ages did not believe that bad deeds could be undone.

3. Church courts used feudal laws to try people for heresy.

4. A king under interdict was generally supported by his subjects.

5. Excommunication was a light punishment that no one feared.

SENTENCE COMPLETION

From the list that follows, select the term that best completes each sentence.

universities   Thomas Aquinas   Romanesque   monks
Bologna   Salerno   Roger Bacon   Gothic

1. An English churchman of the 1200's, —, is considered to be the founder of experimental science.

2. The Church encouraged the development of — to train church officials.

3. In Ireland, — decorated the pages of the *Book of Kells*.

4. At — in Italy, one could study medicine.

5. Founded in 1088, the university in — specialized in law.

6. The writings of the famous scholar — express how both faith and reason are needed to understand God.

7. Churches in the — style have rounded arches.

8. —-style churches have large stained-glass windows.

THE CRUSADES

For many years, European Christians made the long, difficult trip to the Middle East to visit the places where Jesus had lived and taught. Of special importance was the city of Jerusalem, where Jesus was crucified. In the late 1000's, the Seljuk Turks began to interfere with Christian visitors to the Holy Land. The Turks were not Christians but Muslims. Muslims believed in a religion called Islam. Muslims considered Jesus to be a holy man or a prophet, but not God.

The Turks also threatened the Byzantine Empire, which had its capital at Constantinople. The Byzantine Empire was the remaining portion of the old Eastern Roman Empire. The Byzantines were Christians.

1. The Beginning of the Crusades. The Byzantine emperor asked the pope in Rome for help in fighting the Turks. At the Council of Clermont in 1095, Pope Urban II called for a *crusade*, a holy war, against the Turks. Thousands of peasants and knights answered Urban's call.

Peasants made up the first group that set off for the Holy Land. When they reached Asia Minor, most were killed by the Turks.

Thousands of knights followed in 1096. After many bloody battles, they took Jerusalem in 1099. Following this First Crusade, Christians ruled the city until 1187. Then the Turks recaptured it. This event caused the Third Crusade to begin in 1189. Three kings—Richard the Lion-Hearted of England, Fredrick Barbarossa of Germany, and Philip Augustus of France—led their armies against the forces of Saladin, one of the most revered Muslim leaders. The Europeans failed to recapture Jerusalem. Saladin, however, agreed to allow Christian pilgrims to visit the Holy Land.

The Crusades ended in 1291. In that year, the Muslims took Acre, the last Christian-held city in the Holy Land.

For 200 years, Crusaders tried to drive the Turks out of the Holy Land. Kings tried, emperors tried, even children tried. They all failed. All they permanently won in the Holy Land was the right of Christians to visit Jerusalem. This right cost the lives of tens of thousands of Christians and Muslims.

Although the Crusaders did not change much in the Holy Land, they were changed by their experiences. In turn, they introduced new ideas and goods to Europe.

2. Results of the Crusades. The Crusades changed Europe forever. People who had never traveled far from their homes jour-

Routes of the First Four Crusades

Choose the item that best answers each question.

1. Which of the following areas was divided between Christian and Muslim rulers? (*a*) England (*b*) France (*c*) Spain (*d*) Italy

2. In which *two* nations or organizations did Crusades not start? (*a*) England and France (*b*) Holy Roman Empire and Italy (*c*) Spain and Egypt

3. Which pair of areas were in Muslim hands during the Crusades? (*a*) Byzantine Empire and Italy (*b*) Holy Roman Empire and France (*c*) North Africa and Asia Minor (*d*) England and Scandinavia.

neyed hundreds of miles to the Middle East. They came into contact with Byzantines, Turks, and Arabs. The culture of these eastern peoples were more advanced than the culture of Europe.

a. *Increased trade.* The Crusaders liked many of the new things they saw. They brought silks, spices, sugar, and other goods home with them as well as new ideas about how to live. To satisfy the demand for eastern goods, a brisk trade developed between Europe and the Middle East. Several seafaring cities in Italy—particularly Venice and Genoa—controlled this trade and profited greatly from it.

b. *Growth of towns.*   Towns in other parts of Europe also grew larger. Townspeople began turning out goods for the eastern trade. Skilled and unskilled workers came to towns to look for employment. Many serfs ran away from manors to seek a better life in the towns. If a serf could keep from being found by his or her master for a year and a day, the serf would become a free person. It was easier to hide in towns than in the countryside.

Among the most important centers of trade during the Middle Ages were Venice, Genoa, Pisa, and Naples. Located on the Italian seacoast, these cities came to control most of the trade between Europe and the eastern Mediterranean.

In Belgium, Bruges and Ghent became the leading commercial cities of northern Europe. They produced and sold woolen cloth and imported the products of Asia and the Middle East from the Italian cities.

The trade of the North Sea and the Baltic Sea was controlled by the north German cities of Bremen, Hamburg, and Lübeck. In the 13th century, those and other German cities formed a commercial organization called the *Hanseatic League*.

c. *Growth of the middle class.*   The businesspeople in the towns became the new *middle class* of Europe. They looked to the kings of their countries for protection. Kings always needed money for defense and public works, such as roads. Roads connected towns and helped trade. To get money, kings gave special rights and privileges to the townspeople. Thus, the townspeople often sided with the king in disputes with his vassals, the lords.

The increase in the power of the towns led to a decrease in the power of the lords. The feudal system of giving land in return for promises of loyalty and service began to lose its importance. Money became more important. Kings were able to gain more money and power than the lords.

 ESSAY QUESTION

Explain why a serf might want to run away from a manor.

WRITING SENTENCES

Use each of the words below in a sentence.

1. Holy Land   **4.** trade

2. Urban II   **5.** townspeople

3. Crusades

THE CHANGING POWER OF MONARCHS

During the time of the Crusades, changes took place in the way the nations of Europe were governed. The monarchs, or rulers, gained power. They increased their landholdings and won the loyalty of more of their subjects.

1. Government in England.   After William of Normandy conquered England in 1066, royal power was strengthened. He ordered the preparation of a *Domesday Book*, a survey of England's people and property. This was used to give the king information about all sources of revenue and wealth in the country. The royal government collected taxes, decided important court cases, and asked for advice from lords to get their support.

    a. *Common law.*   King Henry II, who ruled from 1154 to 1189, strengthened the justice system. The judges he appointed traveled around the country deciding cases. Their decisions formed the basis of the *common law*. Such law applied "in common" to all the people.

    b. *Magna Carta.*   John, one of Henry's sons, became king in 1199. To get money to fight the French, he gave up some royal power. When he asked his barons, the important landholders, to pay more taxes, they refused. They forced John to sign the *Magna Carta* in 1215. For the most part, this "great charter" set forth the rights of the barons. More important, many of the rights were also extended to the common people. One right said that a person could not be sent to prison without first receiving a jury trial. By signing the Magna Carta, John accepted the idea that even a king's power is limited by laws.

King John about to sign the Magna Carta.

c. *First Parliament*. From early times, the kings of England had asked their chief vassals for advice about important matters. Edward I, however, was the first king to call on representatives from several different groups—townspeople, knights, churchmen, lords—to give him advice. In 1295, these people met together in the first *Parliament* to make laws for the country. Throughout modern times, Parliament has governed England.

2. The Kings of France. During most of the Middle Ages, French kings controlled only a small amount of land around Paris. The remainder of what is now France was governed by various feudal lords and the English. Through inheritance, marriage, and wars, the kings gradually added to their holdings.

King Philip II ruled from 1180 to 1223. He used his own officials to collect taxes and to act as judges. Through many wars against English kings, Philip greatly increased the royal landholdings.

The lawmaking body of France developed under King Philip IV. In 1302, he called representatives of the Church, the nobility, and the townspeople to sit in the *Estates General*. This body generally followed the will of the king. Philip IV also set up royal courts of law.

a. *Hundred Years' War*. Off and on between 1337 and 1453, the French fought the English. From the time of William the Conqueror, English kings had owned large sections of France. French kings wanted to control French land held by English kings. The conflicts between the French and English kings are known as the Hundred Years' War.

France, 1180

France, 1453

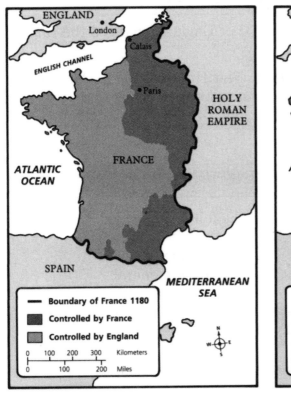

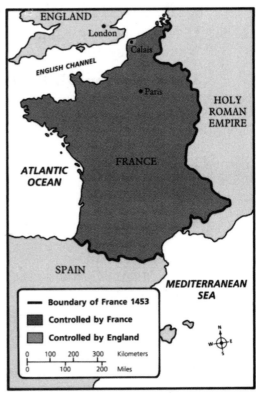

1. Between 1180 and 1453, the French (*a*) invaded England (*b*) lost all of France to the English (*c*) took control of all of France except the port of Calais (*d*) invaded Spain.

2. The major result of the wars between England and France was (*a*) victory for the French (*b*) victory for the English (*c*) victory for the Spaniards (*d*) all of the above.

---

    b. *Joan of Arc.* The French gained an advantage in the war of 1429. Joan of Arc, a peasant girl, believed that voices of the saints told her to help defeat the English. She persuaded Charles, the heir to the French throne, to let her lead an army. Inspired by Joan's presence, French forces won key victories within a few months. Charles was crowned King Charles VII. Joan continued to lead troops into battle until she was captured by enemies of the king in May 1430. She was turned over to the English, who let Church authorities try her for witchcraft. They found her guilty and burned her to death in May 1431.

    In 1453, Charles finally pushed the English out of all but a tiny part of France. As a result of the French victory, the king's power was greatly increased. Charles now controlled almost all of France.

ESSAY QUESTIONS

1. Describe how King Henry II of England changed the English justice system.

2. **PROVE or DISPROVE:** The Hundred Years' War helped French kings to increase their power.

3. Explain how Joan of Arc helped King Charles VII.

DEFINITIONS

Explain the meaning of each of the following terms:

    a. common law   *c.* Parliament
    b. Magna Carta   *d.* Estates General

IDENTIFICATIONS

Identify each of the following people.

    a. William of Normandy   *d.* Edward I
    b. Henry II   *e.* Philip IV
    c. John

CHRONOLOGY

Find the year in which each of the following events occurred. Then arrange them in the order in which they took place.

    a. the beginning of the rule of King Philip II of France
    b. the signing of the Magna Carta
    c. the beginning of the rule of King Henry II of England
    d. the end of the Hundred Years' War
    e. the meeting of the first Parliament
    f. the meeting of the first Estates General

THE BYZANTINE EMPIRE

The Byzantine Empire began as the eastern part of the Roman Empire. After the fall of Rome in 476, the Byzantines kept alive many

Roman ideas about law and government. Roman culture blended with the existing Greek culture of the area. Greek was the official language and Christianity the official religion. The capital of the empire, Constantinople, became a prosperous trading center. It controlled the water route between the Black Sea and the Aegean Sea.

1. The Growth of the Empire. The Byzantine emperors were dictators. They ruled with the support of a well-trained army and navy and an efficient system of secret police and spies. The emperors controlled not only the government but also the eastern Christian Church, known as the Eastern Orthodox Church. Women as well as men ruled the empire.

    a. *Justinian's rule.* Early Byzantine emperors tried to increase the size of their empire. They fought the Germanic tribes that held lands that had been part of the old Roman Empire. Before Emperor Justinian, who ruled from 527 to 565, no one had succeeded in adding much territory. Justinian's armies conquered many lands around the Mediterranean Sea, including Italy, North Africa, and southern Spain.

Justinian constructed churches and public buildings in Constantinople and other cities that he ruled over. He ordered forts to be put up throughout the empire. He also asked officials to compile (gather together) all the laws of Rome and make

Justinian, emperor of the Eastern Roman Empire, shown in a detail from a mosaic.

The interior of the Church of Santa Sophia in Constantinople (now Istanbul), erected by Justinian.

sure that they could be easily understood. The resulting group of laws is known as the Code of Justinian. This code has influenced the legal systems of many present-day European and Latin American countries.

The Byzantines created fine art and constructed great buildings. As their trade prospered, the riches of Constantinople increased. Other Mediterranean trading cities, particularly Venice, watched jealously.

Constantinople was the most advanced city in medieval Europe. Its paved streets were lighted at night. Visitors marveled at its palaces, churches, parks, museums, and schools. Chariot races were held in the Hippodrome. The city was the trade center of the Byzantine Empire. Merchants imported Far Eastern luxury goods and exported them to Italian cities and Russia.

Although skilled workers produced Byzantine luxury goods (such as gold and silver jewelry, perfumes, and fine glass), agricultural production was limited by a lack of farmland.

b. *Decline of Byzantium.* After Justinian's death, his empire could not be kept together. His military campaigns and building programs had left little money in the treasury. The Byzantine army became too weak to fight off invading Arabs, Turks, Serbs, Visigoths, and Lombards. The 7th and 8th centuries were known as the "Dark Ages" of the Byzantine Empire. Much territory was lost to invaders. Despite a brief revival of Byzantine military power in the 9th century, the empire continued to decline. During the next 500 years, the empire shrank until it included only part of Asia Minor, southern Italy, and Greece.

The Byzantine Empire

Indicate whether each statement is *true* (**T**) or *false* (**F**).

1. Between 565 and 1000, the Byzantine Empire grew larger.

2. Egypt and Syria were part of the Byzantine Empire in 565.

3. The Byzantine Empire did not rule any part of Italy, Spain, or North Africa in 565.

4. Greece and Anatolia were part of the Byzantine Empire from 565 to 1000.

5. Venice and Rome were Byzantine cities in the year 1000.

6. Anatolia made up the major part of the Byzantine Empire in the year 1000.

2. The Fall of the Byzantine Empire. In the late 1000's, the Seljuk Turks came out of Asia and attacked the Byzantines. The forces of the Turkish ruler Alp Arslan defeated a huge Byzantine army at the Battle of Manzikert in 1071. The Turks then advanced through much of Anatolia (in Asia Minor). After many years of defending the empire, the Byzantine emperor asked the pope in Rome for help against the Turks. The Crusaders stopped in Constantinople on their way to the Holy Land. In 1204, at the urging of Venice and against the wishes of the pope, the Crusaders captured and looted Constantinople instead of fighting the Turks.

After the Byzantines won back their city in 1261, they could not regain their former strength. Another group of Turks, called Ottomans, started raiding communities around Constantinople. Greece fell, and so did most of Asia Minor. Finally, in 1453, the Ottomans under Sultan Mehmed II captured Constantinople. The Byzantine Empire, which had existed for nearly 1,000 years, came to an end. The Ottoman civilization replaced the Greco-Roman civilization in the East.

THE RISE OF RUSSIA

Between the 400's and 700's, people known as Slavs settled between the Baltic and Black seas. They built towns along the great rivers of the region. Trade made the towns of Novgorod and Kiev prosperous. In the early 800's, Swedish Vikings, the Rus, moved into the Slavic area. They took over the rule of Novgorod and Kiev in the mid-800's. Eventually, the Rus established a state that would be called Russia.

1. The Byzantine Influence. As the Russian state developed, it borrowed much from the advanced culture of the neighboring Byzantine Empire. In the 900's, Eastern Orthodox missionaries persuaded the Russian people to become Christians. Byzantine builders constructed churches in Kiev, the first capital of the Russian state. Byzantine teachers set up schools. Russians used Byzantine models when they developed their law, literature, and art. In particular, the rulers of Russia learned from the Byzantine emperors how to keep the government and the Church under their control.

Russians also borrowed an alphabet to write their language. The Cyrillic alphabet was created by a Byzantine missionary. He combined the Greek alphabet with letters he invented.

2. Russia Under Mongol Rule.   The development of Russia as a Byzantine state came to a halt in the 1200's. Mongol invaders swept in from East Asia and captured one Russian city after another. Kiev fell in 1240. For the next 200 years, Mongols controlled Russia. During this period, Russia had little contact with Western Europe or the Byzantine Empire.

The Mongols let Russian princes govern Russia. They also left the Christian Church alone. As long as the Russians paid tribute (money) each year, the Mongols did not directly interfere, in Russian affairs.

3. Rulers From Moscow.   The city-state of Moscow prospered under the Mongols. A trading and religious center, it was used by

The Growth of Russia, 1300–1584

EXPLAIN: Between 1300 and 1584, the rulers of Moscow made Russia a great nation.

A woodcut of Ivan IV.

The Granger Collection, New York

the Mongols as a central tax collection point. The Mongols let the princes of Moscow act independently as long as they collected enough taxes to pay the tribute.

Under the leadership of Grand Prince Ivan III (ruled 1462–1505), Moscow refused to send any more tribute to the Mongols. At this time, the Mongols were too weak to do much about the rebels in the city. In 1480, the city freed itself from Mongol rule. Ivan III, also called Ivan the Great, ruled Russia with an iron hand. He united other Russian city-states with Moscow. By doing so, he brought a vast territory under his control.

Ivan IV, the grandson of Ivan III, was named the ruler of Russia in 1533 at the age of three. At age 17, he took the title of *czar* (from the Latin *caesar*), or emperor, and ruled until 1584. He too added territory to Russia, particularly lands to the east of Moscow. His cruelty to those who opposed him earned him the name Ivan the Terrible.

Later czars followed Ivan's example of using brutal force to impose their will. While the czars gained power, the Russian people became poorer. Many of their rights and freedoms were taken away from them.

Chapter Review

MULTIPLE-CHOICE

Choose the item that best completes each sentence.

1. The violent and insecure life of Europe after the fall of Rome was caused by (*a*) competition for trade routes (*b*) weak central government and frequent wars (*c*) competition among great empires (*d*) wars between Germans and Mongols.

2. The title the pope gave to Charlemagne was (*a*) king of the Franks (*b*) Holy Roman emperor (*c*) grand prince of Moscow (*d*) prince of the Visigoths.

3. Alfred led the Anglo-Saxons in England in the fight against the (*a*) Vikings (*b*) Normans (*c*) Romano-British (*d*) Celts.

4. The warriors of Viking descent who conquered England in 1066 were the (*a*) Anglo-Saxons (*b*) Slavs (*c*) Normans (*d*) Byzantines.

5. One great achievement of the Byzantine Empire was the (*a*) Donation of Pepin (*b*) rise of the Seljuk Turks (*c*) fall of Constantinople (*d*) Code of Justinian.

6. The cultural development of the Russians was changed by the (*a*) Anglo-Saxons (*b*) Mongols (*c*) Seljuk Turks (*d*) Arabs.

7. Feudalism was based on a system of cooperation between (*a*) lords and vassals (*b*) serfs and peasants (*c*) townspeople and serfs (*d*) factory workers and farmers.

8. The manor was known for its (*a*) lack of defenses (*b*) dependence on towns for food (*c*) location inside towns (*d*) self-sufficiency.

9. The Roman Catholic Church helped spread learning in Europe by (*a*) using excommunication (*b*) exercising authority over kings (*c*) encouraging universities (*d*) rejecting the authority of civil courts.

10. The Crusades helped to weaken feudalism by encouraging the (*a*) growth of towns (*b*) building of Gothic churches (*c*) lords to rebel against their kings (*d*) serfs to remain on their manors.

CHRONOLOGY

Explain the importance of each of the following dates.

1. 1066   5. 1302
2. 1095   6. 1453
3. 1215   7. 1480
4. 1295

THEMATIC WRITING

Reread "Feudalism and the Manorial System" on page 147–150. Then write about *one* of the following themes:

The Obligations of Lords and Vassals
The Organization of Life on a Manor.

FACT/OPINION

Decide which of the following statements are *fact* (**F**) and which are *opinion* (**O**).

1. The empire of Charlemagne included France, Germany, Austria, and Switzerland.

2. Alfred the Great defeated the efforts of Vikings to conquer England.

3. The Franks contributed more to the development of European civilization than did the Normans.

4. William the Conqueror ordered a survey of all people, land, and wealth in England.

5. For medieval warriors, the use of sword and spear required more skill than did the use of the longbow.

6. Feudalism provided social, political, economic, and military organization to Europe during the Middle Ages.

7. Feudalism was weakened by the Crusades.

8. Medieval manors were largely self-sufficient.

9. During the Middle Ages, life in Paris was more comfortable than life in Venice.

10. Europeans preferred to live under strong, central governments.

Connections: Cavalry

Greek cavalry. A frieze (sculptured scene) from the Parthenon.

The charge of *cavalry*, or warriors mounted on horses, was an effective way of fighting for more than 1,000 years, especially against soldiers on foot, or infantry. Alexander the Great used cavalry to defeat the Persians. In turn, mounted Persian archers gave the Roman legions a very hard time. The Huns of Attila, who invaded and terrorized Western Europe, did most of their fighting from the backs of horses. The same was true of the Mongols who conquered China in the 13th century.

During the Middle Ages, battles in Europe were fought by knights clad in steel armor. The armor protected the knight from the blows of most swords, lances, clubs, and arrows. Sometimes even a knight's horse was fitted with armor. A disadvantage of armor was its heavy weight. Because of this, knights lost their speed and mobility in battle.

Knights became easy targets. The Battle of Crécy in 1346 marked the beginning of the end of the knights. The French lost this battle because their knights were massacred by English archers. Three-foot arrows driven by powerful longbows pierced the armor of the French knights.

Soon after, most military leaders returned to the hit-and-run tactics of the Huns and the mounted Persian archers. The light cavalry of the Russian Cossacks and Native American braves of the Great Plains were among the world's greatest horsemen.

Gunpowder, an invention of the Chinese, and the spread of firearms finally ended the era of the cavalry charge.

List *three* groups of people who used cavalry in battle.

DOCUMENT-BASED QUESTION

This question is based on the accompanying documents (1–3). It will improve your ability to work with historical documents.

Historical Context:

The Western Roman Empire had fallen, but other sources of authority took its place during the Middle Ages. Feudalism, the

Roman Catholic Church, and developing national monarchies came to control the lives of peoples across Western Europe.

Task:

Using information from the documents and your knowledge of world history, answer the questions that follow each document. Your answers to each question will help you write the document-based essay.

Document 1.   Study the illustration on page 141.

Charlemagne holds two items. What types of power do these two items symbolize?

Document 2.   Study the illustration on page 147.

What does it reveal about the relationship of the vassal to the lord under the feudal system?

Document 3.   Extract from the Magna Carta (1215):

63. Wherefore we wish and firmly enjoin that the English church shall be free, and that the men in our kingdom shall have and hold all the aforesaid liberties, rights and concessions well and peacefully, freely and quietly, fully and completely, for themselves and their heirs from us and our heirs, in all matters and in all places. . . .

Source: http://www.fordham.edu/halsall/source/magnacarta.txt. Part of Internet Media Sourcebook.

What is King John of England telling his subjects in this passage that ends the Magna Carta?

DOCUMENT-BASED ESSAY

Using information from the documents and your knowledge of world history, write an essay in which you:

- Discuss the power of the kings and emperors.
- Explain how the relationship of the ruler to the ruled changed during the Middle Ages.

CHAPTER 8
Islam and the Muslim Empire

While the Germanic kingdoms and the Roman Catholic Church were gaining strength in Europe, changes were also occurring in the Middle East. In the early 600's, events took place in Arabia that had a major influence on the whole world. This influence is still felt today. The events led to the founding of one of the great religions of the world.

THE BEGINNINGS OF ISLAM

Most of the people of Arabia in the 600's worshipped many gods. They saw no reason to change their ways until they heard the words of a man named Muhammad. He called himself a *prophet* and a teacher. In the religious sense, a prophet is one who brings the teachings of God to others.

1. The First Muslim. In the year 610, Muhammad believed that an angel spoke to him in a vision. The angel called him the "messenger of God." Muhammad then started urging the Arabs to worship one God, called Allah in Arabic, instead of many gods.

Muhammad first told the people of Mecca, his home city, about Allah. He preached that all who believed in Allah are equal and that the rich should give to the poor. Many wealthy and powerful people in Mecca thought Muhammad was a troublemaker. They did not want to give up their old beliefs. To stop Muhammad from preaching, they threatened to kill him. In 622, Muhammad fled to Medina, another city in Arabia. His journey from Mecca to Medina is called the *hegira* (the departure). The people of Medina accepted Muhammad's ideas more readily than did the people of Mecca.

As Muhammad gained followers, he formed an army and marched on Mecca. He forced the people there to acknowledge Allah as their only God. By 632, the year of Muhammad's death, most of the people of Arabia had accepted the ideas of the Prophet. One of the world's great religions had been born. It came to be called Islam, and its followers, Muslims. Islam is Arabic for "surrender to the will of God." Muslim means "one who surrenders to God" or "believer."

Men praying in a mosque in Jakarta, Indonesia.

As a young man, Muhammad had traveled to many areas of the Middle East. It is thought that the beliefs of the Jews and the Christians he met contributed to the development of some of his ideas. Muhammad's teachings about life after death and the moral obligations of Muslims are similar to some beliefs and practices of Jews and Christians. Also, Muhammad regarded many Jewish and Christian religious figures, such as Moses and Jesus, as prophets and holy men. He taught his followers to respect and honor these prophets.

2. Islamic Teachings.   Followers of Islam regard the *Koran* as their holy book. It contains the teachings of Muhammad. The Koran tells Muslims that they must accept Allah as the one true God and Muhammad as his Prophet. They must also pray five times a day and fast (not eat) during the daylight hours in the holy month of Ramadan. Other duties are to give money to the poor and not to eat pork or drink alcoholic beverages. Another important duty is to make a *pilgrimage* (journey) to the holy city of Mecca at least once in a lifetime. The Koran sets down ideas about good and evil, justice and injustice.

Muslims are taught that after death, the soul is rewarded in heaven or punished in hell. Other Islamic teachings stress the equality of all Muslims, regardless of background; respect for parents; and the protection of the weak by the strong. Muslims are also taught that a warrior, or soldier, who dies fighting for Islam is assured of going to heaven.

An organized priesthood did not develop among the Muslims as it did among the Roman Catholics. Men called *imams* lead the faithful in prayer in mosques, the Muslim places of worship.

A page from a 13th-century Koran, which is written in rhymed Arabic.

Muslim men go to mosques on Fridays and holy days. Muslim women worship at home.

THE ISLAMIC WORLD

After Muhammad died, the Arabs continued to spread Islam by military conquest. As the Muslim Empire expanded, the Arabs also developed a great civilization.

1. The Muslim Empire.   When Muhammad died in 632, his close friend and father-in-law, Abu Bakr, was chosen as the leader of the Muslims. He took the title of *caliph*, or successor. Under Abu Bakr, the Arabs started military campaigns against neighboring states. In the mid-600's, they united Arabia under the rule of the caliphs. Then they attacked the Byzantine and Persian empires. Muslim forces easily took the areas that are now the countries of Syria, Israel, and Egypt from the Byzantines. These victories were followed by more successes against the Byzantines in North Africa. Although the Arabs weakened the Byzantine Empire, they did not succeed in destroying it.

   a. *Eastward push.*   By the late 600's, Arab forces had completed the conquest of the Persian Empire. They had captured areas that are now Iraq and Iran and pushed northward into Armenia and eastward into Afghanistan and northern India.

The Muslim Empire, 632–750

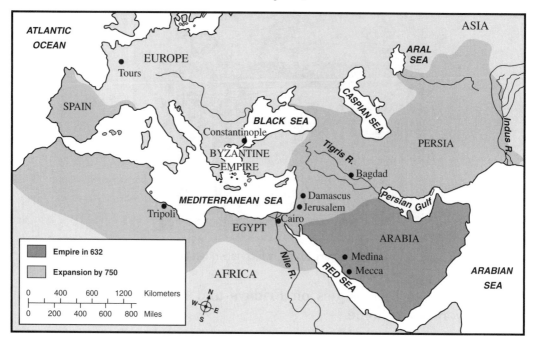

1. Indicate whether each of the following statements is *true* (**T**) or *false* (**F**).
    a. The Muslim Empire extended through Europe, Africa, and Persia.
    b. Cairo, Damascus, and Baghdad were cities of the Muslim Empire.
    c. Spain was part of the Muslim Empire in 632.
    d. Arabia was part of the Muslim Empire in 632.
    e. Tours was a Muslim city.

2. **EXPLAIN:** The Muslim Empire included many different cultures.

---

b. *Westward push.* Arab armies carried Islam into Europe in 711. They quickly conquered the Germanic Visigoths in Spain. But when the Arabs moved into France, they met a major defeat. At the Battle of Tours in 732, an army of Germanic Franks forced the Arabs back into Spain. (The Franks were led by Charles Martel, the grandfather of Charlemagne.) The Muslims remained in Spain until 1492. In that year, Christian forces completed their long reconquest of Spain when they captured Granada, the last Muslim stronghold.

By 750, the Muslim Empire had reached its greatest extent. It included all of the Middle East, Asia to the borders of India and

China, most of Spain, and all of North Africa. In these lands, people of many different cultures lived under the rule of the caliphs. Most of these people were not forced to convert. They voluntarily accepted Islam because they believed in the Muslim moral code or sought opportunities open to Muslims. Some wished to escape special taxes paid by non-Muslims. Conquered peoples who did not convert to Islam were allowed to practice their own religions.

2. Muslim Civilization. Within the borders of their great empire, the Muslims produced a complex, creative civilization. The leading scholars and philosophers studied ideas from many other civilizations. They read works by the ancient Greeks, Hindus, and Persians. The information in these works inspired Muslim thinkers to develop new ideas. For several centuries, Muslim achievements in the arts and sciences were superior to those of Europeans.

   a. *Mathematics.* Arab mathematicians used the zero and a number system developed by the Hindus. When Europeans learned about the number system, they thought the Arabs had invented it. As a result, we call the numerals "Arabic" numerals. Al-Khwarizmi, who lived in the 800's, improved the system of mathematics called algebra. (He may have been the first to use that term.) Another Arab mathematician, Al-Hazan (965–1039), made important discoveries in optics, the study of light rays.

   b. *Medicine.* Muslims excelled in the field of medicine. Physicians such as Rhazes (about 865–932) and Ibn Sina, known in Europe as Avicenna (980–1037), wrote medical encyclopedias. These books were used by doctors in Europe for hundreds of years. Muslim doctors developed advanced surgical procedures and treatments for diseases. Muslim hospitals gave far better care to the sick than did any in Europe in the Middle Ages.

   c. *Literature and philosophy.* In literature, Persian and Indian works had a strong influence on Arab poetry. One of the greatest poets in the Muslim Empire was Omar Khayyam. A Persian, he lived from about 1050 to 1123. His best-known work is a collection of romantic poetry called *The Rubaiyat.* Another famous example of Muslim literature is the *Arabian Nights,* a collection of stories.

   Muslim scholars respected the ideas and learning of people of other faiths. Moses Maimonides, a Jewish doctor born in Spain in 1135, became one of the greatest philosophers of the Muslim Empire.

Prince of Physicians

When only 20 years old, Avicenna (A.D. 980–1037) was already known as the most learned person of his time. Avicenna was a Muslim physician, philosopher, astronomer, and poet. His reputation spread throughout the Islamic and Christian worlds.

Christians called him Avicenna. His Arabic name was Ibn Sina. He was born in Bukhara, a city in Persia. His great intelligence became known at an early age. By the time he was 10, he had memorized the Koran and much poetry. Avicenna studied with excellent teachers, yet he soon surpassed them. He then educated himself. When he was 20, Avicenna had mastered most branches of formal learning, such as law and medicine. He was well known as an outstanding physician.

Political upheavals connected with the rise and fall of dynasties in Persia kept Avicenna moving from city to city. In spite of the turmoil around him, Avicenna continued his work in science, medicine, and philosophy. His fortunes rose when he became court physician to a Persian prince. The prince was so impressed with Avicenna's brilliance that he made the physician his chief minister. In time, however, enemies forced Avicenna out of office and into hiding. He was even put in prison for a while. However, Avicenna's strength of mind and body enabled him to keep writing and working.

Avicenna based many of his ideas about philosophy on the writings of Aristotle, Plato, and other Greek thinkers. He gave later Muslim and Christian philosophers a direction for their thinking.

Many of Avicenna's books were translated into Latin in the 12th century. His most famous work was *Canon of Medicine*. This medical text was used by medical students and doctors throughout the world for more than 600 years. The *Canon* is still used in some parts of Asia. Avicenna also wrote 16 other books on medicine, 68 books on philosophy and theology, 11 on astronomy and science, and 4 books of poetry.

All these books helped to spread Avicenna's influence throughout Europe. He was especially honored by Christian physicians. Among the titles given to him was "Prince of Physicians."

Avicenna diagnosing an illness by a visual examination of a sample of fluids.

Why was Avicenna honored by both Muslims and Christians?

Long periods of peace in the empire made it possible for the Arabs to accomplish much in many fields. A strong government kept order and encouraged learning and trade. Muslims and other people could travel safely throughout the empire. This led to the free exchange of ideas and an increase in knowledge and creativity.

 ESSAY QUESTIONS

1. Describe the rise of Islam and the role played by Muhammad.

2. List *three* important ideas found in the Koran.

3. State *two* similarities among Islam, Christianity, and Judaism.

4. **PROVE or DISPROVE**: As conquerors, the Arabs were more successful in the Middle East than they were in Europe.

5. Name *three* Muslim scholars, and list one important contribution of each.

THE CALIPHS OF DAMASCUS AND BAGHDAD

Each caliph considered himself to have a special tie to the Prophet Muhammad. Because of this relationship, the caliph expected to be honored as the only leader of Islam. Not every Muslim agreed, however.

1. Umayyad Dynasty.   At first, the center of Muslim government was in Mecca. As the empire grew, Muslim military and political organization became more complex. The generals and governors of newly conquered lands became more powerful than the caliphs in Mecca. In 661, the Muslim governor of Syria rebelled, made himself the caliph, and established the Umayyad Dynasty. From Damascus, the new capital, the Umayyad rulers led the Muslim world until 750.

The caliphs of Damascus sent out their armies to add more territory to the empire. Among the peoples they converted to Islam were the Berbers of North Africa. The Umayyads also conquered lands to the east of Damascus. They extended Muslim rule into areas that are today known as Afghanistan and Pakistan.

2. The Abbassid and Fatimid Dynasties.   After a time, some of the conquered peoples grew restless. Revolts broke out in the

740's. In 750, another Arab family overthrew the caliphs of Damascus. Almost all of the Umayyad princes were killed.

a. *Abbassid Dynasty.* The Abbassid family that overthrew the Umayyads in 750 were descendants of Abbas, an uncle of Muhammad. The new rulers decided to move the capital away from Damascus. They ordered a city to be built along the Tigris River in present-day Iraq. Baghdad, the new center of government, became famous for its beauty and the luxurious way of life of the rulers.

The caliphs of Baghdad encouraged cultural, scientific, and economic development. Many great Muslim thinkers and writers lived during the period of the Abbassids.

In time, the Abbassid rulers became too fond of luxury. When they increased taxes to pay for their pleasures, problems developed in the empire. The caliphs began to lose control. Law and order broke down. Bandits attacked the trade routes, cutting off a rich source of income. Opposition to Abbassid rule spread throughout the empire.

Outside forces also threatened the Abbassids over the years. The Seljuk Turks moved into the empire in the 1040's. Then, in 1258, Mongols from Asia conquered Baghdad. This defeat ended the Abbassid Dynasty.

The Abbassids had ruled only the eastern part of the Muslim world. In the west, the *emirs* (rulers) of Cordova governed Spain after 755. They were descendants of an Umayyad prince who had escaped the massacre of his family by the Abbassids. Spain, therefore, was independent of the caliphs of Baghdad.

b. *Fatimid Dynasty.* In the 10th century, all of North Africa broke away from the Abbassids. A new dynasty, called the Fatimid, took control of what are now Tunisia, Morocco, Libya, and Egypt. The Fatimids were descendants of the Prophet through his daughter, Fatima. Their leaders also took the title of caliph and ruled the Fatimid Empire from Cairo in Egypt.

The Muslim world had become divided into three rival empires—the Umayyad, Abbassid, and Fatimid dynasties. Yet the people all shared the Islamic religion, the Arabic language, and a highly advanced culture.

THE RISE OF THE TURKS

Conflicts between Arab and non-Arab Muslims brought about changes in government. In the 11th century, most of the Muslim world came under the control of the Turks. These warriors from Central Asia knew little about literature, art, or science. But they soon accepted the beliefs and advanced culture of Islam. The Turks provided Islam with leaders and new achievements.

1. The Seljuk Turks. One group of Turks called themselves Seljuks after an early leader. They first conquered the lands ruled by the Abbassids. By 1063, Toghril Beg, a grandson of Seljuk, had seized Baghdad and all of the area from Persia to Syria. Although the caliphs of Baghdad continued to hold office, the Turks controlled them.

a. *Alp Arslan.* One of the most able of the Seljuk leaders was Alp Arslan. He and his troops defeated a Byzantine army at the Battle of Manzikert in Syria in 1071. This victory added much of Asia Minor to Alp Arslan's growing empire. He also brought Armenia and part of the Black Sea coast in Russia under Turkish rule. (About this time, the Byzantine emperor asked the pope in Rome for help against the Turks. This request led to the Crusades, discussed on page 156.)

b. *Saladin.* Another great leader of the Seljuk Turks was Saladin. He ended Fatimid rule of Egypt in 1171, captured Damascus, and made himself *sultan* (king) of Egypt and Syria. Saladin also brought portions of Arabia, Yemen, and Iraq under his control.

This remarkable ruler became well-known to Europeans after he captured Jerusalem from its Christian defenders in 1187. Saladin then led Turkish and Arab forces against the armies of three European kings, who headed the Third Crusade (1189–1192). Saladin's skills as a military leader kept the Europeans from recapturing the Holy Land. The best that the Europeans could do was to work out a three-year truce with Saladin. This agreement permitted Christians to travel in safety to Jerusalem.

Even though he had great power, Saladin kept little wealth for himself. According to legend, when Saladin died in 1193, he had only his saddle and a few other possessions to leave to his son.

Although the Europeans continued to organize Crusades, the real threat to the Seljuk Turks came from Asia. A new wave of fierce invaders, the Mongols, was sweeping over the Muslim world.

2. The Mongols. Early in the 13th century, warrior tribes of Mongolia united under the leadership of a chief named Temujin. He became Genghis Khan (Very Mighty King). Under his rule,

Saladin receives the English Bishop of Salisbury in Jerusalem in 1192.

Mongol armies conquered northern China, southern Russia, and Persia. After Genghis Khan died in 1227, his successors continued to extend their power. Eventually, they established a great empire, one of the largest in the world up to that time. The Mongol Empire included China, Russia, portions of southern and Eastern Europe, and much of the Middle East.

In 1258, Hulagu, a grandson of Genghis Khan, captured and looted the city of Baghdad. Hulagu also executed the caliph of Baghdad, thus ending the Abbassid Dynasty. He then invaded Syria and attempted to conquer Egypt. The Mongol advance toward Egypt was stopped at the Battle of Ain Jalut in 1260. (The battle place is in what is now northern Israel.)

The most powerful force in Egypt at that time was a society of professional soldiers, the Mamelukes. These dedicated warriors spent their lives training for battle. Their great victory over the Mongols at Ain Jalut saved Egypt and prevented the invaders from moving farther west. The Mamelukes invited a surviving member of the Abbassid family to Egypt to become the caliph. Egypt then became the center of the Islamic world.

3. The Early Ottoman Empire.   During the 15th and 16th centuries, the Ottoman Turks brought almost all of the Islamic world under the power of their leaders, the sultans. Originally, the Ottomans were subjects of the Seljuk Turks. The Seljuks had given the Ottomans land in Asia Minor on the border of the Byzantine Empire. Gradually, the Ottomans gained control of more and more territory. They took over parts of the Byzantine Empire around Constantinople and moved into Greece and Macedonia.

a. *Janissaries.* Strong Ottoman rulers built up a fierce and loyal army known as the Janissary Corps. To obtain men for the corps, the Turks took Christian boys from villages in southeastern Europe. The boys became Muslims and were legally slaves. They served the sultan for life as soldiers, bodyguards, and royal

The Ottoman Empire

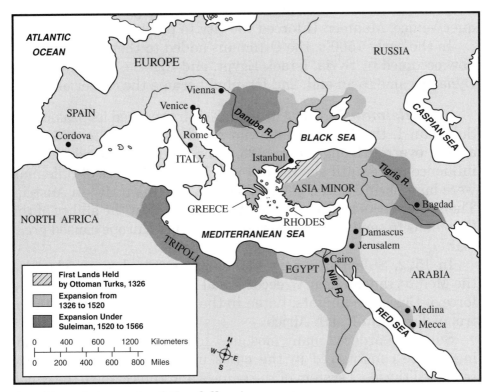

1. Complete each of the following sentences:
    a. The map shows the expansion of the Ottoman Empire between the years — and —.
    b. Tripoli is on the coast of —.
    c. Suleiman added territory in the east along the —.
    d. Jerusalem and Damascus became part of the Ottoman Empire between the years — and —.

2. **PROVE or DISPROVE:** From 1326 to 1566, the Ottoman Turks were conquerors.

officials. They became known for their military skill, ruthlessness, and devotion to the sultans. Janissaries helped govern newly conquered territories.

b. *Mehmed II.* The real founder of the Ottoman Empire is considered to be Mehmed II, who ruled from 1451 to 1481. He destroyed the Byzantine Empire by capturing Constantinople in 1453. He then rebuilt the city, which he renamed Istanbul, and made it his capital. Talented people from all over the known world were encouraged to settle there. Mehmed II wanted Istanbul to be a center of trade and culture.

The armies of Mehmed II seized lands around the western edge of the Black Sea. Then they moved into the Balkans in southeast Europe. To curb the power of Venice, Mehmed II strengthened his navy and attacked other areas of Italy. Although he did not conquer Venice, Mehmed II forced the city to pay him a yearly tax.

In the early 1500's, the Ottomans added to their empire lands now occupied by Syria, Israel, Egypt, and Algeria. The Mameluke Dynasty came to an end, and Istanbul became the center of Islam.

c. *Suleiman I.* The Ottoman Empire reached its peak under Suleiman I, the Magnificent, who ruled from 1520 to 1566. His armies overran Hungary in 1526. (The Turks remained a strong influence there until about 1700.) By 1529, the forces of Suleiman were hammering at the gates of Vienna, the main city in Austria. Their attempt to capture Vienna twice failed. But the ability of the Ottomans to send troops so far into Christian Europe caused great fear.

In 1522, Suleiman's navy had captured Rhodes, an island in the Mediterranean near Greece. It had long been held by a strong force of Christian knights. Later, in the 1550's, the navy took control of Tripoli in North Africa.

Suleiman ordered many mosques, forts, and other great buildings to be constructed in the cities under his control. He also reformed the legal system of the empire and thus came to be called "the Lawgiver" by Muslims. The name "Magnificent" was given to Suleiman by Europeans because he surrounded himself with beautiful furnishings and art.

d. *Decline of the Ottoman Empire.* After Suleiman, less able sultans ruled. In the great naval Battle of Lepanto, a European force, mostly made up of Spaniards and Venetians, defeated the Turks in 1571. Gradually, the Ottoman Empire lost its power in Europe and in North Africa. It did, however, continue to control much of the Middle East until the early 20th century. In

A Christian fleet defeats the Ottoman navy at Lepanto.

the 1920's, what was left of the Ottoman Empire became the nation of Turkey.

An efficient system of government and widespread trade made it possible for the Ottoman Empire to last so long. For most of its history, the empire was rich and powerful. Yet, Islamic culture did not progress under later Turkish rule. The Turks were more interested in military and political affairs than in new ideas. They isolated Islam and prevented it from sharing in the new ideas and inventions that brought Europe into modern times.

CRITICAL THINKING

1. If you were a medieval European, why might you both admire and fear the Ottoman Empire?

2. Reread "2. Muslim Civilization," on pages 177–179. Then write one or two paragraphs to explain why you AGREE or DISAGREE with the following statement: "During the Middle Ages, the Muslim civilization was equal to the civilization found in Europe."

3. Reread "1. The Seljuk Turks," on page 181. Then write a paragraph about Saladin. Tell why you think he was either a weak or a strong leader.

Chapter Review

MULTIPLE-CHOICE

Choose the item that best completes each sentence.

1. Muhammad the Prophet started a new religion called
   (*a*) Christianity (*b*) Islam (*c*) Judaism (*d*) Roman
   Catholicism.

2. Mecca and Medina are in (*a*) Arabia (*b*) Syria (*c*) Egypt
   (*d*) Israel.

3. The holy book of all Muslims is the (*a*) *Rubaiyat* (*b*) Bible
   (*c*) *Iliad* (*d*) Koran.

4. Muslims gather to pray in (*a*) synagogues (*b*) mosques
   (*c*) churches (*d*) temples.

5. The Muslim Empire was ruled by (*a*) caliphs (*b*) emperors
   (*c*) kings (*d*) dukes.

6. As their power expanded, the Turks destroyed the
   (*a*) Byzantine Empire (*b*) Ottoman Empire (*c*) Holy Roman
   Empire (*d*) Gallic Empire.

7. *The Arabian Nights* is an example of Muslim achievement
   in the field of (*a*) literature (*b*) mathematics (*c*) science
   (*d*) philosophy.

8. The Umayyad Dynasty ruled the Islamic world from the city
   of (*a*) Cairo (*b*) Baghdad (*c*) Damascus (*d*) Granada.

9. In the 11th century, the Muslim Empire came under the rule
   of the (*a*) Crusaders (*b*) Seljuk Turks (*c*) Ottoman Turks
   (*d*) Byzantines.

10. After the decline of Mongol power, the Muslim Empire was
    ruled by the (*a*) Mamelukes (*b*) Byzantines (*c*) Seljuk Turks
    (*d*) Venetians.

 ## ESSAY QUESTIONS

1. Identify the *three* rival dynasties that ruled major parts of the
   Muslim world from A.D. 661 to 1000. Specify the dates each
   ruled and the area or region ruled by each.

2. Describe the role played by the Mongols in the history of Islam during the Middle Ages.

3. Explain the importance of each of the following battles:
   a. Battle of Manzikert (1071)
   b. Battle of Ain Jalut (1260)
   c. Battle of Constantinople (1453)
   d. Battle of Lepanto (1571)

4. Describe the establishment of a great empire by the Ottoman Turks.

TIMELINE QUESTIONS

Use the information on the timeline below to answer the following questions.

1. Muhammad started preaching the ideas of Islam about 610. Was that before or after the time of the Umayyad Dynasty?

2. The Battle of Tours occurred in 732. Which Muslim dynasty was in power then?

3. Which *two* Muslim dynasties existed at the same time?

4. Which *one* of the following ruled the Ottoman Empire? (*a*) Mehmed II, 1451–1481 (*b*) Saladin, 1173–1193 (*c*) Alp Arslan, 1063–1072

5. During which years were the Seljuk Turks powerful?

6. Charlemagne ruled between 771 and 814. Which dynasty was important in the Muslim world during that time?

7. William the Conqueror invaded England in 1066. Which groups ruled the Muslim world in that year?

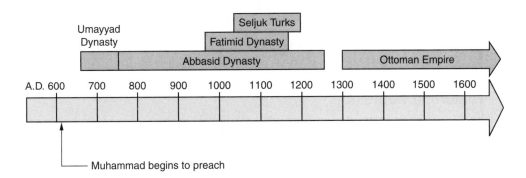

Connections: Islam and the Spread of Ideas

A physician prepares medicine from honey. This page is an Arab translation of an early Greek physician's work.

The Islamic civilization affected many different countries and cultures. Islam drew on the ideas of the Greeks, Romans, Persians, Indians, and Byzantines to help shape its own special civilization.

Islamic warriors and merchants carried their religion and goods to Western Europe. Soon after, Muslim scholars gave new ideas to the Europeans through travel and writings. These scholars did outstanding original work in chemistry, medicine, mathematics, astronomy, and geography. The Muslims built great universities in the cities of Damascus, Cairo, Baghdad, and Cordova. In these centers, advances were made in all areas of learning. For example, mathematicians worked to further develop algebra and trigonometry. Doctors, familiar with ancient Greek writings, did research on diseases such as smallpox and how the disease was spread. Geographers advanced the theory that the world is round.

The achievement of Muslim learning had a great impact on Europeans. Looking at the Muslim experience in education, the Europeans decided to build universities of their own. In time, universities were established in Paris, Cambridge, Oxford, Salerno, and Bologna. These, and other centers of learning, preserved learning in Europe during the Middle Ages and prepared the way for the Renaissance.

1. Complete the following sentence:
   Islamic centers of learning were —, —, —, and —.
2. Name *one* effect Muslim learning had on Europeans.

DOCUMENT-BASED QUESTION

This question is based on the accompanying documents (1–3). It will improve your ability to work with historical documents.

Historical Context:

In the early 600's, changes were taking place in the Middle East that would greatly influence the course of history. The Prophet Muhammad founded a religion called Islam in Arabia. Islam was spread by military conquest, and a great Muslim Empire was created by the rulers who followed Muhammad.

Task:

Using information from the documents and your knowledge of world history, answer the questions that follow each document. Your answers to each question will help you write the document-based essay.

Document 1.   Study the map on page 176.

What continents were included in the Muslim Empire by 750?

Document 2.   Excerpt from *The Koran*, the holy book of the Muslims:

> Surely those who believe [Muslims], and those who are Jews, and the Christians, and the Sabians [ancient rulers of Yemen thought to have been believers in one god]—whoever believes in God and the Last [Judgment] Day and does good, they shall have their reward from their Lord. And there will be no fear for them, nor shall they grieve. (2:62)

By reading this excerpt, what conclusions could one make on how Muslims should treat Christians and Jews living in conquered territories that had become part of the Muslim Empire?

Document 3.   Excerpt from a description of Baghdad written by Benjamin of Tudela, a Spanish rabbi who visited the Muslim city in the 12th century:

> The city of Baghdad is twenty miles in circumference, situated in a land of palms, gardens and plantations, the like of which is not to be found in the whole land of Shinar [in the Bible, a country near the Tigris and Euphrates rivers]. People come thither [to Baghdad] with merchandise from all lands. Wise men live there, philosophers who know all manner of wisdom, and magicians expert in all manner of witchcraft.

> **Source**: *Itinerary of Benjamin of Tudela*, translated by Marcus Nathan Adler. NY: Philipp Feldheim, 1907. Found at http://isfsp.org/sages/ben1.html

How does Benjamin's description of Baghdad indicate its importance in the Muslim Empire?

Document-Based Essay

Using information from the above documents and your knowledge of world history, write an essay in which you:

- Explain how Islam took root in Arabia in the 7th century.
- Describe the religious toleration and cultural richness of the Muslim Empire in the centuries after Muhammad's death.

UNIT IV

GLOBAL INTERACTIONS

CHAPTER 9
The Civilizations of Africa

Africa is the second largest continent in the world, after Asia. It is surrounded by the Atlantic Ocean on the south and west, the Indian Ocean on the southeast, the Mediterranean Sea on the north, and the Red Sea on the northeast. Trade between North Africa and Europe travels over the Mediterranean Sea. The Red Sea aids trade between North Africa and the Middle East.

Much of North Africa is covered by the great Sahara Desert. The area south of this desert is known as sub-Saharan Africa. Its more varied geography includes rain forests, great rivers, grassy plains (savannahs), mountains, and deep valleys. Natural barriers make land travel difficult, while powerful rapids and steep waterfalls impede navigation of the rivers. Because of the diversity of environments and the natural barriers that separate one region from another, the cultures of sub-Saharan African have developed differently through the centuries.

The Egyptian civilization was not the last great one in Africa. South of the Sahara Desert, other major civilizations also developed. Few written records about these civilizations still exist. Most of what we know about them comes from the reports of travelers and traders from Europe and the Middle East.

GHANA, MALI, AND SONGHAI

Between A.D. 300 and 1500, three large empires arose in West Africa. They carried on a brisk trade with the Romans and later

Early Kingdoms of Africa

Indicate whether each of the following statements is *true* (**T**) or *false* (**F**).

1. Mali was the largest empire shown.

2. The Niger River flows into the Indian Ocean.

3. Gold mines were located south of Kumbai Saleh.

4. Kumbai Saleh was located on the Niger River.

5. Major salt deposits could be found north of the Songhai Empire.

6. Ghana was the smallest empire shown in West Africa.

7. The Nile River flows north.

8. Both Mali and Songhai extended to the Atlantic Ocean.

with the Muslims. The wealth of the rulers of these African empires amazed the traders from the north.

1. The Empire of Ghana. The first West African empire was Ghana. As early as A.D. 300, people in ancient Ghana had mastered the art of ironworking. By then, according to ancient legends, the empire had been ruled by 44 kings. Although the empire of Ghana lasted until the end of the 12th century, its period of greatest power was from the 8th to the 11th century.

Ghana's wealth came from gold. Its rulers controlled the supply of gold from nearby mines. Ghanaian traders exchanged gold, ivory, and slaves for salt and copper brought by Muslim traders from North Africa. (People wanted salt to preserve food and to make it taste better. The body also needs salt, especially in a warm climate, to stay healthy.) The Muslim traders carried the gold, jewelry, and leather goods of Ghana to Baghdad and other Islamic cities. In return, the Ghanaians also received cloth and tools.

The kings of Ghana were so rich that they armed their personal guards with gold swords. The kings even covered their horses with blankets made of gold cloth.

Kumbai Saleh, a city of about 15,000 people, was the capital of the Ghana Empire. Aided by his nobles, the king ruled through a strong, centralized government. A large, powerful army backed up his commands. The soldiers carried weapons made of iron.

In the mid-11th century, North African Berber warriors, called Almoravids, conquered Ghana and most of West Africa. Under Almoravid rule, many members of the royal family of Ghana became Muslims. The Almoravids destroyed the capital city of Kumbai Saleh in 1076. This badly weakened the power of the kings. Eventually, the Ghana Empire broke up. A neighboring kingdom absorbed it.

2. The Riches of Mali. In 1235, a Mandingo soldier-hero named Sundiata conquered large areas along the Niger River. The Mandingo people formed the kingdom of Mali. Some of the land they took over had once been part of Ghana. The area included the gold mines of West Africa. These mines made Mali so prosperous that its wealth became famous throughout Africa and elsewhere. (In fact, before the discovery of America, much of Europe's gold came from Mali.) Ivory, cotton, and herds of cattle also contributed to Mali's wealth. By the beginning of the 14th century, Mali had grown into an empire.

Travelers to Mali and its principal city, Timbuktu, were impressed by the many commercial activities and by the law and

A Great King

Mansa Musa, king of Mali, is shown seated on his throne (lower right) in this detail from a European map dated 1375.

The greatest Mali king, Mansa Musa, was a grandson of King Sundiata. Mansa Musa ruled from 1312 to 1337. He was devoted to the Muslim religion. Islam was spread throughout the empire. In 1324, Mansa Musa made a pilgrimage to the holy city of Mecca. He was accompanied on his long journey by 60,000 people. The enormous caravan carried 24,000 pounds of gold loaded on 80 camels. In addition, 500 servants each carried about six pounds of gold. Few kings anywhere had the ability to display such wealth. In the words of an Arab historian, the glittering goods carried in the caravan "almost put Africa's sun to shame."

On his return from Mecca, Mansa Musa brought back many talented people. They included teachers, scholars, artists, engineers, and architects, all of whom helped to make Timbuktu (or Tombuctou) a great center of learning and the arts.

The flourishing of trade and culture in Mali was largely due to Mansa Musa's ability as a king and administrator. For almost two centuries after his death, Mansa Musa's portrait was drawn on maps of Africa. Why? In the minds of people throughout the world, this fabled king symbolized Africa.

Why is Mansa Musa considered important in Africa's past?

order that gave security to everyone. Some visiting Muslims disapproved of the great freedom exercised by the women of Mali. Unlike women in other Muslim lands, Mali women were free to take an active part in the social and cultural life of the empire.

After the death of Mansa Musa, Mali's greatest king, the power of Mali declined. Another great empire that arose in West Africa, the Songhai, conquered Mali.

3. The Songhai Empire.   Songhai grew into the most powerful empire of West Africa. At its peak, it extended eastward from the Atlantic Ocean to near Lake Chad, in central Africa. Songhai's wealth came from its gold trade. Many commercial towns sprang up. In these towns lived craft workers, businesspeople, judges, doctors, and religious leaders.

The Songhai Empire reached its greatest strength at the end of the 15th century. By then, a warrior king of the Songhai named Sunni Ali had conquered large amounts of territory along the Niger River. In 1468, he captured Timbuktu from desert tribal rulers.

Askia Muhammad, the most powerful king of the Songhai Empire, ruled from 1493 to 1528. A devout Muslim, he based his laws on the teachings of the Koran. Askia set up a fair system of

Timbuktu as drawn by a European visitor in 1828.

taxation and encouraged the establishment of Muslim schools. Under his rule, philosophers, scholars, and teachers increased the reputation of Timbuktu as a center of learning. In the 16th century, books sold in Timbuktu brought higher prices than did any other merchandise. Such was the value the people put on learning.

The kings who followed Askia Muhammad were not so strong as he. They could not defend the empire as well against its enemies. As a result, Songhai fell to the army of the sultan of Morocco in 1591.

CRITICAL THINKING

1. **PROVE or DISPROVE:** The fame of Timbuktu was well deserved.

2. Give *two* reasons why Askia Muhammad was regarded as a great ruler.

IDENTIFICATIONS

Identify each of the following:

a. Sundiata
b. Mansa Musa
c. Sunni Ali
d. Askia Muhammad
e. Timbuktu

CITY-STATES IN EAST AFRICA

Starting in the 700's, Arab traders sailed south along the east coast of Africa. They looked for products to trade. The traders also sailed east across the Indian Ocean to India. As trade developed among India, Arabia, and Africa, the merchants became wealthy. The coastal towns where they settled grew into great cities.

1. The Trading Cities. The East African coastal cities of Mogadishu, Malindi, Mombasa, and Kilwa developed into city-states. Each controlled land outside of its city walls. Each had its own ruler, made its own laws, and had a small army. The rulers obtained money by taxing trade goods.

The main trade goods from Africa were ivory, iron, and gold. Asians bought ivory to carve into art objects, chess pieces, and furniture. Iron was sent to India, China, and the Muslim Empire to be made into swords, spears, and daggers.

In return for their products, Africans wanted cotton cloth, glass beads, and porcelain (fine chinaware). African merchants highly prized the delicate cups, bowls, and vases from China.

Control of the gold trade made the city-state of Kilwa rich. In the 13th and 14th centuries, the rulers and merchants of Kilwa built fine palaces and homes. One palace contained 100 rooms, interior courtyards, and an eight-sided swimming pool. It was the largest building in East Africa. Mosques, parks, and fountains added to the beauty of the city. The ruins of Kilwa can be seen today.

2. The Swahili Culture.   Many East Africans of both the interior and the coast spoke the Swahili language. As they came in contact with Arabic and Asian languages, they added words from these tongues to Swahili. The language was written in Arabic script.

Over time, the many different peoples of East Africa adopted customs from one another's way of life. The blending of language and customs produced a new culture called Swahili. Many Swahili people accepted Islam as their religion. Others clung to the old African religions.

Swahili artists, craftspeople, poets, storytellers, traders, and others created a sophisticated way of life in the coastal cities. When the Portuguese arrived in the late 1400's, they were amazed by the cities. They were particularly impressed by the fine quality of Swahili clothing and the cleanliness and comfort of life.

The Portuguese did not favorably impress the Swahili. When the Swahili rejected Portuguese demands for trading rights, the Portuguese attacked. The city-states were destroyed. The trade of the Swahili people and the richness of their way of life disappeared.

GREAT ZIMBABWE

Between the 11th and 15th centuries, a great city and fort were constructed in southern Africa. As the city grew, a thick wall, 30 feet high, surrounded the palaces and other buildings in the city. Both the wall and the buildings were made of fine stonework laid in a variety of patterns. The builders of Great Zimbabwe, as the city was called, were masters of construction. The people of Zimbabwe were also active in the gold and ivory trade of East Africa.

East African Trading Cities

Use information on the map to answer the following:

1. List *four* cities that were part of the Swahili culture.

2. Name the body of water that the Swahili cities faced.

3. How many miles are there between Zimbabwe and Kilwa?

4. Name the largest island shown on the map.

5. In what direction (or directions) would a merchant from Kilwa have sailed to reach Goa?

6. EXPLAIN: The wealth of the Swahili culture came from overseas trade.

---

1. The Way of Life. The people of Zimbabwe considered their kings to be gods. According to tradition, the prosperity of the kingdom depended on the strength and good health of the ruler. Illness or physical weakness on the part of the king might bring

The ruins of Great Zimbabwe of A.D. 1200–1400.

disaster to the people. A king who became ill was required to kill himself so that a healthier ruler could take his place.

Among the privileged people who lived in the palace with the king were his wives and royal advisers. Only these people were allowed to see the king. Ordinary people, such as farmers and soldiers, could not look at the king. The common people lived in small stone houses outside the city wall.

Many of the people of Zimbabwe worked as gold miners. In streams and in pits dug into the earth, they searched for the precious metal so important to the trade of the region. Others hunted elephants for their ivory tusks. As a result of their labor, Zimbabwe became wealthy and powerful.

2. Change and Decline.   The gold and ivory of Zimbabwe were sold to the Swahili trading cities along Africa's east coast. The return trade brought cotton cloth, porcelain, and other eastern goods to Zimbabwe. In time, the Zimbabwe merchants traded directly with China, Persia, and India. By the 15th century, the city had reached its peak of prosperity and power.

Portuguese traders attempted to gain control of the goldfields around Zimbabwe in the 16th century. But the Europeans did not succeed. The Zimbabwe kings kept them at a distance. In fact, no European ever saw the great city. Instead, the kings strictly regulated the trading activities of the Portuguese to protect the best interests of Zimbabwe. The rulers of the coastal cities were not so strong. Portuguese attacks on the Swahili cities ruined Zimbabwe's trade with the east-coast cities.

Great Zimbabwe continued as a city until the 19th century. However, the decline of trade and political fights within the ruling family weakened it. In 1830, Zulu tribes attacked Zimbabwe. The Zulus had migrated from farther south in search of new land. The people of Zimbabwe fled from the invaders, abandoning their great walled city.

ESSAY QUESTIONS

1. Describe the benefits brought by the Swahili culture to the people of East Africa, especially to those in the coastal cities.

2. How did Great Zimbabwe become wealthy? What caused the decline of this kingdom?

THEMATIC WRITING

Reread "2. Change and Decline," on pages 199–200, and write a paragraph about *one* of the following themes:

The Portuguese and Africans
The End of Zimbabwe

THE ARRIVAL OF THE EUROPEANS

The Portuguese were the first Europeans to sail along the West African coast south of the Sahara. The Dutch and the French soon followed. At first, the Europeans came to trade for gold and ivory. Then they began to buy slaves in Africa. They soon set up trading posts and, eventually, colonies along the coast of Africa. The arrival of the Europeans brought profit to some Africans and misery and destruction to others.

1. The Portuguese. In the 1400's, the Portuguese began to look for an all-water route to India and East Asia. They wanted to trade with these areas and to spread Christianity. They did not want to use the land routes controlled by the Muslims and the Italian trading cities. Portuguese ships sailed farther and farther south along the western coast of Africa.

In 1471, the Portuguese reached Guinea, a gold-rich area about midway along the West African coast. The trade that developed with Guinea was so profitable that this section of West Africa came to be called the Gold Coast. To protect their trade from other Europeans, the Portuguese built a series of forts. At the same time, they established contact with the Congo Empire along the Congo River. By converting the African ruler of this empire to Christianity, the Portuguese were able to expand their trade in this region.

In 1488, Bartolomeu Dias, a Portuguese explorer, sailed around the Cape of Good Hope at the southern tip of Africa. Between 1497 and 1498, Vasco da Gama traveled beyond the tip of Africa, up the eastern coast, and across the Indian Ocean to India. By 1509, the Portuguese controlled the Indian Ocean trade routes.

In 1541, Christopher da Gama (the son of Vasco) led an expedition to Ethiopia, a powerful kingdom in northeastern Africa. This contact led to the conversion to Christianity of two Ethiopian rulers. As a result, Portuguese priests were able to build churches in Ethiopia and to gain influence in that country. In 1574, the Portuguese began to settle Angola, a large area on the west coast of southern Africa. On the east coast, Mozambique served as a base for the Portuguese trading ships that sailed to India.

2. The Dutch and the French.   At the end of the 16th century, the Dutch and the French began to compete with the Portuguese for trading rights in West Africa.

   a.   *Dutch traders.*   In 1595, the Dutch built their first trading posts on the Gold Coast. From 1621 to 1637, they took control of most of the territory held by the Portuguese in West Africa. After 1640, the Dutch were the main European traders in the area.

   The Dutch took their most important step by establishing a settlement called Cape Town on the southern tip of Africa in 1652. In 1688, Huguenot (Protestant) groups from France arrived in the Cape Town area. The Dutch (also Protestants) and French settlers intermarried, and a new culture soon developed. The settlers of European descent called themselves Afrikaners. As a result of hard work on their farms and in their businesses, the people prospered. Cape Town grew.

   b.   *French traders.*   In the early 17th century, the French also moved into West Africa. In 1626, they built a settlement called St. Louis at the mouth of the Senegal River. After further exploration of the lands along this river, the French set up several trading posts. Thus began a period of gradual conquest of the Senegal region by the French. In 1643, they built their first settlements on

Europeans in Africa, 15th–17th Centuries

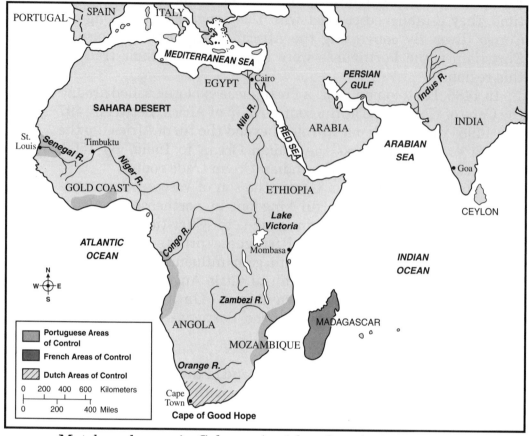

Match each area in Column A with a description in Column B.

Column A	Column B
1. Cape Town	*a.* Portuguese area of control
2. Angola	*b.* French area of control
3. Mozambique	*c.* Dutch area of control
4. Madagascar	
5. Gold Coast	
6. St. Louis	

Madagascar, a large island in the Indian Ocean off the east coast of Africa.

These early efforts at colonization gave Europeans control of some land on Africa's coasts. For the most part, the Europeans did not move very far into the interior of the continent. Strong African rulers, a hot, humid climate, and killing diseases kept most Europeans out. The real conquest of Africa did not begin until the 19th century. By then, Europeans had better-equipped armies than the Africans.

| SENTENCE COMPLETION |

From the list that follows, select the term that best completes each sentence:

gold and ivory	India	Mozambique
Guinea	Angola	Ethiopia
Cape of Good Hope		

1. In 1574, the Portuguese began the settlement of —, a larger area on the west coast of southern Africa.

2. In 1488, Bartolomeu Dias sailed around the — at the southern tip of Africa.

3. Europeans purchased — from the African kingdoms and empires.

4. The expedition of Christopher da Gama led to the conversion of two rulers to Christianity and the growth of Portuguese influence in —.

5. From — on the east coast of Africa, Portuguese trading ships sailed to India.

6. In 1471, the Portuguese reached — , a gold-rich land on the west coast of Africa.

7. Between 1497 and 1498, Vasco da Gama sailed from the east African coast across the Indian Ocean to —.

| IDENTIFICATIONS |

Write a sentence of your own to identify each of the following:

a. Cape Town
b. Huguenot
c. Afrikaners

d. St. Louis
e. Madagascar

THE RISE OF THE SLAVE TRADE

The desire for gold and ivory first brought Europeans to Africa. But in the 17th and 18th centuries, slaves became the major attraction. The slave trade developed into a rich business for Africans, Europeans, and Americans.

1. Slavery in Africa. Slavery had existed for centuries in the African kingdoms. Criminals, people who could not pay their debts, and prisoners captured in wars were often turned into slaves. Some powerful rulers had thousands of slaves. The buying and selling of slaves took place in the markets of many cities, especially in Muslim North Africa.

    a. *African slaveholders.* In general, slaves in Africa were not treated as badly as elsewhere. Those who served wealthy families occasionally became adopted members of those families. Some slaves were given the opportunity to earn their freedom. Those who did had the same social status as people who had never been slaves. The children of free men and slave women were born free. Africans expected their slaves to work hard. But the owners often worked alongside their slaves, doing the same type of labor.

    b. *Arab slave traders.* In many of the African kingdoms, slaves were sold to Arab traders. The Arabs then sold the Africans to masters in Arabia, Persia, and India. Both Africans and Asians profited from the Indian Ocean slave trade. The Berbers of North Africa also purchased slaves from African rulers. Berber traders took slaves across the Sahara to sell in Mediterranean countries. Spain and Portugal especially needed workers. In those countries, long wars between Christians and Muslims had caused a shortage of laborers. Africans were purchased to work on farms, in households, and as common laborers in the cities.

2. Europeans and the Slave Trade. In the 17th century, the trade in slaves changed drastically. Europeans wanted workers for their colonies in North and South America and the West Indian islands in the Caribbean Sea. On *plantations* (large farms) in the colonies, Europeans grew crops to sell in Europe and elsewhere. The main crops were sugarcane, rice, tobacco, and cotton. Many workers were needed to plant, till, and harvest the crops.

    a. *Indian slaves.* At first, Europeans forced Indians to work on the plantations. But there were not enough Indians to do the work, and many died from mistreatment. The Spanish, Portuguese, British, Dutch, and French owners of the plantations then sought workers from West Africa.

    b. *African slave trade.* From the 17th to the 19th century, an enormous number of West Africans were sold to Europeans as slaves. The area between the Gold Coast and the mouth of the Niger River came to be called the Slave Coast. The Portuguese were the first to buy slaves in large numbers. They sent the slaves

Captives were marched from the interior of Africa to the coast, where they would be sold.

to Portuguese plantations in Brazil. By the 1650's, the Dutch, British, and French also controlled slave-trading areas along the west coast of Africa. Arabs and, later, Americans also took an active part in the slave trade. By the 19th century, more than 10 million Africans had been shipped to the Americas.

European slave traders depended on the cooperation of African kings and chiefs. These rulers sold Africans captured in raids on villages in the interior. The captives were taken to slaveholding areas on the coast. From there, the slaves were put on ships.

The voyage across the Atlantic Ocean terrified the slaves. Many had never been away from their villages before, and they were afraid of the unknown. During most of the trip, the slaves were chained belowdecks in spaces too small to allow them to stand erect. They had very little to eat. Many died on the journey from disease or lack of food. Some threw themselves overboard. When the ships reached the Americas, the slaves were sold in public marketplaces.

3. Evils of the Slave Trade.   The slave trade was *racist*. European and American slave owners regarded black African slaves as inferior because of the color of the Africans' skin. Slaves were treated as pieces of property with no rights. They were bought and sold with no respect for their wishes. Often, families were broken up and sold to different masters.

The Africans' loss of language, customs, and religion was one of the worst evils of the slave trade. After their capture, Africans were often separated from others of their tribe or village. On the

The African Overseas Slave Trade

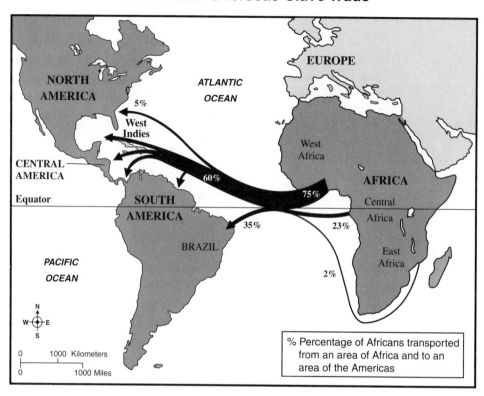

% Percentage of Africans transported from an area of Africa and to an area of the Americas

slave ships and on the plantations, the slaves were often a mixed group of strangers, with different languages and beliefs. They had to learn the language and culture of the slave owners. In so doing, they quickly lost much of their African heritage.

The trade in slaves also changed West Africa in particular. (Other areas of Africa were not so heavily involved in the trade.) The people of West Africa came to depend on the metal tools, cloth, and guns that the traders exchanged for slaves. The possession of quantities of guns may have encouraged more wars among the tribes. Certainly the slave trade took away young, healthy men and women who might have contributed a great deal to their tribes.

4. Racism as a Global Practice. Europeans were not the only people to engage in racist activities. The Chinese regarded Europeans and all other foreigners as barbarians (inferior peoples with little to offer of cultural value). For this reason, European merchants were confined to certain coastal cities and were otherwise restricted in their activities in China.

The Japanese also regarded Europeans and, later, Americans as barbarians. Japan's rulers periodically closed their country to foreigners. To avoid "contamination" by cultures considered to be inferior, Japanese outside of Japan were prevented from returning to their homeland. In addition, the Japanese treatment of the Ainu, a minority people of northern Japan, was marked by a same lack of acceptance of people who were "different."

In Europe, racism was practiced mainly in the form of anti-Semitism, or intolerance toward Jews. In several European countries, Jews were persecuted in a variety of ways. They were barred from certain occupations, forced to wear clothing different from other Europeans, and confined to enclosed areas of cities, called ghettos. Periodically, Jews were expelled from countries. In some places, they were sometimes tortured and killed because of their religious beliefs and identity.

CRITICAL THINKING

PROVE or DISPROVE each statement:

1. The traditional practice of slavery in Africa was not destructive of African culture.

2. Africans, Europeans, and Americans participated in the slave trade in order to develop new colonies.

3. The transportation of slaves across the Atlantic Ocean was cruel and inhuman.

4. The slave trade was the only type of racist activity practiced from the 15th to the 19th centuries.

Chapter Review

▶ MULTIPLE-CHOICE

Choose the item that best completes each sentence or answers each question.

1. The earliest West African empire was (a) Angola (b) Mali (c) Songhai (d) Ghana.

2. A great center of learning in West Africa was the city of (a) Kilwa (b) Kumbai Saleh (c) Timbuktu (d) Cape Town.

3. In the 11th century, West Africa was conquered by the (*a*) Swahili (*b*) Berbers (*c*) Portuguese (*d*) Dutch.

4. The greatest of the Mali kings was (*a*) Askia Muhammad (*b*) Sunni Ali (*c*) Mansa Musa (*d*) Abu Bakr.

5. The Songhai Empire extended east from the Atlantic Ocean to near (*a*) Lake Chad (*b*) the Congo River (*c*) the Red Sea (*d*) the Nile River.

6. A rich trading city in East Africa was (*a*) Kilwa (*b*) Kumbai Saleh (*c*) Damascus (*d*) Timbuktu.

7. The Swahili culture developed on the African coast bordering the (*a*) Red Sea (*b*) Mediterranean Sea (*c*) Atlantic Ocean (*d*) Indian Ocean.

8. Great Zimbabwe was abandoned after attacks in 1830 by the (*a*) Berbers (*b*) Swahili (*c*) Zulus (*d*) Mandingos.

9. Europeans were drawn to Africa by a desire for (*a*) iron and coal (*b*) gold and ivory (*c*) cotton and porcelain (*d*) timber and rubber.

10. Which *one* of the following was a major result of the European involvement in the slave trade? (*a*) Africans were sold to masters in Persia and India. (*b*) The Berbers of North Africa purchased slaves from African rulers. (*c*) Millions of Africans were transported to the Americas to work on plantations. (*d*) Africans became citizens of European countries.

CHART COMPLETION

For each of the empires and cultures listed, provide the information called for in the column heads.

	Years it existed	*Location*	*Main city*	*Main leader(s)*
Ghana				
Mali				
Songhai				

ESSAY QUESTIONS

1. Describe the rise of great civilizations and powerful empires in Africa between 300 and 1500.

2. Name the city-states of East Africa and explain why they were wealthy.

3. How did the Portuguese and Zulus cause the decline of Zimbabwe?

4. Explain the connection between the arrival of Europeans in Africa to the rise of the slave trade in the 17th and 18th centuries.

5. Why do historians and others regard the slave trade as racist?

Connections: Slavery and Africa

A slave is a person who is owned by another person. Slavery has been practiced in many societies throughout history. The Bible records that the Egyptians kept the Hebrews in bondage for many years. The greatness of Greece was, in large part, built on the work of slaves. The Roman Empire depended on the labor of millions of slaves.

Slaves in ancient times were used in many different ways. Slaves were chained to benches in ships and forced to pull oars. Slaves worked in mines and quarries. Some slaves fought as gladiators for the amusement of free citizens. Many slaves worked in the crafts or were household servants. Some were well educated and taught the children of their masters.

Slavery also existed in Africa. Africans became slaves in a number of ways. Prisoners of war—men, women, and children—were forced into slavery. People who broke the law were some-times sold into slavery as punishment.

Slave markets arose in the Muslim cities of Africa. People of all races were offered for sale in these markets. Slaves were usually treated well, especially in North and West Africa. In these areas, children born to slaves often did not become slaves. They were free. Some slaves were able to gain freedom through hard work or by marrying into a free family. Some slaves, like those in ancient Greece or Rome, became tutors. A few even became advisers to kings.

The nature of slavery in Africa changed in the 17th century. European colonists and traders began to arrive in great numbers. Their need for slaves to work on plantations in the Americas and elsewhere caused the rise of a large-scale slave trade. The conditions of slavery worsened. For millions of Africans, it was the beginning of misery and hopelessness.

1. Compare the practice of slavery in Africa with slavery in other places.

2. Why do you think most modern countries have laws prohibiting slavery?

DOCUMENT-BASED QUESTION

This question is based on the accompanying documents (1–3). It will improve your ability to work with historical documents.

Historical Context:

Major civilizations began to develop in Africa south of the Sahara Desert around A.D. 300. They became powerful and prosperous. Beginning in the 1400's, Europeans arrived in Africa, first to trade and then to colonize.

Task:

Using information from the documents and your knowledge of world history, answer the questions that follow each document. Your answers to each question will help you write the document-based essay.

Document 1.   Excerpt from a traditional tale about Sundiata, the founder of the Empire of Mali:

> There are some kings . . . who are feared because they have power, but they know how to use it and they are loved because they love justice. Sundiata belonged to this group. He was feared, but loved as well. He was the father of Mali and gave the world peace. After him the world has not seen a greater conqueror. . . . He had made the capital of an empire out of his father's village [Niani], and Niani became the navel of the earth.

> **Source**: Niane, D.T., *Sundiata: An Epic of Old Mali*. Translated by G.D. Pickett. Longman, 1965, p. 82.

According to this document, what do the people of Mali think about their ruler and the empire?

Document 2.   Excerpt from an account of the city of Mali by the Moroccan traveler and historian Ibn Battuta in 1352:

> Thus I reached the city of Malli [Mali], the capital. . . . The negroes possess some admirable qualities. They are seldom unjust, and have a greater abhorrence of injustice than any other people. Their sultan shows no mercy to anyone who is guilty of the least act of it. There is complete security in their country. Neither traveller nor inhabitant in it has anything to fear from robbers or men of violence. . . . They are careful to observe the hours of prayer, and assiduous in attending them

in congregations, and in bringing up their children to them. On Fridays, if a man does not go early to the mosque, he cannot find a corner to pray in on account of the crowd.

Source: Ibn Battuta *Travels in Asia and Africa*, tr. and ed. by H.A.R. Gibb. London: Broadway House, 1929, pp. 323–324.

According to this document, what characteristics of civilization were present in Mali at the time?

Document 3. Excerpt from a letter of King Afonso I (Nzinga Mbemba) of Congo to the king of Portugal, regarding the slave trade in Congo in 1526:

And we cannot reckon how great the damage is, since the mentioned merchants [Portuguese slave traders] are taking every day our natives, sons of the land and the sons of our noblemen and vassals and our relatives, because the thieves and men of bad conscience grab them wishing to have the things and wares of this Kingdom which they are ambitious of; they grab them and get them to be sold; and so great, Sir, is the corruption and lawlessness that our country is being completely depopulated, and Your Highness should not agree with this nor accept it. . . .

Source: Davidson, Basil. *The African Past: Chronicles From Antiquity to Modern Times*. Boston: Little, Brown and Company, 1964, p. 191.

Based on this document, why did King Afonso write to the king of Portugal?

DOCUMENT-BASED ESSAY

Using information from the documents and your knowledge of world history, write an essay in which you:

- Discuss the type of civilizations that developed in West Africa.
- Explain what happened to this region after Europeans arrived in the 1400's.

Chapter 10
Early Civilizations in the Americas

Europeans knew almost nothing about North and South America until 1493. Although early European explorers claimed to have "discovered" these continents, people had been living in them for thousands of years. Many scientists agree that the ancestors of the people we call Indians, or Native Americans, came to North America from Asia 17,000 to 11,000 or more years ago. Many crossed the Bering Strait, a narrow body of water separating northern Asia from what is now Alaska. During the last Ice Age (which occurred 26,000 to 11,000 years ago), a land bridge connected Asia and Alaska. Over the centuries, waves of migrants crossed the Bering land bridge and moved into all parts of North and South America. The gradual melting of the glaciers eventually caused the land bridge to be submerged beneath the rising sea water of the Bering Strait. It is believed that the ancestors of the Eskimos reached Alaska in boats around 3,000 years ago.

There is some evidence that ancestors of the Indians were preceded by older migrants, during an earlier Ice Age some 73,000 to 56,000 years ago. They arrived in the Americas either by sailing across the Pacific Ocean, possibly from Australia and Polynesia, or by crossing the Bering land bridge. The appearance of these older migrants was similar to that of Polynesians or Australian Aborigines. Eventually they disappeared, absorbed by the larger American Indian population. However, their genetic evidence remains in the DNA of Native Americans.

The newcomers developed many different ways of life. The climate and geography of the areas in which they settled affected the types of houses they built and food they ate. The most advanced Indian cultures existed in Middle America and western South America.

A great many Indians were hunters and gatherers. A number of groups were farmers and lived in communities. They all shaped stone, wood, and bone into tools and weapons. None of the Indian groups used metal, except to make jewelry and ornaments. They did not know about firearms or how the wheel could be used as a tool. Neither did they domesticate animals, except for dogs and birds. Sheep, cattle, and horses were not introduced into the Americas until after 1500.

Routes to the Americas in the Ice Age

PROVE or DISPROVE: The Americas were populated by a single mass migration of early Indians.

THE GEOGRAPHY OF THE AMERICAS

To understand the cultures of the Americas, it is helpful to look at the geography of the two continents. (See page 555.)

The length of the two continents from the Bering Strait to Cape Horn (at the southern tip of South America) is about 11,000 miles. The extreme north of North America reaches into the Arctic Ocean. The extreme south of South America is about 600 miles from Antarctica. Along the western coasts of both continents stretch vast mountain ranges. The two landmasses are bounded by the Atlantic Ocean on the east and the Pacific Ocean on the west.

Both continents have a variety of geographical features. The tundra in the northernmost area of North America is a frozen plain where few plants can grow. Parts of North America in what is now known as Canada and the United States have large forests and woodlands. The central part of North America includes prairies and deserts. There are rain forests in Central America. A long, western mountain range extends from Alaska through North and Central America to the southern tip of South America. The range is known as the Rocky Mountains in North America and as the Andes in South America.

Besides its western mountainous region, South America's main regions include rain forests, tropical scrubland, and grassy plains. A strip of desert stretches between its mountains and its western coast. A larger desert is located in its southern area.

THE OLMECS

The oldest great Mesoamerican civilization—that of the Olmecs—flourished from about 1200 to 400 B.C. It was at its height around the time the Egyptians were declining as a great power.

The birthplace of the Olmec culture was Mexico's Caribbean coast, in the area where Tabasco and Veracruz are located today. Scholars do not know why Mesoamerica's (Mexico and Central America) first civilization originated in such a hot and swampy area. They often compare the Olmecs to the early Mesopotamians because both groups learned to drain marshy areas in order to farm and build on them.

1. Olmec Government and Cities.   Also like the Mesopotamians, the Olmecs gradually united their small farming communities into a state and established a central government to rule it. Olmec society had a rigid class system headed by priest-kings. An elite group of warriors, administrators, and engineers managed important state functions for their rulers. The lower classes consisted of farmers and artisans. Below them were slaves and serfs. They did heavy labor, such as dragging huge blocks of stone from quarries as far as 50 miles away and building temples and creating sculptures for them.

Historians argue that Olmec rulers must have had considerable power and wealth. They were able to organize the construction of the three major urban centers—San Lorenzo, La Venta, and Tres Zapotes. (They have Spanish names now because no record of their Olmec names exists.) The centers contained palaces, religious buildings, and marketplaces. The Olmecs built large, high earthen mounds. Religious ceremonies were held on the flat tops of the mounds.

2. Olmec Culture. Like both the Mesopotamians and the Egyptians, the Olmecs had a writing system, a number system, and a calendar. Their glyph writing is made up of symbols and pictures of real objects. For personal decoration, the Olmecs devised mirrors made of a metal called magnetite. The mirrors may have also been used to light fires by reflecting the sun's rays onto flammable materials.

The Olmecs produced great works of art. The most impressive examples of their skills are massive heads carved from stone. Some are nine feet high and weigh 18 to 20 tons. Anthropologists assume that these sculptures represented priest-kings. Olmec artists also made sculptures of plumed serpents and a creature that was half jaguar and half human. The jaguar was the Olmecs' rain god. Both the plumed serpent and the jaguar were powerful spirits in the religions of later Mesoamerican societies.

So many features of the Olmec civilization recurred in later cultures that some scholars call it the "mother" civilization of Mesoamerica. It also had a strong influence on other societies that existed at the same time. This influence was probably not the result of military conquest. The Olmecs were too few in number to have conquered other groups. Then, too, there is little evidence that the Olmecs occupied other people's lands.

Massive stone head of the Olmec culture, probably representing a sky god.

The Olmecs spread their culture through trade. In fact, they were responsible for most of the trade and cultural exchange that took place between other Mesoamerican groups as well. They created the trade networks through which various groups exchanged such luxury items as jewels for such necessities as corn. As trade items moved from place to place, so too did ideas, customs, and myths.

Scholars do not know why the Olmec civilization ended. Around 900 B.C., some unknown group destroyed the ceremonial center called San Lorenzo. Scholars have various theories about what happened. A rival leader may have tried to drive out the Olmec ruler. A peasant group might have rebelled against harsh treatment by their overlords. After the fall of San Lorenzo, La Venta began to decline. The Olmec state collapsed in about 400 B.C. Olmec culture lived on, however, and developed into new forms.

TEOTIHUACÁN

In about A.D. 300, a city called Teotihuacán arose northeast of what is now Mexico City. The people who built it shared many elements of Olmec culture. Their social scale ranged from priest-kings and their administrators through craftspeople and farmers down to slaves and serfs. They built pyramids and worshipped the plumed serpent and a rain god. Like the Olmecs, they had a calendar, a number system, and a writing system.

City planners laid out Teotihuacán streets in a grid pattern. The east-west streets were at right angles to the north-south streets. The homes of wealthier people were airy and spacious. The walls of some of the buildings were decorated with beautiful murals. Some dwellings were like large apartment houses. Craft workers and artisans lived in them and worked in shops built close by. In the ruins of Teotihuacán, archaeologists have found workshops for many crafts. There are places for tanning leather, making pottery, and carving blades from obsidian to make weapons and tools. (Obsidian is hardened glass from the lava of volcanoes. The edges of thin pieces can be sharpened by chipping and polishing.)

Some 100,000 to 200,000 people lived in Teotihuacán during its most prosperous period. It was larger than most European or Asian cities of the time. At one end of a two-kilometer-long avenue was the gigantic Pyramid of the Sun. It stood 200 feet high and measured 700 feet long on each side. At the other end of the avenue was the smaller Temple of Quetzalcóatl. The ruins of these structures can be seen today.

The people of Teotihuacán established an empire throughout Mesoamerica by means of trade rather than war. Archaeologists have found evidence that these people colonized small areas where important resources, such as obsidian, were mined. Having control of the source of obsidian helped make the people of Teotihuacán the major manufacturers of weapons and tools. Having the main supply of weapons and tools gave them great control over other Mesoamerican societies. As the master traders of the area, they (like the Olmecs) spread their own culture and learned new ways from other groups.

As with the decline of the Olmecs, the reasons for the end of the Teotihuacán civilization are a mystery. Between A.D. 600 and 650, the great city was burned. Possibly an enemy force destroyed it. Nonetheless, its culture survived to be adopted and developed by other peoples.

THE MAYAS, AZTECS, AND INCAS

In what are now southern Mexico, Guatemala, Belize, and Honduras, advanced cultures existed as early as 1200 B.C. Equally high-level cultures developed later in the Andes Mountains in western South America. These New World Indian cultures were as advanced as any in early Mesopotamia and rivaled that of ancient Egypt.

1. The Mayas. Some scholars say that the Mayas created the greatest early civilization in the New World. The first centers of Mayan culture were built in what is now northern Guatemala.

The Mayas were farmers. They cleared small plots of land out of the rain forest. In the hot, humid climate, Mayan farmers grew mainly corn, beans, peppers, and tomatoes. They also raised sweet potatoes, tobacco, cotton, fruits, and cacao (the main ingredient of chocolate).

   a. *Classic Period.* The period of the Mayas' highest level of development lasted from A.D. 100 to 900. These centuries are called the Mayas' Classic Period. During this time, the Mayas built many cities. The largest structures were tall, flat-topped pyramids used mainly for religious purposes. Tombs of rulers and other leaders have also been found in many pyramids.

Some of the buildings seem to have been used as astronomical observatories. From them, priests studied the stars and the movements of the planets. The priests used this information to predict eclipses of the sun and moon. The information also guided the Mayas in the planting of their crops.

In mathematics, the Mayas used the zero and created a number system based on 20. They had a calendar that was as accurate as the one we use today. The Mayas also had a highly developed writing system that has not yet been completely deciphered. Mayan writing used *ideographs*, or symbols, that stood for ideas, dates, numbers, and sounds.

Skilled workers created pottery in many shapes and painted beautiful designs on it. Other workers made objects out of jade. On the inner walls of buildings in religious centers, artists painted colorful murals. Sculptors made intricate stone carvings and sculptures.

In the 800's, the Mayas began to leave their cities. They may have been defeated in wars or have fallen victim to diseases. Perhaps the population grew too large to be fed by the amount of food that could be grown in the area.

b. *Post-Classic Period.* The span of years after the Mayas deserted most of their cities is called the Post-Classic Period. During this period (900–1519), new cities in northern Yucatán (a peninsula that juts into the Gulf of Mexico) became important. These Mayan cities developed into city-states, similar to those of ancient Greece and East Africa. Chichén Itzá is one of the best known of these city-states. The city features a large pyramid. Four staircases, each with 365 steps, lead to the top. The pyramid stands as proof of the great skill of the Mayan builders.

About the year 1200, Toltecs from central Mexico defeated the Mayas. Under the Toltecs, the culture of the Mayas declined. Spanish explorers conquered the remaining Mayas in the early 1500's. By then, most of the great cities had been abandoned and covered by rain forests.

2. The Empire of the Aztecs. In the 1200's, a warlike people called the Aztecs came to central Mexico from the north. During the next 200 years, the Aztecs built an empire by conquering most of central Mexico. They demanded a yearly tax from the conquered people. Aztec power reached its peak in the 1400's.

a. *Tenochtitlán.* The center of the Aztec Empire was Tenochtitlán. This large city was built about 1325 on an island in a lake. Great stone temples and pyramids stood in the center of the city. Stone causeways and bridges connected the city with the

The Mayan and Aztec Civilizations

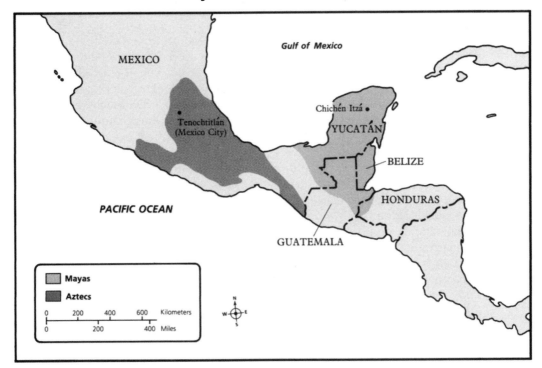

Indicate whether each of the following statements is *true* (**T**) or *false* (**F**).

1. Most of the Mayan civilization was located in Yucatán, Belize, and Guatemala.

2. The Aztec civilization was located in central and southern Mexico.

3. Tenochtitlán was a Mayan city.

4. Part of the Mayan civilization developed on a peninsula.

5. The Aztecs' lands extended south along the Pacific Coast to South America.

---

mainland. By the late 1400's, more than 100,000 people lived in Tenochtitlán. Food for the people of the city was grown on islands floating in the lake. Aztec workers created the islands by piling up mud from the lake bottom.

    b. *Aztec culture.* The Aztecs were very skilled people. They made beautiful objects out of gold, silver, and precious stones. They wove fine cotton cloth. The system of picture writing they used resembles Mayan ideographs.

The Emperor and the Conqueror

In 1519, two men faced each other in the Aztec city of Tenochtitlán. Montezuma II (1466–1520) ruled the powerful Aztec Empire. He was the political, religious, and military head of all the Indian tribes and territories controlled by the Aztecs. Hernando Cortés (1485–1547) commanded a force of 600 Spaniards who had come to conquer Mexico. The conflict between these two men resulted in the fall of the Aztec Empire, the death of Montezuma, and the beginning of Spanish rule in Mexico.

Before this encounter, Montezuma II, emperor of the Aztecs, had extended the empire south to what is now Central America. A builder of many public buildings, aqueducts, and tem-

ples, Montezuma taxed the people heavily to pay for these public works. Further, the religion of the Aztecs required human sacrifices. People picked for sacrifice usually came from conquered tribes. These tribes frequently rebelled against the Aztecs because of Montezuma's harsh rule.

After Cortés landed in Mexico, thousands of Indians joined his expedition to Tenochtitlán. These Indians hated Aztec rule.

Surprisingly, Montezuma welcomed Cortés. Gifts of gold were presented to the Spaniards. Montezuma believed that Cortés was sent by the god Quetzalcoatl. In response to Montezuma's welcome, Cortés quickly entered the city and made Montezuma a prisoner. Shortly afterward, the Aztecs rebelled and forced the Spaniards out of Tenochtitlán. When Montezuma tried to calm his people, they turned on him and stoned him to death. In 1521, Cortés and his Indian allies destroyed the city. After the fall of the Aztec Empire, Cortés built Mexico City over the ruins of Tenochtitlán. Cortés and the Spaniards were the new rulers of central and southern Mexico.

Cortés was one of the greatest of the Spanish adventurers. He showed great skill in founding Spanish towns in Mexico. Cortés also continued explorations and colonization in other parts of New Spain. However, Cortés had enemies who eventually persuaded the king of Spain to remove him from Mexico. Cortés ended his days in Spain, a forgotten and broken man.

Emperor Montezuma welcomes Hernando Cortés to Tenochtitlán in 1519.

Why did both Montezuma and Cortés die unhappy and disappointed?

This artist's reconstruction shows the Aztec Temple of Tenochtitlán.

c. *Aztec religion.* The Aztecs worshipped many gods, including Quetzalcoatl, the feathered serpent. They believed that this god and the gods of the sun, the rain, the wind, and war required the gift of human blood to keep the world alive. To obtain victims to sacrifice, the Aztecs constantly fought wars with other Indian peoples. On special days, prisoners were laid on a temple altar. Then a priest used a sharp stone knife to cut out the heart of each victim. The Aztecs believed that the person whose heart was offered to the gods became a messenger to the gods. The victim was expected to plead with the gods for the well-being of the Aztecs.

d. *Spanish conquest.* In the early 16th century, a few Spanish soldiers led by Hernando Cortés arrived in Mexico. They wanted lands to colonize and the treasure of the Aztecs. By then, Aztec rule had been weakened by revolts of its subject peoples. Many of the rebelling people helped the Spaniards conquer the Aztec Empire. Within two years, Tenochtitlán was destroyed. The Spaniards built Mexico City on the ruins of Tenochtitlán.

3. The Greatness of the Incas. The most powerful of the early American civilizations developed in the Andes Mountains of South America. By the 16th century, the Incas ruled an empire of 12 million people in what are today the countries of Ecuador, Peru, Bolivia, Chile, and Argentina. The people in the Inca Empire belonged to 100 different cultural groups and spoke 20 different languages.

a. *Political and social control.* The Incas worshipped their emperor as a representative of the sun god. He had total

The Inca Civilization

1. List *three* modern countries included in the Inca Empire of 1500.

2. Identify *two* geographic features that you think influenced the Inca civilization.

Ruins of the Inca city of Machu Picchu, high in the Andes Mountains of Peru.

power over everyone and everything in his empire. The government owned and controlled all land and most businesses. Men were drafted into the army or assigned to other types of government service. Some young women received special training in religion so that they could serve in the temples. All men were expected to marry by a certain age. Those who did not choose wives on their own had to marry women selected for them by government officials.

The Incas ruled their empire more successfully than the Aztecs ruled theirs. The different peoples of the empire had to learn about the Inca language, religion, and way of life. The government sent colonists into conquered lands to serve as teachers. Sons of conquered rulers were brought to Cuzco, the Inca capital, for education and to make sure that the conquered rulers did not rebel. After being educated by Inca teachers, the conquered rulers' sons were sent home to rule their people.

b. *Occupations and technology.*   Inca farmers in the Andes Mountains planted crops, particularly potatoes, on terraces. These were flat spaces dug into the sides of mountains. Water was provided through irrigation systems.

The Incas had many skills. Their roads and bridges, among the best in the world at that time, connected all parts of the empire. Inca doctors performed many types of operations, including brain surgery. Craft workers made beautiful gold and silver objects. Stone structures were carefully put together. A thin knife cannot be pushed between the shaped stones of the sections that still stand.

c. *Spanish conquest.* In 1532, Spanish soldiers led by Francisco Pizarro marched into the Inca Empire. They seized the emperor Atahualpa and made him pay a huge ransom in gold. But the treasure did not save his life. By 1572, the Spaniards had completed their conquest of the entire Inca Empire.

CHART COMPLETION

Compare the Incas with the Aztecs and the Mayas by completing the following table.

	Government and organization of empire	Religion	Skills and crafts
Incas			
Aztecs			
Mayas			

 ## MATCHING EXERCISE

Match each term in Column A with its meaning in Column B.

Column A	**Column B**
1. ideographs	*a.* the time of the highest level of Mayan civilization
2. astronomical observatories	*b.* a city-state in Yucatán
3. Chichén Itzá	*c.* places from which Mayan priests studied the stars and planets
4. Classic Period	*d.* the years after the Mayas moved away from their cities in Guatemala
5. Post-Classic Period	*e.* symbols in Mayan writing

CRITICAL THINKING

Write a paragraph to PROVE or DISPROVE the following statement:

The Mayas, Aztecs, and Incas used tools and weapons of sharpened stone. They knew nothing of iron or of wheeled vehicles. Therefore, they did not have advanced civilizations.

NORTH AMERICAN INDIAN CULTURES

Native American tribes developed a wide variety of cultures in what are today Canada and the United States. Unlike the Mayas, Aztecs, and Incas, North American Indians did not build cities and empires. Many lived in villages, but most moved from place to place to find food. Distinctive ways of life developed in each particular geographical area. Four major cultural groups are the Indians of the Eastern Woodlands, the Southwest, the Plains, and the Northwest Coast.

1. Eastern Woodlands Groups. In the forests of southeastern Canada and the eastern United States, Indians lived as hunters and farmers. For both activities, they used tools and weapons made of chipped stone, bone, and wood. Not until the arrival of Europeans in the 1500's did the Indians obtain metal axes and knives.

    a. *Political organization.* One of the largest groups of Indians in the Eastern Woodlands area was the Iroquois. Five tribes formed the Iroquois League of Five Nations: Seneca, Cayuga, Mohawk, Onondaga, and Oneida. (The Tuscaroras later joined the group, making it the Six Nations.) The purpose of the league was to keep peace among the member tribes. The unity and fighting ability of the Iroquois made them very powerful.

    In their tribal councils, the Iroquois practiced a type of democracy. Their elected chiefs acted as servants of the people. The government of the league was in the hands of 50 men called *sachems*. The leading women of the tribes chose the sachems. Each sachem had a voice in the Council of the League, the governing body of the Six Nations.

    Anyone could attend meetings of the council. At these meetings, proposals were presented for acceptance or rejection. After a great deal of discussion and speechmaking, the sachems would reach a decision about each proposal. Some historians believe that the men who planned the government of the United States may have gotten some of their ideas from the way the Six Nations operated.

    b. *Matriarchal society.* Women had a great deal of authority among the Iroquois. A woman headed each clan, or group of related families. The women owned all of the family goods. No one could inherit anything except from his or her mother. Young men and women could not choose whom they would marry. Mothers arranged all marriages.

North American Indian Cultures

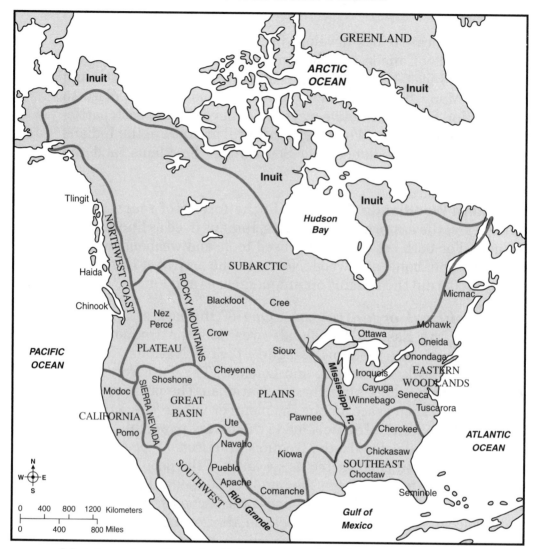

Match each culture in Column A with a location in Column B.

Column A	Column B
1. Iroquois	*a.* Plains
2. Seminole	*b.* Plateau
3. Apache	*c.* Greenland
4. Sioux	*d.* Great Basin
5. Modoc	*e.* Northwest Coast
6. Shoshone	*f.* Southwest
7. Haida	*g.* Eastern Woodlands
8. Nez Percé	*h.* Southeast
9. Inuit	*i.* California

When a man married, he went to live with his wife's clan. However, he remained forever a member of his mother's clan. As such, he had no responsibility for raising or teaching his children. They were brought up by his wife's brothers. Children, in turn, had no responsibility for taking care of aged fathers. When men became old, they went back to their mother's clan.

    c. *Homes and villages.*   The Iroquois called themselves the "People of the Long House." They lived in houses made of bark attached to wooden pole frames. Most of the houses measured about 60 feet long, 18 feet wide, and 18 feet high. Some were as long as 150 feet. Several related families shared each house. A number of houses, arranged in rows, made up a village. A stockade, a high fence made of poles, surrounded the village. Outside the stockade were fields where the women raised corn, squash, and beans. The men hunted, fished, and raided or fought other Indian tribes.

    During the American Revolution (1775–1783), some of the Iroquois tribes sided with the British. After the Americans won the war, they sent troops to punish the Iroquois. This action weakened the Six Nations forever.

2. Southwest Groups.   In the 1500's, Spanish explorers traveled throughout what is now the southwestern part of the United

Iroquois longhouses had bark roofs and sides to keep out the rain. Stockade fences were typically built around Iroquois settlements.

States. They gave the name *Pueblos* to the Indians of the region. *Pueblo* is the Spanish word for "town." Many Pueblo towns still exist. Two have been continuously occupied since about 1150.

a. *Architecture*. The Southwest has a hot, dry climate. Most of the area is covered by deserts and rugged mountains. Both the climate and the land affected the types of houses the Pueblos built and the places in which their houses were located. Using *adobe*, or sun-dried bricks, the Pueblos made flat-roofed houses. Most of the buildings were three or four stories high. Some were very large, containing enough rooms to hold several hundred people. Pueblo houses have been called the first "apartment buildings" in America.

For protection against enemies, some houses were built on ledges under overhanging cliffs. Others stood on top of flat, high-sided *mesas*. Steep, narrow trails led to these villages. The Pueblos did not like fighting. When threatened by enemies, they retreated into their houses through doorways that could be reached only with ladders.

b. *Economy, government, and religion*. The Pueblos lived as peaceful farmers. The men grew corn, beans, squash, and

A Pueblo town near Taos, New Mexico.

cotton. The women cooked, wove cloth, made pottery, and helped build the houses.

A council of religious leaders and clan chiefs governed each Pueblo town. Little law enforcement was needed. The community ridiculed or ignored troublemakers until they behaved properly.

To the Pueblos, religion was very important. Each community had a *kiva*. This underground room served as a religious center and meeting place for men only. Women were not allowed to enter it. Throughout the year, many different ceremonies took place. With special costumes and rituals, the Pueblos hoped to persuade the gods to give them rain and good fortune. They also believed in spirits called *kachinas*. The Pueblos believed that these messengers from the gods lived with the Pueblos for six months of the year. During the other six months, they lived with the gods in the mountains. The Pueblos had the most elaborate religion of all the tribes in the area north of Mexico.

c. *Other peoples.* Sometime after A.D. 1000, invaders from the north threatened the peaceful existence of the Pueblos. These invaders, the Apaches and the Navahos, were hunters. They brought to the Southwest warlike habits and more powerful bows and arrows than the Pueblo possessed. The Apaches and Navahos often attacked Pueblos towns to take food and slaves. The Pueblos were good farmers, traders, and craft workers, but not warriors. They would not fight unless forced to do so to protect their homes.

Long contact with the Pueblos gradually changed the Navahos. They abandoned the ways of the warrior and became farmers. Later, they herded sheep. Learning weaving from the Pueblos, some Navaho men made beautiful rugs and blankets. (The Navaho is the largest group of Native Americans in the United States today.)

The Apaches remained hunters and raiders. Against the Spaniards, Mexicans and, later, the Americans, the Apaches used hit-and-run tactics. They specialized in sudden attacks and then swift retreats into their mountain strongholds. The Apaches were never defeated by military forces. Eventually, in the late 19th century, they agreed to a treaty of peace with the U.S. government.

3. Plains Indians. The grasslands from the Missouri River in the east to the Rocky Mountains in the west are known as the Great Plains. The area extends from Canada in the north to Texas. Most of the Native Americans who lived on the western plains were nomadic hunters. They wandered about, following the movements of large game animals. They had no permanent villages. Carrying their goods with them, they set up camp wherever they happened

The Anasazi

In 1888, at a place called Mesa Verde, a pair of ranchers found a deserted village. It had been built on a ledge of a cliff wall of a canyon in southwestern Colorado. The dwellings in this village were like modern apartment houses. They were three or four stories tall. Here and there, towers rose above the houses. So impressive was this stone and adobe structure that the ranchers named it the Cliff Palace.

Since the discovery of the Cliff Palace, more ancient villages have been found. Most of these are located in an area called the Four Corners, where the borders of Colorado, New Mexico, Arizona, and Utah meet. The dry Southwestern climate has preserved the bones of the former inhabitants as well their belongings.

From fossils and artifacts, anthropologists have pieced together information about these people. Most scholars believe that they are the ancestors of the Pueblo and the Hopi who now live in this area. Historians and archeologists call these ancestors the Anasazi (the ancient ones).

Originally, the Anasazi were hunters and gatherers. About A.D. 100, they began to cultivate corn. To be near their crops, they settled in permanent communities. Lacking a large supply of trees for building material, they made adobe bricks from the desert soil. As communities grew larger and natural water supplies became inadequate for their populations, the Anasazi built simple irrigation systems.

The artifacts the Anasazi left behind show that they were skilled craftspeople. They wove their baskets so tightly that they could carry water and cook in them. They were clever at making nets for snaring animals. One kind of net had a large black spot painted in the middle. Anthropologists believe that the Anasazi stretched it across a dry streambed and then beat bushes to scare out the rabbits. The frightened rabbits would mistake the black spot for a hole and ensnare themselves as they tried to escape through it. Judging from their pottery and fabrics, the Anasazi had a keen sense of beauty.

Anthropologists believe that these people had a complex religion. In the deserted Anasazi villages, they have found kivas. On the walls of some of these underground rooms, artists had painted supernatural figures bestowing rain, seeds, fish, and other good things on the earth. Priests once used the altars and fire pits, which were also found in the kivas, for performing sacred rites.

Historians do not know what disaster struck the Anasazi to make them leave the area within a short time period. They know only that these ancient people began deserting their cities in the late 1200's. A combination of problems may have caused them to look for new homes—a prolonged period of drought, attacks by fierce newcomers, and a dwindling supply of wood for fuel and construction.

to be. Some of these tribes did have particular places to which they returned each winter. Many eastern Plains Indians lived in permanent villages. They farmed and hunted mainly in the spring and summer. Among the best-known Plains Indian tribes were the Sioux, Cheyenne, and Comanche.

a. *Buffalo economy.* The lives of the Plains Indians depended mainly on the buffalo. From the buffalo, Indians obtained the skins they needed for their clothes and tepees. Tepees are the cone-shaped tents in which the Plains Indians lived, particularly during hunting periods. Most of their tools and weapons were made from buffalo bones. Dried buffalo dung provided fuel for campfires.

Until the Spaniards brought the horse to North America, hunting buffalo was difficult. Before the late 1600's, the Indians hunted on foot. They often killed buffalo by driving them over a cliff. Gradually, the Indians acquired horses and learned how to ride. On horseback, the hunters could easily run down the buffalo herds and shoot arrows into the big animals.

Their skill in handling horses and the discipline and organization needed in buffalo hunting helped make the Plains Indians great warriors. Tribes generally fought to avenge a wrong or to get more horses. They also fought for excitement. Acts such as touching an armed enemy with a hand or a special stick or stealing horses from the middle of an enemy camp gave high honor to individual warriors. Such acts were called "counting coup."

b. *Settlers from the East.* Settlers who moved into the Great Plains after the mid-1800's destroyed the Plains Indians' way of life. Farmers, miners, and cattle ranchers pushed the tribes out of their hunting grounds. The buffalo were killed for sport by people who did not need them for food. Soon almost none of the great animals were left. The disappearance of the buffalo weakened the Plains tribes. Little by little, the U.S. Army forced the

Plains Indians were expert at killing buffalo for meat and other purposes.

tribes to move onto *reservations*. The U.S. government had set aside these areas of land for the use of the Indians. The reservation Indians could no longer follow their old ways of life. They came to depend on the government to provide their food, clothing, and shelter.

4. Northwest Coast Indians. On the northwest coast of North America, the mild climate and abundant natural resources made possible the rise of a complex Indian culture. The people who lived in what are today British Columbia, Washington, and Oregon were able to obtain a good living without much effort. They had time and energy to devote to the development of fine arts and crafts and to religious and social ceremonies. Among the most prosperous of the Northwest Coast peoples were the Haida and the Tlingit.

   a. *Village life.* The Northwest Coast Indians lived in villages built along the seashore or the edge of a bay or river. A typical village consisted of eight or more large wooden houses. One house chief also served as the village chief. This was a hereditary position passed on from one male relative to another. Being chief gave a person wealth and prestige.

   The construction of the houses reflected the woodworking skill of the Northwest Coast Indians. So too did the tall, elaborately carved totem poles set up in front of each house. Some totem poles represented the deeds of the chiefs. Other poles held the bones of dead chiefs. Still others showed that some families had special privileges.

   The only crop that the Northwest Coast Indians grew was tobacco. Most of their food came from the water. In their great canoes, some 60 feet long and 8 feet wide, they pursued whales, seals, sea otters, and fish. They made harpoons and other fishing tools of wood and bone and attached shell points. The Northwest Coast peoples also built traps in the rivers to catch salmon and other fish.

   Most Northwest Coast groups were divided into four social classes: chiefs, nobles, commoners, and slaves. Each person was born into a class. An individual could advance to a higher class, however, by showing a certain skill or by acquiring wealth. The way to demonstrate the possession of wealth was to give away one's belongings. This was done at a community feast called a *potlatch*. By striving to gain honor and high standing at a potlatch, chiefs and even whole families sometimes made themselves poor by giving away all they owned.

Haida whalers returning to their village with their catch.

b. Wars. Despite the wealth of the Northwest Coast Indians, they were not always peaceful. Tribal conflicts over sites or fishing places sometimes set off savage wars. Raiding parties took the heads of enemies and mounted them on poles in the village or on canoes. Wars were also fought to capture slaves and goods or to avenge a murder. Sometimes one group, or tribe, set out to kill people to accompany a dead chief on his journey to the next world.

The complex culture of the Northwest Coast tribes was ended not by wars but by diseases. The Indians caught the diseases from European explorers and traders. Eventually, the weakened survivors left their coastal villages to live on reservations provided by the U.S. government.

DEFINITIONS

Reread "1. Eastern Woodland Groups," on pages 225–227. Then write a definition in your own words for each of the following terms:

    a. League of Five Nations
    b. sachems
    c. clan

SENTENCE COMPLETION

From the list that follows, select the term or terms that best completes each sentence in the paragraph.

Spaniards	Cheyenne	buffalo
tepees	Great Plains	Comanche
counting coup	Sioux	horse

The grasslands between the Missouri River and the Rocky Mountains are known as the _(1)_ . The largest and best-known tribes who lived there were the _(2)_ , the _(3)_ , and the _(4)_ . These hunters depended on the _(5)_ for most of the necessities of life. For hunting, they rode the _(6)_ , which had been brought to North America by the _(7)_ . Wherever Indians camped they set up _(8)_ , or skin tents, Warriors showed their bravery by _(9)_ .

WRITING EXERCISE

Reread "2. Southwest Groups," on pages 227–229. Then write a paragraph in response to each of the following questions:

1. How were the ways of life of the Pueblos, Apaches, and Navahos different from one another?

2. How did the Pueblos feel about war?

3. Why were religious ceremonies important to the Pueblos?

SENTENCE CONSTRUCTION

Rearrange each of the following word groups to make correct sentences:

1. the Haida among the Tlingit prosperous peoples most the Northwest of and the were Coast

2. village a eight typical or of consisted houses more wooden large

3. totem some poles dead memorials were chiefs to

4. food water came most of from the their

THE INUIT OF THE FAR NORTH

The Inuit lived in the northernmost region of North America. Named Eskimos by outsiders, they called themselves the Inuit, which means "the people." Many scholars believe that the Inuit originally came from northern Asia. But they crossed into North America long after the Indians in the region moved farther south.

Inuit woman strings fish together. The fish will then be smoked over a low fire. Photographed in 1904.

a. *Nomadic life.* The frozen lands of the Arctic could not support a large population in one place. The Inuit, therefore, lived in small family groups. They were nomads, traveling from place to place in search of animals and fish for food. They had no need for a central government or a complex economy. The Inuit became highly skilled at living a satisfactory life in an extremely harsh environment.

From caribou (North American reindeer), polar bears, whales, seals, smaller game, and fish, the Inuit obtained food and furs and skins for clothing and tents. Bones were used for harpoons, spears, and fishhooks. The Inuit generally lived in tents in the summer. In the winter, they built dome-shaped houses of sod and wood or blocks of snow.

When the Inuit moved to a new area in the winter, they packed their possessions on sleds pulled by dogs. To hunt sea animals, the Inuit used *kayaks*. These are small, one- or two-person boats made of waterproof skins stretched over a wooden frame. The Inuit also used a larger open boat for long voyages and to carry goods.

The long hunting journeys of some Inuit took them as far east as Greenland. There they made contact with Norse colonists who had settled in western Greenland in the 10th century. Historians believe that between 1000 and 1500, the Inuit absorbed these Norse people through intermarriage. Eventually, the Norse colony disappeared. Some Greenland Inuit today are somewhat European in appearance. They may be the descendants of Norse people who lived in Greenland long ago.

b. *Religion.* For the Inuit, as well as for most Native American groups, the world was full of spirits. The Inuit believed that special people called *shamans* had great power to influence the spirits. Shamans used magic to heal sick or wounded people. They also helped hunters by calling the animals to be killed. Inuit legends include many stories about the most skilled shamans.

 MATCHING EXERCISE

Match each term in Column A with its meaning in Column B.

Column A	Column B
1. Inuit	*a.* person believed to have great power to influence spirits
2. Arctic	
3. kayak	*b.* 10th-century colonists in Greenland
4. shaman	*c.* a name meaning "the people"
5. Norse	*d.* a one- or two-person boat
	e. the northernmost region of North America

Chapter Review

▶ **MULTIPLE-CHOICE**

Choose the item that best completes each sentence or answers each question.

1. The Maya, Aztec, and Inca civilizations developed in (*a*) North America (*b*) Middle and South America (*c*) North and Central America (*d*) South America.

2. Human sacrifice was practiced most frequently by the (*a*) Mayas (*b*) Olmecs (*c*) Incas (*d*) Aztecs.

3. Which statement is equally true of Maya, Aztec, and Inca civilizations? (*a*) They were hated by other Indians. (*b*) They had superior metalworking skills. (*c*) They built great cities. (*d*) They hunted and fished with kayaks.

4. The Spanish who conquered the Mayas, Aztecs, and Incas in the 16th century were most interested in (*a*) gold and other forms of treasure (*b*) furs to sell in Europe (*c*) slaves to ship to the West Indies (*d*) new farming techniques.

5. The Iroquois League of Five Nations was an example of (*a*) the evils of kings (*b*) dictatorship (*c*) democracy in government (*d*) commercial expansion.

6. The first "apartment buildings" in North America were built by the (*a*) Sioux (*b*) Navahos (*c*) Apaches (*d*) Pueblos.

7. Horsemanship and discipline made the Plains Indians great (*a*) warriors (*b*) farmers (*c*) builders (*d*) traders.

8. The Plains Indians' way of life was weakened by the (*a*) appearance of the horse (*b*) disappearance of the buffalo (*c*) decline of cattle and sheep (*d*) invention of gunpowder.

9. The woodworking skills of the Northwest Coast Indians were best displayed by their (*a*) houses, canoes, and totem poles (*b*) method of warfare (*c*) potlatches (*d*) selection of chiefs.

10. For centuries, the Inuit lived as (*a*) farmers (*b*) herders (*c*) merchants (*d*) hunters and fishers.

Connections: Roads in Early Civilizations

The empires and kingdoms of the ancient world were held together by roads. The Romans built roads across Europe, North Africa, and the Middle East. Over these highways marched the legions that kept the Roman Peace (*Pax Romana*), the merchants whose trade made the empire prosperous, and imperial couriers with messages from the Caesars to the governors of distant provinces.

The Persian Empire also depended on roads. This far-flung empire extended from Egypt to India. It was tied together by a system of military roads. These roads helped the growth of trade as well. Inspectors called the "Eyes of the King" traveled along these roads to make sure that the governors of all the provinces were carrying out the king's orders.

The Incas of South America also laid down roads from one end of their empire to the other. One great Inca road followed the coast of the Pacific Ocean. Another ran along the crest of the Andes Mountains. Many sections of the roads were paved with stone. Suspension bridges hung over gorges and rivers. These bridges were marvels of engineering for the age in which they were built. Over these roads and bridges, relays of Incan runners rushed messages from one part of the empire to the other. Pack animals carried goods to and from Cuzco, the "City of the Sun."

For the early civilizations of Europe, the Middle East, and America, roads made possible the administration of government, the flow of trade, and the exchange of ideas.

Why were roads as important to the Incas as they were to the Romans and Persians?

ESSAY QUESTIONS

1. Select *one* early American civilization that you find interesting and identify its most important cultural characteristics.

2. Explain why historians compare the early Mesoamerican civilizations with the early civilizations of the Middle East and Europe.

3. Describe the results of interaction between Native American cultures and Europeans.

DOCUMENT-BASED QUESTION

This question is based on the accompanying documents (1–3). It will improve your ability to work with historical documents.

Historical Context:

Many different cultures developed over thousands of years in the Americas. The civilizations interacted with one another in many ways.

Task:

Using information from the documents and your knowledge of world history, answer the questions that follow each document. Your answers to each question will help you write the document-based essay.

Document 1.   Study the illustration below.

What reason for the Aztecs' going to war is shown here?

Aztec practice of human sacrifice.

Document 2.   Excerpt from *The Popol Vuh,* the sacred book of the Quiché Indians, a branch of the ancient Mayas. This excerpt relates to the rise of the Quiché nation in what is now Guatemala.

And it was not at small cost, that they [the Quiché] conquered the fields and the towns; the small towns and the large towns paid high ransoms; they brought precious stones and metals, they brought honey of the bees.

It was not little what they [the Quiché] did, neither were few, the tribes which they conquered. Many branches of the tribes came to pay tribute to the Quiché; full of sorrow they came to give it over.

Source: *The Popol Vuh*, by Delia Goetz and Sylvanus Griswold Morley, from Adrian Recino's translation (1954). Copyright not registered or renewed. Found at http://www.sacred-texts.com/nam/maya/pvgm/index.htm

Based on this document, what was the relationship between the ancient Mayas and the other tribes and towns?

Document 3. Excerpt from the *Constitution of the Iroquois Nations*, which governed the actions of the Iroquois League in the 1500's (originally unwritten but later reconstructed from legend and spoken history):

80. When the Confederate Council of the Five Nations has for its object the establishment of the Great Peace among the people of an outside nation and that nation refuses to accept the Great Peace, then by such refusal they bring a declaration of war upon themselves from the Five Nations. Then shall the Five Nations seek to establish the Great Peace by a conquest of the rebellious nation.

84. Whenever a foreign nation is conquered or has by their own will accepted the Great Peace, their own system of internal government may continue, but they must cease all warfare against other nations.

Source: Constitution of the Iroquois Nation. Found at http://tuscaroras.com/pages/history/about_iroquois_constitution.html. Prepared by Gerald Murphy (The Cleveland Free-Net-aa300) Distributed by the Cybercasting Services Division of the National Public Telecomputing Network (NPTN).

Based on this document, how did the Iroquois League attempt to establish the "Great Peace"?

DOCUMENT-BASED ESSAY

Using information from the documents and your knowledge of world history, write an essay in which you:

- Discuss how early peoples in the Americas interacted with one another.
- Compare the methods used by the Mayas, Aztecs, and Iroquois to impose their will upon neighboring people or to get along with them.

CHAPTER 11
India and East Asia

In the period from the 8th to the 18th century, great changes came to India and East Asia. As invaders conquered the area, the ideas of these outsiders changed old ideas of government and the way people lived.

The outsiders who brought about the changes were Muslims from the Middle East, Mongols from Central Asia, and Manchus from northeast Asia. The Muslims conquered India, and the Mongols and Manchus took over China. They ruled as sultans and emperors and altered the cultures of India and China. The Muslim religion, Islam, challenged the ideas of Hinduism and Buddhism.

China, in turn, greatly influenced Japan and Korea. Even though these two countries adopted much from Chinese culture, each developed a unique culture of its own.

From the 1600's onward, aggressive Westerners forced the large Asian countries, such as China and India, to sign trade agreements. Many of the small countries became Western colonies. Christianity was introduced into many Asian countries.

INDIA UNDER MUSLIM RULE

After the Gupta Empire ended in the middle of the 6th century, India experienced a long period of unrest. Asian invaders from the north and east raided its cities. From the 700's to the 1200's, Muslims from the Middle East attacked India. They wanted to convert Hindus to Islam and add territory to their empire. During this period, local Indian rulers fought against the Muslim advance.

Southern India, called the Deccan, remained in the hands of Hindu rulers. These kings were not defeated by the Muslims until the 1300's.

1. Delhi Sultans. By 1200, Turkish Muslims had conquered large parts of northern India. The Muslims chose Delhi as their capital. All-powerful Muslim rulers called *sultans* founded a Delhi Empire. Later sultans extended Muslim power southward into the Deccan region of India. The Delhi sultans persecuted Hindus and offered benefits and equality to those willing to convert to Islam.

Asia Today

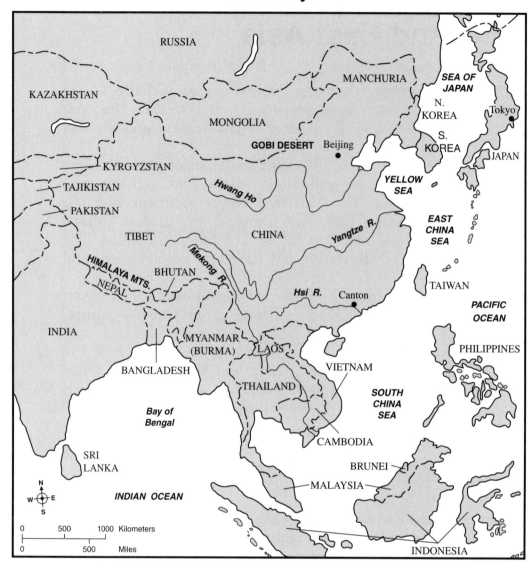

Although many converted, especially those from the lower castes, Hinduism remained the religion of the majority.

    a. *Mongol invasion.* In 1398, Mongols from Central Asia swept into India after conquering Persia, Mesopotamia, and Afghanistan. Led by Timur (or Tamerlane), the Mongol forces captured Delhi, looted the city, and killed most of its people. Within months, Timur left India and headed toward Turkey. His attack so unsettled the Delhi Sultanate that it never regained full control of northern India.

b. ***Portuguese arrival.*** Just 100 years after Timur's invasion, Vasco da Gama, a Portuguese explorer, reached India. The Portuguese built forts on the west coast and encouraged the spice trade. Their main center of trade and settlement in India was Goa. They kept this colony until 1961. The Portuguese introduced Roman Catholicism, but this religion did not win large numbers of converts.

2. The Mogul Empire. In the early 1500's, another invading force of Muslims moved into India.

a. ***Babur.*** Led by Babur, a descendant of Timur, the invaders conquered Delhi in 1526. Babur became the first ruler of the Mogul Empire in India. This empire lasted until the mid-1700's. In addition to his ability as a military leader, Babur was a talented writer and a planner of beautiful gardens. He composed fine poetry and wrote a highly praised account of his life.

After Babur died, rival groups struggled for 20 years to take control of the Mogul Empire. The competition ended in 1556 when Akbar, Babur's grandson, became emperor.

b. ***Akbar.*** Akbar proved to be the best of the Mogul rulers. Between 1556 and 1595, he defeated Hindu armies and extended his empire southward and westward. From his capital at Delhi, Akbar gave his subjects efficient government and justice under fairly administered laws. All his people had the right to appeal to him for final judgment in any lawsuit. As Akbar's fame spread, capable men from many parts of Central Asia came to serve him. These men helped Akbar create a strong, centralized government and a competent civil service (paid government officials in charge of taxation, construction, water supply, etc.).

Akbar allowed the practice of all religions. He tried to end the conflict between Hindus and Muslims. He gave Hindus positions in his government and married Hindu wives. Because he enjoyed religious discussions, Akbar invited Roman Catholic priests to Delhi to explain Christianity to him. Regarded as one of the world's outstanding rulers, Akbar encouraged learning and the growth of art, architecture, and literature.

Akbar died in 1605. By then the Mogul Empire was one of the richest and best-governed states in the world.

c. ***Shah Jahan.*** The Mogul Empire reached its peak of power under Akbar's grandson, Shah Jahan (ruled 1628–1658). During this golden age, many palaces and forts were built. Delhi was greatly beautified. When his beloved wife died, Shah Jahan

The Mogul Empire

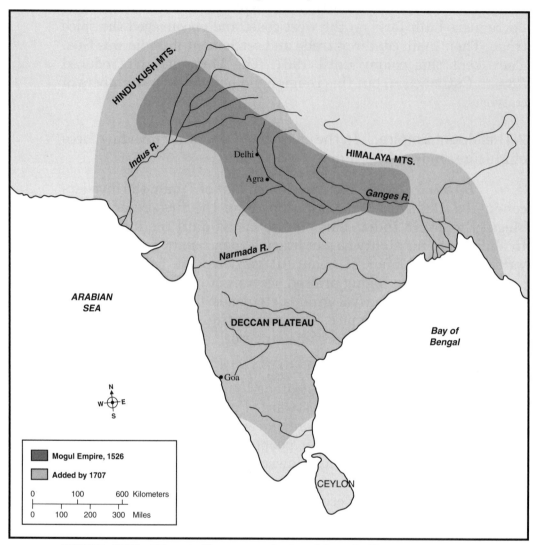

EXPLAIN: The influence of the Mogul Empire on India was greater in 1707 than in 1526.

---

had the Taj Mahal constructed as her tomb. It is considered to be one of the most beautiful buildings in the world. In this period, painting and literature also blossomed. Mogul writers produced histories, memoirs, and poetry.

d. *Aurangzeb.* Shah Jahan became ill in 1658 and his son, Aurangzeb, took over as emperor. Changes occurred quickly. Aurangzeb prohibited the practice of all religions except Islam. He dismissed Hindus from the government, raised their taxes, and destroyed their temples. Aurangzeb began a great war against the Hindu kingdoms in southern India. His aim was to unite all of India under Muslim rule. After years of bloodshed, he failed to subdue all Hindu kingdoms. Aurangzeb died in 1707, the last of the strong Mogul emperors.

After Aurangzeb, the Mogul Empire became weaker and weaker. Wars between rivals for the throne wiped out the Muslim nobility. Law and order broke down. Corruption in government and religious persecution caused rebellions. In 1739, Delhi was looted once again. Invading Persians conquered the city and carried off its royal treasures. The Moguls could not recover from these blows.

e. British arrival.   Earlier footholds set up by Westerners (such as the Portuguese) had also added to the problems faced by Mogul rulers. In 1608, the English had been given permission to trade in India. The French had won trading rights in 1664. Eventually, the British drove out the French. Shortly thereafter, the British took control of India away from the weakened Moguls.

f. Mogul legacy.   The Mogul conquest resulted in centuries of Muslim rule in northern and central India. Religious diversity was increased as some Hindus converted to Islam. By the 17th century, 20 percent of the population of India had become Muslims. The great majority of Indians remained Hindus.

The Taj Mahal at Agra, begun in 1632, was completed in 1649.

Differences in religious belief and the harsh treatment of Hindus by some Muslim rulers have caused the two religious groups to remain hostile to each other through the centuries (to modern times). Language differences also developed. The Muslim conquerors introduced Persian and Arabic to India. Persian became the official language of the Mogul Empire. Hindi, or Hindustani, was spoken by most Hindus. In time, elements of all three languages merged to create Urdu. Urdu is the official language of modern Pakistan.

CHART COMPLETION

Complete the following table.

The Mogul Empire

Emperors	Dates	Most important accomplishment

CRITICAL THINKING

PROVE or DISPROVE: Peace, prosperity, and religious toleration were enjoyed by people in India during the reigns of both Shah Jahan and Aurangzeb.

IMPERIAL CHINA

For nearly 1,000 years after the end of the T'ang Dynasty in A.D. 907, China continued to be a great civilization. Other countries in Asia, the Middle East, and Europe looked with envy at its riches. The Chinese influenced their neighbors with new ideas and inventions. Even foreign invaders adopted China's culture. Four major dynasties—the Sung, Mongol, Ming, and Ch'ing (Manchu)—ruled from 960 to 1912.

1. The Sung Dynasty. The Sung came to power as rulers of China in 960. Throughout the Sung period, tribes of fierce nomads continually threatened China. These warriors came from the deserts and plains beyond the Great Wall, which guarded China's northern border.

A Sung painting showing a shepherd boy
playing a flute while riding a water buffalo.

a. *Division of China.* Early in the Sung period, nomads
from Manchuria fought their way into northern China. The invaders
captured the Sung emperor and began their own dynasty, the Ch'in
Dynasty, in the north. Beijing (Peking) became their capital city. The
son of the captured emperor set up a new Sung capital at Hangzhou
(Hangchow) in southern China. By 1127, China was divided between
the Ch'in Empire in the north and the Sung Empire in the south.

b. *Cultural developments.* Despite this division, advances
in science, technology, and the arts continued under the Sung. An
inoculation against smallpox was developed. The *abacus*, the
world's first adding machine, was invented. Gunpowder came to
be used as a weapon in warfare. Printing with wooden, movable
type resulted in more books becoming available.

Landscape painting reached its highest stage during the Sung
period. Potters became even more skilled in making porcelain during this period. Unusual glazes gave the surfaces of the porcelain
a rich color.

c. *Economic developments.* Trade made the Sung Empire
highly prosperous. Large ships carried cargoes of silk and porcelain to Korea and Japan. The ships also sailed to Southeast Asia,
the Persian Gulf area, and Africa. Prosperity enabled the cities to
become centers of learning and art. Hangzhou, the imperial capital, was larger than most European cities of the same period.
Many of the streets in the capital were paved. An efficient garbage
collection system kept the city clean.

By the 12th century, Sung China may have been the most advanced society in the world. Not everyone, however, shared equally in its benefits. The peasant farmers of the countryside lived in poverty. The government collected taxes from the peasants and forced them to labor on public works. It did little for the peasants in return. The lives of Chinese peasants remained almost unchanged until modern times.

d. *Women in China.* Women in Sung China were considered to be inferior to men and had few rights. In public, wives had to walk ten steps behind their husbands. Among the wealthy, it was fashionable to bind the feet of little girls to keep their feet permanently small. The tight wrappings bent the toes toward the heel. This practice crippled many women. Some could not walk without support.

Military weakness and the corruption of government officials contributed to the downfall of the Sungs. The problems of the Sung rulers continued until the dynasty ended with the Mongol invasion of 1279.

2. The Mongols. In the 13th century, nomadic Mongol horsemen in Central Asia united under a great leader named Genghis Khan. He directed his fierce warriors on a wave of conquest that lasted more than 20 years. Korea, northern China, Central Asia, Persia, the Middle East, and part of Russia fell to the Mongols.

a. *Kublai Khan.* The conquests continued after Genghis Khan died in 1227. Kublai Khan, grandson of Genghis, became the Mongol emperor in 1260 and conquered the Sungs in 1279. He ruled the Mongol Empire, one of the largest ever to exist, until his death in 1294.

Kublai Khan constructed roads and canals and rebuilt the city of Beijing. He gave aid to orphans and old people and provided hospitals for the sick. He also purchased food supplies in times of plenty to store away for use when famine struck.

Kublai Khan's attempts to conquer Indochina, Burma (Myanmar), Java (Indonesia), and Japan failed. Two naval fleets sent against Japan were unsuccessful.

As part of the Mongol Empire, however, China benefited from opportunities for cultural exchange and trade with other Asian countries and with Europe. China's wealth and culture attracted Persian, Arab, and European visitors.

b. *Marco Polo.* During this period, Marco Polo of Venice in Italy came to China with his father and uncle, both merchants. Polo, just 17 years old, became a favorite of Kublai Khan and

Marco Polo about to start on his travels to East Asia in 1271.

remained in China for 17 years. He traveled throughout the empire. After Polo returned to Italy in 1295, he wrote a book about what he had seen. Many people refused to believe his descriptions of the size, wealth, and wonders of China. In time, other Europeans followed Polo's route to China. Marco Polo's book is regarded as a major step in promoting the exchange of goods and ideas between China and the West.

The Chinese never accepted the Mongol culture. They regarded the Mongols as inferior foreigners and barbarians. As Mongol rule weakened, Chinese opposition strengthened. In 1368, Chu Yuan-chang, a Buddhist monk who had become a rebel leader, drove the Mongols out of Beijing. A new Chinese dynasty, the Ming, replaced Mongol rule.

3. The Ming Dynasty. During the years of their rule—1368 to 1644—the Ming emperors strengthened China in many ways. For a time, they supported the silk industry and encouraged trade with other lands. Fleets of newly designed ships sailed to the Pacific and Indian oceans. Beijing, the northern capital, was enlarged and beautified, as was Nanking, the Ming's southern capital. Members of the royal family lived in the Forbidden City, a walled compound of royal palaces, which the Mings built in the center of Beijing.

a. *Foreign visitors.* Portuguese traders and Christian missionaries began to arrive in China in the 16th century. The Portuguese established a permanent settlement in Macao in

The Ming and Manchu Dynasties

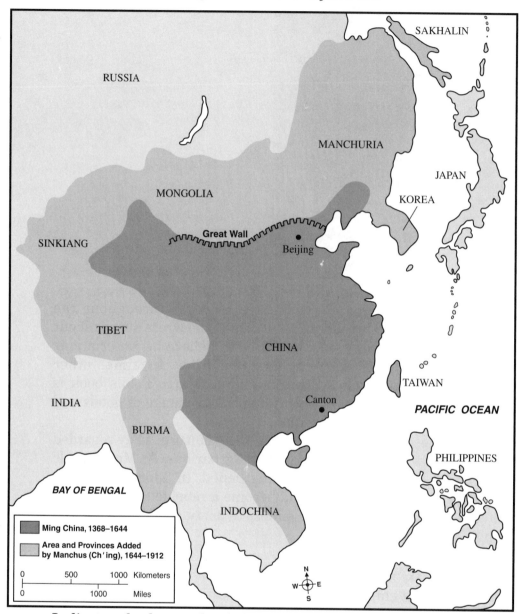

Indicate whether each of the following statements is *true* (**T**) or *false* (**F**).

1. Indochina was part of Ming China.

2. Taiwan was made part of China by the Manchu Dynasty.

3. Manchuria and Mongolia were part of Japan in 1368.

4. Canton and Beijing were Ming cities.

5. The Philippines were not conquered by either the Ming or Manchu dynasties.

southern China. Spanish, Dutch, and English traders followed. But changes were occurring. The Ming no longer welcomed foreigners to China. The government also tried to limit the movements of Chinese beyond their own borders. Confined by the government to Guangzhou (Canton), the European traders introduced to China some New World plants but had little impact on Chinese society and the Chinese economy until much later.

b. *The Manchus.* The policy of isolation, high taxes, and the cruel practices of the emperors created unrest. Peasant uprisings and bandit raids occurred more and more frequently, leading to a breakdown in law and order. Land attacks by Mongol warriors and Japanese sea raids kept the Ming on the defensive. In desperation, the government asked the Manchus for help. The Manchus were nomads from Manchuria. They had been raiding the border areas of China. The Manchus agreed to help the Ming and were allowed to pass through the Great Wall to enter China. With their aid, Ming forces drove the bandits out of Beijing. However, the Manchus then turned against the Ming. They captured the imperial capital in 1644 and established their own dynasty, called the Ch'ing.

4. The Ch'ing Dynasty. The Manchus tried to keep their own language and customs. They had doubts about the loyalty of the Chinese. The invaders made all Chinese men wear their hair in a braid. This single braid made them look different from the Manchus and showed that they submitted to Manchu rule.

The first Manchu emperors were able rulers who followed traditional Chinese forms of government. Until the end of the 18th century, China enjoyed peace and prosperity. Under Ch'ien-lung (ruled 1735–1796), the Ch'ing Empire expanded in size. It included Korea, Mongolia, Manchuria, Tibet, and parts of Indochina. The population of China increased rapidly. Soon it became difficult for farmers to grow enough food for everyone.

The Manchus tried to continue the policy of isolating China from Europe and America. But the Westerners kept coming and asking for trading rights. The Russians came overland. Others—especially the Japanese, Americans, British, French, and Germans—came by sea. (Americans arrived in China in 1784.) Despite the restrictions placed on them by hostile Manchu officials, foreign merchants filled their ships with cargoes of Chinese tea, silk, and porcelain. The Ch'ing, however, did not have the modern weapons they needed to prevent foreigners from taking

A Woman of Power

Tz'u-hsi, the Dowager Empress.

Tz'u-hsi (1835–1908) was one of the most powerful women in Chinese history. For almost 50 years she ruled the Manchu Dynasty and the Chinese Empire with an iron will. To the West, she was known as the "Dowager Empress."

Although Tz'u-hsi had great power and influence, she lacked vision and did not use her power well. After the Taiping Rebellion of 1864 failed, China enjoyed a period of peace. With wise leadership, China might have become a powerful nation in the world. Unfortunately, Tz'u-hsi's greed gave rise to government corruption. For example, she removed funds from naval construction projects in order to build an imperial pleasure garden. This helped to cause China's military defeat by Japan in 1895. In 1898, Tz'u-hsi blocked an attempt to modernize and reform the government.

Tz'u-hsi's greatest mistake in judgment was to support the Boxer Rebellion of 1900. She encouraged the Boxer leaders and used her influence to support the rebels with Manchu troops. The results were disastrous for China. Instead of being driven out, the Western powers crushed the Boxers and forced the Manchu government to pay large amounts of money for damages.

In 1902, Tz'u-hsi began to reform the government, but she died before any real changes occurred.

EXPLAIN: Tz'u-hsi contributed nothing to the welfare of China.

what they wanted. In the 19th century, weak Manchu emperors gave up much Chinese territory to Western nations. Attempts to resist the advance of foreigners led to wars with European nations and Japan. China lost all of these conflicts.

The inability of the Manchus to control the Westerners and Japan and maintain Chinese military strength created unrest. A number of protest groups formed in the 1800's. In 1911, a revolution began. It ended the Ch'ing Dynasty, and China became a republic in 1912.

CRITICAL THINKING

PROVE or DISPROVE each of the following statements:

1. Chinese culture declined under the Sung Dynasty.

2. Mongol rule benefited China.

3. The Ming rulers kept foreign merchants and nomads out of China.

4. Under the Manchus, China's relations with Japan and the Western nations strengthened.

THE RISE OF JAPAN

Japan is a group of islands in the northern Pacific, just east of the Asian mainland. Its history and culture have been strongly influenced by the Chinese. Much of what is known about early Japan comes from Chinese sources. Yet because a body of water separates Japan from the Asian mainland, the island nation developed a unique culture.

Japan has many good harbors on its long, irregular coastline. Many Japanese have turned to fishing and overseas trade. As a result, Japan became a major maritime nation.

Mountains restrict the amount of farmland and limit the number of Japanese who can farm for a living. Japan has always been poor in mineral resources. In modern times, the country has depended on imports of food and raw materials.

1. Development.   People have lived in Japan for thousands of years. The earliest natives of Japan may have been prehistoric immigrants from Korea and other parts of northeast Asia. Some early immigrants to Japan may have come from Malaysia and southern China. The earliest written reference to Japan is in a Chinese history from the 1st century A.D. Korean histories also mention warring clans in Japan. In the 300's, one of these clans, the Yamato, conquered most of the others. Yamato rulers became known as emperors. The present-day emperor of Japan traces his family history back to the Yamato emperors.

Most early Japanese followed the religion called Shinto, "the way of the gods." Shinto honored spirits thought to be found in nature—in forests or mountains, for example. Shintoism was later

Japan

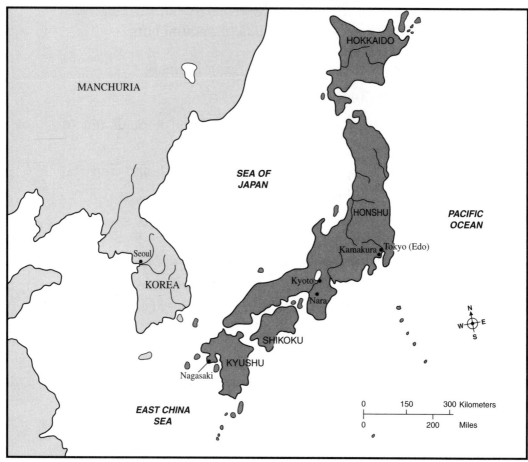

1. Japan has four main islands. Name *two* of these islands.

2. The northernmost city shown on the map is (*a*) Tokyo (*b*) Nara (*c*) Nagasaki (*d*) Seoul.

3. The southernmost city shown on the map is (*a*) Tokyo (*b*) Nara (*c*) Nagasaki (*d*) Seoul.

4. A city in Korea is (*a*) Tokyo (*b*) Nara (*c*) Nagasaki (*d*) Seoul.

---

influenced by Buddhist and Confucian ideas, one idea being the honoring of the spirits of one's ancestors.

In the 400's, Korean travelers and scholars introduced Chinese writing to Japan. The Japanese began to adopt many Chinese ways of doing things. Temple architecture, clothing styles, and methods of preparing food were all influenced by Chinese ideas. Japanese justice was based on Chinese law codes.

The Great Buddha of Kamakura. Cast in bronze in 1252, it is 50 feet in height.

In the mid–500's, Koreans brought the Buddhist religion to Japan. The Buddhist idea of gaining happiness and peace through discipline and deep thought appealed to the Japanese. Many Japanese followed both the Shinto and Buddhist religions.

In 710 at Nara, the Yamatos created a city that resembled the Chinese imperial court. About 180 years later, the capital moved to the present-day city of Kyoto, where it remained until 1868.

The ruling families in Kyoto turned away from Chinese ways and encouraged the development of a distinctive Japanese culture. The women of the imperial court wrote poetry and stories in the Japanese language. One of the best and most famous of the stories is the novel *Tale of Genji* written by Murasaki Shikibu in the early 1000's.

2. The Rise of the Shoguns.   As time passed, the emperors lost authority. Powerful noble families carried out the functions of the government in the name of the emperor. Sometimes the noble families, or clans, fought one another to gain control of the government.

   a. *First shogun*. In 1185, the Minamoto clan defeated its rivals and became the strongest family. Seven years later, the emperor named the leader of the family, Minamoto Yoritomo, the first *shogun*.

   The shogun was the chief military general of the country. He also controlled the country's financial affairs, courts, and government appointments. Most power belonged to the shogun, but he acted as if it came from the emperor. Yoritomo ruled from his palace at Kamakura. Soon Kamakura became more important than the capital of Kyoto. The Kamakura Shogunate lasted from 1192 to 1333.

b. *Feudalism.*   Outside of the capital, large landholders controlled local affairs. These men were members of the *samurai*, or warrior, class. They taxed the peasants who worked the land. The larger, more powerful landholders were called *daimyos*. Their private armies of samurai kept order. In return for pledges (promises) of loyalty and service, samurai received land from a daimyo or the shogun. This exchange of promises for land was like the feudal system that existed in Europe from around 800 to 1400. Feudalism in Japan lasted from about 1000 to 1867.

The samurai followed a strict code of conduct called *Bushido*—the way of the warrior. Above all they prized courage in battle, loyalty to their leaders, and personal dignity. If they dishonored themselves, they committed suicide by means of *seppuku*, or hara-kiri, a ritual to regain one's honor.

c. *Two crises.*   During the Kamakura Shogunate, the Japanese faced two major crises. The Mongol emperor of China, Kublai Khan, decided to invade Japan. In 1274, he sent an army through Korea to invade northern Japan, but the Japanese turned them back. Then, in 1281, the Chinese tried once more. Again they failed when a great storm, a *typhoon*, destroyed many of their ships. The Mongols withdrew. The Japanese called the typhoon "Kamikaze," the "Divine Wind." They felt that they had special protection from the gods.

3. Achievements of the Shoguns.   In the 1330's, the Ashikaga family took control of the government. It ruled until 1568. The Ashikagas did not have a firm hold on the shogunate. Civil war broke out among the noble families. Daimyos became even more important in controlling local areas.

a. *Chinese influences.*   In the midst of the unrest, many developments occurred that continued to influence the culture of Japan. Direct trade with China opened up. Monks introduced a different version of Buddhism called Zen. Zen Buddhists believed that they could gain enlightenment through quiet thought. They practiced great self-control and discipline to rid themselves of emotions and desires. The samurai followed Zen ways to give themselves courage and strength in battle.

Contact with China and Zen ideas promoted new styles of painting and architecture. The arts of arranging flowers and designing gardens also flourished under the Ashikagas. Elaborate

A temple near Kyoto.

tea-serving ceremonies became popular among the nobles and the samurai. *No* plays began to be produced in the 1300's. These dance dramas usually portrayed a religious idea.

   b. *Continual fighting.*   Civil war broke out among powerful daimyos in the late 1400's. The Ashikagas could not stop the fighting. Finally in 1568, one daimyo, Oda Nobunaga, captured Kyoto. He gained the loyalty of a great many nobles in central Japan. But before he could take full control, he was assassinated in 1582.

   Nobunaga's chief general, Toyotomi Hideyoshi, became the ruler. He won the support of the most important daimyos. Then he sent armies to Korea and attempted to invade China. Hideyoshi wanted to create an empire in East Asia. His wish was not fulfilled. After he died in 1598, the Japanese forces returned home from Korea.

   c. *Western influences.*   During the time of the civil war, Europeans first came to Japan. Before the Portuguese arrived in 1542, the Japanese had not had any contact with the West. From the Portuguese, the Japanese learned about muskets. Such weapons changed the way the samurai fought. They now used guns as well as swords.

   Along with the traders came Roman Catholic missionaries. Led by Francis Xavier, who arrived in 1549, Jesuits converted many Japanese to Christianity. Franciscans, who arrived in 1593, expanded the missionary work. Within 30 years, the number of Japanese Christians reached about 250,000 to 300,000.

d. *The Tokugawas.* In 1600, Tokugawa Ieyasu won a great battle over rival daimyos. He then became the ruler of Japan. The emperor appointed him shogun in 1603. The Tokugawa family governed until 1868 from Edo (present-day Tokyo).

The Tokugawas brought peace to Japan. They encouraged the growth of industry and trade. However, in the early 1600's, these shoguns became suspicious of the influence of Christians and European traders. In 1612, the shogun began to persecute Christians in Japan. Missionaries were driven out or killed. Japanese converts were executed by the thousands.

The Tokugawas also restricted the activities of foreign traders. By 1641, all but one port was closed to outsiders. Only ten Chinese ships and one Dutch ship could land each year at the port of Nagasaki. Any Japanese who was away from the country at the time could not return. Japan isolated itself from the outside world for more than 200 years.

Although Japan prospered under the Tokugawa Shogunate, a desire for change developed. Books came in from Europe on the one Dutch trading ship that arrived each year. From these books, samurai scholars learned about Western ideas. They were particularly interested in geography, medicine, and military tactics.

In the 19th century, new ideas and financial problems weakened the Tokugawa shoguns. They could not resist a new effort by Western nations to trade with Japan.

4. The Meiji Restoration. Starting in the late 1700's, Russian, British, French, and American officials tried unsuccessfully to establish relations with Japan.

a. *Commodore Perry.* In 1853, Commodore Matthew Perry of the United States sailed with four ships into Tokyo Bay. Perry presented Japanese officials with a letter from President Millard Fillmore asking for trading privileges. Perry left and the following year returned with more ships. Without modern weapons, the shogun could not resist. He signed an agreement opening Japan to trade with the Western world.

Increased contacts with the West made the Japanese aware of the wealth and military power of Europe and the United States. Japan appeared backward by comparison. As a result, discontent with Tokugawa rule increased.

b. *Meiji Restoration.* In 1867, some of the powerful nobles forced the shogun to resign. The Emperor Meiji took power

Commodore Matthew Perry meeting with the Imperial
Commissioners at Yokohama in 1854.

the following year, thus restoring the position of emperor as the
actual head of government. The rule of the shoguns had ended.
During the Meiji reign (1868–1912), Japan developed into a
strong, modern nation.

Rapid and dramatic changes transformed almost every aspect
of life in Japan. Businesses imported new machinery to manufacture textiles and other goods. New systems of communication
were established. A modern school system gave more Japanese
children an opportunity to obtain an education. A national army
and navy were created. No other nation achieved the goal of mod-
ernization in so short a time.

Japan's first constitution went into effect in 1889. It created a
Diet, or parliament, and recognized the emperor as a god.
Although the emperor had certain powers, a small group of officials exercised the real authority. They set up a strong central government. But they did permit some democratic features, such as
political parties.

To unify Japan and increase national loyalty, the leaders
revived the ancient code of Bushido, the "path of the warrior." It
stressed honor, loyalty, fearlessness, and absolute obedience to the
emperor.

By the beginning of the 20th century, Japan had become a modern industrial and military power. Government leaders felt ready
to compete with Western nations for colonies in Asia.

5. Japanese Culture. Throughout their history, the Japanese
have demonstrated their ability to learn from other peoples and

adapt elements of other cultures. From the 6th to the 9th century, the Japanese modified Chinese culture to shape their own language, art, literature, and government. In the 19th century, the transformation of Japan from a feudal country into a modern, industrialized nation was due to their ability to learn from the technologically advanced West. By drawing upon the political institutions of the United States, Japan again transformed itself. In the 20th century, the militarism and dictatorship of the World War II era was abandoned in order to build a democratic society.

While pursuing these changes the Japanese did not merely imitate others. They developed their own unique civilization.

MATCHING EXERCISE

Match each person in Column A with his or her description in Column B.

Column A	*Column B*
1. Murasaki Shikibu	*a.* a Japanese ruler who wanted to create an empire in East Asia
2. Minamoto Yoritomo	
3. Toyotomi Hideyoshi	*b.* the first shogun of Japan
4. Francis Xavier	*c.* shogun appointed in 1603 who ruled from Edo
5. Tokugawa Ieyasu	
6. Matthew Perry	*d.* the author of *Tale of Genji*
	e. the U.S. commodore who persuaded Japan to trade with the West
	f. a Jesuit who arrived in Japan in 1549

IDENTIFICATIONS

Define or identify each of the following:

a. Ashikagas

b. Shintoism

c. Oda Nobunaga

d. daimyo

e. Toyotomi Hideyoshi

f. Bushido

g. Tokugawa Ieyasu

h. Zen Buddhism

THE KINGDOM OF KOREA

Korea is another East Asian nation with a distinctive and rich culture. For much of its long history, Korea has been dominated by stronger powers. Most often, China or Japan controlled Korea politically and influenced its culture. But the Koreans have managed to keep their own identity.

1. The Early Years.　The first recorded effort at political organization in Korea was made in 194 B.C. A military leader named Wiman set up a state that came to be known as Wiman Choson. It lasted for approximately 80 years, until armies from China destroyed it. The northern part of Korea then became part of the Chinese Empire.

From about A.D. 1 to 900, Korea was divided into three kingdoms. The Chinese culture strongly influenced the kingdom in the northern part of the country. Buddhism, Confucianism, and the Chinese written language were brought to Korea during this period. Japanese culture had a greater effect on the two kingdoms in the south, which were closer to Japan.

From the 10th through the 14th century, a dynasty of Buddhist rulers called the Koryo united all of Korea. (The name Korea comes from the word Koryo.) Although these kings ruled independently, they paid tribute to the Mongol Empire. During the

A 12th-century ceramic jar made in Korea.

Koryo period, in 1234, the Koreans invented movable metal type, using Chinese symbols to print books.

The Koryo period ended in 1392. In that year, the Yi Dynasty established its rule over Korea. The Yi, who followed the teachings of Confucius, built their imperial capital at Seoul. This city served as the center of political rule for most of Korea's history.

A civil service examination system was used to select government officials from a group of scholars trained in Confucian teachings. In this and in other ways, the Koreans continued to draw heavily on Chinese culture. But they did create their own alphabet in the 1440's.

China also gave Korea military aid. With this help, Koreans resisted Japanese forces that invaded their country from 1592 to 1598. During this war, a Korean hero, Admiral Yi Sunshin, built the world's first iron-sided ship. With it, he destroyed much of the Japanese fleet, which was made of wood.

2. The Manchu Influence. The war with the Japanese exhausted the Koreans. As a result, new invaders from Manchuria easily conquered the whole country in the 1630's. (The Manchus then went on to seize control of China.) While the Yi rulers remained on the throne in Korea, they were subject to the Manchu government.

a. *Isolationism.* Korea, following China's lead, isolated itself from the rest of the world. European sailors who became shipwrecked in Korea were usually held prisoner. In 1669, eight sailors escaped from Seoul after 13 years of captivity. When one of the sailors, Hendrick Hamel, returned to Holland, he wrote a book about his experience. This book gave the Western world its first description of Korea.

After 1860, Western nations and Japan tried to force the Koreans to open their ports to trade. The Koreans resisted all such attempts. At the same time, the rivalry between China and Japan over Korea grew. Both wanted control of rich resources in Korea, such as minerals and timber.

b. *End of isolationism.* In 1876, the Korean government finally gave in to Japanese pressure. A trade agreement was signed, opening up several Korean ports to trade. Soon, other nations (such as the United States, Great Britain, and Russia) signed treaties with Korea. Russia, a neighbor of Korea, was, like Japan, especially interested in Korea's resources.

The Manchu government in China resented the growing Japanese influence in Korea. The Manchus attempted to take firmer control of Yi affairs. This conflict between China and Japan led to a brief war in 1894 (the Sino-Japanese War), in which the Chinese were defeated. At the end of the war in 1895, China recognized Korea's independence. Japan had thus ended the Manchu influence in Korea.

3. Japanese Rule.   After the defeat of China, the Japanese began to force a number of reforms on the Yi government. The Russians began to aid the Koreans against the Japanese. Russia wanted control of Korea. Japan wanted Russia out of Korea. The two powers went to war in 1904 (the Russo-Japanese War). To everyone's surprise, the Japanese defeated the Russians on land and sea. In 1910, Japan annexed Korea and ended the Yi Dynasty. Korea became the largest possession in the Japanese Empire.

Japanese rule was harsh. A governor-general directly responsible to the Japanese emperor administered Korea. Freedom of speech and the press and other rights were denied to the Koreans. Schools had to teach the Japanese culture and language and ignore the heritage of Korea. The Japanese used their new colony as a place to raise rice to feed the people of Japan. Japanese businesses were encouraged, while Koreans were discouraged from engaging in such business. The Japanese also established military bases in Korea to aid further conquests in Asia.

In some ways, the Koreans benefited from Japanese rule. The communication and transportation systems were greatly improved. Modern business techniques used by the Japanese helped the economic development of Korea. The advanced educational system that the Japanese established trained many of Korea's leaders.

Korea did not become an independent nation again until 1945, after the defeat of the Japanese Empire in World War II. Even today, Korea continues to be influenced by stronger nations, especially China, Japan, and the United States.

SENTENCE COMPLETION

From the list below, choose the term or terms that best complete each of the sentences that follow.

iron-sided ship   alphabet   movable metal type
Buddhism   Wiman Choson   Confucianism

1. In 194 B.C., a military leader set up a state called —.
2. The Koreans learned about — and — from China.
3. In 1234, the Koreans invented —.
4. In 1440's, the Koreans created their own —.
5. Admiral Yi Sunshin built the first —.

TIMELINE EXERCISE

Use numbers 1–4 from the timeline to indicate when each of the events below occurred.

TIMELINE: KOREA

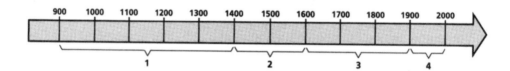

a. Koryo Dynasty (918–1392)
b. Manchu influence began (1630's)
c. War with Japan (1592–1598)
d. Yi Dynasty began (1392)
e. Japanese rule began (1910)

SOUTHEAST ASIA

South of China is the area we now call Southeast Asia. It contains many countries, including Burma (now Myanmar), Laos, Thailand, Cambodia, Vietnam, Indonesia, the Philippines, East Timor, Brunei, and Malaysia. Laos, Cambodia, and Vietnam are known together as Indochina. The whole of Southeast Asia has been greatly influenced by the Chinese and Indian civilizations, particularly by Buddhism.

A warm, wet climate, plentiful rainfall, and the presence of major rivers, especially the Irrawaddy in Myanmar and the Mekong in Vietnam and Laos, provide ample irrigation for the growing of rice and other grains. Tropical rain forests give way to flooded farmlands in much of the region. Bounded on the east by the South China Sea and on the west by the Indian Ocean, the region supports commercial fishing and shipping in these coastal areas. Economic development, especially heavy industry, has been limited by sparse mineral resources.

1. Burma (Myanmar), Siam (Thailand), and Malaya (Malaysia).
Myanmar, Thailand, and Malaysia are neighboring states.

a. *Burma.* Early Burma consisted of a number of small kingdoms. Their culture borrowed many ideas from India, especially the Buddhist religion. Between 1044 and 1287, Burma was united under one ruler. Then Mongols invaded and destroyed the power of the central government. Except for brief periods, Burma remained disunited for 500 years.

In the 1800's, the British took control of the country and made it a part of India. The Japanese ruled Burma from 1941 to 1945, during World War II. After the war, it was returned to the British. Burma declared its independence from Britain in 1948. In 1989, the country's name was changed to Myanmar.

b. *Siam.* People have been living in Thailand (called Siam from 1782 to 1939) for more than 5,000 years. For almost that long, they have been growing rice. Some scholars think that the Thai were the first to grow rice. Buddhism is the major religion in Thailand. About 1238, the Thai people united to form a nation. Since that time, they have been an independent kingdom. They have fought a number of wars to keep out invaders.

In the 1800's, the British and French tried to control Thai affairs. But the Thais prevented them from getting more than trading rights.

c. *Malaya.* Malaya, at the southern tip of the Indochinese Peninsula, contained several small states. Traders traveling between China and India stopped along the Malay coast. In the 1300's, Arab traders came. Gradually, Islam replaced Buddhism and Hinduism as the main religion of the people. The Portuguese arrived in 1509. They were followed by the Dutch and the British.

Entrance to the Buddhist temple of Royal Wat in Bangkok, Thailand.

The British eventually controlled the government of Malaya. In the 19th century, the Chinese and the British developed the tin and rubber industries of the area. Malaya became independent of Britain in 1957. The union of Malaya and the port city of Singapore created Malaysia in 1963. To end political tensions between the Malays and the Chinese majority in Singapore, however, Singapore broke away from Malaysia in 1965.

2. Cambodia. The Khmer settled in Cambodia in ancient times. In the 1st century A.D., they organized themselves into a state called Funan, located in southern Cambodia. By the early part of the 10th century, a powerful Khmer Empire had developed. Its capital, at Angkor, contained large, ornate stone temples and palaces built over several centuries. A large temple complex is Angkor Wat. The Khmer dedicated Angkor Wat to the Hindu god Vishnu.

Hinduism, imported from India, was the main religion of the Khmer. Many of the Khmer also practiced Buddhism. Most of the other peoples of Southeast Asia followed their ancient tribal religions. Such religions involved the worship of ancestors and spirits.

By 1200, the Khmer Empire reached the height of its power. It controlled much of what are now Vietnam, Thailand, Laos, and Myanmar. The Khmer combined military power with a high degree of technology. They invented systems to get water to fields in dry areas. As a result, they were able to grow enough rice to feed

The ancient Khmer temple of Angkor Wat in Cambodia.

the people in their empire. For many reasons, including attacks from Thailand, the empire began to weaken after the 1200's. By the end of the 15th century, the Thais had succeeded in destroying the Khmer Empire. From then until the 1800's, the Thais and the Vietnamese dominated Cambodia.

In 1863, the French conquered Cambodia and controlled it until 1953. The French were briefly replaced by the Japanese during World War II (1940–1945). Then in the 1970's and 1980's, rebel forces backed by China and Vietnam waged war in Cambodia to replace its government. Vietnamese troops invaded the country in 1983 and controlled it until 1989. A new Cambodian government was set up in 1993.

3. Laos. The story of the Lao people began in the 9th century A.D. During that era, their ancestors moved into northern Laos from southwestern China. In the 14th century, a ruler named Fa Ngum established a Lao kingdom called Lan Xang, or "Land of a Million Elephants." Lan Xang included much of Thailand and all of Laos. Fa Ngum made Buddhism the state religion. Lan Xang lasted for more than 350 years despite its conflicts with the Vietnamese to the east and the Burmese and Thais to the west.

The Laotians played a part in destroying the mighty Khmer Empire in the 15th century. They attacked and occupied some lands on the northeastern border of the empire. This contributed to the eventual victory of the Thais and the end of the golden age of the Khmers.

In the early 18th century, Laos split into three kingdoms. They were Luang Prabang in the north, Vientiane on the Mekong River, and Champassak in the south.

The kings of Thailand gained power over most of Laos in the late 1700's. The three kingdoms had to pay tribute to Thailand. In the late 1800's, the French took control of Indochina. Laos became part of the French Empire. In more recent times, the Laotians have been dominated by Vietnam.

4. Vietnam. The Vietnamese are an ancient people with a long history.

    a. *Chinese influence.* The Vietnamese were conquered by the Han dynasty of China around 111 B.C. and remained part of the Chinese Empire for the next thousand years. During that time, the Vietnamese did, however, resist being completely absorbed by the Chinese.

The Vietnamese have been influenced by Chinese culture to a greater extent than almost any other people in Asia. Despite this, the Vietnamese have always regarded China and the Chinese living in Vietnam as a threat to the survival of Vietnam.

    b. *Independence.* Between the 10th and 15th centuries, the Vietnamese broke away from the direct control of China. But they continued to pay tribute to its emperors. In 1288, Vietnam defeated the armies of Kublai Khan when the Mongol ruler attempted to regain control of this portion of Southeast Asia.

In the late 15th century, the Vietnamese began to conquer the lands to their south. These lands were inhabited by the Chams, who had absorbed many aspects of India's culture, including Hinduism and Buddhism. By the 18th century, the Vietnamese had expanded into the Mekong River Delta. The people of this region were also strongly influenced by Indian culture.

    c. *Foreign occupation and revolt.* In the late 1800's, the Vietnamese, like the Cambodians and Laotians, became part of the French Empire. Although the Vietnamese emperor was permitted to maintain his court in the region called Annam, the French governed Vietnam directly. The French also took control of the mineral resources and rubber plantations of the area. During this colonial period, which ended in 1954, the French language and culture and the Roman Catholic religion became popular among the wealthier Vietnamese. The majority of the people remained Buddhist.

From 1940 to 1945, Vietnam was invaded and occupied by Japanese military forces. Following Japan's defeat in World War

II, French rule resumed. Vietnamese rebels defeated the French in 1954. Vietnam was divided into North Vietnam, a Communist state, and South Vietnam, a non-Communist state. Efforts to unite the country caused a bloody civil war in which U.S. forces took part from 1964 to 1973. Vietnam was united under a Communist government in 1975.

5. Indonesia. Located southeast of the Asian mainland, Indonesia is an *archipelago,* or group of islands. Six thousand of its 13,500 islands are inhabited by a mixture of more than 300 ethnic groups. Linguistically and culturally, most Indonesians are part of a larger Indo-Malaysian world, which includes present-day Malaysia, Brunei, the Philippines, and parts of mainland Asia.

The early Indonesians had an agricultural economy based on the growing of cereal crops in a warm, wet climate. Pottery and stone tools were introduced between 2500 and 500 B.C. As a result of increasing interaction with South and East Asia, the Indonesians began to use metals and domesticated farm animals from 500 B.C. to A.D. 500.

Approximately 2,000 years ago, Hindu and Buddhist peoples reached Indonesia from India. Their religions became strongly established on Sumatra and Java, two of the larger islands. In the early centuries A.D., Indian language and culture, along with the Hindu and Buddhist religions, were eagerly accepted by Indonesian rulers and their nobles. Among the ordinary people, however, Hindu concepts such as caste and the inferior status of women were not so easily absorbed. Indianized empires arose from the 7th to the 14th century. The kingdom of Srivijaya ruled large areas of Sumatra, western Java, and much of the Malay Peninsula. It controlled the trade of the region and was a formidable sea power until the 13th century. Its port of Palembang served Chinese and Indian traders and became wealthy. A stronghold of Buddhism, Srivijaya attracted pilgrims and scholars from other parts of Asia.

From the 10th to the 15th century, powerful Hindu states arose in eastern Java. Their wealth came from the sale of spices to Indian and Southeast Asian merchants. The spices were transported to Mediterranean markets by way of the Indian Ocean. The ruler of one of these states, Prince Vijaya, forced Mongol invaders to withdraw from Java in the 13th century. The new dynasty he established became an empire that spread throughout much of the territory of modern Indonesia.

Muslim traders brought Islam to Indonesia in the 15th century. By the 16th century, Islam had become the dominant religion of the islands.

Following Europe's Commercial Revolution, the Portuguese became the main trading power in Indonesia. In the 17th century, they were replaced by the Dutch, who took control of Java by 1750. The Dutch continued to extend their authority over the other islands until the 20th century. Under Dutch rule, Indonesia became united under one government for the first time.

From 1942 to 1945, Indonesia was occupied by Japanese forces. After World War II, Indonesian nationalists fought against a continuation of Dutch rule. In December 1949, the country gained its independence.

6. The Philippines. Also an archipelago, these islands were first populated approximately 30,000 years ago, mainly by Malay peoples. Later migrations took place in repeated movements over several thousand years before and after the first century A.D. The economy of the early Filipinos was agricultural, depending heavily on rice farming. Society was organized into extended family groups headed by chiefs and nobles.

Islam was brought to the Philippines by Indonesian traders, and it spread through the islands in the 16th century. Muslim immigrants founded territorial states ruled by sultans or rajahs.

The Spanish began to colonize the islands in the 16th century, founding Manila, the capital, in 1571. They named the islands for King Philip II of Spain.

In 1898, following the Spanish-American War, the Philippines were ceded by Spain to the United States. U.S. troops repressed a brutal rebellion against American authority from 1899 to 1905. Although three decades later the United States promised independence to the Philippines, World War II intervened. Japanese forces invaded and occupied the islands in 1941. Following World War II, in 1946, the Philippines finally became an independent republic.

 MATCHING EXERCISE

Match each term in Column A with its definition in Column B.

Column A	Column B
1. Indochina	*a.* the name of a people and an empire
2. Siam	*b.* a Lao kingdom known as the "Land of a Million Elephants"
3. Khmer	
4. Angkor Wat	*c.* the peninsula south of China
5. Lan Xang	*d.* a large temple complex dedicated to Vishnu
	e. an early name for Thailand

TRUE OR FALSE

Decide which statements are true and which are false. In each false statement, change the underlined word to make the statement true.

1. Burma was a <u>united</u> country from 1044 to 1287.

2. The Thai have been growing <u>rice</u> for 5,000 years.

3. The main religion of the Khmer was <u>Buddhism</u>.

4. Champassak was a <u>Laotian</u> kingdom in the 1600's.

5. The French influence in Indochina <u>gained</u> strength in the late 1800's.

6. The <u>Vietnamese</u> defeated Kublai Khan in 1288.

7. Vietnam was <u>never</u> influenced by outside cultures.

8. Indochina is <u>east</u> of China.

Chapter Review

MULTIPLE-CHOICE

Choose the item that best completes each sentence.

1. Until the 1300's, the Deccan rulers were (*a*) Hindu (*b*) Buddhist (*c*) Christian (*d*) Muslim.

2. Timur captured Delhi in (*a*) 700 (*b*) 1200 (*c*) 1398 (*d*) 1500.

3. The correct order in which these Mogul emperors ruled is (*a*) Akbar, Shah Jahan, Babur (*b*) Babur, Akbar, Shah Jahan (*c*) Shah Jahan, Akbar, Babur (*d*) Babur, Shah Jahan, Akbar.

4. Shah Jahan promoted the (*a*) creation of beautiful buildings, literature, and art (*b*) destruction of palaces and forts (*c*) appointment of outsiders as government officials (*d*) growth of industry.

5. Under the Sung Dynasty, foreign trade was (*a*) carried on by Mongols (*b*) discouraged (*c*) encouraged (*d*) permitted only with Japan.

6. The Sung emperors ruled China from (a) Beijing (b) Korea (c) Hangzhou (d) Delhi.

7. Kublai Khan ruled all of China from (a) 1279 to 1294 (b) 1227 to 1234 (c) 1260 to 1294 (d) 1337 to 1425.

8. Marco Polo wrote about China under the (a) Sung Dynasty (b) Shogunate (c) Ming Dynasty (d) Mongol Dynasty.

9. Under Ming rulers, foreigners were (a) welcomed into the Forbidden City (b) discouraged from coming to China (c) kept in Macao (d) sent to Japan.

10. The last imperial dynasty to rule China was the (a) Sung (b) Ming (c) Ch'ing (d) Ashikaga.

11. The Manchus expanded their empire to include (a) Mongolia, Manchuria, and Tibet (b) Burma, Thailand, and Malaya (c) Japan, the Philippines, and India (d) Java, Laos, and Cambodia.

12. From the Yamato Clan came Japan's first (a) daimyos (b) emperors (c) samurai (d) shoguns.

13. The first shogun of Japan was (a) Minamoto Yoritomo (b) Murasaki Shikibu (c) Tokugawa Ieyasu (d) Murasaki Ashikaga.

14. Japan became a modern nation under the (a) Tokugawas (b) Ashikagas (c) Meijis (d) Kamakuras.

15. From A.D. 1 to 900, Korea was strongly influenced by the culture of (a) China and Japan (b) Russia (c) India (d) Laos.

16. The Yi Dynasty in Korea followed the (a) Wiman (b) Mongol (c) Koryo (d) Ming.

17. Japanese rule in Korea after 1910 (a) encouraged Korean businesses (b) denied freedom of press and speech to Koreans (c) destroyed the Korean transportation system (d) strengthened Korean military power.

18. The Khmer were ancestors of the (a) Laotians (b) Vietnamese (c) Cambodians (d) Thais.

19. In the late 1700's, the three kingdoms of Laos paid tribute to (a) France (b) Thailand (c) China (d) Japan.

20. Over the years, the Vietnamese have been influenced by the cultures of (a) China, India, and France (b) Japan, India, and France (c) Korea, China, and Japan (d) Myanmar, Laos, and Cambodia.

CHRONOLOGY

Find the dates of each of the following events or periods. Then number the events and periods from 1 to 5 in chronological order.

    a. Akbar ruled India.
    b. Marco Polo lived in China.
    c. Khmer Empire ruled Cambodia.
    d. Minamoto Yoritomo appointed first shogun of Japan.
    e. Koreans invented movable type.

WRITING EXERCISE

Reread "4. The Meiji Restoration," on pages 258–259. Then write a paragraph describing how Japan changed under Meiji rule.

MAP EXERCISE

Use the information from the map "Asia Today," on page 242, to complete each of the following sentences:

1. The — lie between India and Tibet.

2. Three countries that border the Sea of Japan are —, —, and —.

3. Three great rivers of China are the —, —, and —.

4. The Philippines are located in the — Ocean.

5. Two countries watered by the Mekong River are — and —.

6. Vietnam is bordered by three countries. They are —, —, and —.

DOCUMENT-BASED QUESTION

This question is based on the accompanying documents (1–4). It will improve your ability to work with historical documents.

Historical Context:

Beginning in the 8th century, settled Asian societies were significantly transformed by encounters with outsiders. These outsiders

Connections: Dynasty

Until modern times, the Chinese were ruled by dynasties, or families of rulers. The Chou, Ch'in, and Han dynasties ruled in ancient times. The Han dynasty gave China its first really strong government. During the Middle Ages, the T'ang, Sung, and Ming dynasties held power. Invaders who took control of China, such as the Mongols (1279–1368) and the Manchus (1644–1912), also established dynasties.

Some dynasties ruled better than others. From time to time, the Chinese grew dissatisfied and rebelled against their rulers, thus replacing one dynasty with another.

Other societies were also ruled by dynasties, or powerful families. The pharaohs of Egypt belonged to dynasties. Over a period of more than 2,500 years, beginning with Menes (about 2900 B.C.) and continuing to about 300 B.C., there were 30 Egyptian dynasties.

Powerful families also ruled the Roman Empire, although they were not called dynasties. For example, following the death of Julius Caesar in 44 B.C., Augustus, Julius's nephew and adopted son, came to power. Augustus was followed by Tiberius, his stepson, and Caligula, his grandson. Because of their connection with Julius Caesar, these emperors were of the Julian line. The Flavians were the next great family to rule. Later the Roman Empire enjoyed a long period of peace and prosperity during the rule of the Antonines (A.D. 96–180).

Like the Chinese emperors and Egyptian pharaohs, the later Roman emperors were treated as gods. In all societies, imperial dynasties and absolute power went together.

1. List *three* dynasties that ruled China in ancient times.

2. Complete the following sentence: "Over a period or more than — years, Egypt was ruled by — dynasties."

3. Select the correct answer to complete the following sentence: "Among the imperial families that ruled the Roman Empire were the — ."
    a. Julians
    b. Flavians
    c. Antonines
    d. all of these

included such Asian invaders as the Mongols and Manchus, and, later, Western colonial and commercial powers (including Great Britain and the United States).

Task:

Using information from the documents and your knowledge of world history, answer the questions that follow each document. Your answers to each question will help you write the document-based essay.

Document 1. Look at the drawing of the Great Wall of China on page 71.

How successful was this wall in keeping the Mongols and Manchus out of China?

Document 2. Excerpt from *The Travels of Marco Polo,* in which Polo describes Mongol warriors seen during his travels in China, 1275–1292:

> They are brave in battle, almost to desperation, setting little value upon their lives, and exposing themselves without hesitation to all manner of danger. Their disposition is cruel. . . . When there is a necessity for it, they can live for a month on the milk of their mares, and upon such wild animals as they may chance to catch.
>
> No people upon earth can surpass them in fortitude under difficulties, nor show greater patience under wants of every kind.
>
> **Source**: *Travels of Marco Polo, the Venetian*, translated by William Marsden, edited by Thomas Wright. London: H.G. Bohn, 1854.

According to this document, why were Mongol armies so successful as conquerors?

Document 3. Excerpt from a letter of Chinese Emperor Ch'ien-lung to British King George III (1792), rejecting the king's request to expand trade with China:

> You, O King, from afar have yearned for the blessings of our civilization. . . . Our Celestial Empire [China] possesses all things in prolific abundance and lacks no product within its own borders. There was therefore no need to import the manufactures of outside barbarians in exchange for our own produce. . . . Should your vessels touch the shore, your merchants will assuredly never be permitted to land or to reside there, but will be subject to instant expulsion. In that event your barbarian merchants will have had a long journey for nothing.
>
> **Source**: E. Blackhouse and J.O.P. Bland, *Annals and Memoirs of the Court of Peking*. Boston: Houghton Mifflin, 1914, pp.322–331.

According to this document, what was the Chinese opinion of their civilization and that of outsiders, such as the British?

Document 4. Study this Japanese woodcut that depicts Commodore Matthew Perry.

What does the illustration tell us about Japanese feelings regarding Commodore Perry and the United States?

DOCUMENT-BASED ESSAY

Using information from the documents and your knowledge of world history, write an essay in which you:

- Explain the views of settled societies in Asia toward invading nomadic groups.
- Compare these views to how Asian societies such as China and Japan later viewed Westerners.

CHAPTER 12
Europe: Renaissance, Exploration, and Reformation

In the year 1300, civilizations in Asia and the Middle East were creative and alive. In contrast, European civilization seemed unchanged and unchanging. However, strong forces for change were just below the surface of everyday life. When the Crusaders returned from their campaigns in the Holy Land, they brought back exotic goods—spices, jewelry, and other luxuries. They also brought back descriptions of how people lived in other lands. Most important, ideas in government, science, and the arts were brought to Europe from these lands.

As these ideas spread throughout Europe, people's attitudes changed. People became curious about other parts of the world. At the same time, scholars, scientists, writers, and artists became interested in the neglected arts and sciences of ancient Greece and Rome.

Between 1300 and 1700, new ideas and inventions caused Europeans to think and live in different and exciting ways. Talented individuals created great art and literature. Scientific experiments expanded knowledge about the human body and the natural world. Reformers changed the Roman Catholic Church. Other reformers broke away from the Church and created new Christian religions.

Restless adventurers explored new lands and increased trade between Europe and Asia and Africa. This trade created a new class of rich merchants, many of whom supported the arts and sciences. Cities grew powerful at the expense of the feudal manors in the countryside. By 1700, a new Europe had come into being.

THE RENAISSANCE

Renaissance is a French word that means "rebirth." It is used to describe the great renewal, or rebirth of interest in learning and the arts in Europe at the end of the Middle Ages. At that time, people became more interested in the world around them. They accepted new ideas more readily. From the 14th through

Europe, 1300

Indicate whether each statement is *true* (**T**) or *false* (**F**).

1. The Holy Roman Empire controlled much of Central Europe in 1300.

2. The Russian states were part of the Holy Roman Empire then.

3. The Teutonic knights lived on the shores of the Baltic Sea.

4. Part of Spain was controlled by Muslims in 1300.

5. France and England were part of the Turkish kingdoms then.

---

the 17th century, Europeans made great advances in the fine arts, literature, and science. Classic works from Greece and Rome were rediscovered. Starting in Italy in the 1300's, the Renaissance spirit later spread north and west throughout Europe. The Renaissance period is regarded as the beginning of modern times in Europe.

1. Beginnings in Italy. In the 1300's, Italy was a collection of independent city-states. A powerful and wealthy family ruled each one. The pope in Rome, who headed the Roman Catholic Church, controlled the Papal States in central Italy. The Holy Roman emperor of Germany had authority over northern Italy.

No one ruler was strong enough to unify Italy. As a result, Italy during the Renaissance was violent and disorganized. Wars, revolts, political plots, and assassinations occurred often.

Amid this unrest existed great wealth. Trade had brought prosperity to Italy, particularly the city-states in the north. Most of the trade routes from the Middle East and Asia led to the Mediterranean Sea. Italian merchants sent ships to Arab ports to purchase the silks, spices, and jewels of China, India, and other Eastern lands. Riches from this trade poured into such important city-states as Venice, Genoa, Florence, and Milan. Many nobles, merchants, and bankers in these city-states became *patrons* of the arts and sciences. They used much of their wealth to encourage the development of art, literature, science, and philosophy.

2. An Age of Genius. During this exciting and lively period called the Renaissance, people eagerly learned new ideas. They tried different ways of doing things. Some individuals developed great skills in many areas of learning and the arts. Even today, we call such a talented individual a "Renaissance person."

Many of the best-known and most talented of the Renaissance artists and writers lived in Florence. This city-state became Italy's greatest center of beauty, learning, and creativity. In some ways, it was like Athens, the leading city-state of ancient Greece.

a. Artists. Leonardo da Vinci (1452–1519) is regarded as the best example of a Renaissance person. In addition to being a great painter, this genius was a sculptor, an architect, a scientist, and an engineer. His paintings include *Mona Lisa* and *The Last Supper*, both masterpieces. Leonardo was born in Florence. As military engineer of that city-state, he designed part of its defense system. Leonardo also drew plans for machine guns, tanks, airplanes, and many other machines that were yet to be developed. Many of his ideas led to inventions that were made centuries later.

One of the greatest artists of the Renaissance was Michelangelo Buonarroti (1475–1564). Also a Florentine, Michelangelo was a painter, sculptor, architect, and poet. Lorenzo de Medici, ruler of Florence, hired Michelangelo to create many works of art for him. Another famous patron was Pope Julius II. At his command, Michelangelo painted events from the Bible on the walls and ceiling of the Sistine Chapel in Rome.

b. Writers. Another talented Florentine, Niccolò Machiavelli (1460–1527), wrote about government and politics. Impressed by

Leonardo da Vinci, a self portrait.

the leadership of Cesare Borgia, ruler of Rome, Machiavelli wrote a guidebook for rulers, called *The Prince*, based on Borgia's political practices. The book describes the ways a strong ruler might seize and hold power. Citizens were to be given only those rights

The Creation of Adam, detail from the Sistine Chapel's ceiling.

Inspired by Heaven

Michelangelo Buonarroti.

The story of Creation is told in the Book of Genesis in the Bible. It is told again, in pictures, on the ceiling of the Sistine Chapel in Rome. This series of beautiful paintings is the work of an Italian artist, Michelangelo Buonarroti (1475–1564). Michelangelo is even more famous as a sculptor than as a painter. He created huge and powerful statues of Moses and David.

Born near Florence, the 13-year-old Michelangelo was apprenticed to the painter Domenico Ghirlandaio. The boy soon turned to sculpture after seeing the marble statues in the garden of the Medici palace. Lorenzo de Medici, ruler of Florence and patron of the arts, was impressed by Michelangelo's ability and took the boy into his household. For several years, Michelangelo studied sculpture in the school begun by Lorenzo.

Michelangelo, stubborn, moody, and short-tempered, was devoted to his art. His talent developed quickly. He painted, sculpted, and wrote poetry. As an architect, Michelangelo designed many buildings and monuments, including the great dome of St. Peter's in Rome. He was also active in the politics of the day.

Among Michelangelo's patrons were the most powerful men in Europe. Chief among them was Pope Julius II. It was for Julius that Michelangelo painted the Sistine Chapel. Michelangelo painted the ceiling while lying on his back on a scaffold high above the chapel floor. The ceiling was an area of 10,000 square feet. It took Michelangelo four years to complete the paintings.

Michelangelo died at the age of 89, a Renaissance man.

State *three* facts that prove that Michelangelo was a "Renaissance man."

that the ruler wanted to grant. Machiavelli advised leaders to be strong and ruthless when necessary, kind and generous when possible. Machiavelli taught that "it is far safer to be feared than loved." He also believed that "the end justifies the means." In other words, a ruler could use any method to achieve a goal.

Some Renaissance writers came to be known as *humanists*. They wanted people to improve their lives through learning and new experiences. Humanists urged people to study the literature of ancient Greece and Rome. They believed that the classical writers could teach important ideas about life, love, and beauty. Humanists glorified the individual and the world in which they lived. The humanists revived interest in literature and writing.

An early humanist writer was Francesco Petrarch (1304–1374). He wrote poems called sonnets in Latin and Italian. Many of the sonnets express his love for a woman named Laura. Another well-known humanist was Giovanni Boccaccio (1313–1375). He wrote a book of short stories called *The Decameron*. It was created during the time of the terrible Black Death plague in Italy. The stories are told by a group of ten young men and women. They live in an isolated house in the country to escape the plague. The group amuses itself by making fun of many customs of the Middle Ages.

3. The Northern Renaissance.   In the 15th and 16th centuries, new ideas and the love of learning spread beyond Italy. France, Holland, England, and Spain experienced a Renaissance of their own.

a. *Spread of ideas.*   Two inventions greatly helped the spread of ideas during the Renaissance. In the mid-1400's, Johann Gutenberg, a German printer, invented (independently of the Koreans) movable metal type and the printing press. The first European book printed by machine was the Gutenberg Bible. It appeared around 1455. Before the invention of the printing press, books had to be copied by hand. The printing press made it possible for books to be produced more cheaply and accurately and in greater numbers. The increased circulation of books (by Italian and other European writers) introduced more people to the ideas of the Renaissance.

During the Middle Ages, Latin was the written language of the Roman Catholic Church and of scholars and artists in Western Europe. However, other languages had been developing through everyday usage. Italian, Spanish, French, Portuguese, Dutch, German, and English were among the spoken, or *vernacular*, languages. Renaissance writers abandoned Latin and wrote in their vernacular languages. This enabled more people to enjoy and learn from their works. Combined with the printing press, less expensive books written in vernacular languages gave all people the opportunity to become literate and better educated.

Dante Alighieri (1265–1321) was the first to write an important work, the *Divine Comedy*, in a vernacular language. By doing so, he became known as the "father of modern Italian." Some

Western Europeans did not favor the abandonment of Latin. Chaucer, for example, was urged by friends not to write his *Canterbury Tales* in the vernacular. He was warned that the English language was continually changing and that in a few years no one would be able to understand his collection of stories. By rejecting this advice, Chaucer made an important contribution to the development of written English.

b. *Rabelais.* François Rabelais (1494–1553) was a French Renaissance writer and a humanist. He created the comic story of *Gargantua and Pantagruel*, a giant and his son. To be truly knowledgeable, he thought, people should study Latin, Greek, and Hebrew, as well as mathematics and science.

c. *Erasmus and Rembrandt.* Born in Holland, Desiderius Erasmus (1466–1536) became the greatest humanist scholar in northern Europe. His book *Praise of Folly* attacked superstition and ignorance. Erasmus's constant correspondence with scholars in many countries helped to spread humanist ideas. Another product of the Dutch Renaissance was Rembrandt van Rijn (1606–1669). His many paintings of ordinary people and religious scenes are among Europe's greatest works of art. One of the most famous is *The Night Watch*.

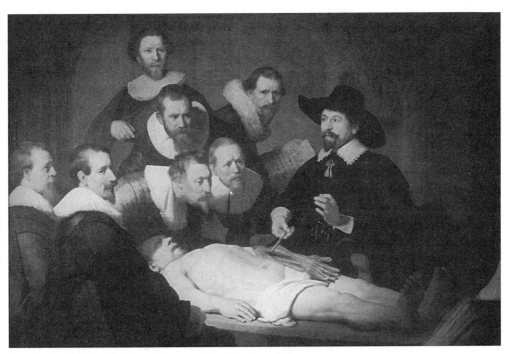

Rembrandt's *The Anatomy Lesson of Dr. Nicolaas Tulp.*

Original Globe Theater, 1598.

d. *Shakespeare*. The Renaissance in England reached its height during the reign of Queen Elizabeth I (1558–1603). Her encouragement of the arts and sciences resulted in a Golden Age. During this time, people with inquiring and creative minds were known as Elizabethans. Foremost among English Renaissance writers was William Shakespeare (1564–1616). Some regard him as the greatest playwright who ever wrote in English. Among Shakespeare's many masterpieces are historical plays such as *Julius Caesar* and *Henry V*, tragedies such as *Hamlet* and *Romeo and Juliet*, and comedies such as *A Midsummer Night's Dream* and *The Taming of the Shrew*. All of these and many more of Shakespeare's plays are still performed.

e. *Cervantes*. The Renaissance reached Spain in the 16th century. Miguel de Cervantes (1547–1616), one of the world's best-known writers, created the famous *Don Quixote*. In this humorous novel, a simple old man believed that he is a knight who must fight in defense of noble causes. Wearing a rusty suit of armor and riding a broken-down horse, Don Quixote sets out to do battle for justice. He is accompanied by his faithful servant Sancho Panza. Through Don Quixote's adventures, Cervantes ridicules romantic and silly ideas about the way of life of medieval knights.

CRITICAL THINKING

Explain why you AGREE or DISAGREE with each of the following statements:

1. A strong central government kept all of Italy peaceful and well organized during the Renaissance.

2. The wealth of the Italian city-states helped artists and writers in Italy.

3. The ruling families of Italy and the popes made no contributions to the growth of the Renaissance.

IDENTIFICATIONS

From the list that follows, select the person who best fits each description.

a. Leonardo da Vinci
b. Michelangelo
c. Francesco Petrarch
d. Giovanni Boccaccio
e. Niccolò Machiavelli

1. I wrote poems called sonnets in Italian and Latin. I expressed my love for a woman named Laura in many of them.

2. I wrote *The Prince*, a book that describes how a strong man might seize and hold political power.

3. I sculpted powerful statues and painted events from the Bible on the walls and ceiling of the Sistine Chapel.

4. In the collection of stories called *The Decameron*, I made fun of many of the customs of the Middle Ages.

5. My paintings *The Last Supper* and *Mona Lisa* are masterpieces. My ideas for inventions were so advanced that they could not be built until centuries after I thought of them.

CHART COMPLETION

Reread "3. The Northern Renaissance," on pages 282–284. Then complete the following table.

The Renaissance Enriches Europe

Nation	Renaissance person(s)	Achievement	Date
England	1.—	—	—
	2.—	—	—
France	—	—	—
Germany	—	—	—
Holland	1.—	—	—
	2.—	—	—
Spain	—	—	—

THE SCIENTIFIC REVOLUTION

During the Renaissance, scientists explored new areas of knowledge and began to think in new ways. Their many inventions and discoveries greatly changed the ways people lived.

1. Scientific Method. For many centuries, scientists had accepted the writing of ancient scholars and the teachings of religious leaders about science and nature. At the end of the Middle Ages, however, scientists began to use new methods to study nature. Conclusions based on observation and experimentation became the basis for scientific work. Statements put forth as facts were accepted as truth only after they had been tested in experiments. These tests and the results were written down so that other scientists could repeat them. Gradually, the *scientific method* of observation, experimenting, and drawing conclusions came into common use. It led to revolutionary advances in the fields of chemistry, physics, mathematics, astronomy, and medicine.

a. Galileo. Two of the most important men to use the scientific method were Galileo Galilei of Italy and Isaac Newton of England. Galileo (1564–1642) built a telescope to study the stars. His observations led him to conclude that the Earth and all the other known planets move around the sun. Because his theory conflicted with the beliefs of officials in the Roman Catholic Church (who thought that the Earth is the center of the universe), Galileo was persecuted for his work. Eventually, he was forced to deny what he had concluded. However, his ideas about the *solar system* came to be accepted by all scientists.

b. ***Newton.*** Isaac Newton (1642–1727) taught mathematics. One of his early achievements was the creation of the system of advanced mathematics called calculus. Newton also developed the law of universal gravitation. This law explained the operation of a force called gravity. It is the force of gravity on every planet that pulls objects toward the planet. Newton also explained how gravity keeps planets in orbit around the sun. With this knowledge, Newton built the foundation of modern astronomy. He is regarded as one of the greatest of all scientists.

2. Scientific Achievements.   Dramatic discoveries were made in the field of medicine. In 1543, a medical student from Belgium, Andreas Vesalius, published a book on human anatomy. To get firsthand information about the human body, Vesalius examined the bodies of dead people. His book was the first to describe correctly the parts of the body.

In 1628, William Harvey, an English doctor, wrote a book explaining how the heart pumps blood through the body. This was the first description of the circulatory system.

Modern chemistry began with the work of Robert Boyle, an Irish scientist. His studies in the mid-1600's proved that air is a mixture of gases. He also studied how animals breathe.

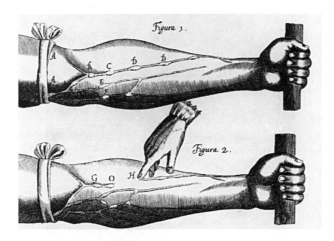

A diagram showing an experiment by William Harvey. Arteries and pressure points in arms are examined. Before Harvey's time, it had been thought that the arteries were empty and served merely as air tubes.

Johannes Kepler (1571–1630), a German astronomer and mathematician, discovered that the planets follow an elliptical (oval-shaped) orbit around the sun. His work is used to explain the paths followed by modern, human-made satellites.

3. Results of the Scientific Revolution.

Respect for the achievements of Renaissance scientists led scholars in other fields to question what had been taught in the past. The scholars tried to apply the scientific method to other areas of learning, such as government, history, and economics. They believed that human intelligence, or reason, could solve any problem and unravel any mystery about the world.

a. *Descartes*.   René Descartes (1596–1650) founded the system of analytic geometry. This French scientist and philosopher expressed his beliefs by saying, "I think, therefore I am."

b. *Locke*.   The 18th century in Europe is known as the Age of Reason. During this period, scholars applied the lessons of the Scientific Revolution to the practice of government. These scholars declared that people should be governed by the same natural laws that scientists had found in nature. They argued that in nature, people are free and have certain *natural rights*. The most important of these rights are life, liberty, and property.

John Locke (1632–1704), an English writer, said that the duty of government is to protect people's natural rights. He believed

John Locke. His political ideas inspired Thomas Jefferson, author of the Declaration of Independence.

that governments that do not protect the natural rights of their citizens could be changed by the people. Locke presented his ideas in a book called *Two Treatises of Government*. This book strongly affected the thinking of Europeans. Locke's ideas also influenced the leaders of the American and French Revolutions in the late 1700's.

c. *Montesquieu*. Charles-Louis de Secondat, Baron de Montesquieu (1689–1755), a French political thinker, admired the English political system. His writings about the separation of governmental powers influenced the writing of constitutions of nations around the world, including that of the United States. He believed that the separation of powers was essential for the preservation of individual liberties. In his 1748 book, *The Spirit of the Laws*, Montesquieu said that administrative powers were the legislative, the executive, and the judicial. These powers were to be divided among different branches of government so that each branch would have power over the other two. This idea has become known as *checks and balances*.

d. *Rousseau*. Jean Jacques Rousseau (1712–1778) was a French-Swiss philosopher, writer, political theorist, and self-taught composer. His writings have influenced millions of people. In *Émile*, he posed new theories of education, stressing the need for "child-centered" instruction. Rousseau's most important work is *The Social Contract* (1762). It outlines the basis for a political order that would be in accordance with nature and would protect the natural rights with which all humans are born. Rousseau believed that people enter into a social contract among themselves, agreeing to surrender all their rights to the community and to submit to the will of the majority. The people create government as a necessary evil to carry out the will of the majority. He wrote that if a government fails in this purpose, the people have the right to overthrow and replace it.

Rousseau's ideas, influenced by those of John Locke, also had an impact on the leaders of the American and French Revolutions. Locke, however, was more concerned with the rights of the individual and limits on the power of government. Rousseau, by contrast, believed that the will of the majority is supreme and that to enforce it governments must have unlimited power. Rousseau's ideas have been used by dictatorships to justify totalitarian rule.

SENTENCE COMPLETION

Complete the following sentences:

1. At the end of the Middle Ages, scientists began —.

2. Statements put forth as facts were accepted as truth only after —.

3. As this scientific method came into common use, it led to —.

4. Two of the most important men to use the scientific method were —.

 MATCHING EXERCISE

Match each name in Column A with the correct description in Column B.

Column A	**Column B**
1. Galileo Galilei	*a.* believed that the Earth and the other planets move around the sun
2. Isaac Newton	
3. Andreas Vesalius	*b.* began modern chemistry
4. William Harvey	*c.* was the first to describe the circulatory system
5. Robert Boyle	*d.* developed the law of universal gravitation
	e. was the first to describe correctly the parts of the human body

CRITICAL THINKING

Reread "3. Results of the Scientific Revolution," on pages 288–289. Then write a paragraph to PROVE or DISPROVE the following statement: "The Scientific Revolution had no effect on what people thought about government."

THE AGE OF EXPLORATION AND DISCOVERY

During the Renaissance, Europeans grew curious about unknown parts of the world. This curiosity was combined with a need and desire for products from Asia. The silks, spices, and jewels of Asia could be obtained only from the merchants of the Italian city-states. The Italians controlled the trade routes across the

Mediterranean Sea. They also charged high prices for the precious Eastern goods. As a result, other Europeans began to search for new, all-water routes to Asia. They sailed south along the African coast and west across the Atlantic Ocean, looking for a new way to Asia. They found new lands, wealth, and adventure.

1. Exploration and Discovery. European nations facing the Atlantic—Spain, Portugal, France, Holland, and England—sent out ships to discover and explore. Portugal began the explorations in the 15th century. Prince Henry the Navigator, a member of the Portuguese ruling family, used his wealth to send expeditions to explore the west coast of Africa. These expeditions led to the growth of the Portuguese trade in African gold and slaves.

   a. *Portuguese explorers.* In 1488, a Portuguese captain named Bartolomeu Dias sailed around the southern tip of Africa. This voyage around the Cape of Good Hope proved that a sea route to the Indian Ocean did exist. Vasco da Gama reached India by following Dias's route around southern Africa and then crossing the Indian Ocean. Da Gama returned to Portugal with a rich cargo of spices and jewels.

   b. *Spanish explorers.* The other Atlantic nations quickly followed the lead of Portugal. In 1492, Christopher Columbus began the first of his westward voyages under Spain's flag. He believed that he had reached Asia or the "Indies," islands off the coast of Asia. Instead, he found new lands that came to be called America.

   Ferdinand Magellan also sailed from Spain. In a voyage that took three years (1519–1521), his expedition became the first to travel completely around the world. Although his ships returned to Europe, Magellan died in the Philippines.

   c. *English, French, and Dutch expeditions.* An Italian named John Cabot explored the parts of Canada known as Nova Scotia and Newfoundland for England in 1497 and 1498. Around 1576, Martin Frobisher explored the Labrador coast of Canada for England. Both Cabot and Frobisher were looking for a northwest passage that would take them around North America to Asia. They did not find it. But the English were the first to establish a permanent European settlement in North America—at Jamestown, Virginia, in 1607.

   An Englishman named Henry Hudson sailed for Holland in 1609. He also tried to find a northwest passage and failed. He did, however, explore much of the area along what is now the Hudson River in New York State.

   Between 1534 and 1541, Jacques Cartier, a Frenchman, explored the St. Lawrence River and eastern Canada. Another

The Age of Exploration and Discovery

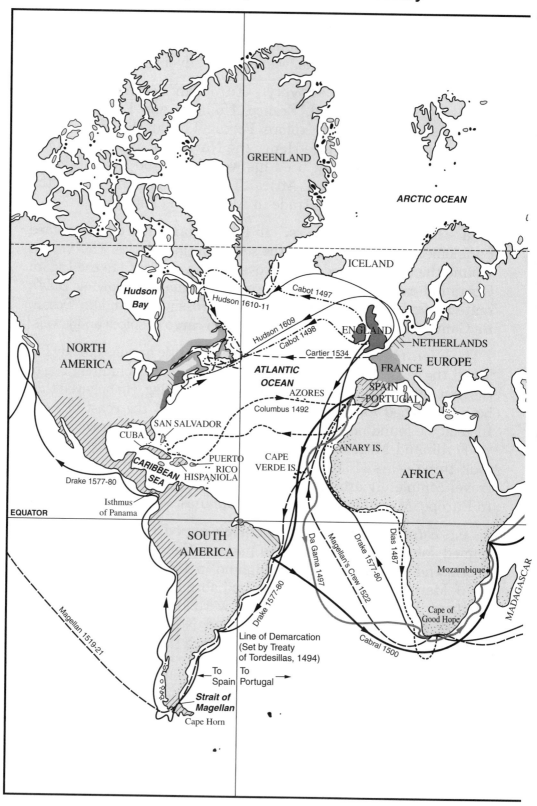

ARCTIC OCEAN

GREENLAND

ICELAND

Cabot 1497

Hudson
Bay

Hudson 1610-11

Hudson 1609

ENGLAND

Cabot 1498

NETHERLANDS

NORTH
AMERICA

Cartier 1534

FRANCE

EUROPE

ATLANTIC
OCEAN

SPAIN

AZORES

PORTUGAL

Columbus 1492

SAN SALVADOR

CANARY IS.

CUBA

PUERTO
RICO

AFRICA

CARIBBEAN
SEA

HISPANIOLA

Drake 1577-80

CAPE
VERDE IS.

Isthmus
of Panama

EQUATOR

SOUTH
AMERICA

Mozambique

MADAGASCAR

Da Gama 1497

Magellan's Crew 1522

Drake 1577-80

Dias 1487

Drake 1577-80

Cape of
Good Hope

Magellan 1519-21

Line of Demarcation
(Set by Treaty
of Tordesillas, 1494)

Cabral 1500

To
Spain

To
Portugal

Strait of
Magellan

Cape Horn

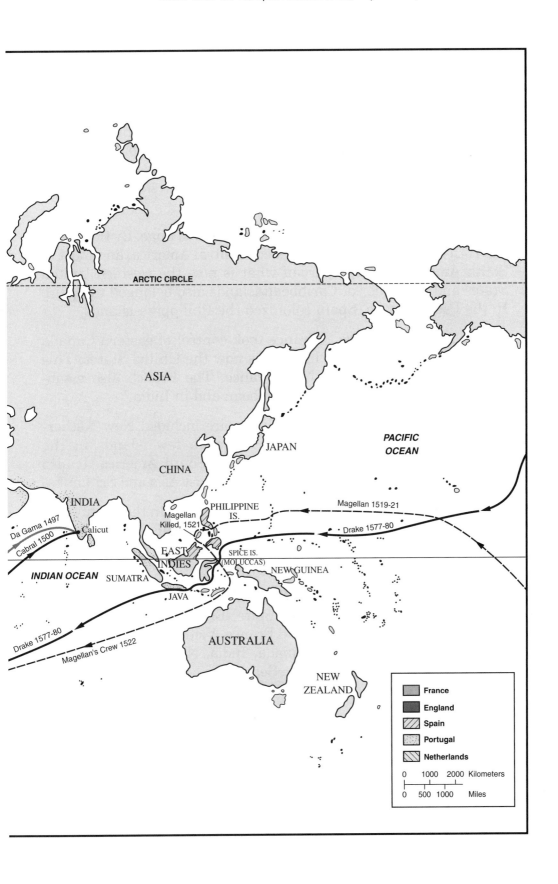

Frenchman, Samuel de Champlain, established a settlement at Quebec in Canada in 1608.

Eventually, the English, French, and Dutch also reached India, Southeast Asia, and East Asia. In these areas, they set up trading posts and colonies.

2. The Rise of Empires. The age of exploration and discovery was followed by an age of colonization and empire building. The Atlantic nations quickly sent government officials, missionaries, and colonists to the lands found by their explorers. Great empires began to grow in the 16th and 17th centuries.

a. *Spanish empire.* Spain's empire was huge. By the end of the 16th century, it included Mexico, Central America, and most of South America. A large part of what is now the western United States and a number of Caribbean islands also belonged to Spain. In the Pacific Ocean, Spain colonized the Philippine Islands.

b. *French empire.* France took control of eastern Canada and the Mississippi Valley in what is now the United States. This large territory was called New France. The French also established trading colonies in the Caribbean and in India.

c. *Dutch empire.* Holland's empire included New Netherland (in what is now New York State), a few islands in the Caribbean, and part of South Africa and South America. It also claimed what are today Indonesia in Southeast Asia and Sri Lanka.

d. *Portuguese empire.* The richest colony in the Portuguese Empire was Brazil in South America. Portugal also controlled trading areas on the coasts of Africa and India.

e. *British empire.* By the 18th century, Great Britain had the largest empire, including 13 colonies on the Atlantic coast of North America. To expand its empire, Britain fought a series of wars against Holland, Spain, and France. Victories on land and sea gave the British control of Canada, India, New Netherland, and several islands in the Caribbean Sea.

f. *Effects of empires.* The building of empires brought great changes to the Atlantic nations and to the lands they colonized. Europeans moved to the newly discovered lands for many reasons. Some wanted more religious freedom than they had at home. Others looked for adventure and new experiences. Whatever their reasons, Europeans brought to their colonies in the Americas and Asia their languages, religions, and cultures. The changes often caused conflicts and bloody wars with the native Americans and Asians.

The lives of Europeans who remained at home were also affected. From the Americas and Asia came new wealth, often in the form of gold and silver. Trade expanded and European cities grew larger and more prosperous. New types of food, potatoes and corn in particular, improved the diet of Europeans. Silk, cotton, and other lightweight fabrics became easier and less expensive to buy. This changed the way Europeans dressed.

The growth of empires also caused competition among the Atlantic nations. Each nation wanted a large empire and the wealth it could bring. Such rivalries resulted in wars for the control of colonies. The most widespread of these conflicts was the Seven Years' War, which lasted from 1756 to 1763. Britain, aided by Prussia, fought France, which was helped by Austria and Russia. Their armies and navies battled over much of the world—in Europe, North America, and India. Britain came out the winner and gained a great deal more territory.

 SENTENCE COMPLETION

From the list below, select the terms that correctly complete the sentences in the following paragraph.

Brazil	New France	India	Africa
Mexico	Indonesia	New Netherland	Caribbean

By the end of the 16th century, Spain's empire included (1) , Central America, and most of South America. A large part of what is now the United States and a number of (2) islands also belonged to Spain. Eastern Canada and the Mississippi Valley were part of (3) . Holland's empire included (4) in North America and what is today called (5) . The richest colony in the Portuguese Empire was (6) . Portugal also controlled trading areas on the coasts of (7) and (8) .

 ESSAY QUESTIONS

1. List the nations that built empires during the age of exploration and discovery.

2. State *two* ways these nations were changed by the growth of empires.

3. The Seven Years' War was one of the first global conflicts of modern times. Name the countries that took part in this war.

THE COMMERCIAL REVOLUTION

The voyages of exploration and discovery ended Italian control of the Asian trade. New trade routes led to important new economic developments in Europe. These economic changes have been called the Commercial Revolution.

1. Global Trade.   Western Europe's major trade routes shifted from the Mediterranean Sea to the Atlantic Ocean. As a result, the Italian city-states gradually lost their economic and political importance. Instead, the capitals of the Atlantic nations became the centers of trade and power. Lisbon, Madrid, Amsterdam, Paris, and London were the cities from which the colonial empires of the Atlantic nations were ruled. To these cities came the new products and riches of the Americas, Africa, and Asia. The dramatic increase in global trade raised Europeans' standard of living.

As trade increased, the economic well-being of Europe became more dependent on the economic growth of the colonies. Businesspeople in Europe *invested* money in sugar and tobacco plantations in America and in coffee plantations in Asia. The *profits* of the investors depended on the success of their overseas business operations. A global economy began to develop.

From the Aztec and Inca lands conquered by Spain came shiploads of gold and silver. Slave ships crossed the Atlantic from Africa to the Americas. European goods were shipped to Africa and the Americas. All this trade helped the growth of businesses in Europe. More goods were made and sold. More money was circulated. Workers received higher wages.

European governments became stronger. Rulers were able to collect more taxes. Increased wealth enabled them to create larger armies and build more ships. In return for trading privileges and special licenses, rulers gained the support of businesspeople. This policy also added to royal wealth and power.

2. Mercantilism.   The increase in global trade led to the development of a new economic theory. It was called *mercantilism*. According to this theory, colonies existed only to enrich their home country. The colonies sent to the home country raw materials needed for its industries. Products manufactured from the raw materials in the home country were sold back to the colonies at a profit. This kept more wealth flowing into the home country than going out of it. Most European mercantilists believed that such a favorable balance of trade would keep a nation prosperous.

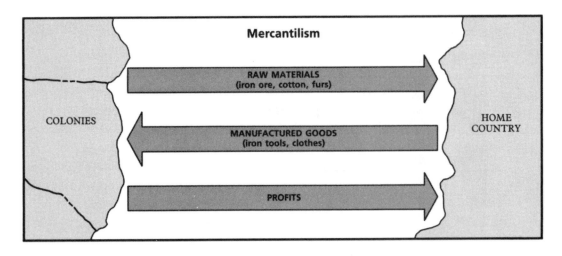

Mercantilists also believed in the use of *tariffs* (taxes on imported goods) to protect home industries from competition. Taxes on imported goods raised the prices of these goods and encouraged people to buy the cheaper goods manufactured in their own country.

Mercantilism helped the industries of European Atlantic nations to grow. It also strengthened royal governments. Through taxation, rulers gained more control over the economies of their countries. This increased national unity. Mercantilism, therefore, made the Atlantic nations of Europe economically and politically stronger.

3. The Rise of Capitalism. The increase in global trade also led to the development of a new economic system. It was called *capitalism*. Merchants used their money (capital) to build new businesses. Manufacturing was one such business. People who used their profits from trade to employ workers to manufacture goods to be sold were called capitalists.

One of the large European industries built by capitalists was cloth manufacturing. Merchant-capitalists paid weavers to make woolen cloth in their homes. Manufacturing goods in the home was called the *domestic system*. The capitalists paid for raw materials and labor and sold finished goods at a profit. In time, capitalists brought workers and raw materials together in central locations to make goods. This step began the *factory system*, which is discussed in Chapter 14.

The rise of capitalism led to a new type of business organization called the *joint-stock company*. To raise large amounts of capital, merchants combined their funds. Each partner received

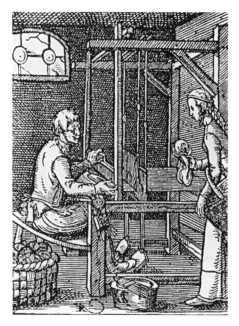

The weaver's wife brings yarn to his loom. An example of the domestic system.

shares, or stock, in the company in return for the money contributed. This money was then invested in a business project, either in Europe or in the colonies. The large investment made possible by the joint-stock company often led to large profits. These were shared among the investors in the form of *dividends*. The size of a partner's dividend depended on the amount of money invested in the company.

The rise of capitalism in Europe made possible the development of large businesses and the production of great amounts of goods. Banks and insurance companies also came into being during this period. Most merchants needed such institutions to protect their money and to share risks in case disaster struck a business venture.

As Europe's capitalist economy developed, bankers created new credit instruments to aid business operations. *Bills of exchange* enabled a merchant in one country to pay for goods purchased in another country. To pay for goods in local transactions, businesspeople were provided with *checks*. Paper money, or *bank notes*, were issued by banks as a substitute for the bulkier gold and silver.

Insurance companies were created by Western European merchants to protect themselves from the loss of ships and goods and other causes of business failure. Each merchant contributed a sum of money called a *premium* to a fund. Merchants who suffered losses were compensated from the fund. As the Commercial Revolution progressed and Europe's capitalist economy grew, banks and insurance companies gained in wealth and power.

MATCHING EXERCISE

Match each term in Column A with the correct definition from Column B.

<table>
<tr><td colspan="2">Column A</td><td colspan="2">Column B</td></tr>
</table>

Column A

1. capitalists
2. domestic system
3. factory system
4. joint-stock company
5. dividends

Column B

a. profits paid to investors
b. merchants who employed workers to manufacture goods
c. workers and raw materials are brought together in central locations
d. groups of merchants who combined funds and received shares
e. manufacturing goods at home

 ## SENTENCE STRUCTURE

Rearrange each of the following word groups to make a correct sentence:

1. the Europeans increase trade in raised   global the of living of standard dramatic

2. a develop to began economy global

3. European stronger became governments

 ## DEFINITIONS

Define each of the following terms.

a. mercantilism
b. favorable balance of trade
c. capitalism
d. global trade
e. Atlantic nations
f. bills of exchange

WRITING EXERCISE

Reread "3. The Rise of Capitalism," on pages 297–298, and write a paragraph to answer the following question: "How did capitalism make the factory system possible?"

THE REFORMATION AND COUNTER-REFORMATION

During the Renaissance, Europeans began to question long-accepted religious beliefs and certain practices of the Roman Catholic Church. Those who challenged, or protested against, the ways of the Church were called *Protestants*. Their demand for reform and religious changes in the Church was called the *Reformation*. This great movement led to the creation of a new branch of Christianity: Protestantism. The Reformation also caused terrible wars and major political changes in Europe.

1. The First Protestants. In 1517, a German monk named Martin Luther posted a document on the door of the church in Wittenberg, a university town. This document is known as the "Ninety-Five Theses." It stated Luther's criticisms of the Roman Catholic Church for allowing the sale of *indulgences*. An indulgence was the promise by the Church to cancel some or all of the punishment a forgiven sinner would suffer in *purgatory* (an intermediate state after death where one waits to go to heaven). In Luther's time, indulgences were issued in return for contributions for the building of St. Peter's Church in Rome. Luther condemned this practice. He claimed that indulgences could neither cancel nor reduce the punishment brought upon oneself by sin.

Luther's criticism of what he considered a bad practice appealed to many Germans and other Europeans. Many Catholics had other complaints about the Church, such as the practice of *nepotism*. Nepotism was the appointment of relatives of high-ranking clergymen to positions in the Church.

At the heart of Luther's plea for reform were three ideas that enraged Church officials. First, a person could be saved and enter heaven through "faith alone." Performing good works or buying indulgences would not guarantee salvation. Second, Luther argued that the Bible was the only guide to salvation that Christians needed. Third, Luther claimed that the interpreting of the Bible by the Church was not necessary. Christians should be able to read and interpret the Bible for themselves.

In 1521, the pope excommunicated Luther. In the next year, Charles V, the Holy Roman emperor and ruler of most of the states of Germany, declared Luther an outlaw.

Luther continued to speak out for reform. His ideas spread rapidly throughout Germany. Knowing the power of the printed word,

Martin Luther. Engraving from the original
picture by Hans Holbein.

Luther translated the Bible into German so it could be read more easily by more people.

All of these actions touched off a long struggle between Luther's supporters and his Catholic opponents. Many German princes sided with Luther against the pope. When Charles V tried to force these princes to remain loyal to the Church, they rebelled. They supported the establishment of a new branch of Christianity based on Luther's teachings. Protestant princes welcomed the opportunity to be independent of the pope and to free themselves from the authority of the Holy Roman Emperor. Some princes seized Church lands and other properties.

The long civil wars in Germany between Catholics and Protestants were finally settled in 1555 by an agreement called the Peace of Augsburg. It allowed each German prince to choose between the two faiths—Catholic or Protestant. The people in the area a prince ruled were required to follow the faith he chose.

Luther's ideas spread from Germany to many other parts of Europe. His ideas became popular in Norway, Sweden, and Denmark.

2. The Spread of the Reformation. Followers of Luther were not the only Protestants in Europe.

a. *Anglicans.* The Reformation came to England in a rather roundabout way. The English king, Henry VIII, was a loyal Catholic. He very much wanted a son to ensure the succession of

The Spread of Protestantism in Europe

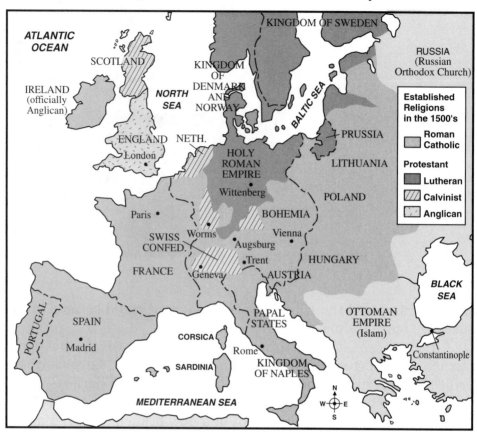

1. **PROVE or DISPROVE:** The rise of Protestantism contributed to religious differences and divisions in Europe.

2. For each country, name the established religion in the 1500's:
   a. England
   b. France
   c. Netherlands
   d. Sweden

---

the Tudor line of kings. His Spanish wife, Catherine of Aragon, had given him a daughter but no son. Henry wanted the pope to grant him a divorce from the aging Catherine so that he could marry someone else who might give birth to a son. When the pope refused, Henry became angry. He appointed an English archbishop who then granted Henry's divorce.

In 1534, Henry broke completely with the Roman Catholic Church. He had Parliament issue the Act of Supremacy. This new law made Henry the leader of a separate church called the Church of England. Thus, Henry made himself more important than the

John Calvin.

pope in regulating church matters in England. Henry closed down the Catholic monasteries and seized much of the land in England that belonged to the Roman Catholic Church. By his actions, King Henry VIII started the movement to make the new Anglican religion the main faith authorized by the English government. However, the ritual forms of worship of the Church of England were very similar to those of the Roman Catholic Church.

   b. *Calvinists.* Between 1536 and 1541, a French lawyer named John Calvin organized Protestant churches in Switzerland. Calvin's ideas were somewhat different from those of Luther. Calvin taught a very strict moral code and was against all but the simplest pleasures. He and his followers believed in a life of hard work and prayer.

   Calvin's ideas spread to Holland, where the Dutch Reformed Church was established. In Scotland, a reformer named John Knox organized the Presbyterian Church in 1560. It too was based on Calvinist teachings.

   French Calvinists were known as Huguenots. The followers of Calvin in England were called Puritans. Both the Huguenots and the Puritans were persecuted. Their religious ideas and strict way of life were quite different from the practices of most French and English people.

   Many Huguenots and Puritans eventually brought their Protestant faith and their belief in hard work to America.

3. The Counter-Reformation. The spread of Protestantism throughout Europe in the 16th century threatened the power and authority of the Roman Catholic Church. Catholic leaders took several important steps to meet this challenge. Pope Paul III called Church officials to the Council of Trent. During three sessions between 1545 and 1563, this council worked out ways to change and improve the practices of the Church. It ended the sale of indulgences and other practices that had been attacked by the Protestants. The training of priests was improved. The council also clearly restated the basic beliefs of the Church.

The success of this *Counter-Reformation* was greatly aided by the Society of Jesus, whose members were known as Jesuits. Ignatius Loyola founded the society in Paris in 1534 (the same year as Henry VIII's Act of Supremacy) to promote Catholicism. Sometimes called "soldiers of Christ," Jesuits were trained as teachers and missionaries. They traveled to all parts of the world to win converts to the Catholic faith. The Jesuit missionary Francis Xavier went to Japan in 1549. Jesuits often accompanied Spanish and French explorers on voyages to the New World.

The Counter-Reformation successfully strengthened the Roman Catholic Church. Protestantism became less popular in Poland, Hungary, and other Eastern European nations. In Italy, France, Spain, and Portugal, Catholicism continued to be the main faith. The Catholic Church went on to become a strong force in South and Central America and parts of North America.

4. Religious and Political Conflicts. When political ambitions became mixed up with religious differences, bloody wars often broke out. Hardly any place in Europe escaped conflict. But England, Spain, France, and Germany were affected the most.

    a. *Spanish Armada.*   Philip II, the Catholic king of Spain, sent the Spanish Armada to attack England in 1588. The Armada consisted of 130 powerful fighting ships and thousands of sailors and soldiers. Its purpose was to prepare the way for an invasion of England by Spanish forces based in Holland. Philip regarded Protestant England, which was ruled by Elizabeth I, as the main enemy of Catholic Spain. By defeating England, he hoped to strengthen both his country and his Church. Philip's plan failed when the small but strong English navy defeated the Armada. England remained Anglican and free from Spanish rule. (Eventually, the Church of England, or Anglican religion, came to be regarded as one of the various forms of Protestantism.)

    b. *French civil war.*   Catholics and Huguenots (French Calvinists) fought a series of civil wars in France from 1562 to 1598. Powerful families of both religious groups wanted the crown. One of the worst incidents of the period was the St. Bartholomew's Day mas-

King Philip II of Spain.

sacre on August 24, 1572. This was a general attack on Protestants in Paris and throughout France. All-out war followed. The conflicts ended when the Huguenot leader, Henry of Navarre, became King Henry IV of France. The first of the Bourbon line, he reigned from 1589 to 1610. To be crowned, Henry needed Catholic support. He had to convert to Catholicism. But as king, he issued the Edict of Nantes in 1598. This law protected the Huguenots from persecution.

c. *Thirty Years' War.*   Perhaps the most destructive of the religious wars in Europe took place in Germany. Known as the Thirty Years' War, it lasted from 1618 to 1648. This struggle between the Catholic and Protestant states of Germany was joined by almost every country in Europe. They all sent armies into Germany. As a result, Germany was nearly destroyed. The Peace of Westphalia ended the war in 1648. Germany remained divided into independent Protestant and Catholic states. This division would prevent Germany from uniting as one country under a national government until the 19th century.

CRITICAL THINKING

Explain why you AGREE or DISAGREE with each of the following statements:

1. The Counter-Reformation had no effect on Europe.

2. The leaders of the Roman Catholic Church did little about the Reformation.

 ## MATCHING EXERCISE

Match each term in Column A with the best choice from Column B.

Column A

1. Martin Luther
2. "Ninety-Five Theses"
3. indulgence
4. nepotism
5. Reformation
6. Protestants
7. Peace of Augsburg

Column B

a. people who challenged certain practices of the Roman Catholic Church
b. a German monk who criticized certain practices of the Roman Catholic Church
c. an agreement that allowed each German prince to choose between Catholicism and Protestantism
d. a document posted on the door of the church in Wittenberg
e. the demand for religious changes that became a great movement
f. the appointment of relatives of high-ranking clergymen to positions in the Church
g. a promise by the Church to cancel punishment for sins already forgiven

WRITING EXERCISE

Reread "2. The Spread of the Reformation," on pages 301–303, and write a paragraph about *one* of the following themes:

1. The Reformation in England

2. John Calvin and the Growth of Protestantism

THE GREAT RULING HOUSES OF EUROPE

The royal families of Europe gained power during the period of the Renaissance and Reformation. Most ruled as *absolute monarchs*. They did not share their power with the people. In most of these countries, there were no parliaments to check the authority of the ruler.

Absolute monarchs tended to believe that they had a divine, or "God-given," right to rule. They believed that they were appointed by God to rule over their subjects and did not have to answer to anyone but God. They felt that the people, in turn, had an obligation to obey God's representative.

1. The Tudors of England. Two famous Tudor monarchs who held great power were Henry VIII (ruled 1509–1547) and his daughter Elizabeth I (ruled 1558–1603). Henry fought a number of wars with France. He promoted trade. Although he imprisoned or killed nobles and officials who disagreed with him, most of his subjects liked him. When the pope refused Henry's request for a divorce, he broke with the Roman Catholic Church. Henry made himself the head of the Church of England.

Elizabeth I also insisted on her own policies. She promoted trade and the founding of colonies in order to get money for the royal treasury. She continued to keep the Church of England separate from the Church of Rome. Her navy prevented Spanish forces from invading England in 1588 and turning it into a Catholic country.

Both Henry and Elizabeth encouraged writers, painters, and the theater. Elizabeth also urged privately owned English ships, called privateers, to attack Spanish ships to seize the cargoes of gold, silver, and gems. The Tudors made England prosperous and strong.

Elizabeth was the last of the Tudors. The Stuart kings who followed her also considered themselves to be absolute monarchs, ones who ruled by divine right. But Parliament was not willing to let the Stuarts have so much power. A great struggle between the lawmakers and the Stuart kings took place in the mid–1600's.

2. The Bourbons of France. Henry IV of Navarre was the first of the Bourbon kings. His son, Louis XIII, ruled as an absolute monarch. He acted to increase French influence in European affairs by intervening in the Thirty Years' War in Germany.

Queen Elizabeth I of England.

Louis XIV came to the throne in 1643 and ruled until 1715. During his long reign, France became the greatest power in Europe. Louis, called the "Sun King" and the "Grand Monarch," made France a center of learning and the arts. Louis also created the magnificent palace of Versailles outside of Paris. People in other countries imitated the French culture of this period. The French language was spoken by educated people throughout Europe.

French industry prospered during this period. But constant wars to add more territory to France and to protect French colonies overseas drained the royal treasury.

King Louis XIV of France.

The Bourbon kings who followed Louis XIV were left with huge debts. Their efforts to find money through heavy taxation would eventually cause the French people to turn against the monarchy.

3. The Hapsburgs. The Hapsburg monarchs ruled over Germany, Spain, and large portions of Central Europe.

    a. *Charles V.* This monarch became the king of Spain in 1516 and Holy Roman emperor in 1519. During his rule, Spain gained a huge colonial empire and great wealth. The Netherlands, southern Italy, Sicily, and, Austria were also parts of Charles' empire. Charles opposed the Reformation in Germany. He declared Martin Luther to be an outlaw and fought the Protestant princes in Germany.

    To defend his empire, Charles repeatedly fought the French over control of portions of Italy. He also defeated attacks by the Ottoman Turks in Eastern Europe and the Mediterranean.

    Illness and weariness with his responsibilities caused Charles to step down as emperor in 1556. Charles's brother, Ferdinand I, became the Holy Roman emperor. Charles's son, Philip II, became king of Spain. When Queen Elizabeth I refused Philip's proposal of marriage, he sent the Spanish Armada to its doomed effort to conquer England in 1588.

    b. *Maria Theresa.* Another strong Hapsburg ruler was Maria Theresa of Austria and Hungary. She sat on the throne from 1740 to 1780. Her husband was made the Holy Roman emperor

Maria Theresa, ruler of Austria and Hungary.

because women could not hold the title. Throughout Maria Theresa's reign, she had to fight to keep other monarchs from taking territory away from her. She succeeded more often than she failed. In 1772, she joined with Russia and Prussia in dividing Poland for the first time. Thus, a portion of that country was added to Austria.

Maria Theresa tried to rule wisely. She promoted reforms such as education for young children and tried to reduce the power of the great landlords in order to benefit the peasants. The Hapsburgs would rule Austria-Hungary until the end of World War I (1914–1918).

4. The Romanovs of Russia. Members of this family ruled Russia from the 1600's to 1917. They turned the country into a powerful nation.

a. *Peter I.* The most influential of the early Romanovs was Peter I (Peter the Great), who ruled from 1689 to 1725. Peter wanted to make Russia more like the countries in Western Europe where the arts and sciences were advancing. He brought teachers, engineers, and craftspeople from Europe to teach the Russians new ways. In a series of wars with Sweden, he won territory along the Baltic Sea. From the ports along the Baltic, which were called "windows on the West," the Russians increased their trade with Europe. Peter moved the capital from Moscow. He built a new capital, St. Petersburg, on the Gulf of Finland.

Peter set up schools and centers for scientific research. He took away much of the nobles' power and put the Russian Orthodox

Peter the Great of Russia.

Church under his control. He built a strong army loyal to him and crushed a revolt of his nobles. These measures strengthened absolutism in Russia.

b. Catherine II. Catherine the Great was the next strong ruler. The German wife of a Russian czar, she deposed her husband and reigned as an absolute monarch from 1762 to 1796. Catherine II continued to "Europeanize" Russia. She encouraged the creation of literature and works of fine art.

Poland was divided up between 1772 and 1795, with a large portion going to Russia. Catherine also added territory along the northern coast of the Black Sea by warring against the Ottoman Empire.

Unlike Maria Theresa, Catherine allowed large landholders to control local governmental affairs. The peasants and serfs had many rights taken away. Serfs were bound to the land and were treated almost as slaves by many masters. Great discontent built up among the peasants, who made up 95 percent of the population of Russia. While the upper classes gained more privileges, the lower classes received nothing to improve their lives.

Chapter Review

▶ MULTIPLE-CHOICE

Choose the item that best completes the sentence or answers the question.

1. The term *renaissance* means (*a*) revolt (*b*) rebirth (*c*) reform (*d*) revise.

2. The Renaissance began in (*a*) Italy (*b*) Germany (*c*) France (*d*) Spain.

3. The achievements of Michelangelo and Leonardo Da Vinci prove that the Renaissance was an age of (*a*) reason (*b*) revolution (*c*) genius (*d*) disorder.

4. The invention that did most to help spread the Renaissance was the (*a*) telescope (*b*) printing press (*c*) airplane (*d*) microscope.

5. Galileo Galilei and Isaac Newton were part of the (*a*) Age of Exploration and Discovery (*b*) Commercial Revolution (*c*) Scientific Revolution (*d*) Reformation.

6. The development of colonial empires by the Atlantic powers and the shifting of trade routes from the Mediterranean Sea to the Atlantic Ocean were results of the (*a*) Age of Exploration and Discovery (*b*) Scientific Revolution (*c*) Reformation (*d*) Counter-Reformation.

7. Two important results of the Commercial Revolution were the (*a*) use of the scientific method and new inventions (*b*) development of a global economy and the rise of capitalism (*c*) spread of the Renaissance through Europe and the rise of Protestantism (*d*) rise of the Anglican religion.

8. Which of the following was NOT a leader of the Reformation? (*a*) Martin Luther (*b*) John Calvin (*c*) Ignatius Loyola (*d*) Henry VIII.

9. An important step taken during the Counter-Reformation was the (*a*) founding of the Society of Jesus (Jesuits) (*b*) acceptance of all Protestant teachings (*c*) increased sales of indulgences (*d*) encouragement of belief in Islam.

10. A country that became the greatest power in Europe in the 1600's was (*a*) Italy (*b*) Russia (*c*) France (*d*) Denmark.

 MATCHING EXERCISE

Match each of the following names in Column A with his occupation in Column B. Some occupations will fit more than one person.

Column A

1. Rembrandt
2. Newton
3. Cabot
4. Cervantes
5. Boyle
6. Knox
7. Cartier
8. Machiavelli
9. Xavier
10. Frobisher

Column B

a. artist
b. writer
c. explorer
d. scientist
e. Protestant churchman
f. Catholic churchman

WRITING EXERCISE

1. Reread "2. Scientific Achievements," on pages 287–288. Write a paragraph giving *three* reasons why the work of Vesalius and Harvey was important to the growth of scientific knowledge.

2. Reread "The Age of Exploration and Discovery," on pages 290–295. Then list *four* ways that the world was changed by the explorers.

 ## ESSAY QUESTIONS

1. Describe the origins of the Renaissance and the role of humanism.

2. Explain the relationship between the invention of the printing press and the "Northern Renaissance."

3. List the results of the Scientific Revolution.

4. Define the term "Commercial Revolution."

5. Describe the rise of capitalism in Western Europe.

6. Explain the difference between the Reformation and the Counter-Reformation.

7. List the great ruling houses of Europe and explain their members' belief in absolute monarchy.

MAP EXERCISE

Review the map on pages 292–293. Then match each explorer in Column A with the nation for which he sailed in Column B.

Column A	Column B
1. Henry Hudson	*a.* Spain
2. Vasco da Gama	*b.* France
3. Ferdinand Magellan	*c.* Portugal
4. Jacques Cartier	*d.* Netherlands
5. Francis Drake	*e.* England

Connections: Who Discovered America?

"In fourteen hundred ninety-two, Christopher Columbus sailed the ocean blue" and "discovered" America. However, Columbus and those who came after him were not the first explorers of the Americas.

In New Hampshire, stones and stone structures bear writing in a language that was used by Phoenician traders who sailed from colonies in Spain.

There are Chinese historians who believe that a Buddhist monk traveled to Mexico in A.D. 459. They point to similarities between the Aztec and Chinese languages, myths, and coins.

Strong similarities exist between the pyramids of ancient Egypt and those pyramids built by the Mayas and Aztecs of America. Travelers from the Middle East may have shared their knowledge and skills with early Americans.

There is some evidence that Brendan, an Irish missionary, came to Newfoundland in the 6th century to convert the people there to Christianity.

Scandinavian stories, called *sagas*, tell us that Vikings from northern Europe crossed the Atlantic about A.D. 1000. Led by Leif Ericson, the Vikings explored and later colonized areas of Newfoundland. Archeological discoveries support these stories.

Some historians claim that a group of explorers led by a Welsh prince reached what is now Alabama in A.D. 1170. The historians point to similarities between certain Welsh words and those of some Indian languages.

No matter who "discovered" America first, Columbus brought the Americas to the attention of the Europeans. He did it at a time when people wanted to know more about the world that they lived in. Europeans were willing to colonize and build new societies in the New World. Columbus helped lay the groundwork for the Age of Discovery and the Commercial Revolution of the 16th and 17th centuries.

Explain each of the following titles:

1. "Vikings Arrive in America"
2. "Missionary Tries to Convert Indians"
3. "Pyramids Found in America"

A Mayan pyramid and temple in Chichén Itzá, Mexico.

DOCUMENT-BASED QUESTION

This question is based on the accompanying documents (1–5). It will improve your ability to work with historical documents.

Historical Context:

Beginning around 1300, there was a great rebirth of interest in learning and in the arts in Europe. This period was called the Renaissance. It produced a scientific revolution, an age of European exploration and discovery, and a religious movement known as the Reformation.

Task:

Using information from the documents and your knowledge of world history, answer the questions that follow each document. Your answers to each question will help you write the document-based essay.

Document 1. Excerpt from *The Book of the City of Ladies* (1405) by the Italian poet Christine de Pizan, calling for the education of women. The book is considered an early feminist text.

> I tell you again—and don't fear a contradiction—if it were customary to send daughters to school like sons, and if they were then taught the natural sciences, they would learn as thoroughly and understand the subtleties of all the arts and sciences as well as sons. . . . [J]ust as women have more delicate bodies than men, weaker and less able to perform many tasks, so do they have minds that are freer and sharper whenever they apply themselves.

> Source: de Pizan, Christine, *The Book of the City of Ladies*, translated by Earl Jeffrey Richards. NY: Persea Books, 1998.

According to this document, what radical notion in the 1400's did Pizan hold about women's abilities?

Document 2. Excerpt from Christopher Columbus's "Letter to Louis De Santangel" (1493), reporting on his first voyage westward for the Spanish crown:

> Sir,—Believing that you will take pleasure in hearing of the great success which our Lord has granted me in my voyage. I write you this letter, whereby you will learn how in thirty-three

day's time I reached the Indies with the fleet which the most illustrious King and Queen, our Sovereigns, gave to me, where I found very many islands thickly peopled, of all which I took possession without resistance for their Highnesses.

All Christendom ought to rejoice . . . both for the great exaltation which may accrue to them in turning so many nations to our holy faith [Catholicism], and also for the material benefits which will bring great gain, not only to Spain, but to all Christians.

> **Source**: *Select Letters of Christopher Columbus*, translated and edited by R.H. Major. 2nd ed. London: Hakluyt Society, 1870.

According to this document, what did Columbus "discover" and what did he believe would be the benefits of his discoveries?

Document 3. Excerpt from Martin Luther's "Speech Before the Diet of Worms" (1521), in which he defends himself before Holy Roman Emperor Charles V and the German princes:

> Since then Your majesty and your lordships desire a simple reply, I will answer without horns and without teeth. Unless I am convicted by Scripture and plain reason—I do not accept the authority of popes and councils, for they have contradicted each other—my conscience is captive [obedient] to the Word of God. I cannot and I will not recant anything, for to go against conscience is neither right nor safe. God help me. Amen.

> **Source**: Bainton, Roland H. *Here I Stand*. Nashville: Abingdon Press, 1950.

According to this document, why did Luther refuse to change his religious beliefs?

Document 4. Excerpt from "Second Treatise of Civil Government" (1690) by John Locke, in which he discusses the rights of man:

> To understand political power, . . . we must consider, what state all men are naturally in, and that is, a state of perfect freedom to order their actions, and dispose of their possessions and persons, as they think fit, within the bounds of the law of nature, without asking leave, or depending upon the will of any other man. A state also of equality, wherein all the power and jurisdiction is reciprocal, no one having more than another.

> **Source**: John Locke, "The Second Treatise of Civil Government" in *Two Treatises of Government*. London, 1690.

According to this document, what was Locke's belief about the natural state of human beings?

Document 5. Study the chart on page 297.

What does it show about the benefits of the policy of mercantilism for a home country?

DOCUMENT-BASED ESSAY

Using information from the above documents and your knowledge of world history, write an essay in which you:

- Discuss the changes in European life and culture that began in the Renaissance.
- Explain how these events transformed the world.

UNIT V

AN AGE OF REVOLUTIONS

CHAPTER 13
Political and Social Revolutions

The ideas of the Renaissance and the Reformation had an important effect on Europeans generally. People believed that they had certain rights. In particular, they started to question some long-standing ideas about government. In the 1660's, challenges arose to the total power of absolute monarchs and to the theory of the divine right of monarchs.

Political struggles developed between monarchs who wished to keep their power and people who wanted the rulers to share their power with them. Often these struggles burst into violence. Such a use of violence or the threat of violence to bring about basic changes in the way a nation is governed is called a revolution.

Revolutionary successes led to the establishment of *limited monarchies* in England and France and republics in the United States and Latin America. Both forms of government usually depend on constitutions that limit the power of rulers and guarantee basic rights to citizens.

Other revolutionary goals were (a) independence from foreign rulers and (b) national unification. North Americans fought for independence from Britain. Latin Americans fought for independence from Spain. Germans and Italians struggled to unify their countries under national governments. Some of the revolutions succeeded, while others failed. Yet all produced great ideas and great leaders.

REVOLUTIONS IN ENGLAND

People in 17th-century England took actions to bring an end to absolute monarchy. In two revolutions, the English limited the power of their kings and made their government more democratic.

1. The Puritan Revolt.   The death of Queen Elizabeth I in 1603 ended the rule of the Tudor family in England.

    a. *James I*.   Following Elizabeth, James I ruled England from 1603 to 1625. He was a member of the Stuart family, which had ruled Scotland for a long time. Tension quickly grew between James and Parliament.

    Members of Parliament resented James because he was a foreigner. They also disliked his many requests for money and his efforts to impose taxes without Parliament's consent. Parliament also distrusted James's desire for an alliance with Spain, which was a Catholic country. James had been raised by Presbyterians. As king of England, he supported the Anglican church. Another cause of friction was James's dislike of Puritans, who held many seats in Parliament. The Puritans were a powerful Calvinist sect. They considered Anglicanism too close to Catholicism and tried to "purify" the rituals of the Church of England. James and Parliament clashed many times throughout his reign of 22 years.

    b. *Charles I*.   Under James's son, Charles I (ruled 1625–1649), relations between the king and Parliament became worse. Like his father, Charles was a strong believer in absolutism and the divine right of kings. He, too, supported the Church of England. Like his father, Charles discriminated against Puritans.

    Charles had little respect for Parliament. When Parliament refused to give him money to build up his military forces, he forced people to lend him money. Those who refused were sent to prison or drafted into the army.

    In 1628, Parliament agreed to give Charles the money he wanted if he signed the *Petition of Right*. This document prohibited the ruler from imposing taxes without the consent of Parliament. It also stated that no person could be sent to prison without having the charges made public. Charles agreed to these provisions but later ignored them. He raised taxes without the consent of Parliament. He also had people arrested and secretly tried in a special court called the Star Chamber. In this royal law court, people were denied a jury. When Parliament objected, Charles dismissed it and ruled alone for 11 years, until 1640.

Charles did not call Parliament into session again until he had exhausted every other way of raising money. The House of Commons was controlled by Charles's Puritan enemies. Their efforts to restrict the power of the king led to more tension. Before granting any new taxes, the Puritans insisted that Charles be less autocratic. In 1642, Charles attempted to arrest some of the Puritan leaders of Parliament. This action touched off the English Civil War, also called the Puritan Revolt (1642–1648).

c.   *Cavaliers vs. Roundheads.* Those who fought for the king were called Royalists or Cavaliers. They included the nobles, many Roman Catholics, wealthy landowners, and supporters of the Church of England.

Those who fought for Parliament were known as Roundheads. (They cut their hair short, while most of the Cavaliers wore their hair long.) Chief among them were the Puritans. Parliament also had the aid of the Scots, who objected to Charles's interference with their Presbyterian (Protestant) religion. Small farmers, merchants, and others who had suffered from the king's policies also supported the Roundheads.

After 1643, Oliver Cromwell, a deeply religious Puritan, led the Roundhead forces. He trained and organized his men into a superior fighting force. It was called the New Model Army. Cromwell's victory over the Royalists in 1648 left Parliament and the Puritans in control of England. Early in 1649, Parliament tried Charles I,

Oliver Cromwell at the time of Charles I's execution.

convicted him of treason, and beheaded him. Absolutism and the monarchy had temporarily come to an end.

2. Commonwealth and Restoration. After he had won the civil war, Oliver Cromwell made England into a republic in 1649. It was called the *Commonwealth*.

a. *Commonwealth and Protectorate.*

In the new government, Cromwell and Parliament shared power. But tension soon developed between the two. Cromwell dissolved Parliament twice and after 1654 ruled as a dictator. He took the title of Lord Protector of England. During the period of the Commonwealth and Protectorate, England had its first, and only, written constitution. It was called the Instrument of Government.

Between 1649 and 1651, Cromwell put down royalist uprisings in Ireland and Scotland. He treated the Irish in a particularly harsh and cruel manner.

Many English people came to resent Cromwell's rule. He closed all theaters and other places of public amusement. He also did not permit any opposition to his religious or political ideas. Heavy taxes and Puritan intolerance of the Anglican religion, to which the majority of English belonged, increased dislike of Cromwell.

b. *The Restoration.*

After Cromwell's death in 1658, Parliament again had the most power. But the majority of the English people wanted a king again. In 1660, Parliament invited the oldest son of Charles I to return to England from his exile on the continent of Europe. The rule of Charles II (1660–1685) is called the *Restoration*. While the monarchy was restored, it was marked by a sharing of power between the king and Parliament. Charles II reigned as a limited monarch.

An important step to protect individual rights was taken during the Restoration period. In 1679, Parliament passed the *Habeas Corpus* Act. It stated that a person who was arrested could obtain a writ, or order, demanding to be taken before a judge within a certain period of time. The judge would then decide whether the person should be placed on trial or released.

Political parties began to develop during the Restoration. Supporters of the king came to be called Tories. Those who wanted Parliament to be stronger than the king were known as Whigs. Limited monarchy, *habeas corpus*, and the rise of political parties contributed to the growth of democracy in England.

The Merry Monarch

In 1658, the lord protector of England, Oliver Cromwell, died. With his death, the hope of a Puritan England vanished. In 1660, the English, dissatisfied with Cromwell's military dictatorship, invited Charles II to become king of England. Eleven years earlier, his father, King Charles I, had been executed by Cromwell.

With great ceremony, Charles II was crowned. His first acts as king were to grant pardons to many of his former enemies and to proclaim religious freedom. He was a tolerant ruler who had no wish to persecute anyone. Throughout his reign of 25 years, Charles managed to control the powerful religious and political groups that threatened to throw England into another civil war. While Charles sympathized with the Roman Catholics, he made peace with the Puritans and the Church of England (Anglicans).

Charles had other immediate problems to deal with. As a result of commercial competition, England went to war with Holland in 1664. A widespread plague struck England in 1665. In 1666, the Great Fire of London destroyed most of the city.

Throughout these troubles, Charles quietly remained in command. In doing so, he acquired more power for the monarchy. Yet, as king, Charles contributed to the growth of democracy in England. For example, he approved the *Habeas Corpus* Act of 1679, which safeguarded citizens from improper arrest and jailing.

Charles recognized that science, mathematics, and technology would be important to the nation's future. In 1662,

King Charles II.

he founded the Royal Society of London, an "invisible university" where scientists such as Isaac Newton, Robert Boyle, and William Harvey could meet, discuss theories, and publish papers.

Charles promoted the arts as well. Music and painting flourished, as did architecture. After the Great Fire, there was a need for good architects to design hundreds of new churches and public buildings in London.

Charles was an easygoing monarch. He played with his dogs and generally enjoyed life. Because of this, people called him the "Merry Monarch." Charles liked horse racing and often rode in races himself. He was a good tennis player. The game became popular again after being out of favor during the Cromwell years.

Charles II died at the age of 55. With his last breath and with some wit, he begged his friends to forgive him for taking such a long time to die.

Give two reasons why Charles II was a popular king.

3. The Glorious Revolution. James II became king of England in 1685. He was the younger brother of Charles II and the last Stuart to rule. A Roman Catholic convert and a believer in absolute monarchy, he was disliked by Parliament. But Parliament was willing to support James because he had Protestant daughters married to Protestant princes who would succeed him. When James's second wife, a Catholic, gave birth to a son in 1688, Parliament became worried. (A son, no matter what age, inherited the throne before a daughter.) Parliament feared that another Catholic king would rule England upon the death of James II. Most members of Parliament agreed that this could not be allowed to happen.

Parliament secretly invited James's daughter Mary and her husband, William of Orange, the ruler of Holland, to rule England as Protestant king and queen. They accepted. When William landed in England with an army and marched on London, James II fled to France. Because William and Mary won their victory without bloodshed, this event is called the *Glorious Revolution*. The monarchs officially began their joint rule in 1689.

The Glorious Revolution of 1688 ended absolute monarchy in England forever. Limited monarchy became the permanent form of government. In 1689, the English *Bill of Rights* made it clear that Parliament would have more power than the kings and queens of England. The bill, also known as the Declaration of Rights, stated that taxes imposed without the consent of Parliament were illegal. It declared that the ruler could not suspend laws passed by Parliament. It prohibited English courts from imposing cruel punishments. It provided for frequent meetings of Parliament and gave all members of Parliament freedom of speech.

DEFINITIONS

Explain the meaning of each of the following terms:

a. Cavaliers
b. Roundheads
c. Commonwealth
d. Restoration
e. Church of England
f. Puritans
g. limited monarchy
h. Glorious Revolution

CHRONOLOGY

State the dates when the following people began their rule of England. Then rearrange the names in their proper chronological order (1–6).

a. William and Mary
b. Charles II
c. Oliver Cromwell
d. James II
e. Charles I
f. James I

WRITING EXERCISE

Write *one* or *two* paragraphs to explain why the Petition of Right, the *Habeas Corpus* Act, and the Bill of Rights aided the growth of democracy in England.

THE AMERICAN REVOLUTION

In 1607, while James I was king, the first permanent English settlement was established in North America, at Jamestown, Virginia. By 1733, the English had created 13 separate colonies along the east coast of North America.

The majority of Europeans in the colonies were from England. They spoke the English language and followed English ways. They felt that they should have the rights and privileges of English citizens in the home country. Eventually, they fought a war to keep those rights.

1. The Road to War. During most of the 1600's, England did not pay much attention to its American colonies. Some actions were taken to control certain types of trade. But the English government was too occupied with events at home to concern itself much with people who lived thousands of miles away. *Salutary neglect* was the term used to describe this policy of limited control of colonial affairs. While it lasted, the colonists became accustomed to ignoring the more restrictive English laws. Chief among these were the *Navigation Acts*, which sought to restrict colonial industry and limit colonial trade with all countries other than England. In 1765, however, a new policy was begun.

From the late 1600's through the mid-1700's, England and France fought a number of wars over colonies in the Americas and Asia. Occasionally, Spain was also involved. The Seven Years' War (1756–1763) was the largest and last of these wars. It was known in England's North American colonies as the French and Indian War. England (called Great Britain after 1707) won all these wars and thereby gained the largest empire. But victory left the British with many debts after 1763. To solve their financial problems, King George III (ruled 1760–1820) and his ministers decided to collect more taxes from the American colonies.

a. *New Colonial Policy.* Many Americans objected to the New Colonial Policy of the British. They particularly disliked the Stamp Act, passed by Parliament in 1765. It required the purchase of government stamps to put on newspapers, pamphlets, legal documents, playing cards, and other items. Americans considered this to be a direct tax. In their view, Parliament had no right to tax them in this way because they were not represented in this lawmaking body. The slogan of the colonial protestors became "No taxation without representation!"

Some Americans openly refused to obey the tax laws. They burned offices where stamps were sold. They stopped buying British products and called a *congress*, or meeting, to protest the Stamp Act. British merchants, hurt by the boycott of their goods, and some members of Parliament called for a repeal of the Stamp Act. George III and his ministers finally agreed.

In 1767, a new set of tax laws, called the Townshend Acts, was passed. Colonial protests and a boycott of British goods again forced a repeal. All taxes except for those on tea were ended in 1770.

b. *Boston Tea Party.* Colonial leaders such as Sam Adams in Massachusetts and Patrick Henry in Virginia worked to stir up anti-British feeling. They and others wanted the American colonies to govern themselves. Their efforts were aided by a new British law passed in 1773. The Tea Act eliminated the tax on tea

In 1765, Americans in New York City protested the Stamp Act.

imported to the American colonies by the British East India Company. This enabled that company to undercut the prices being charged for tea by American merchants and smugglers, making them very angry. When a British ship carrying tea arrived in Boston harbor in late 1773, a group of Americans dumped the tea into the harbor. Similar actions to destroy cargoes of tea occurred in other colonial seaports during the next few months. This is now known as the Boston Tea Party.

The king and his ministers reacted with great anger and took steps to punish Boston. They closed Boston harbor and suspended the government of Massachusetts. They also moved a large number of British troops into the Boston area. The colonists referred to these measures as the *Intolerable Acts*.

Virginia leaders felt that the rest of the colonies should show support for Massachusetts. They called for a meeting of delegates from each colony. The First Continental Congress met in Philadelphia in the fall of 1774. The Congress expressed support for Massachusetts and asked all colonists not to buy British goods. It urged Parliament and the king to stop punishing Boston and to recognize the basic rights of the colonists. Parliament's reply did not satisfy all Americans. Colonists stepped up training of military groups called Minutemen and stored weapons and ammunition in secret locations.

c. *Battles of Lexington and Concord.* In April 1775, British troops marched out of Boston toward Lexington and Concord. Their mission was to arrest American leaders in

North America, 1783

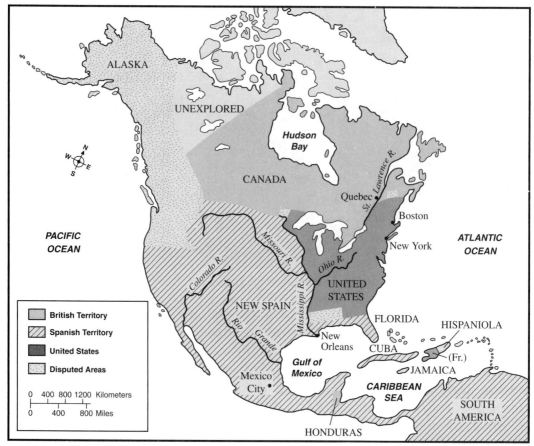

EXPLAIN: In 1783, the newly independent United States had many problems to work out with other nations.

Massachusetts and seize stores of weapons hidden by Americans. Colonial forces resisted the British in Lexington and Concord and shot at the royal troops all along the route back to Boston. The American Revolution had begun.

2. The Beginning of a New Nation. In May 1775, the Second Continental Congress began meeting. The most important decision made by the Congress was to approve the Declaration of Independence on July 4, 1776. This famous document stated why the American colonies should no longer be a part of the British Empire. It also made clear the high value placed by Americans on liberty and individual rights.

The American Revolution lasted for eight years. In spite of many setbacks, the ragged American army finally overcame the

Revolutionary American Documents

British troops and a small band of armed Americans clashed in Lexington, Massachusetts, in April 1775. Following other battles at Concord and at Bunker Hill outside Boston, the Second Continental Congress announced its decision to declare the independence of a new nation, the United States.

1. The Declaration of Independence.

The Declaration of Independence, written mainly by Thomas Jefferson, with the assistance of Benjamin Franklin and John Adams, is a great democratic document. It reflects Jefferson's thinking, influenced by the ideas of the English philosopher John Locke. In it, Jefferson stated that governments must be representative of the people, limited in power by a recognition of basic human rights, and must derive their powers from the "consent of the governed." If any government violates people's natural rights, then the people have the right to "alter or abolish" that government.

After stating these democratic principles, the Declaration lists Americans' many grievances against King George III of Britain. These included dissolving colonial assemblies, stationing British troops in the colonies, and taxing the colonists without their consent.

Published on July 4, 1776, the Declaration provided members of the Continental Army and other Americans with a clear objective for the war they were fighting. Not all Americans, however, agreed upon the need for independence from Great Britain. Scholars believe that approximately one-third of the American colonists actively supported the "Patriot" cause, another one-third were indifferent or uninvolved, and one-third were actively opposed to the rebellion and its goal of independ-ence. Many American "Loyalists" formed regiments that fought in support of the British forces. After the conclusion of the Revolutionary War in 1781, many American Loyalists emigrated to England, Canada, the West Indies, and elsewhere.

2. The U.S. Constitution.

During the *Critical Period* (1781–1789), the newly born United States struggled to deal with political and economic problems that threatened its survival. By 1787, it was believed by many that the Articles of Confederation, the loose agreement among the states approved in 1781, required amendment in order to provide a stronger national government. Delegates from every state except Rhode Island went to Philadelphia in the summer of 1787 to do this. Among them were Benjamin Franklin, James Madison, and Alexander Hamilton. The *Constitutional Convention* was headed by George Washington.

The work of James Madison was especially important to the success of the Convention. Acting as secretary to the Convention, Madison developed a new plan of government. He and other Virginia delegates persuaded the Convention to replace the Articles of Confederation with a Constitution. The document they wrote provided the United States with the framework for a strong national government and protection for basic freedoms. Upon its *ratification* (approval) by the states, the Constitution became the basic law of the United States.

The Constitution consists of the *Preamble*, a main body of seven articles, the Bill of Rights, and 17 more amendments adopted in later years (1791–1992).

The Preamble states that the new U.S. government was established by "we the people." It gives goals to be achieved, such as to form a more perfect union, establish justice, insure domestic tranquility, provide for the common defense, promote the general welfare, and secure the blessings of liberty to ourselves and our posterity (future generations).

Articles I, II, and III establish the *separation of powers* by dividing the powers of government among the executive, legislative, and judicial branches. These articles provide for the Congress to make the laws, the president and vice president to carry out the laws, and the Supreme Court and lower federal courts to interpret the laws.

3. The Bill of Rights. Soon after the Constitution was adopted in 1789, Congress proposed ten amendments. This *Bill of Rights* was ratified in 1791. Originally, they protected citizens from the federal government, but they were later applied to state governments as well. These amendments provide for freedom of religion; separation of church and state; freedom of speech, press, assembly, and petition; the right to keep and bear arms; protection against quartering (forcing citizens to feed and house soldiers); protection of the rights of persons accused of crimes; protection against loss of life, liberty, or property without "due process of law"; and protection against excessive bail and cruel and unusual punishment. The Tenth Amendment provides that powers not delegated to the federal government or denied to the states belong to the state governments and to the American people.

The need to replace the Articles of Confederation with the federal system described above was explained in essays written by James Madison, Alexander Hamilton, and John Jay. The essays were published in a book entitled *The Federalist Papers*.

Those who agreed with the ideas of Madison and the others joined with them in forming the Federalist Party, the first political party in the United States. Opposing them were the Anti-Federalists, especially Patrick Henry and Samuel Adams. They feared that a strong national government might not respect basic rights and liberties. In the 1790's, the Anti-Federalists, or Democratic-Republicans, were led by Thomas Jefferson. Alexander Hamilton became the leader of the Federalist Party.

1. **Compare the roles of Thomas Jefferson and James Madison in the founding of the United States (1776–1791).**

2. **Identify *two* ideas found in both the Declaration of Independence and the U.S. Constitution.**

3. **Explain why you AGREE or DISAGREE with the Founders' belief in the need for a Bill of Rights.**

might of the British. France aided the Americans with money and naval support.

The Peace of Paris formally ended the war in 1783. This recognized the United States of America as a fully independent nation that stretched from the Atlantic Ocean to the Mississippi River and from Canada to Florida. The American success would become an example to other people who struggled for greater freedom.

Revolutionaries in France and Latin American were encouraged by the actions in North America.

CRITICAL THINKING

Explain why you AGREE or DISAGREE with each of the following statements:

1. "The American Revolution was an unnecessary war. It happened only because the American colonists and the British government could not understand each other's point of view."

2. "The issuing of the Declaration of Independence by the Second Continental Congress was the only way the American colonists could have resolved their differences with the British government."

ESSAY QUESTIONS

1. Describe how the British reacted to each of the following colonial actions:
   a. boycott of British goods in 1765
   b. destruction of tea in Boston Harbor in 1773
   c. storing of weapons and ammunition in secret locations in 1775

2. Explain the meaning of the phrase "No taxation without representation."

THE FRENCH REVOLUTION AND THE NAPOLEONIC ERA

The French Revolution (1789–1799) was a major event in the struggle against absolutism in Europe. It produced new and important ideas about government and society. It also brought Napoleon Bonaparte, one of the most remarkable men in history, to the attention of the world.

1. Problems of the Old Regime.   France during the 1700's had three major problems: inequality, insolvency, and injustice.

a. *Inequality.* French society was divided into three groups called estates. The clergy and nobles made up the First and Second Estates respectively. Many of these people lived in luxury, held the most important government jobs, and paid very little in taxes.

The Third Estate (professional and businesspeople, farmers, and laborers) made up 97 percent of the French population. This group paid more than their share of the taxes and did the work that made it possible for the nobles and high church officials to live well. The *bourgeoisie* (middle class) was the most influential group in the Third Estate. They suffered from tariffs on trade, restrictions on manufacturing, and restrictions on business activity. Many wanted the government to leave business alone. Such a policy, called *laissez-faire* (hands off), had been presented by Scottish economist Adam Smith in his book *Wealth of Nations*. From the ranks of the bourgeoisie came the intellectuals (highly educated philosophers and writers) who would begin and lead the French Revolution. These were the leaders of the 18th-century *Enlightenment* or *Age of Reason*. They believed that people had natural rights and should be governed with logic and reason.

The ideas of the French philosophers influenced many people. One of the best-known philosophers was Jean Jacques Rousseau (1712–1778). In his book *The Social Contract*, he presented new theories of government: responsibility to the people and respect for natural rights. The ideas of Rousseau and Montesquieu influenced North American revolutionaries, such as Thomas Jefferson, and South American independence leaders, such as Simón Bolívar.

All three estates were represented in the lawmaking body of France, the Estates General. But this body rarely met. As a result, the majority of French people had no chance to influence the way they were ruled.

b. *Insolvency.* Another great problem of France in the late 1700's was a lack of money. The many wars ordered by Louis XIV against Great Britain and other nations had drained the treasury. France's support of the American revolutionary cause had also been costly. The nobles and clergy refused to pay higher taxes or to give up any of their privileges. As a result, the large and inefficient government was close to being bankrupt.

c. *Injustice.* A third serious problem was injustice. France did not have one set of courts and laws that applied to everyone. The king or his representative could imprison anyone for any reason for any period of time. Once in jail, a person might never be brought to trial, be allowed to apply for bail, or even be charged with a crime.

This 18th-century cartoon shows the Third Estate carrying the burden of the First and Second Estates.

2. The Beginning of the Revolution. When King Louis XVI (ruled 1774–1792) could not raise more money to finance the government, he called the Estates General into session. It met in 1789 for the first time in 175 years. Immediately, there was a problem about voting. Since each estate had only one vote, the First and Second Estates could outvote the Third Estate.

The Third Estate did not like this arrangement. Its members wanted each representative to have a vote. (The Third Estate had 600 representatives; the Second, 300; and the First, 300.) When the First and Second Estates disagreed, the Third Estate withdrew from the Estates General and formed the National Assembly. The representatives from the Third Estate took an oath to provide France with a constitution that would limit the power of the king and give more rights to the people.

Most French people enthusiastically supported the aims of the National Assembly. Threats by the king to arrest the leaders of the Assembly caused riots all over France. On July 14, 1789, an angry crowd stormed and captured a fortress called the Bastille in Paris. The Bastille had been used as a prison for opponents of the government. The crowd then marched on city hall, killed the mayor of Paris, and set up a revolutionary government.

In the countryside, peasants rose up against nobles, burning manor houses on some feudal estates. When the people stopped

In storming the Bastille, Paris revolutionaries also attacked a symbol of the Old Regime.

paying taxes and royal officials fled France to keep from being killed, the government broke down. The king was forced to accept the revolutionary government led by the National Assembly.

The National Assembly changed France in many ways. In August 1789, it adopted the Declaration of the Rights of Man. The declaration provided all people of France with such basic rights as freedom of speech, religion, and the press. It also guaranteed the right of men to participate in the government of France. The National Assembly reformed the legal system. It provided for elected judges, trail by jury, and an end to brutal punishments.

Perhaps the Assembly's most important work was the Constitution of 1791. It reformed the government by establishing a limited monarchy. After Louis XVI accepted the new constitution, the National Assembly was dissolved. A Legislative Assembly was elected to make laws for France.

3. The Republic.   In 1792, the new legislators faced threats from outside France. Prussia and Austria went to war with France to aid the royal family. Later, Britain, Spain, and Holland joined the fight against France.

A powerful extremist group called the Jacobins convinced people that the king had plotted with Austria and Prussia to overthrow the revolutionaries and restore the absolute monarchy. The Assembly was forced to arrest the king and queen. Then the Assembly called for new elections to choose representatives for a National Convention. The Convention drew up a new constitution and created the First French Republic.

a. *Reign of Terror.* The Convention also put Louis XVI on trial for treason. He was found guilty and in January 1793 beheaded. Soon a Committee of Public Safety, led by the Jacobins, directed the government. The leader of the Committee was Maximilien Robespierre. In mid-1793, the Committee began a Reign of Terror. It arrested anyone suspected of opposing the Committee, sympathizing with the monarchy, or aiding the enemies of France. Most of the people who were arrested were killed. Thousands were beheaded by a machine called the *guillotine.* Others were drowned or shot.

In early 1794, the Jacobin leaders turned on one another. Finally, in July 1794, a moderate group in the National Convention had Robespierre beheaded, thus ending the Reign of Terror.

Although the Jacobins created a dictatorship and fostered great fear among people, they did stimulate French patriotism. The majority of people at last felt that the privileges of the aristocracy had ended. They were inspired by the ideals of liberty, equality, and fraternity. Pride was stirred by a song called "The Marseillaise," which became the French national anthem. Most French people stood together to save France from its enemies. By 1795, French armies had not only defended the nation but had conquered parts of Holland, Belgium, and Germany.

b. *The Directory.* In 1795, another constitution placed France under the control of the Directory, a five-member committee. The Directory proved to be corrupt and inefficient. It could not solve the country's serious financial problems. Furthermore, in 1798, the enemies of France gained new strength. Britain, in control of the seas, persuaded other countries to join the fight against France. In the following year, French armies lost land battles in Italy, Switzerland, and Holland. France's future looked dark.

In 1799, an able young general named Napoleon Bonaparte forced the Directory to resign. He then took over the government and brought the French Revolution to an end.

The execution of Louis XVI. The Reign of Terror soon followed.

4. The Napoleonic Era.   Napoleon has always been regarded as a son of the Revolution. His climb from poverty in Corsica, an island south of France, to become the ruler of France was made possible by the Revolution. After 1789, France often looked to men of talent and energy rather than to men of noble birth to be leaders. The qualities that helped Napoleon become France's youngest and most popular general also made possible his rise to become the country's first emperor in 1804. Under his rule, France became a military dictatorship and the most powerful nation in Europe.

a. *Napoleonic reforms.* Between 1802 and 1805, Napoleon increased the efficiency of the French government. He had a new law code prepared. The Code Napoléon made all citizens equal before the law. It provided for trail by jury and religious freedom. The Code Napoléon is still the basis of the French legal system. It has also served as a model for the legal systems of several countries in Europe and Latin America.

Napoleon organized a public school system run by a committee called the University of France. He established the Legion of Honor, an honorary society for people who had performed important services for France.

Napoleon gave France a fair taxation system and set up the Bank of France. This organization coined money and kept the currency stable. It also made sure that economic conditions favored business activity. As a result, France stayed reasonably prosperous.

All of these reforms made the people of France like Napoleon, even though he was a dictator. He gave France order, stability, and the kind of equality that the Revolution had called for. But

Napoleon's Empire, 1812

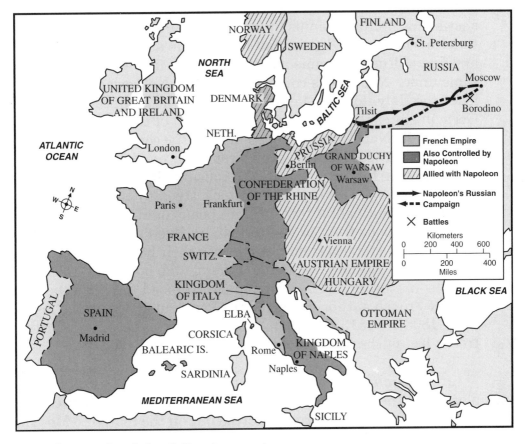

Complete each of the following sentences:

1. In 1812, the French Empire included —, the —, and portions of —.

2. Among the areas also controlled by Napoleon in 1812 were —.

3. In Central Europe, the — Empire was allied with Napoleon.

4. Great — was neither allied with nor controlled by Napoleon.

5. A country in which Napoleon fought a major military campaign in 1812 was —.

Napoleon did not permit freedom of the press. Nor did he give the French peace.

b.   *Foreign expansion.* Shortly after Napoleon took control of the government, he defeated the Austrians and made peace with Britain. But in 1803, the treaty with Britain fell apart. Britain persuaded Austria, Russia, Sweden, and Naples to renew the fight against France on land and sea. The resulting battles are known as the Napoleonic Wars. They lasted from 1805 to 1815. Napoleon showed his military genius by leading the armies of France to victories over Austria, Russia, and Prussia. He also invaded Portugal and Spain. Russia became an ally of France in 1807. Most of Italy came under Napoleon's control. So did the Netherlands. He abolished the Holy Roman Empire. In its place, he grouped most of the German states together in a Confederation of the Rhine.

By 1807, Napoleon controlled most of the countries on the continent of Europe. He had given France an empire. Only Britain, with its powerful navy, was able to continue fighting Napoleon.

To weaken Britain, Napoleon took steps to cut off its trade. Under the Continental System, European countries were ordered not to buy goods from or sell to Britain. Even ships from British colonies were stopped from trading with their home country. Many countries in Europe, including Russia, did not want to follow Napoleon's orders. The Portuguese refused. Their rebellion against French authority started the Peninsular War, which lasted from 1808 to 1813. By then, Spanish, Portuguese, and British troops had pushed Napoleon's forces back into France.

c. *French retreat.*   Partly to punish Russia for not going along with the Continental System, Napoleon invaded that county in 1812. Some 600,000 troops started out on the march to Moscow in June. The French forces occupied Moscow in September. In October, the Russians counterattacked. The French retreated, and in November, winter set in. Only some 100,000 of the French forces survived.

The setback in Russia encouraged all parts of the empire in Europe to rebel against French military rule. In 1813, the armies of Prussia, Austria, and Russia decisively defeated Napoleon at Leipzig (in Germany) in the Battle of Nations. Early in 1814, even many French people turned against the emperor. Finally, in April, Napoleon was captured and exiled to Elba, an island in the Mediterranean.

In March 1815, Napoleon saw a chance to regain power. He escaped from Elba and marched through France. Loyal French soldiers joined his cause. Troops from all over Europe rushed to stop Napoleon. Led by the British Duke of Wellington, the allies defeated Napoleon in June 1815 at Waterloo in Belgium. Napoleon was then exiled to the island of St. Helena in the South Atlantic Ocean. He died there in 1821.

The Napoleonic Era was over. The long wars had caused great bloodshed and destruction throughout Europe. Yet

Napoleon before the Battle of Austerlitz, at which the French defeated Russian and Austrian forces in 1805.

Napoleon's armies had also spread the revolutionary ideals of liberty, equality, and fraternity. These ideals and the Code Napoléon inspired other Europeans to make changes in their governments.

5. The Congress of Vienna.   After Napoleon's defeat in April 1814, the leaders of Europe decided to hold a conference to determine how to keep the peace. They met in Vienna, Austria, beginning in September 1814. Representatives came from most countries in Europe. Even France was allowed to send a delegate. Most decisions were made by officials from Great Britain, Russia, Prussia, and Austria.

Prince Klemens von Metternich, a brilliant Austrian diplomat, dominated the conference. Metternich's ideas would greatly influence European affairs for 30 years.

The Congress of Vienna attempted to keep Europe at peace by establishing a *balance of power* among the nations. It wanted to prevent any one nation from becoming militarily stronger than its neighbors. The decision makers at the Congress also supported the principle of *legitimacy*. Wherever possible, the royal families who had ruled before the French Revolution and the Napoleonic Era were restored to power. A Bourbon king, Louis XVIII, had already been placed on the throne of France. Former ruling families were returned to power in Austria, Prussia, Spain, and the many states of Italy.

Europe After the Congress of Vienna, 1815

Indicate whether each statement is *true* (**T**) or *false* (**F**).

1. In 1815, France was part of the German Confederation.

2. The Papal States were located in central Italy.

3. Poland was part of Russia in 1815.

4. Berlin was located in the Kingdom of Prussia in 1815.

5. Vienna was a city of the Ottoman Empire in 1815.

6. Sardinia included the island of Corsica.

The Congress opposed the efforts of the Poles, Belgians, and other national groups to govern themselves. Any demand for limiting royal power or granting political rights to the common people was rejected. Such ideas were considered to be revolutionary and dangerous.

The decision makers at Vienna did not force France to sign a harsh peace treaty. They wanted the French people to accept the government of Louis XVIII. France lost all the territory it had taken in Europe. Its boundaries were to be the same as they had been in 1792. It kept most of its overseas possessions. But France was made to pay for damages it had done to other nations during the wars. It also had to pay to keep troops of the victorious nations in forts along the borders of France.

The Congress of Vienna ended the era of the French Revolution and Napoleon. Yet the revolutionary spirit did not die in 1815. Throughout the 19th century, demands for political change would lead to violence in France and elsewhere in Europe.

CRITICAL THINKING

Reread "2. The Beginning of the Revolution," on pages 333–334. Then write a letter to King Louis XVI telling him why he should cooperate with the National Assembly.

IDENTIFICATIONS

Explain or identify each of the following terms:

  a. First, Second, Third Estates   e. Jacobins
  b. Declaration of the Rights of Man   f. Reign of Terror
  c. First French Republic   g. Directory
  d. Committee of Public Safety

WRITING EXERCISE

Reread "4. The Napoleonic Era," on pages 336–339, and then write a paragraph in response to each of the following questions:

1. What did Napoleon do to change France for the better?

2. How did Napoleon lose his empire and his crown?

3. List steps taken by the Congress of Vienna to end the era of the French Revolution and Napoleon.

THE LATIN AMERICAN REVOLUTIONS

While the Napoleonic Wars raged in Europe, great changes were occurring elsewhere. The people in the Spanish colonies in the Western Hemisphere did not like the way they were being ruled. They wanted to break Spain's control over them. The successful revolutions in the 13 colonies in North America and in France gave hope to Latin Americans. They were also inspired by the victory of the forces of Toussaint L'Ouverture in Haiti. A former slave, he had led an uprising against the French in 1803.

1. Causes of Discontent.   The colonists and others in the Spanish Empire had several reasons to resent Spanish rule.

   a.   *Trade disputes.*   The Spanish government controlled trade for the benefit of Spain. The colonies had to buy manufactured goods from the home country and sell their products only to Spain. This mercantilist policy kept wealth flowing into Spain. It did little to help the colonists.

   b.   *Inequality.*   The unequal distribution of wealth and power among the Latin Americans created another source of resentment. Spain gave important political and military jobs only to *peninsulares.* These were people who had been born in Spain (which, with Portugal, makes up the Iberian Peninsula). Creoles, colonists born in Latin America to Spanish parents, wanted more power for themselves. They tended to be the wealthy landowners, mine owners, and businesspeople. Mestizos, children of Spanish and Indian parents, also wanted a share of the political power. They tended to work in towns or be overseers on estates. The great mass of people, the peons, were Indians, blacks, and people of mixed heritage. Most peons worked on the great estates and in the mines. They had no land of their own and lived in poverty. They had little hope of achieving wealth or power.

   The desire for revolution was strongest among the Creoles. They were well educated and aware of the ideas behind the revolutions in North America and Europe. For the discontented Creoles, opportunity came in 1808. In that year, the armies of Napoleon Bonaparte conquered Spain. His brother, Joseph Bonaparte, became king of Spain. The Latin American colonists refused to accept French rule. Revolutions broke out in many parts of Latin America. Even after the Spanish king was restored to the throne in 1814, the revolutions continued. Most colonists did not want to return to the old ways. They wanted independence.

2. The Great Liberators. A number of gifted military and political leaders arose in Latin America to organize the revolutions. They directed the separate struggles to create independent nations in different parts of the Spanish Empire.

a. *Mexican revolutionaries.* In Mexico, a village priest named Miguel Hidalgo led his Indian followers in an uprising against Spanish rule in 1810. Hidalgo and his army won a few battles. When they reached Mexico City, the capital, Spanish forces stopped them. Hidalgo and some of his followers were captured and executed. Other revolutionaries continued to fight.

Agustín de Iturbide, a Creole leader, finally won freedom for Mexico City in 1821. Well-supported by the Creoles and the Roman Catholic Church, he united most of Mexico against Spain. Soon after his victory, Iturbide proclaimed himself emperor of Mexico. He was overthrown, and Mexico became a republic in 1824.

b. *Bolívar.* The struggle to free Venezuela began about 1808. Under the leadership of Francisco de Miranda and Simón Bolívar, the struggle achieved success in 1811. But a year later, Spanish forces retook the country. Bolívar escaped to Colombia, and Miranda died in prison.

During the next few years, Bolívar unsuccessfully tried to invade Venezuela and to widen the revolution in Colombia. Finally, he gathered enough support to drive the Spaniards out of

Simón Bolívar, the "Liberator."

Colombia in 1819. The "Liberator," as people called Bolívar, became president of Colombia. He then turned his attention to Venezuela. It again became independent in 1821. Bolívar also aided the struggle against Spanish rule in Ecuador. This war was won in 1822. Ecuador, Venezuela, and Colombia joined together in a nation called Great Colombia. It was governed by Bolívar. He hoped that the nation would be the beginning of a union of all Latin American states.

Study the map on page 345. Then complete the following:

1. Name *three* Latin American areas that were controlled by Spain in 1790.

2. Name a city found in *each* of the following countries:
   Mexico   Argentina
   Brazil   Peru
   Chile

3. Complete the following sentence:
   A major change that occurred in Latin America between 1790 and 1825 was —.

---

c. San Martín. José de San Martín, another great revolutionary leader, was born in Argentina. He organized an army in western Argentina to free Chile. San Martín marched over the Andes Mountains, defeated the Spaniards, and declared Chile's independence in 1818. He then took his forces by sea to northern Peru. It became independent in 1821.

San Martín met with Bolívar in 1822 to determine how best to conquer southern Peru. When Bolívar and San Martín disagreed on strategy, San Martín left Peru. Bolívar took over the government of northern Peru and sent forces to drive the Spaniards out of the south. This section became independent in 1825. It was named Bolivia.

3. Brazil. When Napoleon's soldiers invaded Portugal in 1807, its ruler, John VI, fled to Brazil. This was the huge Portuguese colony in eastern South America. Brazil then became a kingdom. John considered himself to be the head of two countries: Portugal and Brazil. Even after the French were driven out of Portugal, John stayed in Brazil. In 1820, he was finally persuaded to return to Portugal to become a constitutional monarch. John left his son, Pedro, in Brazil to take charge of the government.

New Nations in Latin America, 1825

When the Cortes, the Portuguese lawmaking body, tried to make Brazil a colony once again, the Brazilian Creoles resisted. They persuaded Pedro to become the ruler of an independent Brazil. He agreed and became Pedro I. In 1822, he proclaimed Brazil to be free of Portugal. Since the Portuguese government did not want to fight a war to keep Brazil, the Cortes recognized its independence. Brazil remained a monarchy until 1889, when its ruler, Pedro II, was overthrown and the nation became a republic.

4. Achievements and Problems. Independence brought the Latin American Creoles some of the benefits they wanted. They achieved political power for themselves and freedom from Spanish economic control. They could now trade with all nations. But Bolívar's dream of a united Latin America was not realized. Nationalism, ambitious leaders of individual states, and rugged terrain all prevented the union of the various nations. Furthermore, within nations the Creoles were unable to establish governments to which all citizens would be loyal. As a result, revolutions and dictatorships became common in Latin America.

Independence did little to help the peons. Most of them continued to be poor and without power. As a result, the disadvantaged often turned to violence to bring about change.

Conflicts arose also over the position of the Roman Catholic Church in Latin America. Many Latin Americans wanted their government to take over Church lands and wealth and to distribute them to the poor. Others looked to the Church to help change government policies and make life easier for the poor.

This 19th-century cartoon from *The New York Herald* shows European leaders impressed with American naval might. The caption reads: "Let it be written so it can be read."

The United States supported the revolutions in Latin America. In 1822, the United States and Britain became concerned that some European nations might help Spain win back its colonies. Latin America had become a profitable trading market, and Britain and the United States did not want the market shut off by Spain. Britain suggested that the United States join in a warning to the European powers to keep out of Latin America. The United States decided to put forth a declaration of its own, knowing that Britain's naval power would enforce it.

In December 1823, President James Monroe included in his yearly address to Congress several points that have come to be known as the *Monroe Doctrine*. Monroe stated that the Americas were no longer open for colonization by any European powers. He further declared that any attempt by the European powers to interfere in the affairs of the Americas would be considered "as dangerous to our peace and safety."

Over the years, the United States has involved itself in the affairs of several Latin American countries on a number of occasions. It has usually said that it was applying the principles of the Monroe Doctrine to keep outside forces from gaining a foothold in Latin America. Usually the Latin Americans have resented such interference. They felt that their independence was being threatened.

ESSAY QUESTIONS

1. State *two* reasons why the Latin American colonies wanted to be free of Spain.

2. Explain why the Latin American revolutions began during the Napoleonic Era.

3. Explain why Simón Bolívar and José de San Martín are considered to be the two greatest leaders of the independence movement in Latin America.

4. Describe the role played by Pedro I in Brazil's independence movement.

5. Identify *two* major problems faced by Latin Americans after independence.

MATCHING EXERCISE

Match each "liberator" in Column A with the correct description from Column B.

<table>
<tr><td>Column A</td><td>Column B</td></tr>
</table>

Column A

1. Miguel Hidalgo
2. Agustín de Iturbide
3. Simón Bolívar
4. José de San Martín

Column B

a. He liberated Colombia, Venezuela, and Ecuador.
b. He led Indians against the Spanish in Mexico.
c. He liberated Chile in 1818.
d. He proclaimed himself emperor of Mexico.

THE EUROPEAN REVOLUTIONS OF 1830 AND 1848

The French Revolution and the Napoleonic Era stirred up different kinds of feelings in the people of Europe. Some felt uneasy about the changes and wanted to slow the rate of changes being made. They wanted to conserve their way of life. These people were called *conservatives*.

Other people welcomed the changes and tried to bring about even more. These people were called *liberals*. They tended to support efforts to make governments more democratic.

Conflicts between liberals and conservatives sometimes led to violent clashes. As a result, the governments of many countries in Europe changed drastically.

1. The Revolutions of 1830.   After Louis XVIII died in 1824, Charles X came to the throne of France. He wanted to be an absolute monarch. He angered French liberals by supporting the passage of some very unpopular laws. One law ordered payments to be made to nobles who had lost lands during the French Revolution. The money for the nobles came mainly from the middle class.

In 1830, Charles X and his ministers issued the July Ordinances. Under these laws, the legally elected lawmaking body was dismissed. The right to vote was taken away from most of the eligible French voters. The press was placed under government control.

Barricades in Paris, 1830.

The French revolted. In Paris, the people set up barricades in the streets and fought the king's soldiers. After three days, the government collapsed, and King Charles gave up the throne. Although many in France wanted a republic, a committee of liberals chose Louis Philippe, the Duke of Orleans, to be the new king. A new constitution limited the power of the king and gave the vote to more businessmen in France. As a result, the middle class became more powerful than the nobles.

The Belgians also revolted in 1830. They succeeded in winning their independence from the Dutch. The Poles attempted to gain freedom from Russia. The Italians revolted against Austrian rule. Both of these revolutions failed. However, they reflected the growing power of *nationalism* (dedication to one's own country) in European affairs.

2. The Revolutions of 1848. Conflict between European liberals and conservatives continued. Trouble came again to France in 1848. Although most wealthy men had gained the right to vote, most doctors, lawyers, teachers, artists, and workers could not vote. This caused great dissatisfaction with the government of King Louis Philippe. The king was forced to abdicate. The liberals in power decided to do without a king. France once again became a republic—the Second Republic.

Under a new constitution, the Second Republic was governed by an elected president and legislature. In December 1848, Louis Napoleon, a nephew of Napoleon Bonaparte, was elected president. He wanted to follow in his uncle's footsteps as a glorious ruler of France. Under his leadership, the Second Republic turned into the Second Empire in 1852. President Louis Napoleon became Emperor Napoleon III. He ruled until 1870.

Elsewhere in Europe in 1848, more revolutions took place in Germany, Italy, and Austria. German revolutionaries called for more political rights guaranteed by new constitutions. They also wanted to unify the many German states into one nation. Their efforts failed because of the opposition of Frederick William IV, king of Prussia, the largest German state. Elected representatives of the German states met in the Frankfurt Assembly. They tried to unite Germany by offering to make Frederick William emperor. He refused because a king by "divine right" could not be elected by the people. The Frankfurt Assembly collapsed.

Revolutions to establish republics in Italy and Hungary were beaten down by conservative forces.

No revolution took place in Britain in the 1800's. A series of compromises between liberals and conservatives made gradual reform possible without bloodshed. The Reform Bill of 1832 was the first of these compromises. This new law lowered the property requirements for voting enough to double the number of British voters (males only). Most of the new voters were members of the middle class. In 1867, another reform bill lowered the property requirements still further and gave the vote to working-class men. Conservatives accepted these reforms because they wanted to ensure that change would come to Britain peacefully. Women, however, remained without political rights until 1918.

IDENTIFICATIONS

From the list that follows, select the person who best fits each description.

    a. Charles X   *c.* Louis Napoleon
    b. Louis Philippe   *d.* Frederick William IV

1. I became president of the Second French Republic in 1848 and emperor of the Second French Empire in 1852.

2. I refused the crown offered by the Frankfurt Assembly.

3. I tried to be an absolute monarch in France but was forced to abdicate in 1830.

4. I was the duke of Orleans until I became king of France in 1830.

SENTENCE COMPLETION

Complete the following sentences:

1. Liberals tended to support efforts to make —.

2. Conservatives wanted to slow the rate of —.

3. The French people disliked the July Ordinances because —.

4. The French constitution written in 1830 limited —.

5. In 1830, the Belgians succeeded in —.

6. The Second Republic in France lasted only a short time because —.

7. In 1848, German revolutionaries called for —.

8. In Italy in 1848, a revolution failed to —.

9. The British Reform Bill of 1832 lowered —.

Chapter Review

▶ MULTIPLE-CHOICE

Choose the item that best completes each sentence.

1. The main cause of both the Puritan Revolt and the Glorious Revolution in England was (*a*) the Puritans' hatred of Parliament (*b*) the desire of Stuart kings for absolute monarchy (*c*) the ambitions of William and Mary (*d*) competition between Cavaliers and Roundheads.

2. The most important result of the Puritan Revolt and the Glorious Revolution in England was that (*a*) limited monarchy became the permanent form of government (*b*) Cromwell closed all the theaters (*c*) James II married a Catholic princess (*d*) the Tudors were restored to the throne.

3. The New Colonial Policy of King George III was a cause of the (*a*) Latin American revolutions (*b*) French Revolution (*c*) Revolution of 1830 (*d*) American Revolution.

4. The most important decision made by the Second Continental Congress of the United States was to (*a*) issue the Declaration of Independence (*b*) execute King Charles I (*c*) storm the Bastille (*d*) defend Latin American independence.

5. Among the major problems of the Old Regime in France in 1780 were (*a*) inequality, injustice, and insolvency (*b*) taxation without representation (*c*) conflicts between the king and the Estates General (*d*) military weaknesses.

6. One of the positive outcomes of the French Revolution was the (*a*) Reign of Terror (*b*) spread of the ideas of liberty, equality, and fraternity (*c*) control of France by the Directory (*d*) establishment of a military dictatorship.

7. Among the accomplishments of Napoleon Bonaparte were (*a*) the University of France and the Bank of France (*b*) the Legion of Honor and the Code Napoléon (*c*) both of the above (*d*) none of the above.

8. In most Latin American countries, the desire for independence was strongest among the (*a*) peninsulares (*b*) Creoles (*c*) mestizos (*d*) indios.

9. In Venezuela, the title of "Liberator" was given to (*a*) Agustín de Iturbide (*b*) John VI (*c*) Simón Bolívar (*d*) Pedro I.

10. The European revolutions of 1830 and 1848 resulted from conflicts between (*a*) liberals and conservatives (*b*) Jacobins and Royalists (*c*) Protestants and Catholics (*d*) peasants and nobles.

ESSAY QUESTION

From the list below, select *one* person. Then write a three-paragraph essay about that person by answering the following questions:

1. What was happening at the time that this person lived?

2. What did this person do that was important?

3. How were conditions changed by this person?

Oliver Cromwell	Charles I
Frederick William IV	Napoleon Bonaparte
King George III	Prince Klemens von Metternich
Simón Bolívar	King Louis XVI

TIMELINE EXERCISE

Place each of the events listed below in its correct time period by assigning it the letter A, B, or C.

1601–1700: **A**   1701–1800: **B**   1801–1900: **C**

1. French Revolution

2. Glorious Revolution

3. American Revolution

4. Congress of Vienna

5. Puritan Revolt

6. Latin American revolutions

7. Napoleonic Wars

8. Commonwealth and Protectorate

9. French Second Empire

10. Frankfurt Assembly

DOCUMENT-BASED QUESTION

This question is based on the accompanying documents (1–4). It will improve your ability to work with historical documents.

Historical Context:

The ideas of the Renaissance and Reformation caused people in Europe and, later, in the Americas to question their governments. People wanted a greater voice in how they were governed. Between the 17th and 19th centuries, political struggles led to violent revolutions. The result was the creation of limited monarchies and republics in Europe and the Americas.

Task:

Using information from the documents and your knowledge of world history, answer the questions that follow each document. Your answers to each question will help you write the document-based essay.

Document 1.   Excerpt from the English Bill of Rights, which was enacted by Parliament in 1689 and created a contract between the monarchy and the people:

> That the pretended power of suspending the laws or the execution of laws by regal authority [the monarch] without consent of Parliament is illegal;
>
> That the pretended power of dispensing with laws or the execution of laws by regal authority, as it hath been assumed and exercised of late, is illegal;
>
> That it is the right of the subjects to petition the king. . . .
>
> And that for redress of all grievances, and for the amending, strengthening and preserving of the laws, Parliaments ought to be held frequently.

> Source: *English Bill of Rights 1689,* The Avalon Project at Yale Law School, http://www.yale.edu/lawweb/avalon/england.htm

According to this document, how was the balance of power in the English government changed?

Document 2   Excerpt from the "Declaration of Independence," announcing American independence on July 4, 1776:

> We hold these truths to be self-evident, that all men are created equal, that they are endowed by their Creator with certain unalienable Rights, that among these are Life, Liberty and the pursuit of Happiness.—That to secure these rights, Governments are instituted among Men, deriving their just powers from the consent of the governed,—That whenever any Form of Government becomes destructive of these ends, it is the Right of the People to alter or to abolish it, and to institute new Government, laying its foundation on such principles and organizing its powers in such form, as to them shall seem most likely to effect their Safety and Happiness.

> Source: *The Declaration of Independence* (1776), The Indiana University School of Law, http://www.law.indiana.edu/uslawdocs/declaration.html

According to this document, what rights do people have when their government becomes unjust or repressive?

Document 3.   Excerpt from "The Declaration of the Rights of Man and of the Citizen," approved by the National Assembly of France, August 26, 1789:

> 1. Men are born and remain free and equal in rights. Social distinctions may be founded only upon the general good.

2. The aim of all political association is the preservation of the natural . . . rights of man. These rights are liberty, property, security, and resistance to oppression.

3. The principle of all sovereignty resides essentially in the nation [people]. No body nor individual may exercise any authority which does not proceed directly from the nation.

> **Source**: *Declaration of the Rights of Man (1789)*, The Avalon Project at Yale Law School, http://www.yale.edu/lawweb/avalon/rightsof.htm

According to this document, what should citizens be able to expect from government?

Document 4.   Study the political cartoon on page 346.

What does the cartoon indicate that the United States would do to enforce the Monroe Doctrine?

DOCUMENT-BASED ESSAY

Using information from the above documents and your knowledge of world history, write an essay in which you:

- Discuss ideas about the rights of individuals that developed out of the American and French revolutions.
- Explain why governments are created and what the responsibilities of governments are to the governed.

Connections: Rebellions and Revolutions

From the 17th to the 19th century, revolutions brought great changes to Europe and to the Americas. Absolute monarchies were ended in England and in France. The United States won independence from Britain. Many Latin American nations gained freedom from Spain and Portugal. Constitutions of independent nations were written throughout the Western world. These constitutions outlined the basic political rights that many Americans and Europeans believed in.

The central idea of the American Declaration of Independence—that citizens dissatisfied with their government have the right to change the government—was carried out in one country after another.

Many rebellions also took place in China. However, most of these rebellions brought little change to the farmers and workers of China. Most of the rebellions seemed to accomplish nothing more than to replace one imperial dynasty with another.

The 19th-century Taiping Rebellion in central and southern China threatened to overthrow the Manchu Dynasty. Manchu rule was harsh. Cruel treatment and heavy taxes burdened the farmers. The rebels, called Taipings, wanted a new and fair government. The leader of the Taipings was a southern Chinese who was influenced by Christian teachings. He wanted to establish a "Heavenly Kingdom of Great Peace" in China.

The Taiping forces pushed the Manchu army out of much of central and southern China. At first, the workers and farmers of the region supported the Taipings. However, the rebel government soon treated the people of the lands they conquered with as much cruelty as had the Manchus. The Taiping leader was treated as a god, as the Manchu emperor had been. The Taiping nobles lived in luxury, while the farmers remained poor. As a result, support for the Taipings rapidly weakened. In time, the Manchus overwhelmed the Taiping rebels.

No great political change came to China until 1912, in spite of the formation of many revolutionary societies and frequent bloody upheavals. In that year, Manchu rule was finally ended. Instead of a new dynasty, elected leaders were chosen by the people. The Republic of China was established. Unfortunately, neither the new government nor the Chinese people had any experience with democracy. Within a few years, Chinese warlords would divide the county among themselves. This government would later be threatened by another political movement—the Communist Revolution.

Explain the meaning of the following statement: For centuries, the Chinese were "the most rebellious but least revolutionary of people."

CHAPTER 14
The Industrial Revolution

While the revolutions to change governments were going on, great changes were also taking place in the way people earned a living. People began to turn from farming and working at home to working in factories.

Until the late 18th century, many Europeans were farmers. They produced much of what they needed for themselves. Clothing, shoes, tools, furniture, and most other items were made by hand. Usually one person made an item from start to finish. After the mid-1700's, however, machines began to be used to do the work of individuals. This change occurred first in the textile industry in England.

The changeover from making goods by hand to making goods by machine is called the *Industrial Revolution*. This revolution completely changed how people lived. We are still experiencing its effects.

ADVANCES IN AGRICULTURE, MANUFACTURING, AND TECHNOLOGY

The Industrial Revolution began in Great Britain. That country contained just the right mix of raw materials, laborers, and people with money to finance new businesses to make the development of the factory system possible. Farmers also used new methods and machines to grow more food to feed the factory workers.

1. Changes in Agriculture. In the early 1700's, British farmers began to adopt new ideas about growing crops. These changes made it possible for more food to be grown by fewer farmers.

    a. *Inventions*. Jethro Tull, an English farmer, invented the seed drill in 1701. It planted seeds in rows. Before the use of this machine became common, farmers had scattered seeds by hand across their fields. Tull also invented the horse-drawn hoe to break up the soil between the rows of plants. By using Tull's machines, a farmer could produce more crops and save seeds while using the same amount of land that had always been farmed. Tull's inventions were not widely used until after the 1730's.

b.   *Changes in land use.*   Traditionally, small farmers had at least three fields in which to grow crops. Two were planted each year, and the third was rested (kept fallow) in order to restore its fertility. In the 1730's, Charles Townshend, an English noble, presented a new idea. He argued that the resting field would be just as fertile if certain crops, such as turnips or clover, were planted on it. Turnips or clover returned to the soil those nutrients used up by wheat or barley. Turnips or clover could also be stored to provide food for farm animals in the winter. If the animals could be fed easily, most of them would not have to be killed each fall. Meat and milk would be available year-round.

In the 1700's, large landowners in Britain rapidly expanded the *enclosure movement* that had begun in the 1500's. Landowners "enclosed," or fenced off, public land for their own use. As the landowners took over these lands, small farmers, who had used these fields for years, were driven out.

The enclosure movement and the creation of large fields made the use of new agricultural methods and machinery highly efficient. Large-scale production of British meat, wool, and grains resulted. However, many small farmers could not make a living on the land left to them. Most of them moved away from their farms, seeking work in towns and cities.

In the mid-1800's, new inventions speeded up the harvesting of grain in the United States, Britain, and elsewhere. The reaper, invented by Cyrus McCormick (an American), was one of the most important of the laborsaving devices. With the new machines, a few workers could now take care of larger farms and produce more grain. The increase in food production occurred at a time when the population was increasing and more people were seeking work in factories and in the growing cities.

2. Changes in Manufacturing.   Great Britain had long been a center for the weaving of wool cloth. In the 1700's, after India had been acquired as a colony, the British became interested in the cotton cloth produced in India. The British decided to make cotton cloth at home.

In 1733, John Kay invented the flying shuttle. The shuttle made it possible for one person, instead of two, to operate a weaving loom. More cloth could be woven in less time. This caused a demand for more thread.

In 1764, James Hargreaves invented the spinning jenny. This machine spun thread eight times faster than the old spinning

McCormick's reaper was first used in 1831.

wheel. A water-powered spinning machine was created in 1769. By that time, looms could not weave fast enough to use all of the available thread. Then in 1784, Edmund Cartwright invented the more effective power loom. All of these developments created a demand for more and more raw cotton.

The major supplier of raw cotton for Britain's weavers was the United States. Then with the invention of the cotton gin by Eli Whitney in 1793, cotton became the leading export of the Southern states. The gin made it possible to separate the seeds from cotton fibers much faster than could be done by hand.

Weaving looms became too large to be used at home. Thus, factories were built. Weavers came to work in factories that could house many looms.

At first, factories had to be located beside fast-running rivers or other bodies of water. Falling water was used to power the machines. After James Watt improved the steam engine in the late 1700's, factories switched to burning coal to obtain power. The coal heated water to produce steam. Steam drove the engine. The steam engine made it possible for factories to be located anywhere. Usually they were built near towns. Coal mining became an important industry in Britain.

Iron making also developed rapidly. Iron parts replaced wooden parts in machines. New processes were invented to produce better quality iron for tools, machines, bridges, and other structures.

Invention followed invention in rapid succession. More and more products were made in factories. By the mid-1800's, Britain had become an industrialized nation. By the late 1800's, France, Germany, and the United States had also become industrialized.

Machines produced goods more rapidly and cheaply and in greater quantities than they could be produced by hand. More people could afford to buy more things. Increased sales made factory owners wealthy. As methods of transportation improved, markets for goods opened up around the world. Traders and shippers became wealthy. The new wealth was used to build more factories, create more goods, and open up more markets.

3. The Factory System. Men, women, and children—some as young as five—worked in factories. They generally worked during daylight hours, six days a week. They had only a short time off during the day, at lunchtime. There were no safety devices on the machines to keep the workers from getting hurt.

When workers did not work, they did not get paid. There were no government agencies that helped out during times of unemployment. Wages tended to be low.

Whole families lived in one or two rooms because it cost too much to rent a larger space. Workers' lives were regulated by the rules of the factory owner or manager.

As more factories were built in an area, more workers came to live near the factories. Towns quickly grew into cities.

a. *Interchangeable parts and mass production.* To turn out products that contained many parts, manufacturers decided that the same parts should all be alike. The use of *interchangeable parts* was introduced in 1800. For example, having one worker make only the wheels for a small wagon and another make only

This engraving shows factory workers operating power looms.

the handle, and so on, speeded up production. To put the wagon together, one worker attached wheels to the box on one side and passed it along to another to put the wheels on the other side, and so on. By using this *mass-production* system, a factory could turn out great quantities of an item.

   b. *Assembly line.* In the 20th century, the automobile industry altered the mass-production system through the introduction of the *assembly line*. Workers stood alongside a wide, moving belt. The belt carried the product to each worker in turn. Each worker attached a standardized part to the car being assembled. At the end of the line, a completed car rolled out of the factory. The assembly line is still used in the production of cars and other complex pieces of machinery.

4. Changes in Transportation.   Until the 1800's, a person could travel only as fast as a horse could go, a boat could be paddled or sailed, or his or her legs could move.

   a. *Steamboats.*   One day in 1807, Robert Fulton, an American, ran his boat, the *Clermont*, up the Hudson River from New York City to Albany. It took 32 hours instead of the 96 required by sailboats. The *Clermont*, powered by steam, was the first commercially successful steamboat. By the late 1800's, oceangoing steamboats had become common.

   b. *Railroads.*   In 1814, George Stephenson of England demonstrated the first successful railroad locomotive. It also was powered by steam. Soon railroad tracks crisscrossed Europe and the United States. The railroads, like the other new means of transportation, were important to the success of the Industrial

Fulton's *Clermont*, a paddle wheeler driven by steam.

Revolution. The needs of railroads for coal and iron led to more growth in those industries. Building railroads also created new jobs for farm laborers and peasants. Moreover, less expensive transportation led to lower-priced goods, thus creating larger markets. More sales meant more factories and more machinery. Business owners could reinvest their profits in new equipment, thereby adding to economic growth.

In the United States, railroads contributed greatly to the settlement of the Western portions of the country, the growth of towns and cities, and the rapid movement of Western products to Eastern markets. In Britain and other nations of Western Europe, the railroads contributed greatly to industrialization. Railroads became the major means of transporting people and goods. Those who built and owned the railroads amassed great fortunes and exercised political and economic power.

c. *Automobiles.* About 1885, Karl Benz of Germany created the first automobile powered by an internal combustion motor. The same year, Gottlieb Daimler of Germany introduced a gasoline-powered engine. It was eventually used to run automobiles.

d. *Airplanes.* In 1903, two Americans, Orville and Wilbur Wright, made the first successful flight in a heavier-than-air plane. Charles Lindbergh's solo flight from New York to Paris in 1927 altered people's idea about distance. In one sense, the airplane brought the countries of the world closer together.

5. Iron and Steel. Machines and other products were manufactured with these metals. Iron was used more frequently, at first, because it was less costly than steel, which is stronger. In 1856, however, Henry Bessemer, a British engineer, developed an inex-

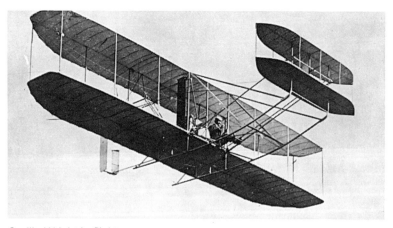

Orville Wright in flight.

pensive way to refine iron into steel. Improvements on the Bessemer process of steelmaking led to the open hearth, electric furnace, and crucible processes. Alloys (combinations of metals) were developed for special types of steel, such as stainless steel. As the uses of steel increased, it became the basic metal of modern industrial society.

America on Wheels

A 1940's photo showing Henry Ford seated in the first car he made, in 1896.

In 1900, the United States was still in the "horse and buggy" age. Few people could afford to buy and own an automobile. Henry Ford (1863–1947) changed that. Ford's Model T car was sold at a price most Americans could afford. Ford made this possible because the Model T was mass-produced. A pioneer of the assembly-line method, Ford was able to produce good cars faster and cheaper than other car manufacturers. In turn, mass production enabled Ford to sell cars at a lower price than that asked by other carmakers.

Beginning in 1908, the large-scale production of low-cost automobiles changed the face of America. Americans began to travel as they had never traveled before. New roads and highways were built. Mass-produced cars, trucks, and buses revolutionized transportation and the way people lived in the United States. People could drive to work from long distances away. Suburbs sprang up around the cities.

Henry Ford made an even greater contribution to American industry. In 1914, Ford announced that he was doubling the wages of skilled workers in his factories. He knew that the increased wages would give his workers greater purchasing power. They could not only buy new models of cars, they could also buy more of the goods being produced in other factories. The "Ford Idea" soon spread to other industries throughout the United States. People came to understand that mass production depended on mass purchasing power.

Henry Ford also became known as a *humanitarian*. He and his son, Edsel, established the Ford Foundation. It grants funds to help universities, medical schools, and hospitals. It also finances studies related to problems such as international peace, civil liberties, and world hunger.

List *three* achievements of Henry Ford.

6. Changes in Communication. Technology greatly improved the ability of people to communicate rapidly over long distances. In the 1830's, several men, including two in Britain (Charles Wheatstone and William Cooke) and one in the United States (Samuel F.B. Morse), introduced the telegraph. Messages were sent miles over electrical wires in the form of sound codes. Within 30 years, Cyrus Field linked North America and Europe through a transatlantic cable.

Alexander Graham Bell of Canada and the United States completed work on his telephone in 1876. This device was readily accepted by businesses and private individuals, particularly in the United States.

The wireless telegraph, invented by Italian scientist Guglielmo Marconi in 1895, further speeded up communications. He sent a message by radio waves across the Atlantic in 1901.

The radio was made possible by the inventions of John Fleming (of Britain) and Lee De Forest (of the United States) between 1909

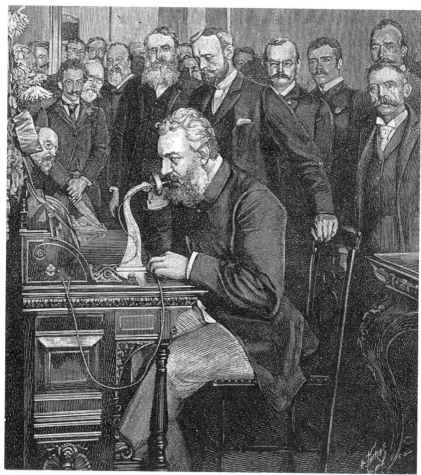

Alexander Graham Bell opening the New York City–to–Chicago telephone line.

and 1912. Radio broadcasts were first offered on a regular basis in 1920. The use of the radio quickly spread everywhere.

Another major communication device was made possible by the inventions of Vladimir Zworykin, a Russian-born American. In 1923, he invented tubes for broadcasting and receiving pictures through radio waves. Six years later, he demonstrated the first practical television system.

7. Changes in Power Sources.   Water power had long been used to run machines. Then people began making use of the power in steam produced by boiling water. Wood or coal was burned to heat the water.

In the early 1800's, natural gas began to be used to provide light and heat in factories. Much later it was piped into homes. Petroleum (oil) became an important power and fuel source after 1859. In that year, Edwin Drake drilled the first oil well in the United States.

In 1800, Alessandro Volta, an Italian, created the first electric battery. Michael Faraday, a British scientist, moved a magnet inside a wire coil and generated an electric current in 1831. This experiment led to the invention of the *dynamo*, an electric generator that transforms mechanical energy into electricity. The first electric generator was put into operation in 1832.

Thomas A. Edison, an American, invented the electric light-bulb in 1879. In 1882, electric generators began to be used to light city streets in London and New York. Edison (1847–1931) was one of the greatest inventors and industrial leaders in history. His best-known achievements were electric lighting, the phonograph, and improvements to the telephone, telegraph, and motion pictures. Edison also created one of the first modern research laboratories. As a businessman, he created new companies to manufacture and sell his products. He obtained thousands of patents (legal rights to products he invented) from two dozen nations. Edison is regarded as one of the manufacturing pioneers who helped make the United States an industrial world power.

IDENTIFICATIONS

Identify each of the following people:

a. Charles Townshend
b. Cyrus McCormick
c. John Kay
d. James Hargreaves
e. Edmund Cartwright
f. James Watt
g. George Stephenson
h. Orville and Wilbur Wright
i. Alexander Graham Bell
j. Guglielmo Marconi

CHRONOLOGY

Give the date when each of the following machines or devices was invented:

1. seed drill
2. flying shuttle
3. spinning jenny
4. water-powered spinning machine

5. power loom
6. cotton gin
7. wireless telegraph
8. electric battery

ESSAY QUESTIONS

1. Trace the growth of the factory system.

2. Explain the connection between mass production and the assembly line.

3. Describe in one or two paragraphs how your life has been affected positively and negatively by *one* of the following inventions. Be sure to include specific details.

    telephone   airplane   automobile
    television   electric generator

EFFORTS AT REFORM

The Industrial Revolution brought many benefits to factory owners and workers in Great Britain, elsewhere in Europe, and in the United States. A higher standard of living developed because jobs, money, and a wider variety of goods became more readily available. But the growth of industry also caused major new problems.

Working conditions in factories were often unhealthy and dangerous. Workers received low wages for long hours of toil. They had no wage protection if factories shut down.

The Industrial Revolution changed the ways families lived. Women were especially affected. They were mostly unskilled laborers. Woman were paid half or less than half of what men received. In 1844 in England, excessive working hours for women were outlawed.

The employment of children and women was in large part carried over from an earlier pattern. Husband, wife, and children had always worked together in cottage industries. Thus, it seemed nat-

The home of a factory worker in Manchester, England.

ural to continue this pattern. Men who moved from the countryside to industrial towns and cities took their wives and children with them into the factory or mines. The desire for this family work often came from the family itself. The factory owner Jedediah Strutt was opposed to employing children under age ten but was forced by parents to employ children as young as seven.

The Factory Acts that limited the work hours of children and women also led to a new pattern of work. Men were expected to earn most of the family income by working outside the home. Women, in contrast, took over daily care of the family and performed low-paying jobs, such as laundry work, that could be done in the home. Working at home for pay made it possible for women to continue to help with family survival.

Industrial cities tended to be dirty and ugly. The areas where the workers lived were particularly gloomy. The workers' homes were close together and usually poorly constructed. Crime and sickness reached a high level in these slum districts. Air and water pollution were often severe in industrial cities. London, for example, became notorious for its thick fog, created by the coal and wood smoke from factory chimneys mixed with other industrial waste. The Thames River became filled with foul-smelling waste. Reform-minded people in government, universities, and religious organizations became concerned about these problems.

1. The Labor Union Movement.   Workers in particular occupations or industries joined together in organizations called *unions* to discuss working conditions and other concerns with employers.

While acting as a group, the workers could put more pressure on an employer to raise wages or improve working conditions than a single individual could.

Union members elected representatives to present their requests or demands to an employer. This process is called *collective bargaining*. If an employer did not grant their requests or demands, the workers might *strike*. They would stop working until they got what they wanted. Sometimes unions organized a boycott of an employer's product. Unions urged consumers not to buy the product until the employer came to an agreement with the union.

To stop a strike, an employer might hire strikebreakers to replace the striking workers. Police or military troops might be called in to end a strike. Some employers tried to weaken union causes by *blacklisting* outspoken members. This list, which was sent to other employers, branded selected workers as undesirable employees. Blacklisting meant that the selected workers could not get jobs in their usual line of work.

a. *European unions*. British workers could not legally organize unions until 1824. Efforts to form a national union in the 1830's had only short periods of success. Until 1871, attempts to form unions were forcefully discouraged by the government as well as by factory owners.

Unions in France did not become strong until the 1880's. The German labor movement gained power in the 1890's. The Industrial Revolution did not take hold in Russia until the late 1800's. As a result, labor unions did not become important there until the early 1900's.

b. *U.S. unions*. In the United States, the labor union movement followed a course similar to that in Great Britain. Early efforts at unionizing specific types of workers succeeded for only a short time. Unions did not become legal in the United States until 1842.

In 1869, the Knights of Labor was founded in the United States. Its members included skilled and unskilled workers, women, and blacks. The Knights called for an eight-hour workday, the banning of child labor, and other reforms. After a few unsuccessful strikes and some violent incidents, the Knights declined in power. The American Federation of Labor (AFL), officially founded in 1886, became the most important national labor organization. It joined with the Congress of Industrial Organizations (CIO) in 1955. The AFL-CIO continues to be the most powerful labor organization in the United States. The majority of unionized workers belong to the AFL-CIO.

An 1890 poster showing the emblem of the United Mine Workers of America.

In Britain in 1901, liberals and trade unionists joined forces to form the Labour Party. It won a number of seats in Parliament in the elections of 1906. The Labour Party became a major force in British politics in the late 1920's and remains so today. Labor unions on the European continent also developed political parties that elected representatives to legislative bodies.

In time, mainly after the 1920's, unions and other reform groups won support for many laws that benefited workers. Child labor laws protected children. Standards for maximum hours of work and minimum wages were established. Sanitary and safety conditions in factories were improved. Compensation payments for on-the-job injuries, old-age pensions, and unemployment insurance lessened workers' financial worries.

2. The Socialist Movement. Some workers and liberals in the 19th century believed that a new form of government was the best way to fight the evils of the Industrial Revolution. These people developed a system of political and economic ideas called *socialism*. Socialists believed that factories, mines, stores, and farms should be owned by the people as a whole rather than by individuals. Socialists attacked the practice of producing goods for profit. Instead, they wanted the goods that everyone needed to be produced at prices everyone could afford. Most important, socialists demanded that governments serve the needs of all the people and not just those of wealthy landowners and industrialists.

a. _Owen_. Wealthy industrialist Robert Owen (1771–1858) became one of the best-known socialists in Britain. He wanted to make life better for working people. To show how society could be reorganized, Owen conducted a practical experiment. He bought a cotton mill in Scotland and provided safe, healthy working conditions for his employees. He refused to hire child laborers. Owen also turned the nearby town of New Lanark into a model community with good schools and a high standard of living.

Owen and other 19th-century socialists who believed as he did were called _utopians_. They tried to establish perfect communities in which the people as a whole owned all the factories and stores and shared all the goods produced. Owen succeeded in doing this in New Lanark. But other utopian communities he tried to set up in Britain and the United States failed. Most people could not cooperate and work together for the common good to the degree required to meet the standards of the utopian socialists.

b. _Blanc_. French socialist Louis Blanc (1811–1882) owned a newspaper. In his writings, he attacked the French government for giving industrialists too much freedom. Blanc believed that the government should set up workshops and run them. Blanc also had the idea that workers should produce according to their ability and be paid according to their needs.

Not all socialist ideas proved to be successful or even practical. By the 20th century, however, socialist ideas had become powerful in European politics. Socialist-led governments have been elected many times in Britain, Germany, Norway, Sweden, Denmark, and France.

3. The Communist Movement. Karl Marx was a 19th-century German revolutionary who lived much of his life in London. His solutions to the problems of industrialization were more radical than those proposed by labor unions and socialists. In 1848, Marx and a friend named Friedrich Engels published a pamphlet titled the _Communist Manifesto_. The ideas it stated came to be called scientific socialism, or _communism_.

Marx blamed the problems faced by workers on capitalism. Under the capitalistic system, business owners put up money, or capital, needed to bring workers, machines, and raw materials together to produce goods. Workers receive wages for their labor. Capitalists gain profits on their investments. Marx claimed that it was unfair for workers who produce goods to get less for their labor than the capitalists got for their investments. According to

The Father of Communism

Karl Marx.

Few 19th-century theories have had as much influence in the world as those written by Karl Marx (1818–1883). Marx, a German writer and economist, was the founder of modern communism.

Karl Marx was born into a middle-class family. As a university student, his attacks on government policies prevented him from becoming a teacher. Instead, he became a newspaper editor and writer. In 1843, he moved to Paris, where he met Friedrich Engels, another German writer. Together, they helped form the Communist League. Engels also worked with Marx on several articles and books about politics.

In 1848, Marx moved back to Germany, where he published a journal for democratic reform. With the collapse of the revolution of 1848 in Germany, Marx fled to London. With financial help from Engels, now a factory manager, Marx was able to spend most of his time there writing.

Marx's most famous works are the *Communist Manifesto* (1848) and *Das Kapital* (Capital), the first volume published in 1867. In much of this work Marx was aided by his friend Engels.

The *Manifesto* outlines those social, economic, and political theories that became known as *Marxism*. Marx believed that society was shaped by a class struggle between workers and capitalists. The workers produced goods. The ruling class controlled the means of producing those goods, such as the labor of the workers, factories, and natural resources. Therefore, according to Marx, the owners *exploited* the workers for their own gain. Marx believed that the means of production should be publicly, not privately, owned. Economic equality would occur and lead to social equality. The class struggle would disappear.

Marx urged the workers of the world to overthrow the capitalist system in order to build a classless society in which all people would be equal.

By the end of the 19th century, the followers of Marx's theories had split into two major camps—Communists and socialists. The socialists believed that democratic methods could be used to replace the capitalist system. The Communists believed that revolution, armed if necessary, was the only way to wipe out the capitalist system.

Why is Karl Marx called the "father of communism"?

Marx, workers and capitalists were enemies locked in an endless conflict. He referred to this conflict as a "class struggle."

For Marx, the solution to the problems caused by capitalism was revolution. He urged the workers of every nation to rise up and smash the capitalistic system.

The theories developed by Marx and Engels appealed to many people, especially those who saw no other solution to problems such as poverty and unemployment. But the worldwide revolution that Marx predicted never occurred. Instead, conditions for workers gradually improved. By the beginning of the 20th century, the standard of living for most people in the Western world had begun to rise higher than ever before.

In Russia, a bloody revolution in 1917 brought Communist leaders to power. This revolution was caused by the inability of the Russian government to stop the terrible suffering and problems brought about by World War I. Communists also took over the government of China, in 1949 after a long civil war. Neither Russia nor China had gone through the Industrial Revolution at the time of the Communist takeovers. Workers never began to control either country. The government in China remains a dictatorship. Russia was a dictatorship until late 1991, when the Communist system collapsed.

CRITICAL THINKING

1. **PROVE or DISPROVE:** Karl Marx and Friedrich Engels proposed practical solutions to the problems caused by the Industrial Revolution.

2. Reread "1. The Labor Union Movement," on pages 367–369, to find out what is wrong with each of the following statements. Then rewrite each as a correct statement.
    a. Unions have nothing to do with collective bargaining.
    b. The Knights of Labor eventually combined with the Congress of Industrial Organizations.
    c. British labor unions formed the Conservative Party in 1901.
    d. Increased political power did nothing for workers.

SENTENCE COMPLETION

Complete each of the following sentences:

1. Socialists believed that —.

2. Robert Owen and other 19th-century socialists were called utopians because —.

3. Louis Blanc believed that the government should —.

4. Socialist-led governments have been —.

ESSAY QUESTION

Explain what Karl Marx and Friedrich Engels meant by their slogan: "Workers of the world, unite! You have nothing to lose but your chains."

SCIENTIFIC AND MEDICAL ADVANCES

Along with the practical inventions of the Industrial Revolution came advances in science and medicine. Scientists developed ideas that explained more about the workings of the natural world. Medical specialists found cures for certain illnesses and helped people live longer, healthier lives.

1. Scientific Knowledge. John Dalton (1766–1844), a British schoolteacher, influenced the field of chemistry. He stated that atoms are the smallest parts of elements and that each element is made up of one kind of atom. Dalton also said that the atoms of one element are different from the atoms of all other elements. He devised a system of atomic weights. Hydrogen, the lightest element, was the standard to which all other elements were compared. Dalton's theories were not entirely correct. But his work laid the foundation for modern atomic theory.

Nineteenth-century scientists also contributed to the field of physics. Michael Faraday (1791–1867) demonstrated that magnetism can produce electricity. His work made it possible to turn mechanical power into electrical power and to create electric generators. Wilhelm Roentgen (1845–1923) announced the discovery of X-rays in 1895. Marie Curie (1867–1934) discovered two radioactive elements: radium and polonium.

Charles Darwin (1809–1882), a British naturalist, changed many people's ideas about how new forms of plants and animals came into being. He said that they develop from earlier forms over a long period of time. This process is called *evolution*. Darwin's basic ideas are set forth in his book *On the Origin of Species by Means of Natural Selection* (1859). In the never-ending struggle for food, Darwin said, the plants and animals that are best suited to obtain food to survive and reproduce adapt to changes in their environment. Those that have difficulty finding enough to eat

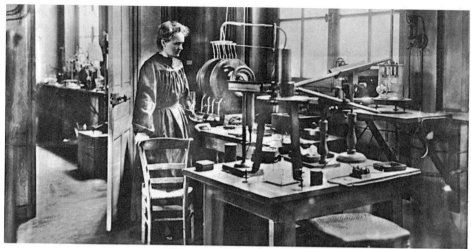
Marie Curie in her laboratory.

eventually die out, because they do not adapt. Through "natural selection," or "the survival of the fittest," animal and plant forms change over time.

Many scholars in the 19th century did not agree with Darwin's ideas. Some people still do not think that his theories can be proved.

An Austrian monk, Gregor Mendel (1822–1884), experimented with pea plants. He wanted to find out how certain characteristics, such as color, are passed on to new generations. His work on inheritance greatly influenced the field of genetics in the 20th century.

2. Medical Advances. Throughout the 19th century, many discoveries in the field of medicine improved the health and well-being of everyone. Edward Jenner (1749–1823), a British doctor, introduced the practice of *vaccination* to prevent smallpox. Before the use of vaccinations, this disease killed most people who contracted it and left ugly scars on those who survived.

The work of Louis Pasteur (1822–1895), a French scientist, explained why the vaccination works. Pasteur's experiments proved that some microorganisms known as bacteria, or germs, cause diseases. A weak solution of disease-causing germs, a vaccine, can be injected into people to keep them from getting certain diseases. Pasteur developed vaccines to treat rabies and anthrax in humans and animals.

Bacteria can also cause grape juice to turn into wine, and milk to turn sour. Pasteur found that heating milk kills the bacteria. This process is called *pasteurization*. It is commonly used today to keep milk from spoiling quickly.

A German doctor, Robert Koch (1843–1910), expanded the knowledge of how germs cause diseases. He identified the germs

Louis Pasteur.

that cause tuberculosis and a number of other dreaded diseases. He developed a method of isolating and growing bacteria. Koch found that germs can be killed by sterilization and that certain diseases can be prevented by keeping drinking water clean.

Pasteur's ideas about germs influenced Joseph Lister (1827–1912), a British surgeon. In 1865, Lister began to use strong chemicals—*antiseptics*—to kill bacteria in operating rooms. This practice prevented infections in patients after surgery.

Earlier, William T.G. Morton (1819–1868), an American dentist, had developed a way of making surgery safer and easier for patients. In 1846, Morton gave the first demonstration of the use of ether as an *anesthetic*, or painkiller, in surgery. He proved that the reduction of pain during surgery prevented shock and speeded the recovery of patients.

The advance of scientific knowledge in the 19th century revolutionized the practice of medicine. The treatment of patients improved. Many diseases could now be prevented or made less severe.

DEFINITIONS

Write a sentence to explain the meaning of each of the following terms:

a. atom   *d.* pasteurization
b. evolution   *e.* antiseptic
c. vaccination   *f.* anesthetic

MATCHING EXERCISE

Match each name in Column A with an accomplishment in Column B.

Column A
1. John Dalton
2. Michael Faraday
3. Wilhelm Roentgen
4. Marie Curie
5. Charles Darwin
6. Gregor Mendel
7. Edward Jenner
8. Louis Pasteur
9. Joseph Lister
10. Robert Koch

Column B
a. developed the theory of evolution
b. identified the germ that causes tuberculosis
c. demonstrated the value of using antiseptics in surgery
d. devised a system of atomic weights
e. introduced the practice of vaccination to prevent smallpox
f. discovered X-rays
g. influenced the field of genetics
h. demonstrated that magnetism can produce electricity
i. discovered radium
j. proved that germs cause diseases

CULTURAL DEVELOPMENTS

The Industrial Revolution also affected cultural activities during the 19th century. Painters, musicians, and writers created new and different forms of expression. These reflected the changes in lifestyles and attitudes brought about by the growth of industry and the movement to cities.

1. Painting. Painters expressed themselves in a variety of styles.

   a. *Romanticism.* Many artists in the late 18th and early 19th centuries painted in the *Romantic style.* They created a world of dreams and fantasies rather than scenes of everyday life. The beauty of nature was a favorite theme. John Constable (1776–1837) and Joseph Turner (1775–1851) of Great Britain painted beautiful landscapes. Jean François Millet (1814–1875) of France created an idealized version of peasant life.

   Romanticism was closely linked to nationalism. The great Spanish painter Francisco Goya (1746–1828), for example, por-

Cézanne's *Portrait of a Peasant.*

trayed the struggle of the Spanish people against the armies of Napoleon. Eugène Delacroix (1798–1863), the greatest of the French Romanticists, was also inspired by current events. In *The Massacre at Chios*, he revealed his sympathy for the Greeks' fight for independence from the Turkish Empire in the 1820's.

b. *Realism.* During the second half of the 19th century, Romanticism gave way to a style of painting called *Realism.* Artists such as Gustave Courbet (1819–1877) of France tried to show life as it really was. Courbet's *Woman With a Parrot* and *The Stone Breakers* shocked some people who thought the works were too realistic. Honoré Daumier (1808–1879), another French Realist, drew political cartoons. He attacked corruption in politics and spent six months in prison for a caricature of King Louis Philippe. Realism reached a peak in the works of Édouard Manet (1832–1883) of France. In his *Death of Maximilian*, Manet showed the actual moment of the execution of the French emperor of Mexico by rebels.

c. *Impressionism.* In the 1860's and 1870's, a completely different style of painting began in France. It was called *Impressionism.* Impressionists wanted to show the effect of light on their subjects. They generally used much brighter colors than the Romanticists and Realists. In creating their scenes of natural views of everyday life, they used small dabs of pure color placed side by side. The eye blended the colors and "saw" the objects the artist had painted. Leading Impressionists were Claude Monet (1840–1926), Pierre Auguste Renoir (1841–1919), and Edgar Degas (1834–1917).

d. *Post-Impressionism.* The Impressionists were followed by the Post-Impressionists. They concerned themselves with form, space, and blocks of colors rather than with representing what a subject actually looked like. Paul Cézanne (1839–1906), Vincent van Gogh (1853–1890), and Paul Gauguin (1848–1903) led the Post-Impressionist movement.

2. Music. Romanticism and nationalism also affected the main type of music that was created in the 19th century—Romantic music.

a. *Romantic music.* The greatest Romantic composer was Ludwig van Beethoven (1770–1827), a German. He created idealistic, emotional works for individual musical instruments as well as for full orchestras.

Another German, Richard Wagner (1813–1883), composed operas featuring heroes and gods from German folklore. He made Germans proud of their history and legends. *The Ring of the Nibelung*, a cycle of four operas, is one of Wagner's most famous works.

In Italy, Giuseppe Verdi (1813–1901) created great operas. Among his masterpieces are *Rigoletto*, *La Traviata*, and *Aida*. A

Richard Wagner.

Ludwig van Beethoven.

strong nationalist, he supported the Italian struggle for unification under a central government.

Nationalism also inspired the great Russian composer Peter Ilich Tchaikovsky (1840–1893). His *1812 Overture* is a musical description of Napoleon's retreat from Moscow, which led to a Russian victory over the French invaders. Jean Sibelius (1865–1957) of Finland and Edvard Grieg (1843–1907) of Norway also wrote important nationalistic music.

b. *Impressionistic music.* Impressionism was reflected in music as well as in painting. The French composer Claude Debussy (1862–1918) tried to create poetry and visual images with his compositions. *Prelude to the Afternoon of a Faun* and *La Mer* are two of his best-known impressionistic works.

3. Literature. Poems, novels, and plays could be classified as either Romantic or Realistic.

a. *Romantic literature.* Focusing on life in the past, folklore, or the beauty of nature, Romantic literature stirred the emotions and took the reader away from the worries of everyday life.

Samuel Taylor Coleridge (1772–1834) and William Wordsworth (1770–1850) were among the leading British Romanticists. Coleridge's "Rime of the Ancient Mariner" concerns supernatural punishment and man's place in nature. Wordsworth's poetry praised the beauty found in nature.

Sir Walter Scott (1771–1832) of Scotland wrote great adventure stories. His novels *Ivanhoe*, *The Talisman*, and *Quentin Durward* returned readers to the Middle Ages and battles fought by heroic knights in shining armor. Alfred, Lord Tennyson (1809–1892) also wrote about the Middle Ages. His *The Idylls of the King* is a collection of poems about King Arthur and his knights.

The French writer Alexander Dumas (1802–1870) created exciting and popular adventure novels. Two of his most famous works are *The Three Musketeers* and *The Count of Monte Cristo*.

An American, James Fenimore Cooper (1789–1851), created novels about the impact of frontier settlers and Native Americans on one another. *The Deerslayer* and *The Last of the Mohicans* are among his most famous works.

b. *Realistic literature.* Realist writing began in France. Realists described everyday life and its problems. *Madame Bovary* by Gustave Flaubert (1821–1880) gives readers a detailed picture of the French middle class in the 19th century. Émile Zola

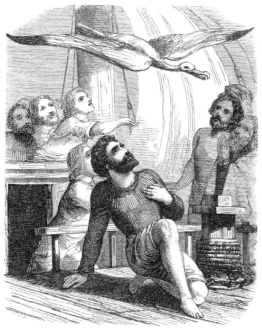

An illustration from Coleridge's "Rime of the Ancient Mariner" (*left*). The death of King Arthur, an illustration from *The Idylls of the King* by Tennyson (*right*).

(1840–1902) attacked social conditions in 19th-century France in novels such as *Nana* and *Germinal*.

The British Realist Charles Dickens (1812–1870) described conditions in debtors' prisons, poorhouses, and courts. *Oliver Twist* and *David Copperfield* are two of his novels about poor people. The Irish dramatist George Bernard Shaw (1856–1950) criticized the social attitudes and customs of his day in many of his

Huckleberry Finn.

Mark Twain.

plays. Two of his well-known works are *Major Barbara* and *Pygmalion*.

Another dramatist, Henrik Ibsen (1828–1906) of Norway, also commented on old-fashioned ideas about how people should behave. *A Doll's House* and *An Enemy of the People* are two of his best-known plays.

Russia and the United States also produced Realist writers. Leo Tolstoy (1828–1910) is one of Russia's most famous authors. He wrote *War and Peace*, a long novel about the effect of Napoleon's campaign in Russia on five families. Mark Twain (1835–1910), whose real name was Samuel Clemens, used humor to poke fun at American society. His best-known novels are *The Adventures of Tom Sawyer* and *Adventures of Huckleberry Finn*.

CRITICAL THINKING

1. Reread "1. Painting," on pages 376–378. Then write a paragraph describing how the subject and style of Romantic paintings are different from the subject and style of Realist paintings.

2. Reread "2. Music," on pages 378–379. Then match each of the following composers with his correct description.

Ludwig van Beethoven   Peter Ilich Tchaikovsky
Edvard Grieg   Richard Wagner
Jean Sibelius   Claude Debussy
Giuseppe Verdi

   a. In addition to composing operas, such as *Rigoletto* and *Aida*, I supported Italy's struggle for unification under a central government.
   b. I wrote music that appealed to the nationalistic feelings of the people of Norway.
   c. I made Germans proud of their history and legends when I wrote *The Ring of the Nibelung*.
   d. My *1812 Overture* describes Napoleon's retreat from Moscow.
   e. My *La Mer* is an example of Impressionism in music.
   f. I am a composer from Finland.
   g. I am the greatest of Romantic composers.

CHART COMPLETION

Reread "3. Literature," on pages 379–381. Then provide the information required in the following table.

19th-Century Writers

	Name	*Name of one work*	*Dates lived*

British:
  Romantic
  Realist			

French:
  Romantic
  Realist			

American:
  Romantic
  Realist			

Chapter Review

▶ MULTIPLE-CHOICE

Choose the item that best completes each sentence.

1. The term *Industrial Revolution* refers to (*a*) armed revolts by factory workers (*b*) the collapse of industries in Europe and America (*c*) the changeover from making goods by hand to making goods by machine (*d*) the use of nuclear power.

2. The Industrial Revolution began in (*a*) Germany (*b*) France (*c*) the United States (*d*) Britain.

3. The factory system made possible (*a*) increased production of farm products (*b*) improvements in education (*c*) mass production of manufactured goods (*d*) more home production.

4. James Watt affected the location of factories by his improvements in the (*a*) airplane (*b*) automobile (*c*) steamboat (*d*) steam engine.

5. Technology includes (*a*) the invention of machines (*b*) the creation of fine paintings (*c*) the education of philosophers (*d*) legal decisions.

6. A powerful labor organization in the United States today is the (*a*) Labor Party (*b*) Knights of Labor (*c*) AFL-CIO (*d*) Republican Party.

7. Two famous 19th-century socialists were (*a*) Samuel Morse and Cyrus McCormick (*b*) Robert Owen and Louis Blanc (*c*) John Fleming and Edwin Drake (*d*) Charles Darwin and Gregor Mendel.

8. Karl Marx was a (*a*) utopian socialist (*b*) scientific socialist (*c*) labor unionist (*d*) Impressionist.

9. Experiments that proved that germs cause diseases were the work of (*a*) Louis Pasteur (*b*) Edward Jenner (*c*) Joseph Lister (*d*) Henry Ford.

10. Two styles that appeared in 19th-century painting, music, and literature were (*a*) Unionism and Capitalism (*b*) Romanticism and Realism (*c*) Socialism and Communism (*d*) Socialism and Capitalism.

THEMATIC WRITING

Select *two* of the following themes. For each, write one or two paragraphs of explanation:

1. The Industrial Revolution began in the late 18th century.

2. The factory system made goods cheaper and more available.

3. Technology improved transportation and communication.

4. The labor union, socialist, and Communist movements offered different solutions to the problems caused by the Industrial Revolution.

5. Medical advances helped people in the 18th and 19th centuries.

ESSAY QUESTION

Read the paragraph below carefully. Then answer the question that follows.

In Britain, the Factory Act of 1819 banned the employment in cotton mills of children under 9 years of age. It also limited to 12 hours the workday of children between the ages of 9 and 16. In 1842, another law banned employing girls and boys under the age of 10 in mines. Five years later, the Ten Hours Act set a 10-hour workday for children under the age of 18 in all textile mills.

What does this paragraph tell you about a particular problem brought on by the Industrial Revolution?

GRAPH INTERPRETATION

Examine the three graphs below. Then answer the following questions.

1. What information on the graphs shows that Great Britain was more industrialized than the other nations in 1831 and 1850?

2. How did the production of coal and iron in France compare with the production of coal and iron in Belgium in 1831 and 1850?

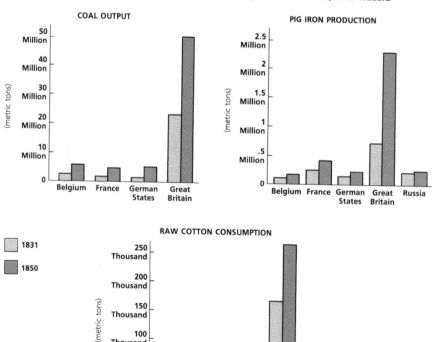

Production in Belgium, France, Germany, Great Britain, and Russia

3. How do we know that Belgium had few factories for the production of cotton cloth in 1831 and 1850?

4. What do the graphs tell us about Russia's industrial capacity in 1831 and 1850?

Connections:
The Industrial Revolution Spreads

The Industrial Revolution started in Britain about 1750. New sources of power and the use of machinery caused a series of changes in agriculture and industry. This led to the rise of the factory system, mass production, and modern capitalism. New inventions and systems changed the way people lived and worked.

Almost all of these changes took place in the Western world, mainly in North America and Europe. Most of the people of Africa, the Middle East, and Asia continued to depend for their livelihood on the kinds of farming and animal herding that they had practiced since ancient times.

As a result, the West and the nonindustrial regions of the world grew farther apart in all areas of culture, especially in values and attitudes. Europeans and North Americans came to believe strongly in change and "progress" through the use of science and technology. Asians and Africans continued to believe that the world was unchanging and that there was a need to be always in harmony with nature.

Such differences led to mutual distrust and dislike. Westerners regarded the peoples of the nonindustrialized regions as weak and inferior. During the 19th century, Europeans used their superior military power to take control of large portions of Asia and Africa.

The Meiji emperor (who ruled from 1867 to 1912) and his officials encouraged the transformation of Japan's agrarian economy into a developed, industrial one. In the 19th century, Japan's transportation and communication networks were improved by means of large governmental investments. The Japanese government also directly supported the prospering of businesses and industries, especially the large, powerful family businesses called *zaibatsu*. The textile industry grew the fastest, remaining the largest Japanese industry until World War II.

Industrialization did not begin in most of Asia, Africa, and the Middle East until the 20th century. Once started, many nations of these regions made great gains in industrializing. As this process continues, a greater understanding and appreciation of different cultures has grown.

Complete the following sentences:

The — began about 1750. Great changes took place in the Western world, mainly in — and —. Most of the people of —, the —, and — remained agricultural.

DOCUMENT-BASED QUESTION

This question is based on the accompanying documents (1–5). It will improve your ability to work with historical documents.

Historical Context:

As political revolutions brought new governments in Europe and the Americas, an economic revolution was also taking place. This revolution saw a changeover from making goods by hand to making goods by machine. The Industrial Revolution, as it was called, brought widespread economic progress but also produced many social problems.

Task:

Using information from the documents and your knowledge of world history, answer the questions that follow each document. Your answers to each question will help you write the document-based essay.

Document 1. Excerpt from *The Condition of the Working Class in England in 1844*, by Friedrich Engels:

> Nobody troubles about the poor as they struggle helplessly in the whirlpool of modern industrial life. The working man may be lucky enough to find employment, if by his labor he can enrich some member of the middle classes. But his wages are so low that they hardly keep body and soul together.
>
> The only difference between the old-fashioned slavery and the new is that while the former was openly acknowledged the latter is disguised. The worker appears to be free, because he is not bought and sold outright. He is sold piecemeal by the day, the week, or the year. Moreover he is not sold by one owner to another, but he is forced to sell himself in this fashion.

Source: Engels, Friedrich, *The Condition of the Working Class in England in 1844*. NY, 1887. (First published in 1844.)

According to this document, how is the industrial worker like a slave?

Document 2. Excerpt from testimony given in 1842 to a commission of the British Parliament investigating child labor. The testimony was given by Ellison Jack, an 11-year-old girl who worked in a coal mine:

I have been working below three years on my father's account; he takes me down at two in the morning and I come up at one and two next afternoon. I go to bed at six at night to be ready for work next morning. . . . I have to bear my burden up four traps, or ladders, before I get to the main road which leads to the pit bottom. My task is four to five tubs; each tub holds 4.25 cwt [47 pounds]. I fill five tubs in 20 journeys. I have been beaten when I did not do what was demanded. Am very glad when my task is done, as it sure fatigues.

Source: Report of the Children's Employment Commission of 1842, from www.hoodfamily.info/coal/coalbearers.html

According to this document, how would you characterize this child's experience with the Industrial Revolution?

Document 3.   Look at the illustration on page 367.

What does it show about living conditions of factory workers in England?

Document 4.   Look at the poster on page 369.

What does the poster suggest is a benefit for workers in joining a labor union?

Document 5.   Excerpt from a 1889 essay by American industrialist Andrew Carnegie, discussing industrialization, competition in business, and society:

Under the law of competition, the employer of thousands is forced into the strictest economies, among which the rates paid to labor figure prominently, and often there is friction between the employer and the employed, between capital and labor, between rich and poor.

The price which society pays for the law of competition, like the price it pays for cheap comforts and luxuries, is also great, but the advantage of this law [is] also greater still, for it is to this law that we owe our wonderful material development. . . . We accept and welcome therefore, as conditions to which we must accommodate ourselves, great inequality of environment, the concentration of business, industrial and commercial, in the hands of a few, and the law of competition between these, as being not only beneficial, but essential for the future progress of the race.

Source: "Wealth" by Andrew Carnegie, *North American Review*, No. CCCXCI, June, 1889.

According to this document, why does Carnegie believe that society should accept the inequalities of industrialization?

DOCUMENT-BASED ESSAY

Using information from the above documents and your knowledge of world history, write an essay in which you:

- Discuss the social changes brought about by the Industrial Revolution.
- Evaluate both the suggested reforms and actual reforms carried out to alleviate some of the problems brought about by the Industrial Revolution.

CHAPTER 15
Nationalism and Imperialism

In the middle of the 19th century, two new nations—Germany and Italy—came into being. While they were struggling to unify, Great Britain was growing stronger. Its industries made it wealthy, and its army and navy made it powerful.

As Europe gained strength, the nations of East Asia became weaker. Japan was the exception. It joined in the Industrial Revolution and developed into the most powerful Asian nation. China kept its ancient civilization and imperial government. But its economy came to be controlled by Westerners. India and Southeast Asia were turned into European colonies.

Europeans also moved into Africa. The colonies set up in that large continent provided raw materials and mass markets for European industries.

Europe was Westernizing the world. Its culture and power were felt everywhere. In fact, the Age of Nationalism and Imperialism could also be called the Age of Europe.

THE UNIFICATION OF GERMANY AND ITALY

People who speak the same language and share a common culture tend to feel a sense of unity. If they live in one general area, they may have a strong desire to be joined together in one nation under one government. These feelings of cultural pride, loyalty, and patriotism are called *nationalism*.

Among the Germans and Italians, nationalistic feelings became very strong in the 19th century. These feelings led to a struggle to unify the separate states into which each nation was divided. By 1871, strong nationalistic leaders in Germany and Italy had succeeded in establishing central governments in both nations.

1. Blood and Iron. Prussia was the largest and most powerful German state. Many Germans believed that unity could be gained only under Prussian leadership. The Frankfurt Assembly had attempted to unify Germany in 1848. Its offer to King Frederick William IV of Prussia to be emperor of all of Germany had been

Otto von Bismarck, the Iron Chancellor.

refused. He did not want a crown given to him by revolutionaries and liberals.

Otto von Bismarck continued the struggle for unification. After he became the chief minister of Prussia in 1862, he followed a policy called "blood and iron." This meant that he would not hesitate to use war to achieve his aims of unifying Germany and expanding its power. To accomplish this, he turned Prussia into a militaristic state with a powerful, well-trained, and disciplined army. Bismarck ruled Prussia as a dictator from 1862 to 1867.

The major obstacles to Germany unity were Austria, France, and the princes who ruled the German states. Austria, and France opposed the unification of Germany because they feared having a large, strong nation on their borders. The German princes did not want to give up their power to a national government. To remove these three obstacles, Bismarck started three wars.

a. *War with Denmark.* In 1864, Denmark took over an area between it and Prussia called Schleswig. Bismarck and Austria objected and invaded Schleswig to free it from the Danes. The Danes lost and turned over Schleswig and Holstein, the province just to the south of Schleswig, to Prussia and Austria. Bismarck persuaded Austria to govern Holstein, while Prussia ruled Schleswig.

b. *War with Austria.* The two powers quarreled over the administration of the provinces. The disagreement led to the

Austro-Prussian War of 1866. Prussia won the conflict that is often called the Seven Weeks' War. Its easy defeat of Austria demonstrated Prussia's military strength. The defeat also ended Austria's ability to control the future of Germany.

To extend Prussia's political power, Bismarck in 1867 organized the North German Confederation. It brought together most of the German states under Prussia's leadership. The Prussian army's ability to win victories had impressed the princes who ruled the north German states. Only four states (all in southern Germany) chose not to be part of the confederation. Mainly Roman Catholic, the south Germans feared domination by the Protestant north Germans.

c. *War with France.*   To encourage the southern states to join with the north, Bismarck started a third war—this time with France. He stirred up anti-French feeling in both northern and southern Germany.

Emperor Napoleon III of France was also eager for a war. He wanted to stop Prussia from gaining more power. In addition, the emperor hoped that a military victory over Prussia would make him more popular with the French people.

The public cause of the war was a dispute between France and Prussia over the selection of a German prince to be king of Spain. By trickery, Bismarck made it look as if both countries had insulted each other. (He did this by rewriting the *Ems Dispatch*, a telegram dealing with the problem.) Newspapers in France and Prussia demanded war. France declared war in July 1870. The south German states blamed France for the situation and came to the aid of the North German Confederation. The Franco-Prussian War, therefore, was really a war between France and all of Germany.

German armies invaded France and surrounded Paris. A large French army under the personal command of Napoleon III was defeated, and the emperor was taken prisoner. In January 1871, Paris surrendered. The Germans had won a quick and total victory.

The Treaty of Frankfurt ended the war. Under its terms, France gave Germany the border provinces of Alsace and Lorraine. Both were rich in coal and iron ore. France also had to pay a large sum of money to Germany. German troops remained in France until the money had been collected.

Following the great victory of 1871, Bismarck called princes and nobles of all the German states to a meeting in the French town of Versailles. There, with much ceremony, the south German states became part of the North German Confederation. The

The Unification of Germany, 1871

Complete each of the following sentences:

1. The largest German state was —.

2. The German state next to Denmark was —.

3. To the west, Alsace and Lorraine border —.

4. The two empires bordering the German Empire were —.

German Empire was born. King William I of Prussia was proclaimed the kaiser (emperor) of all of Germany. Bismarck was named the chancellor, or prime minister. He had succeeded in his plan to unify Germany and turn it into a powerful nation. The policy of "blood and iron" had worked.

2. The Risorgimento in Italy. The attempt to unify Italy during the Revolution of 1848 had failed. The army of Giuseppe Garibaldi had been defeated by French troops requested by the pope, who had opposed unification.

In 1852, a rebirth of the unification movement began. This dramatic period was called the "risorgimento." Count Camillo Cavour led the drive for unification. Cavour was the prime minister of

Piedmont. Located in northern Italy, Piedmont was part of Victor Emmanuel II's Kingdom of Sardinia. Cavour believed in constitutional monarchy and in industrial growth. He strengthened the economy of Piedmont by encouraging the building of factories and railroads and by increasing trade with other countries. Piedmont had to be made economically and politically stronger so that it could win Italian territory from Austria.

The Unification of Italy, 1859–1870

Complete each of the following sentences:

1. The Kingdom of Sardinia included — and the island of —.

2. Most of southern Italy was part of the Kingdom of the —.

3. The year in which most of the Italian states were united with Piedmont was —.

4. The city of — did not become part of the Italian nation until 1870.

5. Two powerful nations that bordered the Italian states were — and —.

The major obstacles to Italian unification were Austria and the pope. Austria controlled portions of northern Italy and had no wish to give them up. The pope ruled the Papal States of central Italy. A strong national government would threaten Church ownership of these lands.

Cavour moved first against the Austrians. He arranged a secret alliance with France and then provoked a war with Austria. When Austrian troops invaded Piedmont, the French aided the Italians. The war ended with a treaty signed by France and Austria in July 1859. Piedmont received the state of Lombardy, previously controlled by Austria.

The Austrian invasion of Piedmont had increased nationalistic feeling in the Austrian-controlled areas of northern Italy. Rebellions broke out in Tuscany, Parma, and Modena. The people of these states demanded to be joined with Piedmont. Knowing that France supported Piedmont, Austria agreed. By early 1860, Piedmont controlled all of Italy except the Kingdom of the Two Sicilies (in the south), the Papal States (in the center), and Venetia (in the northeast). The foundation for an Italian nation had been built.

3. The Return of Garibaldi. In May 1860, Giuseppe Garibaldi landed in Sicily with an army of 1,000 soldiers called Red Shirts. His nationalist soldiers soon took control of the entire Kingdom of the Two Sicilies. Cavour sent the Piedmont army to aid Garibaldi's forces and capture the Papal States. Rome, however, was left untouched. The pope was protected by the French army that occupied the city. Garibaldi then transferred control of the areas held by his Red Shirts to the king of Sardinia. As a result, Victor Emmanuel II was declared king of Italy in March 1861. Cavour died in June, before his dream of unification could be fully realized.

Italy became Prussia's ally in 1866 before the Seven Weeks' War with Austria. The Prussian victory ended Austrian rule of Venetia, and the province was taken over by Italy.

During the Franco-Prussian War in 1870, the French withdrew their troops from Rome, and Italian troops took control. Rome became the capital city of the Kingdom of Italy.

4. After Unification. In the years following unification, Germany and Italy developed quite differently.

a. _Germany._ Bismarck made Germany into one of the strongest nations of Europe. German military and naval power

Garibaldi helps Victor Emmanuel II pull on the "boot" of unified Italy in this political cartoon of 1861.

was greatly increased. Many natural resources, especially coal and iron ore, aided the growth of industries. Productive farms and factories and a good school system gave Germans a high standard of living and a high rate of literacy.

Bismarck had no use for democracy. A legislature existed in Germany, but the kaiser held supreme authority in the government. Labor unions and political parties had little power. Bismarck weakened the unions by giving German workers social insurance benefits, such as old-age pensions and compensation payments for injury or illness. The German social insurance laws were the first passed by any country.

b. *Italy.* After unification, Italy faced many problems. With few natural resources, industry developed slowly and the economy remained weak. Great amounts of money were spent to build up the army and navy. Much of the population suffered from poverty and illiteracy.

Italy was organized as a democracy. A constitution limited the power of the king and provided for an elected parliament to make laws. However, only a small part of the male population had the right to vote. Many of them traded their votes for money. This behavior led to widespread corruption in the government. An additional problem was the refusal of the Roman Catholic Church to recognize the national government. The pope resented the seizure of the Papal States.

In one way, Germany and Italy were alike. Nationalism grew stronger in both countries. This led to the desire to gain glory by competing with other nations for colonies overseas. Between 1871 and 1914, the German Empire and the Kingdom of Italy spent large amounts of money and sacrificed many lives in the race for colonies.

ESSAY QUESTIONS

1. Describe the roles of Bismarck and Cavour in the unification of Germany and Italy.

2. State *two* ways in which the development of Germany and Italy differed in the years following unification.

CRITICAL THINKING

Reread "4. After Unification," on pages 394–396. Then explain why you AGREE or DISAGREE with the following statement:

> Between 1871 and 1914, both Germany and Italy developed democratic national governments capable of solving their economic problems.

SECTIONALISM VERSUS NATIONALISM IN THE UNITED STATES

In the 19th century, the United States became a powerful, prosperous nation. Americans were proud of their victory over Great Britain in the War of 1812. They believed that their destiny was to settle the entire area from the Atlantic Ocean to the Pacific Ocean and from Canada to the Gulf of Mexico. It seemed only right to them that they should win a large area of land from Mexico in the Mexican War (1846–1848). But by mid-century, nationalism had been weakened by a force called *sectionalism*.

1. The Rise of Sectionalism. By 1850, different ways of life had developed in the various parts of the United States. Industries and cities had grown up mainly in the Northeastern states. The South and West were primarily agricultural. Western farms tended to be of medium size.

a. *Slavery.* Agriculture in the South was dominated by large plantations worked by slaves. The slave system was regarded by many people, particularly in the North, as a great evil. One small but influential group called *abolitionists* demanded the immediate end to slavery and the freeing of all slaves. Although few Northerners became abolitionists, most believed that slavery should not be allowed to spread outside the Southern states. In particular, Northerners thought that slavery should be kept out of the lands won from Mexico in the Southwest and West.

b. *Tariffs.* Slavery was not the only issue that divided North and South. The tariff policy of the United States government also caused conflict between the two sections. (A tariff is a tax on goods imported from other countries.) Northern businesspeople wanted to protect their growing industries from foreign competition. They demanded that Congress pass laws that created high tariffs. Southerners opposed such laws. High tariffs increased the cost of imported goods because the amount of the tariffs was added to the price of the goods. Southerners traded mainly with Europe, exchanging cotton, tobacco, and other agricultural products for manufactured goods. High tariffs made the goods the Southerners wanted to buy more expensive.

Tension between North and South greatly increased between 1850 and 1861. Sectional differences caused many Southerners to feel more loyalty to the South than to the United States as a whole. Political differences deepened between proslavery, low-tariff Democrats and antislavery, high-tariff Republicans.

The Northern states outnumbered the Southern states and had a larger population. This gave the North more power in Congress. By 1860, many Southerners felt that they had little future under a national government dominated by the antislavery North. Southerners threatened to *secede*, or withdraw, from the United States and establish a country of their own.

2. The Civil War. In November of 1860, Abraham Lincoln, a Republican, was elected president of the United States. In the next three months, seven Southern states seceded from the United States (the Union). South Carolina, Mississippi, Louisiana, Florida, Alabama, Georgia, and Texas united, forming the Confederate States of America. In April and May of 1861, these seven states were joined by North Carolina, Virginia, Tennessee,

North and South, 1860–1861

Complete each of the following sentences:

1. Three Union states were —, —, and —.

2. The Confederacy included all states from — in the North to — in the Southeast and — in the West.

3. California was a — state.

4. The New Mexico Territory was loyal to the —.

5. Oregon became a state in —.

---

and Arkansas. Fighting between the Confederate States and the Union broke out on April 12, 1861. Although he did not want a war, President Lincoln opposed the secession of the Southern states. He believed that the Union had to be preserved.

The Civil War, which lasted until 1865, was a terrible struggle, marked by great bloodshed and destruction. The worst damage was done in the Southern states, where most of the fighting took place. The Northern victory in April 1865 forced the Southern

The Battle of Gettysburg, in Pennsylvania, a turning point for the North in the Civil War. Confederate forces charged up Little Round Top, which was held by the 20th Maine Regiment. Union forces stopped a Confederate invasion of the North.

states to rejoin the Union and ended slavery and the prewar way of life in the South.

President Lincoln wanted to reunite the Northern and Southern states quickly in order to "bind up the wounds of the nation." Before he could accomplish this goal, he was assassinated in April 1865.

After Lincoln's death, the reunification process was controlled by a group in Congress called the Radical Republicans. To weaken the Democratic Party, they made it difficult for the South to rejoin the United States. During that period known as Reconstruction (1865–1877), the Southern states were treated as conquered territories. They were occupied by Northern troops. Many white Southerners lost their political rights. This harsh treatment kept sectional bitterness alive long after the Civil War had ended. Nationalism in the United States did not again become strong until the end of the 19th century.

 ESSAY QUESTIONS

1. Explain how sectionalism weakened nationalism in 19th-century America.

2. Describe how *two* major issues caused tension between the North and South between 1850 and 1861.

MULTIPLE-CHOICE

1. Which *one* of the following sets of states seceded from the United States in 1860–1861? (*a*) New York, New Jersey, Pennsylvania (*b*) Florida, Alabama, Georgia (*c*) Washington, Oregon, California (*d*) North Dakota, Arizona, Utah.

2. Which *one* of the following was a result of the Civil War? (*a*) Slavery ended. (*b*) The prewar way of life in the South ended. (*c*) President Lincoln was assassinated. (*d*) all of the above.

 ## DEFINITIONS

Explain the meaning of each of the following terms:

a. plantation   *e.* Confederacy
b. abolitionist   *f.* Union
c. tariff   *g.* Reconstruction
d. secede

GRAPH INTERPRETATION

Look at the graph on page 401. Use the information on the graph to answer the following questions.

1. What was the numerical difference in railroad miles in the North and South?

2. What was the numerical difference in population in the North and South?

3. What advantages did the North have over the South in terms of manufacturing and natural resources?

4. If you had been a Southerner in 1861 and had looked at this graph, would you have been confident that the South could win the war? Why or why not?

North vs. South: A Comparison

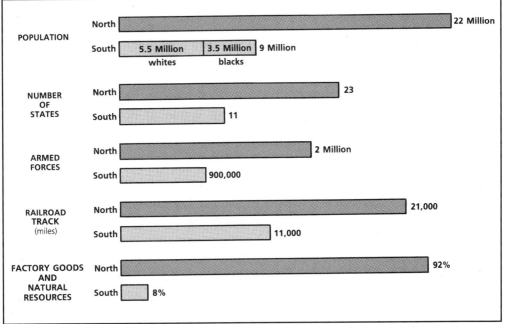

EMPIRE BUILDING IN THE 19TH CENTURY

The United States and the major industrial countries of Europe all acquired colonies in the 19th century. The areas they took over were in Asia, Africa, and Latin America. Some nations, such as Great Britain, already controlled large areas of the world. Others, such as Germany, did not get started in the race for possessions until after 1870.

The period from the 1850's until about 1910 is called the Age of Imperialism. *Imperialism* is the policy of extending authority and control over another territory or country.

1. Causes of Modern Imperialism. Many developments led to imperialism.

    a. *The Industrial Revolution.* The Industrial Revolution increased the wealth of many nations. To remain prosperous, they wanted to be sure that they had readily available supplies of raw materials for their factories. They also looked for new markets for the products that their industries turned out. In addition, businesspeople sought places where they could invest their profits and make even more money. All these needs were met by acquiring colonies.

b. *Militarism.* Colonies required protection by the military forces of the imperialist nations. Supply bases and fortifications were built to defend the citizens of the imperialist nations against native rebellions and attacks by the forces of other imperialist nations.

c. *Nationalism.* The strong sense of nationalism in most European and North American countries in the 1800's led to efforts to make the countries strong. Acquiring colonies also made citizens of the home countries feel powerful and gave them a sense of pride.

d. *Racism and religious views.* Many people in Western countries believed that their civilization was superior to the way of life of the peoples in East Asia, India, and Africa. Westerners wanted to bring the benefits of their ways to others. They also wanted to teach non-Christians about Christianity. For many Europeans and North Americans, such feelings helped to justify imperialism.

2. The Great Empires. Britain owned the largest number of colonies. In 1800, it controlled Canada, part of India, Australia, New Zealand, British Honduras (now Belize, in Central America), and several islands in the Caribbean. In addition to the places mentioned, by 1900 Britain controlled much of Africa, the rest of India, British Guiana (now Guyana, in South America), much of Southeast Asia, Hong Kong, and a number of islands in the Mediterranean and the Pacific.

By the late 1800's, France also had a sizable empire. It controlled much of North and West Africa, Indochina, several islands in the Caribbean, and French Guiana in South America.

Germany entered the race for colonies after 1870. It then picked up sections of Africa and islands in the Pacific. After 1871, Italy also acquired pieces of Africa.

Belgium, Holland, Portugal, and Spain each had a few colonies. The United States acquired territory in the late 1800's and early 1900's. Japan actively spread its authority in East Asia from the 1890's to the 1940's.

3. Imperialism in India. During the 1700's, the Mogul Empire in India became weaker and weaker. At the same time, the British and French East India trading companies gained strength. They competed with each other for control of trade in India.

Rulers of a subcontinent. Englishmen stopping for tea in India.

a. *British East India Company rule.* The major aim of Britain's East India Company was to profit from selling Indian cotton cloth, silk, and sugar to other countries. Victory over France in the Seven Years' War (1756–1763) left Britain as the major power in India. The portions of India not governed directly by Britain were ruled by Indian princes. These local leaders eventually signed treaties that placed their states under British protection.

With some restrictions placed on it by the British government, the East India Company ruled India until 1857. The Company built telegraph, railroad, and irrigation systems. In addition, it set up a postal service and a number of schools. The Company also organized a large army of Indian soldiers, called *sepoys*, to defend its interests. Missionaries arrived to teach Hindus and Muslims about Christianity.

Although many of the changes helped Indians, in general the Indians resented British interference. East India Company officials did not allow Indians to hold high-level positions in the company. Schools taught English and Western ideas and paid little attention to the long history and advanced culture of the Indians. Most of the British tended to treat Indians as inferiors.

b. *Sepoy Mutiny.* Resentment turned into revolt. In 1857, some sepoys refused to use the cartridges supplied for their new rifles. The cartridges were greased and had to have an end bitten off before they could be inserted into the rifles. The sepoys

The Age of Victoria

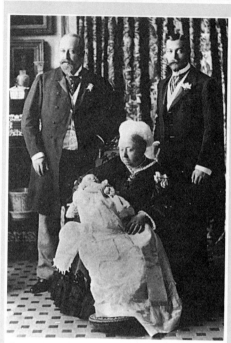

Queen Victoria and royal family members.

Queen Victoria reigned in Britain for 63 years. When the 18-year-old Victoria became queen in 1837, horse-drawn carriages and wagons and sailing ships were the chief means of transportation. Railroads were a novelty. Before she died at the age of 81 in 1901, automobiles were chugging along the streets of London, a network of railroads crisscrossed Britain, and swift ocean liners driven by steam crossed the Atlantic.

The young Victoria knew the Duke of Wellington, who had defeated Napoleon at Waterloo in 1815. She also knew the generals who, in 1914, were to command the British forces in World War I.

The Victorian Age in Great Britain was a period of rapid change. The Industrial Revolution was at its height. The rapid growth of cities marked the age. In 1837, about 18 million people lived in Great Britain, most of them on farms. In 1901, more than 37 million people lived in the nation, most of them living and working in cities.

The Victorian Age was also a period of relative peace. While Victoria reigned, Britain was involved in only one international conflict, the Crimean War (1853–1856). However, as a growing power, Britain did wage various campaigns in winning and defending her colonies.

The growth of industry within the nation and the expansion of the empire led to British prosperity. A proof of this Victorian prosperity was the Great Exhibition of 1851. Inside the Crystal Palace, a huge glass hall, Britain, her colonies, and other nations exhibited their best products and inventions. It was the world's first international exhibition. More than any other event of the time, it demonstrated the Victorian belief in progress.

Queen Victoria and her husband, Prince Albert, believed in hard work, self-discipline, and family life. As such, Victoria and Albert became respected symbols of their era. As the years passed, a Victorian state of mind developed. To the people, religion and a serious attitude toward life were important.

Prince Albert died in 1861 at the age of 42. Victoria had loved him deeply. She mourned him for the rest of her long life.

Why was the Victorian Age such a remarkable period?

Indian infantry supported by an elephant-drawn artillery battery. British officers led these units. This is a late 19th-century photo.

believed that the grease was made of beef or pork fat. Muslims could not eat pork, and Hindus considered cattle to be sacred.

A group of sepoys stationed near Delhi mutinied. They killed their British officers and captured the Indian capital. Soldiers in other areas joined in the revolt. The British, with great difficulty and reinforcements from home, put down the rebellion by the end of 1858.

After the Sepoy Mutiny, the British government took over the administration of India. The East India Company lost its power. A British viceroy (governor) was appointed to head the Indian government. Then, in 1876, Queen Victoria became empress of India.

The British continued India's economic development. They built new industries and more railroads. Despite these benefits, the living standard of most Indians remained low. The population increased, but the food supply did not keep pace. This caused frequent famines.

c. *Toward independence.* These conditions contributed to the growth of a movement for independence. The Hindus formed the Indian National Congress in 1885, while Muslims created the Muslim League in 1906. Important 20th-century leaders in the National Congress were Mohandas K. Gandhi and Jawaharlal Nehru. Mohammed Ali Jinnah headed the Muslim League. Gandhi persuaded many Indians to practice passive resistance. His followers refused to obey British laws, serve in the armed forces, pay taxes, or cooperate with British officials until their demands for independence were met. Gandhi, called "Mahatma," or the "great one," also urged nonviolence. Despite arrests and beatings by the police, his followers did not attempt to use force, even to defend themselves.

Independence finally came in 1947. The British had been weakened by World War II. They were also embarrassed by world

Jawaharlal Nehru (left) and Mohandas K. Gandhi.

support for Gandhi's passive resistance campaign. In the hope of avoiding a civil war, the British divided India into Muslim and Hindu countries. Muslim Pakistan consisted of areas carved out of northwestern and northeastern India. (The northeast is now the country of Bangladesh.) Nehru became the first prime minister of the Republic of India, while Ali Jinnah took the title of governor general of Pakistan.

 SENTENCE COMPLETION

Complete each of the following sentences:

1. The East India Company was important in Indian history because —.

2. Among the benefits brought to India by the British were —.

3. In general, Indians resented the British because —.

4. The Sepoy Mutiny was an important event because —.

5. Indians wanted independence because —.

6. To gain independence for India in the 20th century, Mohandas K. Gandhi and Jawaharlal Nehru —.

4. Imperialism in China. Although the ancient culture of China was known for its learning and art, the country had not started to industrialize by the 19th century. The Ch'ing, or Manchu, emperors were not interested in learning about Western technology. They did not feel that the European "barbarians" could teach them anything. As a result, the Chinese lacked modern weapons. This left them unable to resist the demands of Western nations for more trading privileges in China.

Europeans were attracted to China by the rich profits they hoped to make there. The huge Chinese population offered a supply of cheap workers and a market for European goods. Also, natural resources, such as coal and iron ore, could be developed.

a. *Opium War.* Modern imperialism began in China with the Opium War (1839–1842). Opium, a habit-forming drug, was produced in India. British traders sold great quantities of it in China, and many Chinese became addicted. Large amounts of money flowed out of China into British hands. In 1839, Chinese officials tried to stop the opium trade. They destroyed 20,000 chests of the drug and imprisoned the British traders who were selling it. The British replied by sending an invasion fleet to China. Without a navy and modern weapons, the Chinese could not hold out against the British military power. China was defeated. Its government was forced to sign the Treaty of Nanking in 1842.

As a result of this treaty, the British and other foreigners gained new privileges in China. Foreign traders had been permitted to live and work in the port of Canton. The treaty forced the Chinese to open four more ports to Westerners. Moreover, the port of Hong Kong was given to Britain. Tariffs were reduced. *Extraterritorial rights* were granted to foreigners living in the treaty ports. This meant that foreigners accused of crimes could be tried in their own courts and by their own laws rather than by those of China.

b. *Taiping Rebellion.* China's troubles did not end with the 1842 treaty. In 1850, the Taiping Rebellion broke out. Rebels wanted to overthrow the emperor because the Manchu had allowed China to become weak. It took the government 14 years to crush the rebellion, and it had to ask Westerners for help. In the midst of the civil war, in 1856, the British again attacked China. The British wanted additional trading rights, as did the French, who joined the fight. Together, they easily defeated the Chinese.

c. *Foreign interests.* The Treaty of Tientsin (1858) made the Chinese open 11 more ports to Westerners. Also, foreign traders and missionaries were allowed to move into the interior of

Imperialism in Asia and the Southwest Pacific, 1900

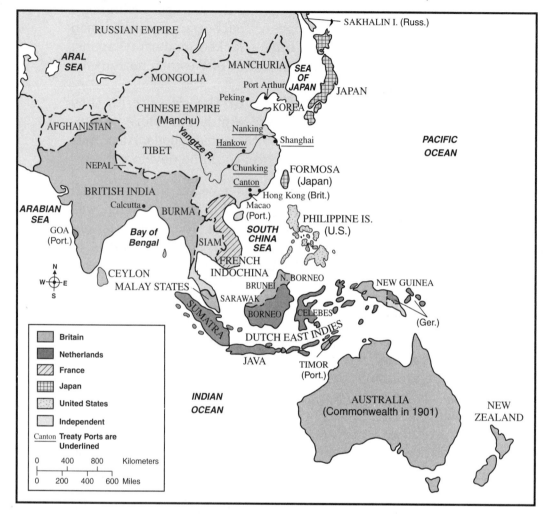

1. **PROVE or DISPROVE:** Great Britain controlled more of Asia in 1900 than did any other non-Asian county.

2. Match each area in Column A with the nation that controlled it in Column B.

Column A	Column B
1. India	a. Japan
2. Sumatra	b. United States
3. Indochina	c. Britain
4. Formosa	d. Netherlands
5. Philippine Islands	e. France

China. The treaty also provided that opium could once again be imported into China.

During the second half of the 19th century, China lost colonial states all around its borders. Britain took Burma, while France assumed control of Cambodia, Laos, and Vietnam. Russia gained territory in the north and the right to run a railroad through Manchuria.

In 1894, China and Japan clashed over Korea. Japan easily defeated the Chinese forces. The peace treaty in 1895 awarded Taiwan and some nearby islands to Japan.

The United States did not take control of any portion of China. But Americans did a great deal of business in China. The U.S. government wanted to protect this trade. In 1899, Secretary of State John Hay asked the European nations and Japan to agree to respect one another's trading rights in China. This desire of the United States for equal rights for all nations with interests in China was called the "Open Door Policy."

d. *Boxer Rebellion.* Many Chinese hated the foreigners who had humiliated their country. A group called the "Righteous and Harmonious Fists" formed to drive all "foreign devils" out of China. Westerners called the members of this group "Boxers." The Boxers killed a number of Europeans and Americans. In 1900,

Group of armed members of the Boxers.

Boxers attacked embassies in Beijing. European and American troops in Beijing held off the attackers for several weeks. Finally, an international force of U.S., British, French, German, Russian, and Japanese troops marched on Beijing. They saved the embassies and crushed the Boxer Rebellion. To make peace, the Chinese government agreed to pay a huge sum of money to the foreign nations and to give them additional privileges in China.

e. *Chinese Republic.* Patriotic Chinese blamed the Manchu ruler for China's troubles and demanded reforms. They wanted China to industrialize and to have a government more responsive to the wishes of the people. In 1911, a revolution led by Dr. Sun Yat-sen overthrew the Manchus and made China a republic. The Kuomintang, or Nationalist Party, tried to follow Sun Yat-sen's "Three Principles of the People" as it set up the new government. The principles called for freeing China from foreign control, establishing a democratic government, and improving the economy. The Chinese had a difficult time putting these ideas into effect.

 ESSAY QUESTIONS

1. Explain how each of the following events helped foreigners gain power and land in China.

    Opium War
    Treaty of Nanking
    Treaty of Tientsin

2. What was the Open Door Policy?

The Father of Modern China

Sun Yat-sen (1866–1925) was a Chinese revolutionary leader and statesman. He is considered by many to be the founding father of modern China. Following the overthrow of the Manchu Dynasty in 1911, Sun became the first president of the newly established Republic of China.

Born to a peasant family, Sun received a few years of schooling before leaving China at age 13. He went to live with an older brother who had become a prosperous merchant in Hawaii. Sun continued his education there, but in 1883 he returned to China to attend college in Hong Kong. Eventually, in 1892, he earned a medical doctor's license from the Hong Kong College of Medicine. After a brief period of medical practice in Hong Kong, Sun turned to politics.

He developed a political philosophy known as the "Three Principles of the People." It is based upon Sun's admiration for the American economic system and the ideas of Alexander Hamilton and Abraham Lincoln. He was inspired by the portion of Lincoln's Gettysburg Address that spoke of "government of the people, by the people, for the people."

Dissatisfaction with the government of China under the Manchu Dynasty led Sun to organize reform groups of Chinese exiles in Hong Kong, by then a British colony. In 1894, Sun founded the Ying Zhong (Revive China) Society. It became a platform for future revolutionary activities.

In 1895, a coup Sun had plotted failed, so he fled China. For the next 16 years, Sun was an exile in Europe, the United States, Canada, and Japan. He raised money for his revolutionary parties and financed uprisings in China. In Japan, he became the leader of several anti-Manchu Chinese groups, until the Japanese government expelled him to the United States.

On October 10, 1911, a military uprising at Wuhan began a revolution that would end more than 2,000 years of imperial rule in China. Sun had had no direct involvement in the revolution so far. However, he immediately returned to China from the United States when he learned of the rebellion against the Manchu emperor.

Representatives from the southern provinces elected Sun president of the provisional government of the new Republic of China (which came into existence on January 1, 1912) and president of the Kuomintang (Nationalist Party). The provisional government had no military forces with which to compel the support of the northern provinces, which had not yet joined the revolution. A warlord named Yuan Shikai controlled a private army in northern China. Sun gained Yuan's support by resigning and offering him the presidency of the new republic. Yuan then sided with the revolution, forced the last emperor to abdicate, and became president.

As president, Yuan's dictatorial methods caused opposition to develop. In 1913, Sun led an unsuccessful revolt against Yuan Shikai and was forced to seek asylum in Japan.

Sun returned to a divided China in 1917. In 1923, he was elected president of a self-proclaimed national government in Canton, in southern China. Convinced of the need to unite China by military force, Sun established the Whampoa Military Academy to build and train a Nationalist army. The commandant of the Academy was Chiang Kai-shek, a follower of Sun and one of the leaders of the Kuomintang.

While warlords with private armies fought one another in northern China, the government of the new republic struggled to survive in the south. Sun pursued a policy of active cooperation with the Chinese Communists, who also wanted control of China. Sun believed that the unification of China, followed by a period of political education, would lead to the development of democracy.

On March 12, 1925, Sun died of liver cancer at the age of 60 while traveling from Canton to Beijing for peace and unification talks with northern regional leaders. Sun Yat-sen's death was followed by a power struggle within the Kuomintang. Chiang Kai-shek emerged as the leader of the Nationalist Party. When the Communists and the Kuomintang split in 1927, a long civil war began. Both sides claimed to be the heirs of Sun Yat-sen. In 1949, Mao Zedong and his Communists took control of China. Chiang Kai-shek and the Kuomintang leadership fled to the island of Taiwan.

Sun Yat-sen (*seated*) with Chiang Kai-shek in 1924 at the Whampoa Military Academy.

1. Explain why you AGREE or DISAGREE with those who regard Sun Yat-sen as the Father of Modern China.

2. Describe the American influences on Sun Yat-sen.

5. Imperialism in Africa.   Ever since the days of the Portuguese explorers in the late 1400's, Europeans had taken African land for colonies. But strong efforts to add to their holdings did not take place until the early 1800's. By 1900, very little of Africa remained out of European hands.

   a. *French colonies.*   The French took over Algeria in North Africa in 1830. They said they wanted to stop pirate raids in the Mediterranean. In 1878, with the approval of Great Britain, France gained control of Tunisia. This country is also in North Africa, to the east of Algeria. Germany opposed the French desire to own Morocco, to the west of Algeria. The dispute was finally settled in France's favor in 1911. France also acquired vast areas of West and Central Africa.

   b. *British colonies.*   Great Britain took the largest portion of Africa. It had scattered holdings in West Africa—Nigeria, the Gold Coast, Sierra Leone, and Gambia. Most of Britain's possessions were in the eastern half of Africa. They stretched in an almost unbroken line from Egypt in the north to the Cape of Good Hope in the south.

   The British were very interested in the Suez Canal, which opened in 1869. It had been built through Egypt to link the Mediterranean and Red seas. British ships used the waterway to shorten the voyage between Britain and India. The Turkish ruler of Egypt owned the largest number of shares in the company that built the canal. In 1875, Britain gained control of the canal by buying the Egyptian stock. Seven years later, Britain stepped in to settle a rebellion in Egypt and stayed on to rule the country.

   Just to the south of Egypt is the Sudan. Although France had wanted to add this area to its empire, the Sudan became a colony of Britain in 1898.

   Britain also gained control of Uganda and British East Africa (now Kenya), in the 1880's. But its richest African colonies were in the south. South Africa had been acquired from the Dutch during the Napoleonic wars in the early 1800's. Its Dutch farmers, called Boers, resented British rule. They moved north in the hope of escaping the British.

   In 1867, diamonds were found near the Boer territory. The mine became the richest source of diamonds in the world. Gold was discovered in a nearby area in 1886. A leading developer of the gold and diamond industries in southern Africa was Cecil Rhodes, an Englishman. He promoted British interests in Africa and dreamed of a "Cape-to-Cairo" railroad to link all of Britain's territories from the south to the north. The railroad was never built,

British troops attacking Boer defenders in 1899.

but Rhodes expanded British rule into Rhodesia (what is now Zimbabwe and Zambia).

The Boers revolted against British rule in 1899. It took British forces three years to defeat the guerrilla fighters. In the hope of preventing future uprisings, the Boers were given more political rights. Boer areas joined with British areas in 1910 to become the Union of South Africa.

c. *Other colonies.* Germany and Italy came late to the race for colonies in Africa. In the 1880's, Germany claimed German East Africa (now Tanzania). At about the same time, Germany acquired Togo and Cameroon, both in West Africa. In 1898, it had received South West Africa (now called Namibia). Italy acquired Libya in North Africa and part of Somaliland in the northeast.

Portugal and Spain also held pieces of Africa. King Leopold of Belgium owned a large portion of Central Africa, the Congo, as his personal colony. In 1908, the king was forced to give up the colony because of his harsh treatment of the Africans. The Belgian government then ruled the area.

Two African countries remained independent throughout the colonial period. They are Liberia in the west and Ethiopia in the east. Liberia had been founded in 1847 by former slaves from the United States.

Imperialism in Africa, 1914

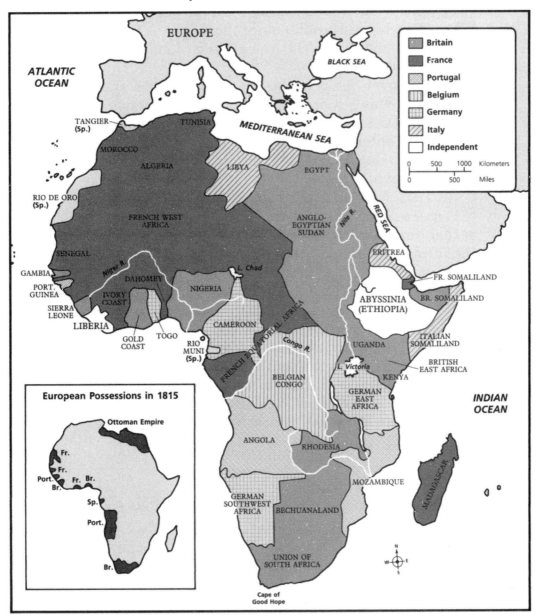

1. Why is it correct to say that the British in 1914 had the "lion's share" of Africa?

2. Which nation owned the most territory in northwest Africa?

3. Name *two* nations in Africa that were independent in 1914.

6. U.S. Imperialism. The United States started its empire in 1867 when it purchased Alaska from Russia. Americans had long been interested in Hawaii—since the 1820's. A revolt there, led by American planters in 1893, brought the islands under U.S. control five years later.

Victory over Spain in the Spanish-American War (1898) gave the United States control of the Philippine Islands and Guam in the Pacific Ocean and of Puerto Rico in the Caribbean. The United States had entered the war to help Cuba gain its independence from Spain. But for years afterward, the U.S. government dominated Cuban affairs.

In 1903, President Theodore Roosevelt encouraged the people of Panama to revolt against the government of Colombia. (Panama at that time was a province of Colombia.) As a reward for assisting the rebels, the United States gained control of the Panama Canal Zone. It then built a canal to shorten the distance ships had to travel between the East and the West coasts of the United States.

The United States also dominated the governments and economies of other Latin American countries through a policy called *Dollar Diplomacy*. This policy encouraged U.S. businesses to invest in the development of countries and to build factories in them. Then, if the business interests were threatened or harmed by the countries, U.S. troops would be sent in to protect American lives and property. The United States also tried

HELD UP THE WRONG MAN

"What will we do with it?"—a cartoon published in 1898 after the defeat of Spain (*left*). President Theodore Roosevelt strong-arming Colombia (*right*).

to regulate events in the Caribbean and Latin America to protect the Panama Canal.

Between about 1912 and 1934, the United States applied the ideas behind Dollar Diplomacy as it interfered in the affairs of several countries in Latin America. Chief among these countries were Nicaragua, Haiti, the Dominican Republic, and Mexico.

In 1917, the United States purchased the Virgin Islands from Denmark. This action completed the building of the U.S. Empire.

CRITICAL THINKING

1. **PROVE or DISPROVE:** U.S. imperialism began with the Spanish-American War.

2. Why do you think many Latin Americans resented Dollar Diplomacy?

7. Japanese Imperialism.   At the end of the 19th century, Japan used its increased military power and industrial strength to take over parts of East Asia. It fought a war with China over Korea in 1894–1895. Victory over China gave Japan ownership of Taiwan and the Pescadores Islands. Korea officially kept its independence, but Japan actually controlled it until 1945.

The Russo-Japanese War (1904–1905) also ended in a Japanese victory. As a result, Japan took over portions of China that had been controlled by Russia. Participation in World War I

Japanese artillerymen and a siege gun that was used to shell Russian-held Port Arthur and Russian ships.

(1914–1918) enabled Japan to acquire German-held islands in the Pacific Ocean. (Germany had lost the war.)

The Japanese Empire reached its peak in the early 1940's. During the 1930's and 1940's, the government built what is called the Greater East Asia Co-Prosperity Sphere. Japanese military forces conquered much of China and Southeast Asia and many islands in the Pacific. Conflict with the United States and its European allies in World War II (1941–1945) resulted in the defeat of Japan and the loss of its empire in 1945.

8. Retreat From Imperialism. Few colonies are left in the world today. A strong spirit of nationalism arose in the colonies after the end of World War II in 1945. This spirit forced the imperialist nations to realize that the colonies had rights too. Also, Great Britain and France were badly weakened by the war. They could no longer afford to administer and defend their colonies. Some colonies had to fight wars to win their freedom. Others achieved independence through peaceful agreements with the ruling country.

The imperialist nations did bring some benefits to their colonies. They introduced modern technology and built roads, railroads, bridges, schools, and hospitals. Their rule was often honest and efficient. But the colonized peoples had fewer rights in their own lands than did the imperialist masters. Colonial people were treated as second-class citizens. They were ruled by governments they did not choose and by laws they did not make. Their traditional ways of life were disrupted by the impact of Western ways. Eventually, most Europeans and Americans came to regard imperialism as evil.

Chapter Review

MULTIPLE-CHOICE

Choose the item that best completes each sentence.

1. Otto von Bismarck was responsible for the unification of (*a*) Japan (*b*) Germany (*c*) Italy (*d*) the United States.

2. To achieve the unification of Germany, Prussia fought wars against (*a*) Spain, Italy, and Holland (*b*) Denmark, Austria, and France (*c*) Sweden, Belgium, and Russia (*d*) Norway, Denmark, and Russia.

3. In Italy, the drive for unification was called the (*a*) Reconquista (*b*) Renaissance (*c*) Reformation (*d*) Risorgimento.

4. The leaders most responsible for the unification of Italy were (*a*) Frederick William IV and Otto von Bismarck (*b*) Napoleon I and Napoleon III (*c*) Count Camillo Cavour and Giuseppe Garibaldi (*d*) Queen Victoria and Prince Albert.

5. The Franco-Prussian War began in (*a*) 1848 (*b*) 1866 (*c*) 1870 (*d*) 1890.

6. The American Civil War was brought on by a struggle between forces called (*a*) nationalism and sectionalism (*b*) imperialism and sectionalism (*c*) nationalism and industrialization (*d*) imperialism and colonialism.

7. The desire of European nations to build empires between 1850 and 1910 is known as (*a*) the policy of blood and iron (*b*) modern imperialism (*c*) risorgimento (*d*) globalization.

8. The nation that controlled the largest empire was (*a*) Italy (*b*) France (*c*) Germany (*d*) Britain.

9. The policy of Dollar Diplomacy was used to extend the power of the United States in (*a*) Asia (*b*) Africa (*c*) Latin America (*d*) Europe.

10. Two nationalist leaders who fought against imperialism were (*a*) Abraham Lincoln and Theodore Roosevelt (*b*) Mohandas K. Gandhi and Sun Yat-sen (*c*) Cecil Rhodes and King Leopold (*d*) Queen Victoria and Jawaharlal Nehru.

 ESSAY QUESTIONS

From the list below, select *one* person. Write a two-paragraph essay about that person by answering the following questions:

1. How did this person help his country?

2. Why do you approve or disapprove of steps taken by this person to achieve his goals?

> Camillo Cavour
> Cecil Rhodes
> Otto von Bismarck

CRITICAL THINKING

1. Explain the meaning of each of the following terms and give a specific example for each.

    nationalism
    sectionalism

2. How do you think the history of the United States might have been different if the Confederate States of America had won the Civil War?

3. Explain why you think imperialism was GOOD or BAD for the people of India, East Asia, and Africa.

Connections: Imperialism

Imperialism comes about when a strong nation with military power takes control of a weaker nation or people. Imperialism has always played a part in world affairs. However, the imperialism practiced by the great civilizations of the ancient world was different from the imperialism of modern times.

The Assyrians, Persians, Greeks, and Romans all had their empires. They conquered neighboring or distant lands and made them colonies. The purpose of the ancient empire builders was to gain wealth by seizing the goods of the conquered peoples and by taxing them. The Romans were the greatest imperialists of ancient times. Their empire included most of Europe and portions of North Africa and the Middle East. From all these areas, slaves and loot poured into Rome.

Modern imperialism was a direct result of the Industrial Revolution. Industrialized nations such as Britain, France, Italy, and Germany sought sources of raw materials, new markets for manufactured goods, and places to invest business profits. To meet their needs, the industrialized nations of Europe competed furiously with one another to gain colonies in nonindustrial regions. Asia and Africa were the Europeans' main targets. Modern imperialism reached its peak during the 1870–1914 period. During those years, Great Britain built the largest empire. Britain's colonies and the regions it controlled nearly circled the globe.

1. State *one* difference between ancient and modern imperialism.

2. Explain the boast of 19th-century Britons, "The sun never sets on the British Empire."

DOCUMENT-BASED QUESTION

This question is based on the accompanying documents (1–5). It will improve your ability to work with historical documents.

Historical Context:

The Industrial Revolution gave rise to two powerful political forces in the 19th century—nationalism and imperialism. Nationalism led to the founding of two new nations in Europe—Italy and Germany. Imperialism led to the Westernizing of the world by European powers.

Task:

Using information from the documents and your knowledge of world history, answer the questions that follow each document. Your answers to each question will help you write the document-based essay.

Document 1. Excerpt from Italian political leader Giuseppe Mazzini's "Duties Towards Your Country," which is characterized by his nationalist feelings:

> O, my brothers, love your Country! Our country is our Home, a house God has given us, placing therein a numerous family that loves us, and whom we love; a family with whom we sympathize more readily and whom we understand more quickly than we do others; and which, from its being centered around a given spot, and from the uniform nature of its elements, is adapted to a special branch of activity.
>
> Before men can *associate* with the nations of which Humanity is composed, they must have a national existence. . . . It is only through our country that we can have a recognized *collective* existence.

> **Source**: Mazzini, Giuseppe, *An Essay On the Duties of Man Addressed to Workingmen.* NY: Funk & Wagnalls, 1898. (First published in 1844.)

According to this document, what are the underlying concepts that characterize nationalism?

Document 2. Excerpt from *Confession of Faith* (1877) by British businessman Cecil Rhodes, in which he characterizes the British:

> I contend that we [the British] are the finest race in the world and that the more of the world we inhabit the better it is for the human race.

Africa is still lying ready for us, and it is our duty to take it. It is our duty to seize every opportunity of acquiring more territory, and we should keep this one idea steadily before our eyes that more territory simply means more of the Anglo-Saxon race, more of the best, the most human, most honourable race the world possesses.

> **Source**: Cecil Rhodes, *Confession of Faith* (1877), found on www.sianews.com/modules. php?name= News&file=article&sid=1882

According to this document, why did Rhodes believe British imperialism would be good for Africa and the rest of the world?

Document 3.   Excerpt from a letter written by Chief Machemba of the Yao people of East Africa to Hermann von Wissmann, a German military commander, in 1890:

If it should be friendship that you desire, then I am ready for it, today and always; but to be your subject, that I cannot be. . . . I do not fall at your feet, for you are God's creature just as I am. I am Sultan here in my land. You are Sultan there in yours. Yet listen, I do not say to you that you should obey me; for I know you are a free man. As for me, I will not come to you, and if you are strong enough, then come and fetch me.

> **Source**: Quoted in A. Adu Boahen. *African Perspectives on Colonialism*. Baltimore: Johns Hopkins University Press, 1987.

Based on reading this document, what can you conclude about how Africans viewed European imperialism?

Document 4.   Study the maps on page 415.

What do the maps indicate was the result of European imperialism in Africa?

Document 5.   Look at the left-hand political cartoon on page 416.

What does this cartoon, titled "What will we do with it?" suggest about the acquisition of the Philippines by the United States?

DOCUMENT-BASED ESSAY

Using information from the above documents and your knowledge of world history, write an essay in which you:

- Discuss the rise of nationalism and imperialism in Europe during the 19th century.
- Explain how European nationalism and imperialism affected the rest of the world.

UNIT VI

A HALF-CENTURY OF CRISIS

CHAPTER 16
World War I

As the 20th century began, Europeans had reason to be hopeful. They felt powerful and in control of the economy of the world. Their colonies were giving them wealth and prestige. Factories turned out ever-increasing quantities of a wide variety of products. New inventions kept improving the way people lived. All seemed well until Europe stumbled into war in 1914.

This "Great War," as it was called, involved most of the major countries of the world. Some individuals, such as President Woodrow Wilson of the United States, hoped that the war would make the world "safe for democracy." Others feared that the world would be changed for the worse.

The problems caused not only by the fighting but also by the peace settlement did bring about changes. New countries came into being. Relationships between the leading powers were altered. The people of Russia, Italy, and Germany turned to dictators to solve their problems. The 20th century became a time of struggle between democracies and dictatorships.

CAUSES OF WORLD WAR I

For any event, there are old causes that developed over time. There are also new happenings that trigger an event. These causes and happenings are known as long-range causes and immediate causes.

In the early 1900's, a number of forces affected relations among the countries of Europe. These forces were imperialism,

423

On the eve of World War I, most Europeans were unaware that their way of life was about to end.

nationalism, militarism, a system of entangling alliances, and international anarchy. Over time, tensions had been created that threatened to erupt into violence. In 1914, a tragic act in an out-of-the-way city in southeastern Europe set in motion events that turned into a world war.

1. Long-Range Causes. There were a number of long-range causes of World War I.

    a. *Imperialism and nationalism.* The tension created in the world by imperialism was strongly linked to nationalism. Many people in each nation of Europe felt themselves to be superior to the peoples of other nations. This attitude created a desire to rule over lands beyond their own borders in Europe and elsewhere. For example, Russia, Turkey, and Austria-Hungary competed for control of the Balkan nations of south-eastern Europe. Germany and France nearly went to war over the right to possess Morocco in North Africa. Russia and Japan fought over Korea.

    Nationalism also led to the rise of Pan-Slavism and Pan-Germanism. Pan-Slavism was the name given to the desire of Russia to protect Slavic people living anywhere in Europe. Pan-Germanism referred to Germany's desire to be the protector of all German-speaking people in Europe. Russia, therefore, supported Serbia, a Slavic nation, in conflicts with Austria-Hungary. Germany backed Austria-Hungary against Russia. The rulers of Austria-Hungary were German. Also, German was the official language of the multiethnic Austro-Hungarian Empire. On occasion, these desires conflicted, resulting in strained relations.

b. *Militarism.* A policy of militarism caused the governments of larger European countries to build up their armies and navies. These countries believed that having a large military force gave them prestige and power. Many also acted as if the best way to solve problems between nations is by the use of military force. Militarism created fear and distrust in Europe. The British had the best and biggest navy. But they became alarmed by Germany's efforts to strengthen its navy by building more and bigger ships. Germany was suspicious of Russia's plans to modernize its army. Distrust led to an arms race.

c. *Entangling alliances.* The tensions created by imperialism and nationalism and the distrust caused by militarism led to the establishment of a system of entangling alliances. To be safe from their rivals, European nations entered into agreements to help their allies in the event of war.

Before 1914, two major alliance systems had been put together. Germany, Austria-Hungary, and Italy formed the Triple Alliance. Eventually, they were joined by the Ottoman Empire (Turkey) and Bulgaria. Most of these nations were known in World War I as the Central Powers. The opposing prewar system was the Triple Entente. Its members were Britain, France, and Russia. During World War I, they were later joined by Japan and many other nations. Collectively, these wartime allies were called the Allied Powers. Instead of increasing security, the alliance systems made it almost certain that a clash between any two nations would draw others into the conflict.

d. *International anarchy.* Finally, in the early 1900's, the nations of Europe tended to act independently. They showed no concern for how their actions would affect their neighbors. This problem was known as international anarchy. It meant that no practical way existed to prevent a war if two or more nations had a dispute with one another. Europe seemed to be sitting on a time bomb.

2. Immediate Causes. In June 1914, Archduke Francis Ferdinand and his wife visited the Balkan city of Sarajevo to inspect military training sessions. He was the heir to the throne of the Austro-Hungarian Empire. Sarajevo was the capital of Bosnia, an area populated by South Slavs. These people were unhappy living under the rule of Austria-Hungary. Many wanted to be united with Serbia. The language and culture of the South Slavs was similar to that of the

Europe, 1915

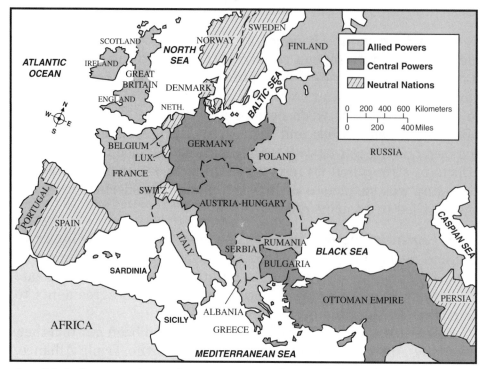

1. List *three* nations that were members of the Allied Powers in 1915.

2. List *three* nations that were members of the Central Powers.

3. List *three* neutral nations.

4. Why do you think Germany and Austria-Hungary were called Central Powers?

Serbs. Also, the South Slav lands bordered Serbia. The Serbs wanted to acquire the South Slav lands in order to enlarge Serbia and gain a port on the Adriatic Sea. Some Serbian officials urged the South Slavs to revolt against Austria-Hungary. Through Francis Ferdinand's visit to Sarajevo, the Austro-Hungarian government hoped to keep the South Slavs within the empire. It was believed that the presence of the archduke, a popular figure, would inspire the South Slavs to be more loyal to the Austro-Hungarian Empire.

During their visit to Sarajevo, a member of a Serbian nationalist group shot and killed the archduke and his wife. The government of Austria-Hungary blamed the government of Serbia for the murders. Backed by Germany's offer of unlimited support, Austria-Hungary presented a set of demands to Serbia. One called

The assassination of Archduke Francis Ferdinand and his wife on June 28, 1914.

for the dismissal from the Serbian government of officials opposed to Austria-Hungary. Serbia rejected the demands.

On July 18, 1914, Austria-Hungary declared war on Serbia. The system of entangling alliances quickly brought other nations into the conflict. Russia came to the aid of Serbia. This caused Germany to declare war on both Russia and France. When German forces moved through neutral Belgium to get to France, Britain declared war on Germany (August 4, 1914). (Despite the Triple Alliance, Italy did not support Germany. Instead, it remained neutral until 1915, when it joined the Allied Powers.) What had started as a limited conflict in the Balkans quickly exploded into the First World War.

ESSAY QUESTIONS

1. List the *five* long-range causes of World War I.

2. Select *one* of these causes and explain why it created problems.

3. Explain how the murder of Archduke Francis Ferdinand started World War I.

CRITICAL THINKING

Explain why you AGREE or DISAGREE with the following statement: "The long-range causes of World War I do not now exist. None of these forces could bring about a war in today's world."

GLOBAL CONFLICT: 1914–1918

World War I involved most major nations in the world and lasted four years. The battles took place in Europe, Africa, and the Middle East and on both the Atlantic and Pacific oceans. New weapons—such as the machine gun, the airplane, the tank, and poison gas—caused great destruction and killed millions of people. It was a war that changed the world.

1. The Western Front. The most important battles of the war were fought in Europe, primarily in France. German armies struck through Belgium and invaded France. Their attempt to capture Paris was stopped at the Marne River in September 1914. From 1915 to 1917, the British and French fought the Germans in one bloody battle after another. Even though tens of thousands were killed, very little territory changed hands.

Both sides dug trenches that stretched for miles. The troops lived and fought in them. They endured the miseries of filth, dampness, lice, and disease. Added to these awful conditions was the danger of being killed by machine gun, rifle, or artillery fire. By 1917, the British, French, and German armies had become exhausted, but no one was willing to give up.

Czech soldiers serving in the Russian Army during World War I. The soldiers are occupying a trench on the Eastern Front.

2. The Eastern Front.   The Central Powers won many victories in Eastern Europe. The forces of Austria-Hungary and Bulgaria defeated Serbia and occupied that country in 1915. In the same year, the Ottoman Turks stopped a British attempt to capture the Dardanelles (the passage between the Mediterranean Sea and the Black Sea) and invade Turkey. The loss of so many Australian and New Zealand troops attempting to capture Gallipoli, on the Turkish coast, made this campaign a disaster for the Allies.

German and Austrian armies invaded Russia. Russian losses and suffering were so great that the Russian people lost their will to fight. In 1917, a revolution overthrew the czar. But the new government kept Russia in the war. This action proved to be unpopular, and another set of leaders—the Communists—gained power. In March 1918, they signed the Treaty of Brest-Litovsk with Germany and withdrew Russia from the war. Germany gained a great deal of Russian territory and valuable natural resources. Just as important, it no longer had to fight on two fronts.

3. Africa and the Middle East.   During the first year of the war, the Allies occupied most of the German colonies in Africa. Only in German East Africa (now Tanzania) did a German force hold out against British troops.

In Egypt, British forces successfully defended the Suez Canal from attacks by the Turks. But British efforts to liberate Syria and Iraq from the Ottoman Empire failed. Not until 1917 were Arab nationalist forces able to weaken Ottoman control of the Middle East. Arabs, with British support, attacked Turkish forts in what are today Saudi Arabia and Israel. The Arab actions helped the British take over the cities of Jerusalem, Baghdad, and Damascus.

4. The War at Sea.   To cripple Germany economically, the British blockaded the German coast. All ships carrying goods to German ports were seized. This caused a great shortage of food in Germany. In the Battle of Jutland in 1916, the German fleet attempted to break the North Sea blockade. But the Germans were defeated by British ships, which controlled the seas until the end of the war. The Germans did, however, slip many light cruisers and submarines past the blockade to raid Allied shipping. Attacks by German submarines proved to be especially damaging. By 1917, Britain also was suffering from food shortages.

5. The United States and the War.   At the beginning of the war, the United States tried to stay neutral. It did not officially take sides, but its sympathies favored the Allies.

The sinking of the British passenger ship *Lusitania* by a German U-boat (submarine) with the loss of many American lives caused much anti-German feeling in the United States.

a. *German submarine warfare.* As the war continued, attacks by German submarines on U.S. ships caused the loss of many American lives. President Woodrow Wilson warned the German government to respect U.S. rights as a neutral. Despite this warning, Germany turned to a policy of unrestricted submarine warfare in late January 1917. It was a desperate effort to cripple the Allies. The new German policy sank many more U.S. ships and killed more Americans. Anti-German feelings increased.

b. *Zimmermann Note.* Another action by Germany deepened American anger. In January 1917, the German foreign secretary, Arthur Zimmermann, sent a telegram to the government of Mexico. Called the Zimmermann Note, it asked for Mexican help if Germany and the United States went to war. In return, Germany offered to aid Mexico in conquering the states of Texas, Arizona, and New Mexico. The British found out about the note and told the Americans. U.S. newspapers printed it in March 1917.

c. *Sympathy for democracies.* A major concern of many Americans was whether democracy could survive in Europe if Britain and France lost the war. The Central Powers were regarded as undemocratic and militaristic. President Wilson believed that helping the Allies to win would make the world "safe for democracy." At Wilson's urging, Congress declared war on Germany on April 6, 1917.

MATCHING EXERCISE

1. Match each of the German actions in Column A with a consequence or result in Column B.

Column A	Column B
1. unrestricted submarine warfare	*a.* Americans feared for the future of democracy.
2. Zimmermann Note	*b.* American lives and property were lost.
3. militaristic government	*c.* Americans were angered by a threat to the southwestern states.
	d. Americans wanted to colonize German lands.
	e. Americans wanted Germany's natural resources.

2. From Column A above, select the German action that you think is the *main* reason why the United States entered World War I. Explain your choice.

6. The End of the War. In late June 1917, the American Expeditionary Force started arriving in France. For a number of months, the U.S. soldiers completed their training and occasionally served as replacements in the front lines. The presence of

Allied infantry in front-line trenches waiting to go "over the top."

fresh fighting men and the increased quantities of supplies lifted the spirits of the French and British troops. Then, in June 1918, the Americans saw heavy action in the battles of Château-Thierry and Belleau Wood. They helped the British and French forces stop the last great German offensive of the war. A few months later, U.S. troops pushed the Germans out of St. Mihiel, which the Germans had held since 1914.

Discouraged by the continuing military reverses, the German people revolted against their government. Kaiser Wilhelm II resigned and fled to Holland. Germany became a republic, and its new leaders asked for peace. The armistice (agreement to stop fighting) of November 11, 1918, ended World War I.

7. The Peace Conference.   In January 1919, the Allied leaders met in France to draw up the official peace treaty. The resulting Treaty of Versailles, signed in June, set forth the conditions for peace between the Allies and Germany. Regarded as unfair by many people, its terms came to be hated by the Germans.

The most important leaders at the peace conference were President Woodrow Wilson of the United States, Prime Minister David Lloyd George of Britain, Premier Georges Clemenceau of France, and Premier Vittorio Orlando of Italy. Wilson wanted the Germans to be treated fairly. His ideas, publicized in January 1918, were known as the Fourteen Points. They called for a "peace without victory." Wilson also wanted an end to secret treaties, freedom of the seas for all nations, and the reduction of weapons. The other Allied leaders wanted revenge and as much territory and wealth as they could force Germany to give them. The French, in particular, wanted to make sure that Germany would never again be strong enough to invade France.

The Treaty of Versailles included a war guilt clause, which Germany had to accept. This clause made Germany responsible for starting World War I. The treaty also punished Germany in other ways. It had to pay huge *reparations* (money for damage done during the war) to the Allied nations. The Allies divided all of Germany's overseas colonies among themselves. Portions of Germany itself were also given away. France took back Alsace and Lorraine. Part of northeast Germany (the Polish Corridor) was added to Poland. Important industrial areas and mineral resources in western Germany were placed under Allied control. German military forces were greatly reduced in size. The terms humiliated the German people.

Separate treaties with the other Central Powers broke up the Austro-Hungarian Empire and created new countries in Eastern

War in the Air

Lieutenant Eddie Rickenbacker and his Spad.

Edward Vernon ("Eddie") Rickenbacker (1890–1973) was the most famous American air ace in World War I. As a fighter pilot, he shot down 22 German planes and four observation balloons in less than a year.

Rickenbacker was born in Columbus, Ohio. One of eight children, he was forced to leave school when his father died. The 16-year-old Rickenbacker studied automotive engineering through a correspondence school while working in a garage. Four years later, he was an automobile sales manager. Interested in racing as a way to sell cars, Rickenbacker became a successful driver. He turned professional in 1911 and drove in several Indianapolis 500 races. By 1917, he had become a leading driver in the United States.

On the United States' entry into World War I, Rickenbacker volunteered to fly for the Army. Considered to be too old (at age 26) to be a flyer, Rickenbacker was assigned as a driver in General John J. Pershing's staff. General Pershing was the commander of the U.S. forces in Europe.

After repeated attempts to transfer to the flying corps, Rickenbacker was finally accepted for flight training and became a pilot. He was assigned to the 94th Aero Pursuit Squadron, the first U.S. air unit to serve on the Western Front. This squadron was credited with 69 enemy planes and balloons shot down, the largest number of any American unit. Rickenbacker headed the list of aces.

In September 1918, Rickenbacker became commanding officer of the squadron. By the end of the war, he held the rank of major. He was awarded the Congressional Medal of Honor and other honors from the grateful American and French governments.

After the war, Rickenbacker returned to the automobile industry, where he pioneered the use of four-wheel brakes; small, light engines; and balloon tires.

In 1938, Rickenbacker bought the small and struggling Eastern Airlines. As president of Eastern for 21 years, he led the company to success and prosperity.

How did Eddie Rickenbacker become a World War I hero?

Europe After World War I

Review the map "Europe, 1915," on page 426. Compare it with this map. Then answer the following questions:

1. Name *five* new countries that were carved out of western Russia.

2. What country did Serbia become part of ?

3. Did Rumania gain or lose territory?

4. After World War I, what area separated the two parts of Germany?

5. What country was once the northern part of Austria-Hungary?

Europe. Various nationalist groups had persuaded the peacemakers to let them determine their own futures as independent countries. Among these new nations were Finland, Poland, Czechoslovakia, and Yugoslavia.

The Allied leaders agreed to President Wilson's demand for the establishment of a League of Nations. Its purpose was to prevent future wars by finding peaceful solutions to international problems. Unfortunately, it would have no way to enforce its decisions.

The United States Senate rejected the Treaty of Versailles and the League of Nations. The senators who opposed the treaty feared that membership in the League might involve the United States too deeply and easily in European problems. The U.S. decision further weakened the League.

In general, the peace agreements did little to solve the problems that had caused World War I. Instead, they created new tensions in Europe.

IDENTIFICATIONS

Explain or define each of the following terms.

a. Western Front
b. Eastern Front
c. Treaty of Brest-Litovsk
d. blockade
e. Zimmermann Note

f. armistice
g. Treaty of Versailles
h. reparations
i. League of Nations

ESSAY QUESTION

Reread "7. The Peace Conference," on pages 432, 434–435. Then explain why the French, in particular, wanted revenge against Germany and how they tried to keep Germany weak.

Costs of World War I

SOLDIERS KILLED IN ACTION*		COST IN MONEY*
1,700,000	Russia	$18 Billion
1,400,000	France	$26 Billion
950,000	Great Britain	$38 Billion
600,000	Italy	$13 Billion
115,000	United States	$22 Billion
1,950,000	Germany	$40 Billion
1,200,000	Austria-Hungary	$21 Billion

*Approximate Figures

CHART INTERPRETATION

Use the information on the chart above to answer the following questions.

1. Complete each of the following sentences:
    a. The nation that lost the most soldiers in World War I was —.
    b. The nation that lost the fewest soldiers in World War I was —.
    c. The nation that spent the most money in World War I was —.
    d. The nation that spent the least money in World War I was —.

2. What fact found on the chart supports the following statement? "The Russian Revolution of 1917 was largely due to the failure of the government of Czar Nicholas II to get Russia out of World War I, as many people had demanded."

THE RISE OF DICTATORSHIPS

World War I caused severe social and economic problems throughout Europe. In Russia, Italy, and Germany, postwar difficulties led to the rise of dictatorships.

1. Communism in Russia. The March 1917 revolution that ended the rule of the czars had many causes. The immediate cause was the hardships brought on by World War I. But the long-range causes had existed for many years.

Compared to Western Europe, Russia was a backward nation both politically and economically. The Romanov czars ruled as absolute monarchs. They did not allow a separate lawmaking body to be created. Moreover, the Industrial Revolution came late to Russia. Serfs, or farm laborers, made up more than 75 percent of the population. Most of them were tied to the land, much as the serfs of the Middle Ages had been. The landowning nobles controlled their lives.

a. *Reforms.* One czar, Alexander II (ruled 1855–1881), did make some changes. He decided that Russia would be stronger and more modern if he freed the serfs. In 1861, the serfs were given certain rights and the opportunity to buy land of their own. The new freedom did not benefit the peasants a great deal. Most remained poor and illiterate.

Nicholas II of Russia on the deck of his yacht.

Throughout the 19th century, various groups and individuals had tried to change the government of Russia. But their efforts to introduce democratic or socialistic ideas had failed. Helping the serfs did not satisfy these reform groups. They wanted a voice in the government. When peaceful means failed, some tried violence. In 1881, a terrorist's bomb killed Alexander II. The new czar, Alexander III, used harsh measures to stamp out any suspected opposition. He persecuted liberals and members of minority groups—Jews, in particular.

b. Revolution of 1905.   As industries came to Russia in the late 1800's, more people became factory workers. They and middle-class business owners began to demand more rights. Reformers saw a chance to change things after Russia was defeated in the Russo-Japanese War (1904–1905). In January 1905, workers marched to the czar's palace to present their demands. Troops fired on the marchers, killing many. This did not stop the demonstrations. Strikes were called. Street fighting broke out. Finally, in October, Czar Nicholas II agreed to allow a duma, a parliament, to be elected. But the new system did not work well. The czar, not wanting to share his power, dismissed the first two dumas. Members of the third one proved to be more willing to cooperate with the czar.

The Revolution of 1905 did little to solve Russia's problems. Unrest continued. It reached a peak during World War I. Defeats in battle and the loss of hundreds of thousands of men at the front, combined with food shortages, made the Russian people desperate. They demanded an end to Russia's participation in World War I. Czar Nicholas II failed to do this. Nor did he do anything about the starvation and poverty caused by the war.

c. March Revolution.   In March 1917, the Russian Revolution began. Nicholas II was driven from his throne. Moderate leaders—Prince George Lvov and Alexander Kerensky—took control of Russia. They spoke to the people about constitutions, democracy, and reforms. However, they too failed to take Russia out of the war. The hunger and misery continued.

d. November Revolution.   Finally, in November 1917, a second revolution occurred. It was led by V.I. Lenin. He promised the Russian people what they wanted most—peace, bread, and land. Lenin's party, the Bolsheviks (later called Communists), took over the government. One of their first acts in 1918 was to take Russia out of World War I by signing the Treaty of Brest-Litovsk with Germany. Later in 1918 they executed Czar Nicholas II and his family.

Lenin speaking to soldiers and workers.

Meanwhile, the Communists fought various groups of anti-Communists in a bloody civil war. As the fighting continued, Lenin reorganized the government and economy of Russia. He tried to follow the ideas of Karl Marx. Workers and peasants elected representatives to local and regional councils called "soviets." Workers were encouraged to take over factories. Peasants seized the estates of nobles. Then the government declared that it owned all industries, banks, railroads, and land.

Organized religious worship was discouraged, and *atheism* (the belief that God does not exist) became official government policy. Class differences were ordered to be ended. Russians were encouraged to address one another as "comrade." The Communist Party was the only political party allowed to exist. It remained firmly in control of government and society until the late 1980s. In 1922, Russia changed its name to the Union of Soviet Socialist Republics—the Soviet Union.

e. **Soviet Union under Stalin.** After Lenin died in 1924, Joseph Stalin gradually took control of the Soviet Union. Stalin built up Soviet industry through a series of Five-Year Plans. He also forced peasants to give up their land and work on *collective farms*. The forced collectivization caused the intentional deaths of millions of these peasants by starvation. Also, the industrialization campaign emphasized heavy industry and military goods at the expense of consumer goods. It was not until the 1950s that the Soviet standard of living began rising. The Soviet industrial and agricultural policies raised the standard of living of most Russians to a level higher than it had been under the czars.

Rule by terror and force reached a peak under Stalin. He would not tolerate any form of disagreement with his policies. Millions of Russians and other Soviet peoples were put to death or imprisoned on Stalin's orders. He is considered to have been one of the cruelest dictators in world history.

CHRONOLOGY

For each of the following years, state an important event that took place in Russia:

    a. 1861   *e.* 1918
    b. 1881   *f.* 1922
    c. 1905   *g.* 1924
    d. 1917

SENTENCE COMPLETION

Complete each of the following sentences:

1. The immediate cause of the end of the rule of the czars was —.

2. Two important ways Lenin changed Russia were — and —.

2. Fascism in Italy.

Many Italians were very angry about the way they had been treated in the peace agreements that ended World War I. They believed that they should have received more territory in return for the large number of Italian soldiers killed in the war. Also, Italy faced severe economic problems in the 1920's. Unemployment and high prices caused great hardship.

The democratic Italian government found it difficult to solve these problems. The political parties in the parliament would not work together for the good of Italy. No leader had the strength and prestige to make the system work. Italians began to lose faith in democracy. One man, Benito Mussolini, the leader of the Fascist Party, appeared to have solutions to problems facing Italy. As a result, many Italians began to support his policies.

    a. *Rise of Fascist Party.* The Fascist Party, founded by Mussolini in 1919, was composed mainly of unemployed soldiers. Members of the party believed in nationalism and militarism. Most important, the Fascists were determined to replace the dem-

Benito Mussolini speaking before a crowd of
Fascist youth.

ocratic government of Italy with a dictatorship. To achieve their
goals, the Fascists beat up and sometimes killed those who
opposed them.

In October 1922, Mussolini and 10,000 armed Fascists marched
on Rome. They hoped to force the premier to resign. The king
feared that a civil war would break out if he attempted to stop the
march. He asked Mussolini to become premier.

b. *Mussolini in power.* As head of the Italian government,
Mussolini remade Italy into a Fascist dictatorship. All other
political parties were outlawed. Secret police arrested critics of
the government. Strikes were forbidden. The government regulated all economic activities. Newspapers and radio stations operated under strict government censorship. The Fascists also took
complete control of the schools. Children were taught that the
individual existed to serve the state, the nation. Boys trained to
be good soldiers. Girls were expected to become mothers of large
families.

Mussolini did strengthen Italian industry and agriculture. But
wages fell, hours of work increased, and taxes rose. Although most
Italians benefited from the order and stability Mussolini provided,
they lost many of their personal freedoms.

CRITICAL THINKING

Explain why you AGREE or DISAGREE with each of the following statements:

1. The Italians were right to accept the leadership of Benito Mussolini.

2. The changes brought to Italy by the Fascists greatly benefited the Italian people.

3. Nazism in Germany.   After World War I, the Germans made a strong attempt to establish a democratic government in Germany. But the Weimar Republic, as the new government was called, faced great problems. Many Germans blamed the Weimar leaders for agreeing to the terms of the hated Treaty of Versailles. Also, widespread unemployment, rapidly rising prices, and the burden of the huge war debt made the German people resentful. Just as the economy improved, the Great Depression of 1929 brought new hardships. Businesses failed, and more people were thrown out of work.

Extremist groups in Germany opposed the Weimar Republic. To many, communism seemed to offer a better way of life. Those who disliked both communism and democracy were drawn to the Nazi Party, led by Adolf Hitler.

a. *Rise of Nazi Party*.   Hitler had served in the German army during the war. He had been wounded and decorated for bravery on the Western Front. The defeat of Germany filled Hitler with shame and bitterness. He hated the democratic leaders of postwar Germany for having surrendered to the Allies.

Hitler was a highly skilled politician. A brilliant public speaker, he easily won support from German audiences. The program of the Nazi Party was based on nationalism, militarism, and racism. Hitler told the Germans that they were a superior race, destined to rule the world. He assured his listeners that they were not responsible for Germany's defeat in the war or its economic problems. He claimed that Communists, socialists, and democrats had betrayed Germany. Hitler singled out Jews for special hatred. He blamed them for all the problems existing in Germany and the world. The Jews thus became *scapegoats*. They were to be treated with great brutality.

In 1923, Hitler and his followers attempted to seize control of the government of the German state of Bavaria. The Beer Hall Putsch

Bank notes in Germany in the 1920s were so worthless that they were used as waste paper.

(revolt), as it was called, failed. Hitler was sent to prison. While there, he wrote the book *Mein Kampf* (My Struggle). It set forth Hitler's racist ideas and his plans for aggression and world domination.

The Nazis became more popular in the early 1930's because they seemed to offer solutions to the economic problems brought on by the Great Depression. The Nazis gained a large number of seats in the legislature. Then in January 1933, Hitler was offered the office of chancellor of Germany, which he took.

b. *Hitler in power.*   Hitler quickly ended democratic government and turned Germany into a dictatorship known as the Third Reich. As *führer* (leader), Hitler had unlimited power. He controlled everything: industrial and agricultural production, education, newspapers, and radio broadcasts. Hitler's orders were enforced by the S.S., a private army of black-uniformed "Storm Troopers," and by the Gestapo, or secret police. Children had to join the Hitler Youth organization to learn to be "good Nazis."

The Third Reich became one of the most brutal dictatorships in the history of the world. All opposition to the Nazis was crushed. Political enemies, Slavs, gypsies, the handicapped, gays, and millions of Jews were sent to concentration (prison) camps. These eventually became death camps where people were murdered on arrival or were worked, starved, or tortured to death.

Adolf Hitler with admiring supporters at Nuremberg, Germany, in 1933.

Under Hitler, Germany gained power but at a great cost to the German people. They had most of their rights and freedoms stripped from them.

TRUE OR FALSE

Indicate whether each of the following statements is *true* (**T**) or *false* (**F**).

1. The leaders of the Weimar Republic were unpopular in Germany after World War I.

2. The Nazi Party offered Germans an alternative to both communism and democracy.

3. Hitler told the Germans that they were to blame for their defeat in World War I.

4. The Third Reich was one of the world's most brutal dictatorships.

Chapter Review

Choose the item that best completes each sentence or answers each question.

1. Which one of the following was *not* a long-range cause of World War I? (*a*) nationalism (*b*) imperialism (*c*) militarism (*d*) communism.

2. Which one of these actions started World War I? (*a*) the Russian Revolution of 1917 (*b*) the murder of Archduke Francis Ferdinand (*c*) the German invasion of Russia (*d*) the Russo-Japanese War of 1905.

3. The two alliance systems that fought each other in World War I were the (*a*) Nazi Party and Fascist Party (*b*) Allied Powers and Central Powers (*c*) Pan-Slavists and Pan-Germanists (*d*) Dual Alliance and Entente Cordiale.

4. Trench warfare was most common on the (*a*) Western Front (*b*) Eastern Front (*c*) Middle Eastern Front (*d*) Balkan Front.

5. A major cause of the U.S. entry into World War I was the German (*a*) invasion of Belgium (*b*) victory in Russia (*c*) annexation of Alsace-Lorraine (*d*) policy of unrestricted submarine warfare.

6. The American Expeditionary Force landed in France in (*a*) June 1917 (*b*) June 1918 (*c*) January 1919 (*d*) February 1920.

7. The most important result of the peace conference after World War I was the (*a*) Zimmermann Note (*b*) Treaty of Versailles (*c*) Treaty of Brest-Litovsk (*d*) Peace of Paris.

8. Following the Russian Revolution of 1917, the first Communist leader of Russia was (*a*) Lenin (*b*) Marx (*c*) Stalin (*d*) Engels.

9. Italy was organized as a Fascist dictatorship by (*a*) Lenin (*b*) Hitler (*c*) Mussolini (*d*) Stalin.

10. Germany was organized as a Nazi dictatorship by (*a*) Lenin (*b*) Hitler (*c*) Mussolini (*d*) Stalin.

CRITICAL THINKING

Reread "Causes of World War I," on pages 423–427. Then read the following statement carefully and answer the questions after it:

> Article 231, the War Guilt Clause, of the Treaty of Versailles: "The Allied and Associated Governments affirm and Germany accepts the responsibility of Germany and her allies for causing all the loss and damage to which the Allied and Associated Governments and their nationals have been subjected as a consequence of the war imposed upon them by the aggression of Germany and her allies."

1. Explain why you think Article 231 of the Treaty of Versailles was fair or unfair to Germany.

2. Write your own version of Article 231.

 ## ESSAY QUESTIONS

Reread "The Rise of Dictatorships," on pages 437–444. Then write answers to the following questions.

1. State *two* things that Hitler and Stalin had in common.

2. State *three* reasons for the rise of dictators after World War I.

Connections: War

The Romans destroy Carthage.

More than 10 million combat troops died in World War I. It was the first "global war" of modern times. The military forces of the Allies and the Central Powers fought each other in Europe, Africa, and the Middle East, and on the seas. Destruction of property and disruption of lives were on a scale larger than anything people had ever seen before.

In some ways, however, the first global war in the 20th century was different from the "total wars" of ancient times. During the third Punic War (149–146 B.C.), the Romans had one objective—to totally destroy Carthage. And that is what they did. The city of Carthage was leveled. The fields around it were plowed up and covered with salt so that nothing would grow. The surviving people were sold as slaves. A curse was placed upon the site. Finally, Hannibal, the leader of Carthage, was hounded from one refuge to another until he committed suicide.

The Huns who invaded Europe in the 4th and 5th centuries destroyed everything in their path. The Huns were nomads who lived by raiding and plundering. A Roman writer described them as being more like beasts than men. The Huns' ferocity filled the people of Europe with terror. In A.D. 451, the Romans finally stopped the Huns in the Battle of Châlons.

The Mongols were another group of fierce nomads. They conquered China in the 13th century and then moved westward across Asia. Eventually, the "Golden Horde" overran Russia, Bulgaria, Poland, and Hungary. Genghis Khan led the Mongols until his death in 1227. He was merciless in victory. Believing that he could never win loyalty from the peoples he conquered, he slaughtered thousands of them to better control his empire. Piles of human skulls more than six feet high frequently marked the routes of the Mongol armies.

Despite the use of modern weapons such as the machine gun, tank, airplane, and poison gas, the armies of World War I did not match the savagery of the warriors of ancient and medieval times. Whole towns and cities with their civilian populations were not totally destroyed. The merging of global war and total war would not happen until World War II.

What is the difference between a global war and a total war?

DOCUMENT-BASED QUESTION

This question is based on the accompanying documents (1–5). It will improve your ability to work with historical documents.

Historical Context:

Early in the 20th century, the forces of nationalism, imperialism, and militarism were causing problems among the leading powers of Europe. Tensions continued to rise. Then, in 1914, events led to the conflict known as the Great War, or World War I. Millions of lives were lost, billions of dollars were spent, and Europe was changed forever.

Task:

Using information from the documents and your knowledge of world history, answer the questions that follow each document. Your answers to each question will help you write the document-based essay.

Document 1. Excerpt from a lecture given by French peace activist Frédéric Passy in 1895, warning about the situation in Europe:

> I need hardly describe the present state of Europe to you. The entire able-bodied population are preparing to massacre one another; though no one, it is true, wants to attack, and everybody protests his love of peace and determination to maintain it, yet the whole world feels that it only requires some unforeseen incident, some unpreventable accident, for the spark to fall in a flash . . . and blow all Europe sky-high.
>
> Source: Frédéric Passy quoted in *Nobel: The Man and His Prizes.* 3rd edition. NY: American Elsevier Pub. Co., 1972, pp. 493–494.

According to this document, what attitude existed in Europe in the years leading up to World War I?

Document 2. Excerpt from *All Quiet on the Western Front* (1928), a novel by the German writer Erich Maria Remarque, who drew upon his own experiences as a soldier in the German army:

> I am young, I am twenty years old; yet I know nothing of life but despair, death, fear, and fatuous [foolish] superficiality cast over an abyss of sorrow. I see how peoples are set against one another, and in silence, unknowingly, foolishly, obediently,

innocently slay one another. I see that the keenest brains of the world invent weapons and words to make it yet more refined and enduring. . . . What will happen afterwards? And what shall come out of us?

Source: Remarque, Erich Maria. *All Quiet on the Western Front.* translated by. A.W. Wheen. NY: Ballantine Books, 1982, pp. 262–264.

Based on this document, what does Remarque indicate was the state of mind of the ordinary soldier in World War I?

Document 3. Excerpt from the speech given by President Woodrow Wilson, on April 2, 1917, asking Congress to declare war on Germany and the other Central Powers:

The world must be made safe for democracy. Its peace must be planted upon the tested foundations of political liberty. We have no selfish ends to serve. We desire no conquest, no dominion. We seek no indemnities for ourselves, no material compensation for the sacrifices we shall freely make. We are but one of the champions of the rights of mankind. We shall be satisfied when those rights have been made as secure as the faith and the freedom of nations can make them.

Source: Woodrow Wilson, *War Messages*, 65th Congress, 1st Session. Senate Doc. No. 5, Serial No. 7264, Washington, D.C., 1917; pp. 3–8.

According to this document, why was the United States entering the war?

Document 4. Excerpts from the Treaty of Versailles, signed on June 28, 1919, officially ending World War I:

231. The Allied and Associated Governments affirm and Germany accepts the responsibility of Germany and her allies for causing all the loss and damage to which the Allied and Associated Governments and their nationals have been subjected as a consequence of the war imposed upon them by the aggression of Germany and her allies.

232. The Allied and Associated Governments . . . require, and Germany undertakes, that she will make compensation for all damage done to the civilian population of the Allied and Associated Powers and to their property during the period of the belligerency.

Source: *Peace Treaty with Germany*, 66th Congress, 1st Session, Senate Doc. No. 49. Washington, D.C., 1919.

Why might the German people have felt angry about the terms of the peace treaty?

Document 5.   Study the photograph on page 443.

What is the photo suggesting about the way Germany responded to its problems after World War I?

DOCUMENT-BASED ESSAY

Using information from the above documents and your knowledge of world history, write an essay in which you:

- Discuss the causes and consequences of World War I.
- Explain how the results of the war prepared the way for another world war.

CHAPTER 17
World War II

The hope that the League of Nations could keep the peace after World War I faded rapidly. The dictators who came to power in Europe and the militarists in Japan refused to be stopped by words. The League had little except words to use as weapons.

Finally, at the end of the 1930's, the democratic nations of Europe took a stand against Nazi Germany. World War II broke out. It lasted from 1939 to 1945 and was the most terrible war the world had yet seen. The conflict seemed to affect almost every part of the planet. It also revealed the worst actions that humans can take against one another: total war and the mass murder of religious and ethnic groups.

After the war, most of the nations of the world again tried to find a way to keep the peace. They established the United Nations.

DICTATORSHIP VS. DEMOCRACY

In the 1930's, war again threatened Asia and Europe. Japan, which had become more militaristic, moved against China and other areas in East Asia. Fascist Italy and Nazi Germany also put their aggressive plans into effect in the mid-1930's. Little was done by the democratic nations or the League of Nations to stop the military actions.

1. Japanese Aggression in Asia. Japan has few natural resources. To run its industries, it must obtain raw materials from other countries. In the 1920's and 1930's, the industrial and military leaders of Japan developed a long-range plan to acquire sources of raw materials. The plan called for conquering East Asia. Control of China was the most important aim of Japan's East Asia Co-Prosperity Sphere.

In September 1931, the Japanese seized Manchuria, a region of northeast China. Renamed Manchukuo, it was given its independence in 1932. But in fact, Japan actually controlled the government. Few nations objected as the Japanese began to use the rich natural resources of their new colony.

In 1937, Japan opened a full-scale attack on China. Japanese forces quickly overran much of the northern part of the country.

Japanese troops in China carrying off some spoils of war.

They captured the capital, Nanking. But General Chiang Kai-shek, head of the Chinese government, refused to surrender. He moved his Nationalist forces into western China and set up a new capital. The Japanese then realized that the war in China would be a long one. (The Sino-Japanese War lasted from 1937 to 1945.)

The League of Nations condemned Japan's aggression. The United States, the Soviet Union, and other nations also protested Japan's actions and gave aid to China. Since no nation was willing to use military force against Japan, the Japanese continued their conquests in China. In 1940, they also moved into northern Indochina.

2. The Spanish Civil War.   During the 1930's, Spain also became a battleground. In 1931, the Spanish people changed their government from a monarchy to a republic. The Republican government was liberal. It proposed many political and economic reforms. Nationalists in the Spanish army opposed the new government. General Francisco Franco led a revolt against the republic in 1936. He had the support of right-wing elements in Spain. These included wealthy businesspeople, high-ranking religious leaders, and Spanish Fascists. Franco promised them he would defend Spain against communism and socialism.

Thousands of loyalists, including volunteers from other countries, joined the Republican armies to fight against Franco and the rebel Nationalists. Both Benito Mussolini, Fascist dictator of Italy,

Emperor Haile Selassie of Ethiopia.

and Adolf Hitler, Nazi dictator of Germany, wanted a Nationalist victory in Spain. They sent planes, troops, and weapons to General Franco. But the Republican forces did not receive much aid from the democratic nations. Their fear of becoming involved in a war was stronger than their desire to help democracy survive in Spain. Only the Soviet Union sent some aid to the Republicans. The Republican forces could not hold out against the Nationalists.

In March 1939, the rebels captured the capital city of Madrid. The Spanish Republic fell, and General Franco became dictator of Spain. His Falangist (Fascist) Party remained in power until Franco's death in 1975.

3. Fascist Aggression in Africa. Mussolini's great dream was to rebuild the Roman Empire. As a first step toward achieving this goal, he ordered the invasion of Ethiopia in October 1935. An independent nation, Ethiopia bordered Italian Somaliland in East Africa. Ethiopia had few modern weapons to use against the well-equipped Italian army and air force.

Emperor Haile Selassie of Ethiopia pleaded with the League of Nations to help. The League asked member nations not to sell food and war materials to Italy until it withdrew from Ethiopia. But many nations ignored the League, so the attempt at economic pressure failed. Italy continued the war against Ethiopia, which fell in May 1936.

4. Nazi Aggression in Europe. Hitler had promised the Germans that he would tear up the hated Treaty of Versailles. In 1935, he started a series of actions that violated the terms of the treaty. He began to draft men into the German army to increase its size. He also organized an air force. No one took steps to stop the illegal German rearmament—not the League of Nations, Britain, France, nor the United States.

a. *Into the Rhineland.* In 1936, Hitler again violated the Treaty of Versailles. He sent German troops into the Rhineland. This border area between France and Germany was supposed to be demilitarized (free of all armed forces). Hitler had ordered his military commanders to withdraw their troops if the French showed any signs of opposition. Although the French wanted to take action, they could not get the British to back them. Therefore, nothing was done, and Hitler controlled the Rhineland.

b. *Into Austria.* Following a period of expansion of German war industries and military forces, Hitler annexed Austria in 1938. By taking control of this German-speaking country, Hitler added to Germany's size and power. The *Anschluss* (union) of Germany and Austria was another step prohibited by the Treaty of Versailles. Once again, no country took any action against Nazi Germany.

c. *Into Czechoslovakia.* This small, democratic nation in Eastern Europe had been created out of the Austro-Hungarian Empire in 1918. More than 3 million Germans lived among 15 million Czechs. The German-speaking population was centered mainly in the Sudetenland in western Czechoslovakia. In 1933, Hitler sent Nazi agents into the Sudetenland to stir up riots against the Czech government. Unrest continued for several years. Then in 1938, Hitler demanded that the Sudetenland Germans be given the right to decide whether they would remain part of Czechoslovakia or unite with Germany. He backed up his demands with the threat of an invasion.

To prevent a war, a conference was held in the German city of Munich in September 1938. Prime Minister Neville Chamberlain of Britain and Premier Édouard Daladier of France met with Hitler and Mussolini. The participants in the Munich Conference decided to give the Sudetenland to Germany. In return, Hitler promised that he would not attempt to take over any more territory in Europe. Abandoned by its British and French allies, Czechoslovakia was forced to yield. Chamberlain returned to Britain and announced that he had preserved "peace in our time."

During the 1930's, British and French leaders often followed the policy of giving in to the dictators in order to avoid war. Called *appeasement*, this policy did not prevent World War II. It merely confirmed the belief of the dictators that the democratic nations were too weak and frightened to stop them.

British Prime Minister Neville Chamberlain (far right) arrives in Munich,
September 30, 1938.

In March 1939, Hitler broke the promise he had made at the Munich Conference. He took over the remainder of Czechoslovakia. Britain and France finally realized that Hitler intended to dominate Europe. They abandoned the policy of appeasement and decided to resist any further Nazi aggression.

 ESSAY QUESTIONS

1. **EXPLAIN:** The East Asia Co-Prosperity Sphere was Japan's master plan for conquest.

2. List *three* places invaded by Japanese forces from 1930 to 1940.

3. List *three* ways Hitler violated the Treaty of Versailles.

TRUE OR FALSE

Indicate which of the following statements are *true* (**T**) and which are *false* (**F**):

1. The League of Nations dealt effectively with the Ethiopian crisis.

2. Ethiopia could not match Italy's military power.

3. Mussolini wanted to be a modern Caesar.

4. Ethiopia conquered Italy in 1936.

SENTENCE COMPLETION

Reread "2. The Spanish Civil War," on pages 452–453. Then complete the following sentences:

1. In 1931, the Spanish people —.

2. General Francisco Franco led —.

3. Both Mussolini and Hitler wanted —.

4. The Republican forces did not receive —.

5. In March 1939, the Nationalist rebels —.

MATCHING EXERCISE

Match each person in Column A with his title in Column B.

Column A	Column B
1. Chiang Kai-shek	*a.* prime minister of Great Britain
2. Francisco Franco	*b.* emperor of Ethiopia
3. Haile Selassie	*c.* general and head of China
4. Neville Chamberlain	*d.* premier of France
5. Édouard Daladier	*e.* general and dictator of Spain

CHRONOLOGY

Many aggressive actions took place between 1931 and 1939 in Europe, Asia, and Africa. Determine the year in which each of the following actions occurred.

1. invasion of Manchuria   4. annexation of Austria

2. full-scale invasion of China   5. takeover of Czechoslovakia

3. takeover of the Rhineland   6. takeover of Ethiopia

CRITICAL THINKING

1. Why do you think many regard the Spanish Civil War as a test that the democratic nations failed?

2. **PROVE or DISPROVE:** The policy of appeasement was a failure.

GLOBAL CONFLICT: 1939–1945

As the 1930's ended, war seemed ready to break out at any moment. The world waited to see what Hitler, Mussolini, and the Japanese would do next. Everyone hoped that any conflicts would not spread. But the most knowledgeable people feared that a general war would be the only way to stop the dictators' aggressions.

1. The Beginning.   To make sure that he had support for his war plans, Hitler allied Germany with Italy and Japan. The Rome-Berlin Axis was formed in 1936. An agreement with Japan was also completed in 1936. The formal military and economic alliance creating the Rome-Berlin-Tokyo Axis was signed in 1940.

The anti-Communist Hitler unexpectedly signed a nonaggression pact with the Soviet Union in 1939. Both countries pledged not to attack the other.

Now Hitler felt that he could go ahead with his plans to take over Europe. On September 1, 1939, German forces poured into Poland. Britain and France demanded that the attack be called off. (Britain had signed a mutual assistance treaty with Poland in late August.) Hitler refused. On September 3, Britain and France declared war on Germany. World War II had begun—just 25 years after the start of World War I.

The Soviet Union took advantage of the situation and in mid-September attacked Poland from the east. The Soviets also seized Latvia, Lithuania, and Estonia on the Baltic Sea. These three small countries became part of the Soviet Union. Finland also felt Soviet blows. Although it fought hard, Finland lost territory to the Soviet Union in 1940.

Poland fell in less than a month. Germany and the Soviet Union divided the country between them. Hitler then turned his attention west to new conquests.

2. Blitzkrieg.   Throughout the winter of 1939–1940, Hitler built up German strength. Then, in the spring, Hitler turned his *blitzkrieg* (lightning-war) tactics against other nations. Troops and artillery in motorized vehicles quickly overran enemy positions. Aided by planes and tanks, they crushed the opposing forces and moved on. Speed and mobility characterized blitzkrieg tactics. The fixed, stationary fronts of the trench warfare of World War I belonged to the past.

In April 1940, German forces took over Norway and Denmark. A month later, they conquered Belgium and Holland. Hitler then

Blitzkrieg. German tanks and infantry, supported by dive-bombing aircraft, attack Poland. A Polish cavalry unit counterattacks.

ordered the invasion of France. After stiff resistance, the French surrendered in June 1940. At this point, Italy entered the war against the democracies.

The Germans divided France into two parts. The north, Occupied France, was directly controlled by German forces. Pro-German French officials administered the south, which was called Vichy France (from the name of its capital city). Marshal Henri Pétain headed the antidemocratic Vichy government. The *Milice*, a French fascist paramilitary organization, repressed opposition.

Many French people regarded those who cooperated with the Vichy government as traitors. Some French leaders escaped to North Africa and Britain. General Charles de Gaulle collected the French in Britain into an organization called the "Free French." He urged all French people to resist the Germans in any way they could.

3. Setbacks and Successes. After the fall of France, Britain stood alone against the dictators. The United States continued to be neutral. It did send food and arms to the British. Britain was also aided by its colonies and the former colonies that had maintained close ties with the home country.

a. *Battle of Britain.* Hitler stepped up preparations to invade Britain. In August 1940, the German air force started its mass bombings of British cities, industrial areas, seaports, and military installations. Even though the bombings caused many deaths and great destruction, Prime Minister Winston Churchill inspired the British to keep on fighting. For a period of ten months, fierce air battles were fought over Britain. During this Battle of Britain, the Royal Air Force destroyed large numbers of German planes. By June 1941, the air raids eased off. Britain seemed safe from a land invasion.

b. *The Eastern Front.* Hungary and Rumania joined the Berlin-Rome-Tokyo Axis in late 1940. Bulgaria then joined early in 1941. By May 1941, Yugoslavia and Greece had been crushed. Germany controlled the whole of the Balkans. Only small bands of resistance fighters continued to oppose the enemy.

German light bombers in a raid over England.

The Lion of Britain

Winston Churchill giving his "V for Victory" sign during World War II.

Sir Winston Churchill (1874–1965) was one of the world's greatest government leaders. As Great Britain's prime minister during World War II, he led the British people in their "finest hour" against the Axis powers of Germany, Italy, and Japan. Later, he was of the first to recognize the great dangers of the Cold War.

World War II began in 1939. On May 10, 1940, Winston Churchill was appointed prime minister. The future looked dark for the nation. Churchill said, "I have nothing to offer but blood, toil, tears, and sweat." His speeches were among his strongest weapons in encouraging the British to fight alone after the fall of France.

After the United States entered the war in 1941, Churchill helped to build the "grand alliance" of Britain, the United States, and the Soviet Union. His influence with the Allies in waging the war against the Axis powers was considerable. U.S. President Franklin D. Roosevelt and Churchill met many times to plan the strategies to defeat the Axis. Relations between Churchill and Joseph Stalin, the premier of the Soviet Union, were not as good. Churchill urged President Roosevelt to take actions that would stop the spread of communism in postwar Europe.

In 1945, Germany surrendered. In that same year, Churchill's political party was defeated in the general election. Out of office, Churchill continued to warn Britain, the United States, and other Western nations of Soviet ambitions and the threat of communism. In a 1946 speech at Fulton, Missouri, Churchill used the term "iron curtain" to describe the rise of Soviet satellite nations in Eastern Europe.

While out of office, he began to write his six-volume history, *The Second World War*. It was completed in 1953. He became prime minister again in 1951. He devoted himself to seeking world peace. In 1953, Queen Elizabeth II made him a knight for his many services to Britain. Sir Winston was also awarded the Nobel Prize for Literature for his many published books and speeches.

Churchill resigned as prime minister in 1955 because of poor health. He wrote another major work, *A History of the English-Speaking Peoples* in four volumes (1956–1958). In 1963, the U.S. Congress declared Churchill an honorary U.S. citizen.

Why is Winston Churchill regarded as Britain's greatest statesman?

World War II in Europe

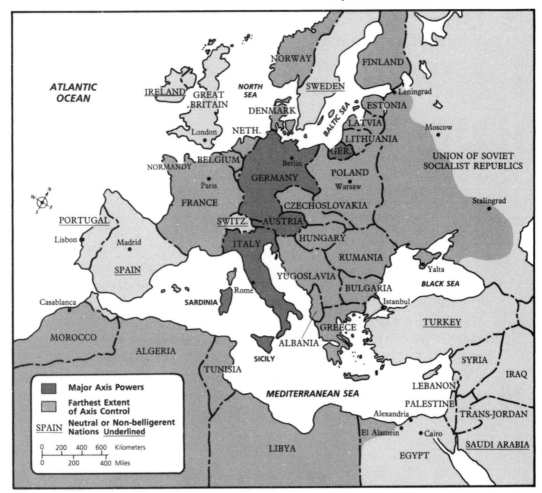

Complete each of the following sentences:

1. During World War II, the major Axis powers in Europe were —.

2. Axis control extended into the nations of —.

3. Neutral nations included —.

In June 1941, Hitler tossed aside the nonaggression pact with Stalin and invaded the Soviet Union. The Germans wanted the Soviet Union's large grain-producing areas and oil resources. German forces advanced east almost to Moscow. Britain and the United States quickly came to the aid of the Soviets, sending arms and food. In December 1941, the Soviet army counterattacked. This action and the harsh winter weather temporarily halted the German attack.

CRITICAL THINKING

1. **EXPLAIN:** The Battle of Britain was Hitler's first failure.

2. **EXPLAIN:** By 1941, Nazi Germany dominated the continent of Europe.

4. The War Against the Jews. Hitler's victories gave him the opportunity to establish a "New Order" in Europe. He planned to colonize Eastern Europe by Germans. Farms, factories, and businesses were to be assigned to deserving members of the German "master race." The original owners—Russians, Poles, and other "inferiors"—were to work as slave laborers to produce food and goods for Germany. This fate became all too true for millions of Europeans of all nationalities and culture groups. Most of these victims were transported to factories inside the dreaded concentration camps.

Hitler's hatred of Jews touched off great waves of persecution. The Nuremberg Laws of 1935 took away the citizenship rights of German Jews. During the "Night of Broken Glass" (November 9, 1938), Jews throughout Germany and Austria were beaten and killed. Their homes, shops, and places of worship were looted and smashed. Many Jews then fled to other

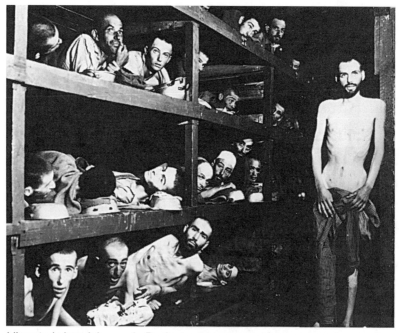

Liberated slave laborers in Buchenwald concentration camp.

parts of Europe to escape the misery of life in the Third Reich. (Some also went to Britain and North and South America.) As the Nazis overran Europe, Jews once again found themselves under Hitler's authority. This created what the Nazis called "the Jewish problem." In January 1942, Nazi leaders officially decided to murder all Jews in Europe. At the Wannsee Conference, Nazi leaders set forth their plan for the "final solution to the Jewish problem."

In every country they conquered, the Nazis rounded up Jews and sent them to death camps. (Some resisted, of course, but the Nazi might was too great for small groups to overcome.) One of the largest and best-known camps was Auschwitz in Poland. In this place alone, some 1 million Jews were murdered. In all, the Nazis killed at least 6 million Jews and an equal number of Poles, Russians, Gypsies, and others.

The Nazi plan to murder all of the Jews of Europe is an example of *genocide*. Genocide is the deliberate destruction of an entire cultural or religious group. The *Holocaust* is the term people now apply to this terrible event in history.

5. The United States and the War. Throughout the 1920's and the 1930's, the United States kept out of international disputes. It did, however, participate in several weapons-reduction conferences.

a. U.S. neutrality. When Hitler and Mussolini started on their aggressive paths, the United States declared its neutrality and its wish to isolate itself from overseas conflicts. At the request of President Franklin D. Roosevelt, Congress passed the *Neutrality Act of 1939*.

b. Lend-Lease. After World War II began in 1939, the United States took steps to help Britain hold off Hitler's forces. The United States offered to sell arms if Britain would transport the weapons in its own ships and pay cash for them. *Cash and Carry* was the term used to describe this policy. Throughout 1940 and 1941, the United States found a variety of ways to maintain its neutrality and still send aid to Britain. The *Lend-Lease Act of 1941* authorized the president to lend or lease goods to any nation whose defense was deemed necessary to the defense of the United States. The Soviet Union also received aid after it was attacked by Germany in 1941.

c. Anti-Japanese trade ban. Japanese aggression against China in the late 1930's called forth strong protests from U.S.

The battleship USS *Arizona* (*center*) on fire after the Japanese bombed it in Pearl Harbor.

officials. After France and Holland fell to the Nazis, Japan made plans to take over French colonies in Indochina and the Dutch East Indies. (The Dutch East Indies is now Indonesia.) To stop such Japanese actions, U.S. President Franklin D. Roosevelt banned the export of materials vital to Japanese industry. The ban went into effect in July 1940 and covered such materials as petroleum, petroleum products, and scrap metal.

As Japan's oil supplies dropped, the country became desperate to obtain more supplies. Throughout 1941, Japan tried to persuade the United States to change its policies. The United States refused. In early December 1941, Japanese military leaders ordered an attack force of ships and planes to head for U.S. targets.

d. War. During the early morning hours of December 7, 1941, Japanese planes bombed the American naval base at Pearl Harbor in Hawaii. Most of the U.S. Pacific fleet was destroyed or severely damaged, as were most of the planes on the base. The United States could not now stop the Japanese from taking over East Asia and key islands in the Pacific.

An aroused United States wholeheartedly supported President Roosevelt's request for a declaration of war on Japan. On December 8, Congress complied. Just three days later, Germany and Italy declared war on the United States. Now Americans faced major wars in both Europe and Asia.

CRITICAL THINKING

1. **PROVE or DISPROVE**: Hitler's "New Order" was a racist and imperialistic program.

2. **PROVE or DISPROVE:** By 1941, war between the Axis Powers and the United States had become impossible to avoid.

6. Allied Strategy in Europe. In January 1942, the United States, Britain, the Soviet Union, and 23 other nations signed the Declaration of the United Nations. These Allied Powers pledged to cooperate with one another to defeat the Axis Powers. The Allies decided to concentrate first on winning the war in Europe. Enough supplies and soldiers would be channeled to the Pacific command to try to keep the Japanese from enlarging their empire.

   a. *North Africa.* By winning the Battle of El Alamein in Egypt (from July to November 1942), the British kept the Germans from taking over the Suez Canal. In November, Allied forces invaded Morocco. By May 1943, the whole of North Africa was in Allied hands.

   b. *Eastern Front.* In late 1942, the Soviets stopped the German advance in Russia. The Germans suffered a major defeat at Stalingrad (now Volgograd) in January 1943. But the Germans found the strength to hold their positions throughout most of 1943. In the fall, the Russians began pushing west toward Germany and south into the Balkans. They did not stop until they reached Berlin in April 1945.

   c. *Italian campaign.* The Allies invaded Sicily in July 1943. Late in July, Mussolini was forced out of office and imprisoned by the Italian king and leading army officers. (He was later shot by anti-Fascists.) A new Italian government signed an armistice with the Allies in September. German forces continued the fight in Italy, however. Rome fell to the Allies in June 1944. But the Germans held on to northern Italy until May 1945.

   d. *D-Day.* The greatest seaborne invasion of modern times was launched on June 6, 1944 (D-Day). Under the command of U.S. General Dwight D. Eisenhower, Allied troops crossed the English Channel and landed in Normandy, France. They relentlessly pushed the German forces out of France, Belgium, and Holland. In December 1944, the Germans broke through the Allied lines in the Battle of the Bulge in Belgium. But the Allied

The Supreme Allied Commander

Eisenhower speaks to paratroopers of the 101st Airborne Division before D-Day.

Dwight David Eisenhower (1890–1969) was the 34th president of the United States. During World War II, he served as the supreme commander of Allied forces in Western Europe.

"Ike," as he was called, came from a poor family in Kansas. In 1915, Eisenhower graduated from the U.S. Military Academy at West Point. This was the first step in what was to become a lifelong profession.

In World War I, Eisenhower served as commander of a tank training center. In the years between the two wars, Eisenhower held many military posts. By 1941, Eisenhower had become a colonel and was made chief of staff of the Third Army. His skill and ability in maneuvering large numbers of troops and equipment in war games earned him a promotion to brigadier general. His record impressed General George C. Marshall, the U.S. Army chief of staff. After the United States entered World War II in December 1941, General Marshall moved Eisenhower into a series of high-level military jobs, mostly in the area of strategic planning. All of the jobs, including *Operation Torch*, the Allied invasion of French North Africa, required the highest type of planning and organization skills.

In December 1943, Eisenhower was appointed supreme commander of all Allied forces in Europe. At this peak in his military career, Eisenhower planned the operation that was necessary to win World War II. *Operation Overlord* was the code name given to the planned invasion of German-held Western Europe by the Allies.

On D-Day, June 6, 1944, American, British, French, and other Allied soldiers landed on the beaches of Normandy in France. The Allies, under Ike, had begun the assault on Hitler's empire that would end with Germany's surrender in May 1945.

After World War II ended, Eisenhower came home to a hero's welcome. President Harry S Truman assigned Ike the job of U.S. Army chief of staff. In this role, Eisenhower scaled down the huge wartime army to meet peacetime needs.

After leaving the army in 1948, Eisenhower served as president of Columbia University. In 1952, the Republican Party persuaded Ike to run for the presidency of the United States. He did, and won. As president from 1953 to 1961, Eisenhower enjoyed great popularity. During his two terms in office, the nation was prosperous and at peace.

Why is Dwight D. Eisenhower regarded as one of the greatest military leaders of World War II?

U.S. troops wade ashore at Normandy on D-Day, June 6, 1944.

forces counterattacked and thrust the Germans back into Germany.

In March 1945, the Allies moved into Germany. As the Russians entered Berlin, Hitler committed suicide. On May 7, the new German leaders surrendered. The next day, the end of the war in Europe—V-E Day—was officially declared.

7. Allied Strategy in the Pacific.   The Allies won their first victory in the Pacific in May 1942. The Battle of the Coral Sea kept the Japanese from invading Australia. The second naval victory in 1942, the Battle of Midway, stopped the eastward advance of Japan.

   a. *Island-hopping.*   In the Pacific, the Allies followed a strategy termed "island-hopping." They chose key islands to attack and then used them as bases to invade others. Enemy forces on bypassed islands were cut off from supplies and support. Names such as Guadalcanal, Tarawa, Kwajalein, and Iwo Jima became familiar as places where bloody battles were fought.

   In the fall of 1944, American forces under the command of General Douglas MacArthur landed in the Philippines. Shortly afterward, the U.S. Navy destroyed the main strength of the Japanese Navy in the Battle of Leyte Gulf.

   b. *Mainland battles.*   Chinese forces, with American aid, kept the Japanese from overrunning all of China. British and

World War II in the Pacific, 1941–1945

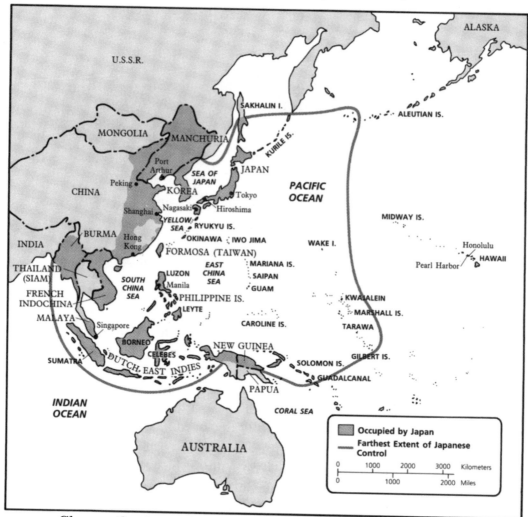

Choose the item that best completes each sentence or answers each question.

1. Which country was partially occupied by Japan? (*a*) Thailand (*b*) India (*c*) China (*d*) Mongolia

2. A country or area not occupied or controlled by Japan was (*a*) Korea (*b*) Manchuria (*c*) French Indochina (*d*) Australia.

3. Two cites in Japan are (*a*) Manila and Port Arthur (*b*) Hong Kong and Singapore (*c*) Hiroshima and Tokyo (*d*) Pearl Harbor and Peking.

4. In which general direction is Midway Island from Japan? (*a*) north (*b*) south (*c*) east (*d*) west

5. Which county was the westernmost one controlled by Japan? (*a*) Burma (*b*) New Guinea (*c*) Kwajalein (*d*) Thailand

Hiroshima after the explosion of the atomic bomb.

Indian troops kept the Japanese out of eastern India. But almost all of Southeast Asia remained under Japanese control throughout the war.

c. *Bombing of Japan.* After June 1944, U.S. bombers flew over Japan at will. They caused great destruction in Tokyo and other major cities. In April 1945, U.S. troops landed on the island of Okinawa, just 350 miles from Japan.

Before the Allies invaded Japan, they tried to persuade the Japanese government to surrender. Japan refused, so on August 6, 1945, an American plane dropped an atomic bomb on the city of Hiroshima. This one bomb leveled between four and five square miles of the city and killed more than 80,000 people. On August 8, the Soviet Union declared war on Japan. The Japanese still refused to give up. On August 9, a second atomic bomb was dropped, this time on Nagasaki. The Japanese now realized that the Allies had the power to destroy their homeland. They signed surrender documents on September 2, 1945—V-J Day.

The terrible war that had claimed the lives of some 50 to 60 million people had finally come to an end. The Allies had already taken some steps to keep the peace.

The Big Three at Yalta: Seated from left to right, Churchill, Roosevelt, and Stalin.

8. Wartime Diplomacy. Throughout the war, President Franklin D. Roosevelt and Prime Minister Winston Churchill of Great Britain met frequently. They cooperated in making plans for conducting the war. Premier Joseph Stalin of the Soviet Union was kept informed of Allied strategy. General Chiang Kai-shek, the head of China, also met with the Allied leaders.

One of the most important meetings of the war was held at Yalta in southern Russia in February 1945. Stalin, Churchill, and Roosevelt worked out the peace terms for Germany and the organization of post-war Europe. They agreed to divide Germany into four occupation zones. Britain, France, the United States, and the Soviet Union would each administer a zone. Since Berlin, the German capital, was located in the Soviet zone, they divided it too into four zones. Germany was to be disarmed and its war criminals punished. War crimes included participation in the mass murder of Jews and other peoples. New borders were established for Poland. The Allies were to help Poland and the other Soviet-occupied Eastern European nations to solve their problems by democratic means. (This did not happen.)

Another agreement of long-lasting importance was the pledge to set up the United Nations. This world peace organization would replace the League of Nations. The U.S. Senate approved the UN Charter in July 1945.

9. Post-War Occupation.   General MacArthur and U.S. troops directed the postwar occupation of Japan. A new constitution turned Japan into a democracy and stripped Emperor Hirohito of his divinity. Japan was not allowed to have military forces except for defensive purposes. The Allies tried Japanese war criminals, executing some and imprisoning others.

Soviet troops, which had liberated most countries of Eastern Europe from Nazi rule, stayed in these countries. Most of Eastern Europe turned Communist. Because these countries usually followed Soviet leadership in economic and political matters, they were called *satellite nations*.

MATCHING EXERCISE

Match each term in Column A with its meaning in Column B.

Column A	**Column B**
1. Axis Powers	*a.* Hitler's plan for Europe
2. nonaggression pact	*b.* a Nazi death camp
3. blitzkrieg	*c.* Germany, Italy, Japan, and their allies
4. Vichy	
5. Battle of Britain	*d.* an agreement between Hitler and Stalin
6. "New Order"	
7. Auschwitz	*e.* a series of air battles lasting from August 1940 to June 1941
8. Pearl Harbor	
9. D-Day	*f.* lightning war
10. Hiroshima	*g.* the Allied invasion of France on June 6, 1944
	h. the capital of the pro-German government of France
	i. the first city on which the United States dropped an atomic bomb
	j. the U.S. naval base attacked by Japan on December 7, 1941

Chapter Review

MULTIPLE-CHOICE

Choose the item that best completes each sentence.

1. Japanese aggression in Asia began with the seizure in 1931 of (a) Burma (b) Manchuria (c) Malaya (d) Thailand.

2. In 1937, Japan began a full-scale attack on (a) China (b) India (c) the Philippine Islands (d) Laos.

3. In the 1930's, Hitler and Mussolini aided Franco during the civil war in (a) France (b) Spain (c) Italy (d) Portugal.

4. The African country conquered by Fascist Italy in 1936 was (a) Egypt (b) Morocco (c) Ethiopia (d) Algeria.

5. Adolf Hitler violated the Treaty of Versailles by his seizure of (a) Bulgaria and Rumania (b) Spain and Italy (c) Austria and Czechoslovakia (d) Yugoslavia and Albania.

6. World War II began on September 1, 1939, when Nazi Germany invaded (a) Poland (b) the Soviet Union (c) France (d) Great Britain.

7. Two countries that the Nazi blitzkrieg failed to conquer were (a) Norway and Denmark (b) Britain and the Soviet Union (c) France and Belgium (d) Holland and Greece.

8. Hitler's "New Order" was based on the belief that the Germans were a (a) conquered race (b) disadvantaged race (c) master race (d) inferior race.

9. The nation brought into World War II by the Japanese attack on Pearl Harbor was (a) the United States (b) the Soviet Union (c) the Republic of China (d) India.

10. The last Axis nation to surrender to the Allies was (a) Germany (b) Italy (c) Japan (d) Hungary.

CRITICAL THINKING

Read the statement below and then answer the questions that follow. The excerpt, from a letter by a Nazi official, summarizes Hitler's instructions for the Nazi rule of Eastern Europe.

> The Slavs are to work for us. In so far as we don't need them, they may die. Therefore compulsory vaccination and German health services are unnecessary. Education is dangerous. It is enough if they can count up to 100. Every educated person is a future enemy. Religion we leave to them as a means of diversion. As for food, they won't get any more than is absolutely necessary. We are the masters. We come first.

1. Imagine that you are living in Eastern Europe during World War II. Explain why you would LIKE or DISLIKE life under Nazi rule.

2. Write a letter to Adolf Hitler. Tell him how you think the Slavic peoples of Eastern Europe should be treated.

 ## ESSAY QUESTIONS

1. Reread "Dictatorship vs. Democracy," on pages 451–455. Then write a paragraph on the failure of appeasement.

2. State *two* important changes the "New Order" was supposed to bring to Europe.

3. Explain why Japan attacked Pearl Harbor.

4. Describe the main events that led to Allied victory in World War II.

5. List major agreements made at the Yalta Conference.

POLITICAL ANALYSIS

Propaganda presents slanted, or biased, information to help or hurt a cause. In wartime, governments often use propaganda in the form of posters to make the public feel patriotic and willing to support the war effort. Study the examples below of German and Allied propaganda posters. Then answer the questions that follow.

A

B "Help Hitler build. Buy German Goods."

1. Which picture ("A" or "B") represents Allied propaganda?

2. Which picture ("A" or "B") represents Axis propaganda?

3. The artist who drew picture "A" is appealing to which emotion?
    - *a.* admiration for national leaders
    - *b.* hatred of the enemy's political system
    - *c.* fear of danger to loved ones
    - *d.* love of county

4. What is the artist who drew picture "B" urging people to do?
    - *a.* support the national leaders
    - *b.* grow crops to feed soldiers
    - *c.* fight against a brutal enemy
    - *d.* enlist in the armed forces

5. Select one picture, "A" or "B." State what you think the artist wants people to believe. Explain why you AGREE or DISAGREE with the artist.

Connections: Fascism and Nazism

Benito Mussolini and his Fascists ruled Italy from 1922 to 1943. Adolf Hitler's Nazi Party held power in Germany from 1933 to 1945. Nazism and Fascism were two of the most destructive dictatorships the world has ever known. For propaganda purposes, both of these 20th-century political systems employed symbols and ideas used by people of ancient times.

Mussolini promised to restore to Italy the ancient glory of the Roman Empire. As the emblem of the Fascist Party, he used the *fasces*, a symbol of authority in ancient Rome. (The *fasces* was a bundle of elm or birch rods bound tightly around an ax. It symbolized the authority of the government.) Mussolini's foreign policy was directed at gaining control of lands that were once part of the Roman Empire. For example, he wanted to turn the Mediterranean Sea into an "Italian Lake."

Hitler went even further. As the emblem of his party, he used the *swastika* (a cross with the ends of its arms extended clockwise at right angles). The early Mesopotamians used the swastika on their coins. The early Christians, the Byzantines, the Navahos in North America, and the Mayas in Central and South America all used the swastika. To those peoples, it was a symbol of good fortune, prosperity, or the continuation of life. Under the Nazis, the swastika became a symbol of terrorism and death.

Hitler encouraged the Germans to identify with the legendary gods and heroes of their early tribal history. To recreate the spirit of the ancient age, Hitler organized huge pageants and parades. Thousands of followers marched to the pounding of drums and the blaring of horns, carrying banners and standards of medieval design. Hitler favored the music dramas of Richard Wagner. To the Nazis, Wagner's medieval themes and heroic music inspired their dreams of conquest.

More than any other 20th-century political philosophies, Nazism and Fascism were rooted in the distant past.

1. Why do you think Benito Mussolini was so interested in the Roman Empire?

2. The greatest medieval German ruler was the Holy Roman Emperor Frederick Barbarossa (Red Beard). He ruled from 1152 to 1190. According to legend, Frederick never died. Instead, he sleeps inside a mountain. The legend says that at Germany's time of greatest need, Frederick will awaken and rule again. Why do you think Adolf Hitler was fascinated by this legend?

DOCUMENT-BASED QUESTION

This question is based on the accompanying documents (1–5). It will improve your ability to work with historical documents.

Historical Context:

The hopes for world peace that followed the end of World War I faded rapidly. Before long, the aggressive policies of Fascist Italy, Nazi Germany, and militaristic Japan plunged the world into another global conflict. World War II broke out in 1939.

Task:

Using information from the documents and your knowledge of world history, answer the questions that follow each document. Your answers to each question will help you write the document-based essay.

Document 1. Excerpt from *Fascism: Ideas and Institutions* (1935), by Italian dictator Benito Mussolini, stating the ideas behind his movement:

> The Fascist conception of life stresses the importance of the State and accepts the individual only in so far as his interests coincide with those of the State. The Fascist conception of the State is all-embracing; outside of it no human or spiritual values can exist, much less have value.
>
> Fascism does not, generally speaking, believe in the possibility or utility of perpetual peace. War alone keys up all human energies to their maximum tension and sets the seal of nobility on those peoples who have the courage to face it. All doctrines which postulate peace at all costs are incompatible with Fascism.

> **Source**: Mussolini, Benito, *Fascism: Ideas and Institutions*. Rome, 1935. Found at http://www.dickinson.edu/~rhyne/232/Nine/MussoFundamentalIdeas.html

According to this document, what are the important principles of Fascism?

Document 2. Excerpt from a speech by British Prime Minister Neville Chamberlain defending the Munich Agreement that allowed Germany to annex part of Czechoslovakia, given before Parliament, October 3, 1939:

I have nothing to be ashamed of. Let those who have, hang their heads. We must feel profound sympathy for a small and gallant nation in the hour of their national grief and loss.

In my view the strongest force of all was . . . that unmistakable sense of unanimity among the peoples of the world that war must somehow be averted. The peoples of the British Empire were at one with those of Germany, of France and of Italy, and their anxiety, their intense desire for peace, pervaded the whole atmosphere of the conference, and I believe that that, and not threats, made possible the concessions that were made.

Now that we have got past [the Czechoslovakia question], I feel that it may be possible to make further progress along the road to sanity.

Source: From Great Britain, *Parliamentary Debates,* Commons, Vol. 339 (October 3, 1938).

Based on this document, why did Chamberlain consent to the Munich Agreement?

Document 3. Study the illustration on page 458.

How does it show why the German blitzkrieg was so successful?

Document 4. Excerpt from a speech given by President Franklin D. Roosevelt before Congress, in January 1941, 11 months before the United States entered World War II:

In the future days, which we seek to make secure, we look forward to a world founded upon four essential human freedoms. The first is freedom of speech and expression—everywhere in the world. The second is freedom of every person to worship God in his own way—everywhere in the world. The third is freedom from want. . . . The fourth is freedom from fear.

That is no vision of a distant millennium. It is a definite basis for a kind of world attainable in our own time and generation. That kind of world is the very antithesis of the so-called new order of tyranny which the dictators seek to create with the crash of a bomb.

Source: "Annual Message to Congress," January 6, 1941. Found at http://www.fdrlibrary.marist. edu/4free.html

Explain why Roosevelt was speaking to the American people about essential freedoms.

Document 5.   Excerpt from *The Diary of a Young Girl,* by Anne Frank (1929–1945), a young Jewish Dutch girl who would die in a concentration camp during the Holocaust:

> It's difficult in times like these: ideals, dreams, and cherished hopes rise within us, only to be crushed by grim reality.
>
> It's utterly impossible for me to build my life on a foundation of chaos, suffering, and death. I see the world being slowly transformed into a wilderness. I hear the approaching thunder that, one day, will destroy us too. I feel the suffering of millions. And yet, when I look up at the sky, I somehow feel that everything will change for the better, that this cruelty too shall end, that peace and tranquility will return once more.

> **Source**: Anne Frank, *The Diary of A Young Girl: The Definitive Edition.* Otto H. Frank and Mirjam Pressler (eds.), translated from the Dutch by Susan Massotty, copyright © 1995 by Doubleday, a division of Random House, Inc. Used by permission of Doubleday, a division of Random House, Inc.

What do Anne Frank's words suggest about how the human spirit deals with difficult times?

DOCUMENT-BASED ESSAY

Using information from the above documents and your knowledge of world history, write an essay in which you:

- Discuss the aggressive nature of the policies and actions of the Axis powers before and during World War II.
- Explain the response of the Allies to the actions of the Axis powers.

UNIT VII

THE NUCLEAR AGE

CHAPTER 18
The Cold War and
Other Conflicts

Peace did not come easily to the world after the end of World War II in 1945. Almost immediately, tension developed between the United States and the Soviet Union. The existence of nuclear weapons caused fears that any conflict might touch off a nuclear war. In an effort to prevent global destruction, the major powers agreed to limit arms production. The late 20th century was a time of great insecurity. It was also a time of great progress.

SUPERPOWER RIVALRIES

At the end of World War II, most of the countries involved in it were exhausted from the struggle. The two nations that emerged from the conflict as the strongest were the Soviet Union and the United States. Although the Soviets had suffered enormous losses, their country was still powerful. The United States had not been invaded and had suffered fewer casualties.

These two countries, which became known as *superpowers,* had very different systems and goals. The Soviet Union was controlled by a Communist dictatorship, which aimed to spread communism to other areas of the world. The United States, a democracy, wanted other peoples to have the political and economic freedoms its people enjoyed.

1. Expansion and Reaction. When the war ended, Soviet troops were occupying much of Eastern Europe. In order to create a buffer zone to protect the U.S.S.R. from invasion, the Russians remained where they were. Over the next two years, they established Communist governments in several Eastern European countries: Poland, Hungary, Rumania, Bulgaria, and Czechoslovakia. The Soviets also occupied the eastern half of Germany, which became known as East Germany. (Yugoslavia and Albania, at first closely associated with the Soviets, would each break away and follow an independent Communist course.) All these countries were known as Soviet satellites because they depended on the Soviet Union for military and economic aid. The governments of the Eastern European nations were dictatorships, supported by secret police and other security services. They maintained command economies, with the centralized control typical of Communist countries.

The United States and its Western European allies watched with dismay as these developments occurred. Fearful of the further spread of communism, Americans adopted a policy of *containment* —that is, keeping the Soviet Union contained so that it would not expand further.

a. *Truman Doctrine.*   The first serious containment measure involved Greece and Turkey. A civil war had broken out in Greece in 1946. Greek Communists were trying to overthrow the government and ally Greece with the Soviet Union. Meanwhile, the Soviets were pressuring Turkey to give up part of its territory. President Harry S Truman (who had succeeded Franklin D. Roosevelt when the latter died in April 1945) decided to act. Early in 1947, he announced what came to be called the Truman Doctrine: The United States would "support free peoples" who were resisting takeovers by outside forces. Truman requested $400 million of economic and military aid to strengthen Greece and Turkey, which Congress granted. This aid helped end the Communist threat to Greece and Turkey.

b. *Berlin Blockade.*   In 1948, the Soviets again tested the will of the Western Allies to contain the spread of communism. This time the test came in Berlin.

After the war, East Germany was controlled by the Soviet Union. West Germany was controlled by the Allies. While Berlin was located in East Germany, the Soviets occupied and governed only one section of it. Britain, France, and the United States held the rest of the city, called West Berlin.

In an effort to force the British, French, and Americans out of Berlin, the Soviets shut down all highways and railroad lines to West Berlin from West Germany. The city was blockaded. It could not receive supplies by land. Rather than try to break the block-

A cargo plane of the Berlin Airlift about to land in West Berlin.

ade by sending in troops and possibly starting a war, the United States and its allies decided to airlift supplies to Berlin.

In spite of great difficulties, the Berlin Airlift kept the people of the city from starving by bringing in tons of food, clothing, and fuel every day. After 321 days, the Soviets ended the blockade and once again opened up the land routes across East Germany. The Berlin Airlift demonstrated Allied determination to oppose Soviet moves. It was a great technological achievement, accomplishing what Soviet aviation experts said could not be done. For the first time in aviation history, an entire city was supplied by air through a long, bitterly cold German winter. Western technology and ingenuity had triumphed.

c. *Point-Four Program.* As part of the effort to oppose further Soviet expansion and contain communism, President Truman proposed a program to give technical assistance to developing nations. Under this Point-Four Program, American money and technical specialists were provided to help developing nations in Africa, the Middle East, Asia, and Latin America. Projects were begun to increase agricultural production, improve government administration, advance education, and promote public health.

 ESSAY QUESTIONS

1. List the countries that became Soviet satellites after World War II.

2. What was the Truman Doctrine?

3. Why do you think the Berlin Airlift was considered a victory for the United States and a defeat for the Soviets?

2. European Economic Recovery.

At the end of World War II, much of Europe lay in ruins. People faced tremendous tasks: rebuilding their cities, growing enough food for their people, and restoring factories, roads, and harbors that had been destroyed. In elections held shortly after the war, the Communists, promising quick relief, made impressive gains in war-torn Italy and France. These conditions prompted further U.S. action.

a. *Marshall Plan.*

In June 1947, U.S. Secretary of State George Marshall announced a program to help Europe. Called the Marshall Plan, it asked all of the nations of Europe to get together and work out a plan for their own recovery. The United States pledged money to carry out the plan. Although the Communist countries could have participated in the Marshall Plan, they chose not to. Stalin, the Soviet dictator, accused the United States of using the plan to wage economic warfare against the Soviet Union. Between 1948 and 1952, the United States gave $12 billion to the 16 Western European countries that joined the program.

Western Europe recovered and went on to achieve the greatest prosperity it had ever known. It is believed that this American aid prevented Western Europe from turning Communist.

b. *European Union.*

The cooperation that began under the Marshall Plan drew Western European countries together in other ways. In 1957, six of these countries, agreeing to follow common policies that would increase trade among them, created the European Community (EC). They later renamed the organization the European Union (EU). By 2004, 25 nations had become members. The EU has become a major economic force in the world.

In 1998, the EU formed the European Central Bank to set a common monetary policy. Since 2002, 12 members—Austria, Belgium, Finland, France, Germany, Greece, Ireland, Italy, Luxembourg, the Netherlands, Portugal, and Spain—have given up their national currencies in favor of a single currency: the euro.

3. Cold War Military Alliances.

By the late 1940's, the United States and the Soviet Union were engaged in a rivalry known as the Cold War. The two superpowers never fought each other directly, however. Tensions between the two countries caused disputes in other countries.

Secretary of State George C. Marshall boards President Truman's plane after attending a meeting of foreign ministers in London in 1947.

a. *NATO.* In 1949, the United States, Canada, Britain, France, Belgium, the Netherlands, Norway, Denmark, Italy, Luxembourg, Iceland, and Portugal formed the North Atlantic Treaty Organization (NATO). They agreed to defend one another from Soviet attack. In the following decades, Greece, Turkey, West Germany, and Spain joined these countries. The United States stationed armed forces in Europe under NATO command.

b. *Warsaw Pact.* In 1955, the Soviet Union, Bulgaria, Czechoslovakia, East Germany, Hungary, Poland, and Rumania organized a miliary alliance called the Warsaw Pact to protect Eastern Europe from NATO countries.

c. *More recent developments.* In 1991, after the collapse of the Soviet Union, the Warsaw Pact was dissolved. NATO, however, did not disband. Instead, it reorganized to counteract threats from the Balkans and the Middle East. In order to send its forces quickly to trouble spots in these and other parts of the world, NATO's military units were made more mobile. NATO also focused more on political influence than on military action. New member nations were welcomed into NATO. Reunited Germany joined in 1990. Several former Communist countries in Eastern

Military Alliances in Europe During the Cold War

Indicate whether each statement is *true* (**T**) or *false* (**F**).

1. During the Cold War, Spain and Portugal were members of the Warsaw Pact.

2. Greece, Turkey, Italy, and West Germany were NATO members.

3. Britain and Norway were neutral nations.

4. The U.S.S.R. was the largest Warsaw Pact nation.

5. Poland, Czechoslovakia, Hungary, Rumania, and Bulgaria lay between the U.S.S.R. and the Western European NATO nations.

6. Yugoslavia was not a member of the Warsaw Pact.

Europe, seeking protection against possible aggression from Russia, applied for membership. In 1999, NATO accepted the Czech Republic, Poland, and Hungary as members. Seven more Eastern European nations (Bulgaria, Estonia, Latvia, Lithuania, Rumania, Slovakia, and Slovenia) were admitted to NATO in 2004.

4. The Nuclear Threat and Disarmament. For decades after atomic bombs were dropped on Japan in 1945, the world lived in fear that nuclear weapons would be used again. The United States was the only nuclear power until 1949. In that year, the Soviet Union exploded its first atomic bomb. The two superpowers then engaged in a frantic *arms race*, competing with each other to develop ever more powerful weapons in greater and greater quantities.

Other nations soon joined the "nuclear club." During the next 20 years, Britain, France, and, later, China, India, and Pakistan all exploded nuclear devices. During the 1960's, dozens of countries agreed to limit aboveground testing of nuclear devices. In another agreement, a number of nations pledged to keep such weapons out of the hands of countries that did not yet possess them.

a. *Peaceful coexistence.* After the first crises of the Cold War, American and Soviet leaders began to work out ways of easing tensions. In 1959, President Dwight D. Eisenhower invited Premier Nikita Khrushchev to visit the United States. Through friendly talks, they reached some understandings. There was hope for *peaceful coexistence*—getting along without fighting. Many people believed that the superpowers could compete economically and politically without going to war.

b. *U-2 Incident.* Three international crises in the early 1960's delayed progress toward better relations. The first occurred in 1960, when the Soviets shot down an American U-2 plane flying over the Soviet Union. It had been photographing Soviet military bases. Soviet anger resulted in the cancellation of meetings with American diplomats in Paris. A planned visit by Eisenhower to the Soviet Union was also canceled.

c. *Berlin Wall.* The second international crisis came a year later, in 1961. During the night of August 13, the East Germans constructed a barrier between East and West Berlin. The Communist government wanted to stop the flight to the west of people seeking more freedom and greater economic opportunity.

Within days, a thick wall was built. East Berliners could no longer travel freely to West Berlin. After stopping the flow to the West of skilled workers, East Germany relaxed economic controls and achieved some economic growth. Efforts to escape continued, however. Many East Berliners were killed or arrested by border guards while attempting to get past the wall. Others managed to reach freedom in the West.

The Berlin Wall remained a barrier and a symbol of oppression until 1989, when the borders of East Germany were once again opened and the wall was torn down.

d. *Cuban Missile Crisis.* A third international incident, the Cuban Missile Crisis of 1962, brought the two superpowers to the edge of war. In 1959, Fidel Castro had led a successful revolt against the dictator of Cuba. Within two years, Castro had turned Cuba into a Communist country and allied it with the Soviet Union. In the fall of 1962, the United States found out that the Soviet Union was placing medium-range nuclear missiles in Cuba. This island is just 90 miles from Florida. President John F. Kennedy demanded that the missiles be removed. After some hesitation, Khrushchev agreed if the United States would publicly promise not to invade Cuba. It was also agreed secretly that the United States would remove from Turkey missiles that Khrushchev regarded as a threat to the Soviet Union.

e. *Détente.* In the 1970's, Soviet and U.S. leaders tried harder to lessen tensions. They pursued a policy called *détente*. This French word means "the relaxation of strained relations." In 1972, President Richard M. Nixon visited Moscow, the first U.S. president to do so. While in Moscow, he and the Soviet leader, Leonid Brezhnev, signed several agreements. They pledged to cooperate in the fields of science and technology, exploration of outer space, and the improvement of trade relations. The most important agreement the two men signed came out of the Strategic Arms Limitation Talks (SALT I), which had taken place between 1969 and 1972. The agreement called for reducing the number of certain offensive and defensive nuclear weapons.

SALT II meetings took place between 1973 and 1979. The treaty that resulted limited the number of long-range bombers and missiles. It was not approved by the U.S. Senate because of the Soviet invasion of Afghanistan in late 1979. Relations between the two countries cooled again. They kept economic, cultural, and diplomatic contacts to a minimum.

SENTENCE COMPLETION

1. For decades after atomic bombs were dropped on Japan, the world feared that —.

2. The Cuban Missile Crisis occurred when —.

DEFINITIONS

Define each of the following terms:

a. Marshall Plan   e. NATO
b. Truman Doctrine   f. Warsaw Pact
c. *détente*   g. Cold War
d. containment

CRITICAL THINKING

Reread "4. The Nuclear Threat and Disarmament," on pages 485–486. Then answer the following question: "Should the nations that possess nuclear weapons prevent the spread of these weapons to other nations?" Give reasons to support your answer.

COLD WAR CONFLICTS

Although the United States and the Soviet Union did not go to war against each other during the Cold War, they took sides in many other conflicts. By doing so, they hoped to influence the outcomes in their favor.

1. The Rise of Communism in China.   Although China had become a republic under Sun Yat-sen, it remained a country in turmoil. In the 1920's, after Western countries refused to provide aid, the Chinese turned to the Soviet Union. The Soviets provided funds and advisers, and many Chinese adopted Communist principles.

   a. *Civil War.*   Chiang Kai-shek, the Chinese leader who succeeded Sun in 1925, was at first sympathetic to communism. Nevertheless, he soon turned against it. A civil war soon broke out between Chiang's forces, called Nationalists, and Chinese Communists. The latter found a strong leader in Mao Zedong. Mao believed that China's huge peasant population was the key to successful revolution. When he and his followers took control of an area, they won support by taking land from the rich and giving it to the poor. Chiang fought back, forcing Mao to lead 100,000 Communists on a "Long March" into the interior. Lasting almost two years, this retreat to avoid being captured or killed by the Nationalists took more than 50,000 lives. After reaching northern China, the Communists gradually built up their military strength.

When Japanese troops invaded China in 1937, Chiang and Mao agreed to cooperate to defeat their common enemy. But when World War II ended in 1945, the Nationalists and Communists resumed their civil war.

Chiang lost the support of many people. They considered his government to be corrupt and dictatorial. The Nationalists favored the landlords and factory owners over the peasants and workers. In 1949, the Communists won the conflict and set up the People's Republic of China. The Nationalist forces escaped to Taiwan and set up a government there.

b. *China under Mao.* As head of the Communist Party, Mao ran the government as a dictator. Chou En-lai served as the premier. Mao quickly moved to nationalize industries. He began a series of Five-Year Plans for economic development under government control. These plans emphasized heavy industry—iron and

Thousand of Mao posters are carried on the first anniversary of the founding of the People's Republic of China, October 1, 1950.

steel, chemicals, electric power, and machinery—but neglected consumer goods. This rapid industrialization caused pollution of China's air and water.

In 1958, Mao announced a "Great Leap Forward." He forced the peasants to combine their lands in huge agricultural communities called communes. In these communes, the government owned everything. The peasants owned nothing. Mao was attempting to increase agricultural production. Instead, strong peasant resistance to the commune system reduced output. Those who protested were "reeducated" in prison camps or killed.

c. *Cultural Revolution.*   Although agricultural and industrial production did eventually increase, Mao's plans did not modernize China as fast as some people wanted. To keep his critics— teachers and other intellectuals, the middle class, and Communists who were not sufficiently radical—under control, Mao launched the "Great Cultural Revolution" in 1966. It soon became an upsurge by Chinese students and workers against the bureaucrats of the Chinese Communist Party. The goals of the revolution were to eliminate all political opposition to Mao and to make Maoism (Mao's interpretation of the teachings of Marx and Lenin) China's sole ideology (governing ideas and policies).

Between 1966 and 1968, Mao encouraged revolutionary groups of students, called Red Guards, to take power from the Chinese Communist Party leaders and national and local authorities. During the chaos and violence that followed, many died and millions more were imprisoned. Schools and universities were closed. Millions of teenagers were forcibly relocated from their cities to the countryside. Government officials were removed from office. The study of the ideas of Confucius was discouraged. Loyalty to the nation, rather than the family, was encouraged. Mao's teachings became the main guide for Chinese thinking and living.

Some peasants and sections of the army fought against the Red Guards. Law and order was breaking down. Economic progress was slowing. Mao called a halt to the revolutionary actions in 1968.

d. *Foreign relations.*   When Mao Zedong had set up the Communist government in China, the Soviet Union gave it aid. The two countries presented a united front against the Western democracies. But in the late 1950's, China began to disagree with Soviet Communist aims. China also resented later Soviet efforts to cooperate with the United States. Disputes over territory were followed by armed clashes on the long Soviet-Chinese border. Finally, in 1963, the Chinese broke off relations with the Soviets.

U.S. President Richard Nixon (*right*) in China in 1972, meeting with Chairman Mao Zedong.

Although Canada, France, Great Britain, and others had established diplomatic relations with Communist China, the United States had not. It had supported Nationalist China on Taiwan. Then in the early 1970's, President Richard Nixon took steps to recognize the People's Republic of China. In 1972, he visited mainland China. Seven years later, the United States and China established full diplomatic relations with each other.

When the United States recognized Communist China, it broke off official relations with Nationalist China. The two countries remained friendly, however, and Taiwan continued to receive some military aid from the United States.

MATCHING EXERCISE

Match each name or term in Column A with a description or definition from Column B.

Column A
1. Mao Zedong
2. Chiang Kai-shek
3. Long March
4. Chou En-lai
5. Taiwan
6. Great Leap Forward
7. Great Cultural Revolution
8. Red Guards

Column B
a. Communist move to northern China in 1934
b. head of Communist China
c. location of Nationalist government
d. premier of People's Republic of China
e. Nationalist leader
f. Communist students
g. plan to modernize China
h. attempt to enforce Maoism

2. War in Korea. After Japan was defeated in 1945, Korea (a Japanese possession) was divided. Soviet troops occupied the north. U.S. troops occupied the south. The dividing line between South Korea and North Korea was the 38th parallel (line of latitude). The South developed an anti-Communist, representative form of government that soon turned into a dictatorship. The North became Communist. Each section hoped to unite the whole country under its rule.

a. War begins. In June 1950, North Korean troops crossed the 38th parallel and invaded South Korea. U.S. President Harry S Truman called on the United Nations to take action. The UN declared North Korea to be guilty of aggression. The UN then asked members for troops to fight in Korea. The United States rushed in U.S. soldiers from bases in Japan. Fifteen other UN member nations also sent fighting units. U.S. General Douglas MacArthur was appointed commander of the UN forces.

b. UN counterattack. By early September, the North Koreans had nearly pushed the UN forces off the Korean peninsula. Within three weeks, however, a counterattack swept the North Koreans back across the 38th parallel. UN troops moved on north toward the Yalu River, the border between North Korea and China. At this point, in November 1950, Chinese soldiers poured into North Korea. The Chinese wanted a Communist victory. They also wanted to prevent UN troops from coming too close to their

U.S. machine-gun crew in Korea.

own border. Chinese and North Korean forces pushed the UN troops back toward the 38th parallel. For the rest of the war, the fighting centered around this line.

In April 1951, President Truman dismissed General MacArthur. He accused the general of publicly demanding a war policy that was opposed to the president's orders. MacArthur wanted to invade China to wipe out communism in Asia. Truman feared that such an action would bring about a full-scale war with China and the Soviet Union. He did not want to get trapped in a major conflict in Asia that would expose Western Europe to a takeover by the Soviets.

In July 1951, truce talks began. Throughout 1952 and into 1953, the talks and the fighting went on. Finally, in July 1953, an armistice was signed.

c. *Post-war developments.* Since 1953, South Korea has developed considerable economic power and has moved toward increased democracy. In contrast, North Korea has remained a rigid Communist dictatorship. By the early 21st century, its economy had become deficient, sometimes unable to supply the North Korean people with sufficient food, electrical power, medical services, and other essential goods and services.

North and South Korea formally ended the Korean War in 1991 by signing a nonaggression treaty. Korea remains divided near the 38th parallel, and the United States continues to keep armed forces in South Korea. In 2005, the United States announced its intention to reduce the number of American troops

The Korean War

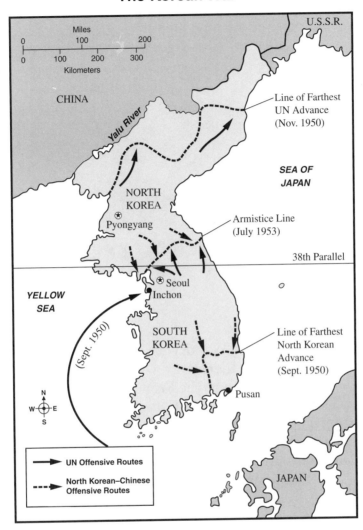

stationed in South Korea. To guard against the possibility of a future threat by North Korea, the United States would install sophisticated high-tech weapons and warning systems. Also, increased South Korean investments improved North Korea's economic prospects.

    ## ESSAY QUESTIONS

1. Explain how the United States got involved in the war in Korea.

2. Discuss the outcomes of the Korean War.

Ho Chi Minh.

3. War in Vietnam.   After World War II, France wanted to resume control of its colonies in Indochina, which Japan had occupied. In Vietnam, one of these colonies, the French were opposed by a nationalist group led by Ho Chi Minh. A Communist, he wanted to free his country from imperialist control. The Soviet Union aided Ho Chi Minh, while the United States backed the French. Fighting between the French and Vietnamese lasted for eight years. In 1954, the Vietnamese won an important battle and the war at Dien Bien Phu.

   a.   *A divided Vietnam.*   Representatives from several countries, including Vietnam, France, the United States, and the Soviet Union, met in Geneva, Switzerland, to draw up a peace treaty. It divided Vietnam at the 17th parallel. Communists controlled North Vietnam, and anti-Communists controlled South Vietnam. Elections were to be held in 1956 to choose a government for the whole of Vietnam. The United States and South Vietnam did not sign the agreements, and the elections were never held.

   North Vietnam, under the leadership of Ho Chi Minh, encouraged South Vietnamese Communists to wage guerrilla warfare against the South. Known as the Vietcong, the guerrillas hoped to bring down the government of the South and unite the country under Communist rule.

   b.   *U.S. involvement.*   South Vietnam asked the United States for help. President Dwight D. Eisenhower sent a few hundred nonfighting advisers and observers. By 1962, under

U.S. troops under enemy fire in South Vietnam.

President John F. Kennedy, the number of American advisers in Vietnam had increased to several thousand.

Soon afterward, during the presidency of Lyndon Johnson, the situation changed: The United States began sending in combat troops. This move grew out of the so-called Domino Theory. If all of Vietnam became Communist, many American leaders believed, then the rest of the countries in Southeast Asia would do so too. The countries would fall to communism like a row of dominoes, and would make up a unified anti-American bloc.

In 1964, U.S. Navy destroyers in the Tonkin Gulf off the coast of North Vietnam reported that they had been fired upon. President Johnson asked Congress for extensive war powers, which it granted. Johnson then ordered U.S. planes to bomb North Vietnam. He sent more and more troops to South Vietnam. At peak strength, there were more than 536,000 American troops in combat against the Vietcong and North Vietnamese forces.

c. *End of the war.* As Americans took over more of the fighting, a strong antiwar movement developed in the United States. The loss of large numbers of U.S. soldiers with no victory in sight caused many American citizens to demand peace. People around the world criticized the United States for becoming involved in what they considered to be a civil war.

In 1969, President Richard Nixon started to withdraw U.S. troops. That same year, the United States began negotiations to

Southeast Asia, 1970

Match each nation in Column A with it capital city in Column B.

Column A	Column B
1. Laos	a. Phnom Penh
2. North Vietnam	b. Saigon
3. Thailand	c. Vientiane
4. Cambodia	d. Bangkok
5. South Vietnam	e. Hanoi

end the conflict. A cease-fire was arranged in 1973, and the last U.S. troops left Vietnam. Fighting between the North and the South broke out again, however, and South Vietnam was too weak to win. Finally, in 1975, North Vietnam claimed victory and united the whole country under a Communist regime.

Communists also took control of Cambodia and Laos. But the kind of Communist unity foreseen by the Domino Theory did not develop. Vietnam, Cambodia, and Laos each developed along different lines, with internal problems that prevented each from being a strong force in Southeast Asia.

CHRONOLOGY

For each year listed below, state an important development in Southeast Asia.

1954   1973
1969   1975

END OF THE COLD WAR

In the 1980's, the Soviet bloc underwent major changes. By the end of the decade, communism had lost its hold and the Cold War was over.

1. Changes in the Soviet Union.   In 1985, Mikhail Gorbachev became the Soviet leader. He began *perestroika,* a program to reorganize the Soviet economy. Increasing numbers of citizens were angry about chronic shortages of consumer goods due to excessive defense spending. Also resented were the limited opportunities for economic advancement under the Soviet system. Gorbachev gave citizens the right to set up their own businesses. He told heads of large factories to make their plants profitable. Another reform, *glasnost*, called for freedom of speech and the press.

Because of these reforms, Soviet relations with the West improved. In 1987 and in 1991, the United States and the Soviet Union signed major nuclear arms reduction treaties. Gorbachev ordered Soviet forces out of Afghanistan in 1989 and ceased supporting Marxist governments and movements around the world.

The economic reforms in the Soviet Union led to increased shortages of necessary goods and services. Some Communist leaders disapproved of Gorbachev's reforms and tried to remove him. In August 1991, Russian president Boris Yeltsin and thousands of demonstrators stopped such an attempt and forced these Communist rebels to resign. All Communist Party activities were suspended.

a. *Collapse of the Soviet Union.*   Gorbachev continued his reforms, but various republics, including Russia and Ukraine, declared their independence. Gorbachev resigned at the end of 1991. Most of the former Soviet republics formed the Commonwealth of Independent States. These events brought about the end of the Cold War.

b. *Yeltsin's Russia.*   After the fall of the Soviet Union, the leaders of the republics tried to develop new political systems and to solve economic problems. In Russia, President Boris Yeltsin worked for democracy and a free market economy. Yeltsin won the national elections of 1993 and 1996. A new constitution was approved. Some Russians prospered, but millions lived in poverty. Yeltsin resigned in 1999. Voters elected Vladimir Putin president in 2000.

c. *Putin's Russia.*   President Putin did much to stabilize the Russian government. By 2002, Russia had balanced its budget and was able to pay its foreign debts. But Russia's new market economy was now vulnerable to the financial ups and downs of other countries. Many Russian companies failed when Western markets fell in 2002. Nonetheless, many experts believed that Russia was on its way to becoming a healthy market economy.

Vladimir Putin easily won the 2004 presidential election. His authoritarian leadership has brought criticism from the United States. Putin has increased presidential power, imprisoned political opponents, and closed newspapers critical of his regime. The continuing war against separatist rebels in the province of Chechnya also has caused concern. The loss of life from Chechen terrorist acts in Russia has drawn worldwide attention. In addition, the criminal activities of the Russian mafia, including drug and weapons trafficking, are regarded as a threat to international security. The Russian economy, however, continues to progress.

2. Changes in Eastern Europe.   Until 1989, the Soviet Union closely supervised the governments of its Eastern European allies. Occasional revolts against the Communist system by groups within the satellite countries were crushed by the U.S.S.R. In 1953, Soviet tanks ended protests by East Berlin workers. Many East Germans fled to the West through West Berlin. It was to halt this flow that the East German government built the Berlin Wall in 1961. Soviet troops put down prodemocracy movements in Hungary in 1956, and in Czechoslovakia in 1968. Protests and strikes by Polish workers, students, and intellectuals in 1956, 1968, 1970, and 1976 were also quickly put down.

a. *Solidarity movement.*   In 1980, new threats to the Polish government arose. Workers, under the name of Solidarity and led by Lech Walesa, demanded trade unions free of Communist control and a reexamination of Poland's alliance with the Soviet Union. At first, the government agreed to some changes. The workers continued to make demands. Then Polish authorities, encouraged by the Soviets, outlawed Solidarity in 1981. They arrested Walesa and thousands of others and imposed military rule on the country. These harsh actions drew strong criticism from the United States and other Western countries. Walesa was released in 1982, and martial law was lifted in 1983.

Mikhail Gorbachev changed the way that the Soviet Union dealt with its satellites. He abandoned the Brezhnev Doctrine, which had stated the right of the Soviets to interfere in any satellite state to protect communism. Thus in 1989, when dissatisfaction with economic and political conditions led to protests all over Eastern Europe, the U.S.S.R. did little in response.

In Poland, rising prices and shortages of consumer goods led to protests. The Communist Party yielded to the people's demands for free elections in 1989, which the Solidarity movement won. One of its leaders, Tadeusz Mazowiecki, formed the first non-Communist government in a satellite country. In 1990, Lech Walesa was elected the president of the country. Poland, however, continued to have economic problems. Poles had to endure high rates of unemployment, shortages of consumer goods, and rising prices. As a result, many former Communists were elected to parliament in 1993. Still, Poland led the former Communist nations of Eastern Europe in economic growth and the development of private enterprise.

b. *Other freedom movements.* By 1989, citizens in other Eastern European countries also had recognized that communism was failing to provide goods, services, and freedom such as are enjoyed in the West. In Hungary, Czechoslovakia, Albania, and Bulgaria, demands for free elections led to the peaceful end of Communist rule. In contrast, the Communist leader of Rumania, Nicolae Ceausescu, was overthrown and executed.

In East Germany, too, the people demanded greater personal freedom and economic opportunity. In 1989, they forced the East German government to open the Berlin Wall and allow unrestricted travel across its borders with West Germany. Opposition political parties formed and negotiated with the government for a new constitution. In 1990, free elections in East Germany led to the fall of the Communist Party from power. In October of that year, East and West Germany were reunited. Gorbachev consented to the German wish that Germany be allowed to join NATO. Unified Germany has struggled with the costs of rebuilding the less developed economy of the former East Germany. Social and political tensions have accompanied tax increases, high unemployment, and slow economic growth. Nevertheless, Germany remains one of the leading political powers in Europe.

The Berlin Wall being demolished.

 ESSAY QUESTIONS

1. How did the Marshall Plan save Western Europe from communism?

2. What led to the end of communism in Eastern Europe?

3. State the importance of *each* of the following:
   a. Long March of Chinese Communists, 1934–1935
   b. Great Cultural Revolution in China, 1966–1968
   c. President Richard Nixon's visit to China, 1972

CRITICAL THINKING

1. Reread "2. War in Korea," on pages 491–493, to find out what is wrong with the following statements. Then rewrite each as a correct statement.
   a. In June 1950, the United States invaded North Korea.
   b. UN troops moved across the Yalu River in November 1950 and defeated a force of Chinese troops.
   c. The Korean War ended in 1953 with the complete defeat of North Korea and the fall of its government.

2. Read *"c. End of the war,"* on pages 495–496. Then write a let-ter to General Thieu, the last president of South Vietnam, explaining why you AGREE or DISAGREE with the following statement: "The United States was ultimately responsible for the defeat of my country."

3. Reread "1. Changes in the Soviet Union," on pages 497–498. Then PROVE or DISPROVE the following statement: "Mikhail Gorbachev's policies of *perestroika* and *glasnost* caused the fall of the Soviet Union."

Chapter Review

> **MULTIPLE-CHOICE**

1. Two American economic programs designed to stop the spread of communism were (*a*) the Truman Doctrine and Brezhnev Doctrine (*b*) the Berlin Blockade and Berlin Wall (*c*) the Marshall Plan and Point-Four Program (*d*) *perestroika* and *glasnost*.

2. The state of tension between the Communist and non-Communist nations in the 1950's is called the (*a*) Cold War (*b*) Nuclear War (*c*) Hot War (*d*) Ideological War.

3. The opposing alliance systems formed by the United States and the Soviet Union after World War II were the (*a*) Common Market and COMECON (*b*) European Union and European Community (*c*) SALT I and SALT II (*d*) NATO and Warsaw Pact.

4. After 1950, the United States fought wars against Communist expansion in (*a*) Greece and Turkey (*b*) China and Japan (*c*) Korea and Vietnam (*d*) Hungary and Rumania.

5. After World War II, three nations that were split into sepa-rate Communist and non-Communist states were (*a*) Germany, Italy, and Japan (*b*) Poland, Greece, and Tur-key (*c*) Germany, Korea, and Vietnam (*d*) Britain, Spain, and Portugal.

6. The proper chronological order of the following events in China is (*a*) U.S. recognizes Communist China; Chinese-Soviet split; Nationalists escape to Taiwan (*b*) Nationalists

escape to Taiwan; Chinese-Soviet split; U.S. recognizes Communist China (c) Chinese-Soviet split; Nationalists escape to Taiwan; U.S. recognizes Communist China (d) Chinese-Soviet split; U.S. recognizes Communist China; Nationalists escape to Taiwan.

7. Two leading Communist leaders in Asia after 1945 were (a) Chiang Kai-shek and Sun Yat-sen (b) Ho Chi Minh and Mao Zedong (c) V.I. Lenin and Mikhail Gorbachev (d) Hu Jintao and Junichiro Koizumi.

8. The civil war in Vietnam ended in (a) 1964 (b) 1975 (c) 1978 (d) 1985.

9. When the Soviet Union collapsed in the early 1990's, most former Soviet republics (a) joined the European Union (b) rebuilt the Warsaw Pact (c) became members of NATO (d) formed the Commonwealth of Independent States.

10. Between 1953 and 1968, the Soviet Union faced revolts in the satellite countries of (a) East Germany, Hungary, and Czechoslovakia (b) Cuba, Bulgaria, and Yugoslavia (c) Albania, Turkey, and Greece (d) Poland, West Germany, and Italy.

THEMATIC WRITING

Reread pages 491–496. Then write a statement of two or three paragraphs about *one* of the following themes:

1. Communist aggression in Asia

2. Successes and failures of the United States in halting Communist expansion in Asia

POLITICAL CARTOON INTERPRETATION

Reread "4. The Nuclear Threat and Disarmament," on pages 485–486. Then study the cartoon below and answer the questions that follow.

"Let's Get A Lock For This Thing"

Source: "Let's Get a Lock For This Thing," from *Herblock: A Cartoonist's Life* (Time Books, 1998).

1. Identify the 1962 crisis to which the cartoon refers.

2. How did this crisis bring the United States and the Soviet Union to the brink of war?

3. How was a war avoided?

4. Why did this crisis threaten the entire world?

5. What other Cold War crises occurred in the early 1960's?

Connections: Hot and Cold Wars

From the late 1940's to 1991, a Cold War (a state of tension and competition) existed between the United States and the Soviet Union. In Korea (1950–1953) and Vietnam (1960's–1975), Cold War tensions erupted into military conflict between the United States and Communist countries aided by the Soviet Union.

This type of long rivalry has taken place before. The political power and independence of the ancient Greek city-states were brought to an end by the long conflict between Athens and Sparta. In the 5th century B.C., Athens, the home of democracy and the arts, regarded itself as the leader of Greece. Sparta, a monarchy devoted to military training and little else, opposed Athens' attempt to dominate Greece. Tensions between them exploded into the Peloponnesian War (431–404 B.C.). In the space of 25 years, the city-states and their allies drained themselves of strength and resources. The Greek city-states were then unable to resist conquest by Macedonia, a kingdom north of Greece, in 338 B.C.

A similar long conflict took place between the Roman and the Parthian empires. The Parthians ruled over what is now Iraq, Iran, and much of the land bordering western India until A.D. 224. For centuries, the Parthians kept the Romans from marching east beyond Syria. Neither side could conquer the other. Border towns and surrounding lands would change hands as victories were won by one side or the other. As a result, little was accomplished by either of these empires other than the deaths of thousands of soldiers and civilians.

1. How was the Cold War similar to and different from the Peloponnesian War?

2. What resulted from the wars between Rome and the Parthian Empire?

DOCUMENT-BASED QUESTION

This question is based on the accompanying documents (1–5). It will improve your ability to work with historical documents.

Historical Context:

Two nations emerged from World War II as superpowers and as rivals—the United States and the Soviet Union. For nearly half a century, the rivalry between the Western democracies (led by the United States) and the Communist bloc nations (led by the Soviet Union) threatened global peace.

Task:

Using information from the documents and your knowledge of world history, answer the questions that follow each document.

Your answers to each question will help you write the document-based essay.

Document 1.   Excerpt from Prime Minister Winston Churchill's "Iron Curtain Speech," March 5, 1946, discussing the political situation in postwar Europe:

> From Stettin in the Baltic to Trieste in the Adriatic, an iron curtain has descended across the Continent. Behind that line lie all the capitals of the ancient states of Central and Eastern Europe. Warsaw, Berlin, Prague, Vienna, Budapest, Belgrade, Bucharest and Sofia, all these famous cities and the populations around them lie in what I must call the Soviet sphere, and all are subject in one form or another, not only to Soviet influence but to a very high and, in many cases, increasing measure of control from Moscow.

> **Source:** Winston Churchill, "Iron Curtain Speech," Westminster College, Fulton, Missouri, March 5, 1946. Found at http://history1900s.about.com/library/weekly/aa082400a.htm

According to this document, what does Churchill mean by the term "iron curtain"?

Document 2.   Study the map on page 484.

The Soviet Union sought to control the countries of Eastern Europe. What geographical reason does the map show for this Soviet desire?

Document 3.   Excerpt from an address to the U.S. Congress by President Harry S Truman, March 12, 1947, setting forth a Cold War foreign policy called the Truman Doctrine:

> At the present moment in world history nearly every nation must choose between alternative ways of life. . . . One way of life is based upon the will of the majority, and is distinguished by free institutions, representative government, free elections, guarantees of individual liberty, freedom of speech and religion, and freedom from political oppression. The second way of life is based upon the will of a minority forcibly imposed upon the majority. It relies upon terror and oppression, a controlled press and radio, fixed elections and the suppression of personal freedoms. I believe that it must be the policy of the United States to support free peoples who are resisting attempted subjugation by armed minorities or by outside pressures.

> **Source:** President Truman, "Address to Congress," March 12, 1947. Found at http://www.cnn.com/SPECIALS/cold.war/episodes/03/documents/truman/

Based on this document, why did the United States want to prevent countries from falling under Communist control?

Document 4. Excerpt from Soviet leader Mikhail Gorbachev's book *Perestroika* (1987), suggesting a new direction in his country's foreign policy:

> There is a great thirst for mutual understanding and mutual communication in the world. It is felt among politicians, it is gaining momentum among the intelligentsia, representatives of culture, and the public at large. . . . The restructuring is a must for a world overflowing with nuclear weapons; for a world ridden with serious economic and ecological problems; for a world laden with poverty, backwardness and disease; for a human race now facing the urgent need of ensuring its own survival.
>
> We are all students, and our teacher is life and time. . . . We want people of every country to enjoy prosperity, welfare and happiness. The road to this lies through proceeding to a nuclear-free, non-violent world.

> **Source**: Gorbachev, Mikhail, *Perestroika: New Thinking for Our Country and the World.* NY: Harper & Row, 1987, pp. 253–254. Copyright © 1987 by Mikhail Gorbachev. Reprinted by permission of HarperCollins Publishers.

According to Gorbachev, why was *perestroika,* or a restructuring, of Cold War policies needed?

Document 5. Excerpt from an address to the Czech people by their newly elected president, Vaclav Havel, January 1, 1990:

> We had all become used to the totalitarian system and accepted it as an unchangeable fact and thus helped to perpetuate it.
>
> We have to accept this legacy as a sin we committed against ourselves. If we accept it as such, we will understand that it is up to us all, and up to us alone to do something about it. We cannot blame the previous rulers for everything, . . . because it would blunt the duty that each of us faces today: namely, the obligation to act independently, freely, reasonably and quickly. Let us not be mistaken: the best government in the world, the best parliament and the best president, cannot achieve much on their own. . . . Freedom and democracy include participation and therefore responsibility from us all.

> **Source:** Vaclav Havel, "New Year's Address to the Nation," January 1, 1990. Found at: http://chnm.gmu.edu/history/faculty/kelly/archive/new/havel1990.htm

According to this document, what was Havel telling Czech citizens about their responsibilities under all types of government?

DOCUMENT-BASED ESSAY

Using information from the above documents and your knowledge of world history, write an essay in which you:

- Discuss the causes of the Cold War and why it was fought.
- Explain why the Cold War ended as it did.

CHAPTER 19
The Changing World

In the late 20th and early 21st centuries, change seemed to happen faster than ever before. In the world of politics, new nations came into being seemingly overnight. Conflict erupted quickly, too, both in recently formed countries and in older, more established ones. In some cases, tension grew out of demands for greater democracy. In others, warfare erupted in regions divided by religious and tribal differences.

POLITICAL DEVELOPMENTS

After the end of World War II in 1945, governments and boundaries in many parts of the globe underwent drastic change. China, as discussed in Chapter 18, became a Communist nation. Japan was occupied by the United States, which had defeated it in the war. Almost all of the colonies of Britain, France, the Netherlands, and the United States gained their independence. But these changes did not mean the end of tension. Not only Korea and Vietnam, but also the Mideast, Latin America, and Europe witnessed serious conflict.

1. Asia. At the end of World War II, most of Japan's industries and cities lay in ruins. The U.S. occupation force acted quickly to put Japan back on its feet. A new constitution, calling for a democratically elected legislature, was put into effect in 1947. A prime minister directed the government.

The official peace treaty between Japan and most of the Allies was signed in 1951. (The Soviet Union signed a separate agreement with Japan in 1956.) The treaty took away all of Japan's former colonial possessions and allowed Japan to rearm for defensive purposes only. (Some possessions—Okinawa, for one—were returned in 1972.) In 1952, the United States and Japan signed a mutual defense pact. It allowed U.S. troops to stay in Japan for an indefinite time.

Japanese industry, with aid from the United States, grew rapidly in the 1950's and afterward. The automobile and electronics industries were especially successful. The country is now one of the major economic powers in the world. By the 1990's, some

Japanese products were dominating Asian and other markets around the world. Japanese companies invested heavily in businesses overseas. But political corruption, inflation, and rising unemployment led to a downturn in the nation's economic fortune in the late 1990's and early 2000's.

In other nations of Asia, economic progress was uneven. In the forefront were the so-called Pacific Rim nations—those along the coast of the Pacific Ocean. In the 1990's, industrialization transformed such countries as South Korea, Taiwan, and Singapore.

In South Asia, however, progress was slow. India, burdened by a huge population and few examples of technology, did manage to increase its food supply and extend the life expectancy of its people. But poverty and illiteracy remained big problems. By the 21st century, however, India had become a center of computer components and other high-tech industries. Foreign investment increased. U.S. and other Western firms have set up service centers in India and exported thousands of jobs there. Religious strife between India's dominant Hindus and minority Muslims also remained a problem. In addition, conflict with its neighbor Pakistan created tension throughout the whole of Asia. In the 1990's, both countries tested atomic weapons, posing a threat to the world's balance of nuclear power. More recently, however, India and Pakistan have increased efforts to reduce tensions between them.

China continued to maintain a Communist government. In the 1980's, many young Chinese protested in favor of greater democracy. In May and June of 1989, thousand of students demonstrated in Beijing's Tiananmen Square. The government ordered the military to use force to end the students' protests. Many young people were killed or arrested. Throughout the world, people raised questions about the future of human rights in China. The persecution of political dissidents and religious minorities continued, and thousands remained in prison.

But dramatic economic change did come to China. To stimulate its backward economy, China encouraged capitalism and free markets. Private business ownership and foreign investment in China expanded. State-owned industries were sold. China's economy grew at a rate that amazed Western observers. In 2005, China's rate of economic growth reached a spectacular 9.5 percent. Western and Japanese business firms built factories in China and sold their products in the expanding Chinese market. A huge dam project to supply electric power was begun on the Yangtze River. The wealthy British colony of Hong Kong was returned to China in 1997. Despite the development of a market economy, however, the Communist Party has remained firmly in power in China.

Chinese workers assembling automobiles in Shanghai.

In addition to human rights concerns, China's growing military power has worried Western leaders in the 21st century. Determined to be the top military power in East Asia, China has been building up its naval and air forces. This has been viewed as a threat to Taiwan and a challenge to U.S. and Japanese interests in the area. A top Chinese general attracted worldwide attention in 2005 when he publicly discussed the possible use of nuclear weapons in any future conflict with U.S. forces.

2. Africa. In 1945, only four independent nations existed in Africa. By 2000, there were almost 60. Most gained their freedom in the 1960's. Some had to fight for years, while others claimed their independence peacefully. Most African nations have governments that are democratic in form and have two or more political parties. But many are ruled by only one political party. Military leaders govern as dictators in a number of countries.

    a. *South Africa.* One African country, South Africa, underwent important change in the late 1900's. For years, it had been ruled by a white minority. Toward the black majority, the country's rulers maintained a policy called *apartheid*, the Afrikaans word for "apartness." This policy required strict separation of the races, as well as placing severe economic and political restrictions on black and mixed-race South Africans. Laws obliged blacks to

Nelson Mandela celebrating his 1994 election.

carry passes, prevented them from voting, and made them subject to arrest at any time.

Finally, in 1992, a majority of white South Africans voted to end apartheid and minority rule. After the adoption of a new constitution, the country held multiracial elections for the first time, in 1994. A black South African leader, Nelson Mandela—who had spent years in prison for leading anti-apartheid protests—was elected president. South Africa under his successor, Thabo Mbeki, however, still faces massive problems, including soaring unemployment and a high crime rate. In addition, South Africa in the 21st century has had the world's highest rate of AIDS (acquired immunodeficiency syndrome).

b. *Civil wars.* Elsewhere in Africa, especially in the region south of the Sahara, unrest has plagued several countries. In Sudan, a civil war has pitted the Muslim north against the non-Muslim south. By the start of the 21st century, the combined effects of civil war and famine had cost the lives of almost 2 million people. In January 2004, the Sudanese government and southern rebels signed an agreement to share the country's oil-producing wealth. But fighting between rebels and the Sudanese government in Sudan's western Darfur region has caused the deaths of tens of thousands of people.

In Somalia, rival clans fought each other throughout the 1990's and early 2000's. A provisional government was established in 2004.

In the Democratic Republic of Congo, a rebellion overthrew the country's dictator in 1997. Several neighboring countries—among them Rwanda, Burundi, Angola, and Uganda—sent in troops, some to overthrow Congo's new president, others to support him. Despite a series of peace agreements in 2002, a new constitution establishing a power-sharing interim government in 2003, and the scheduling of elections in 2006, fighting between the Congolese government and local militias continued.

Rwanda had long known conflict between its two main ethnic groups, Hutus and Tutsis. In the early 1990's, the Hutus went on a rampage, massacring more than half a million Tutsis and forcing almost 2 million more to flee the country. A shaky peace was arranged in 1996, and people hoped that it would last.

In 2002, the government of Zimbabwe allowed black militants to seize white-owned farms. Many people were killed. Thousands were left homeless. Opposition to the dictatorship of President Robert Mugabe has caused continuing violence. Moreover, the economy of Zimbabwe has been severely damaged.

c. *African Union.* An association of African countries called the Organization of African Unity (OAU) was formed in 1963. In its early years, it aimed chiefly to end colonialism. More recently, the OAU has tried to help African nations settle their conflicts and spread democracy and human rights. The OAU, renamed the African Union (AU) in 2001, now has 52 members. The AU sent troops to western Darfur in 2005 in an effort to reduce ethnic violence there.

TRUE OR FALSE

Indicate whether each statement is *true* (**T**) or *false* (**F**).

1. Nelson Mandela favored the policy of apartheid.

2. Sudan is a country divided between Muslims in the north and non-Muslims in the south.

3. Rival clans fought a civil war in Somalia.

4. Rwanda was torn by a major conflict between Hutus and Zulus.

5. The violence in the Democratic Republic of the Congo has involved other African nations in a struggle between the government and rebel militias.

Africa Since 1945

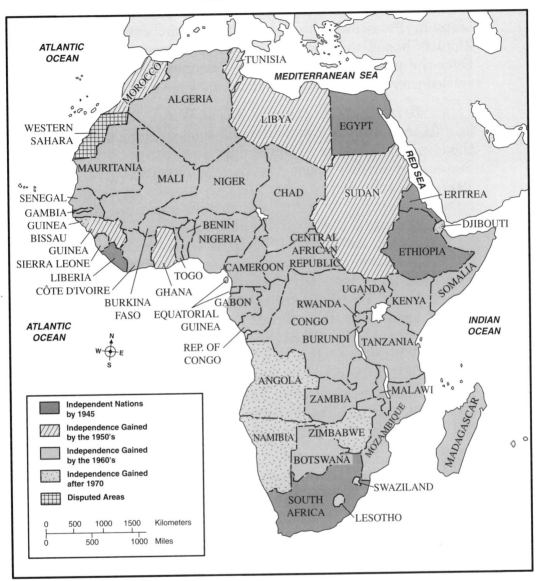

1. Name *two* African nations that gained independence during *each* time period below.
    a. by 1945
    b. 1950's
    c. 1960's
    d. after 1970

2. **EXPLAIN**: Between 1945 and the present, colonialism in Africa disappeared.

3. Identify *three* African nations that have experienced continuing violence in the late 20th and early 21st centuries.

3. Israel.   In the late 1800's, Theodor Herzl, an Austrian Jew, founded the Zionist movement. Its aim was to create a Jewish state in Palestine, the center of ancient Jewish civilization. Zionists hoped that Jews would be free from persecution there. Over the years, thousands of Jews bought land in Palestine and settled there. They farmed and set up some industries.

a. *British rule.*   During World War I, the British fought against the Ottoman Empire, which then ruled Palestine. To keep the loyalty of Zionists in the Middle East, Russia, and the United States, the British issued the Balfour Declaration in November 1917. This statement set forth British support for a Jewish homeland in Palestine. After the war, Britain was given responsibility for administering the government of Palestine.

During the 1920's and 1930's, the rise of Nazism and Fascism in Europe caused many Jews to immigrate to Palestine. The Arabs who lived there resented the growing numbers of Jews settling among them. In 1936, Arabs stepped up attacks on Jews and turned against British officials in Palestine. A bloody civil war raged for three years. Then in 1939, the British issued a document called a White Paper. It limited Jewish immigration for five years and restricted land purchases by Jews from Arabs. The White Paper pleased neither Jews nor Arabs. But World War II soon broke out, pushing the Palestine question into the background. Both sides aided the British against the Axis powers.

b. *Israeli independence.*   After the war, the British again let only a small number of Jewish refugees into Palestine. The pressure mounted as Jews struggled to enter Palestine and the Arabs tried to keep them out. The British decided to turn the Palestine problem over to the United Nations. In late 1947, the UN decided to end British control over Palestine. The area would be divided into a Jewish state and an Arab one. Jerusalem, which has holy places sacred to Jews, Christians, and Muslims, would be put under international supervision. (This last provision did not work out in practice. Until 1967, Jerusalem was divided between Israel and Jordan.)

The Jews set up a democratically elected government directed by Prime Minister David Ben-Gurion. They proclaimed themselves an independent state—Israel—in May 1948. Many native Palestinian Arabs fled to neighboring Arab states. The Arab states refused to recognize Israel as an independent country. Armies from five Arab nations immediately attacked.

Israel successfully defended itself against the larger Arab forces. A UN mediator, the American Ralph Bunche, helped set up terms for peace in 1949 because the Arabs refused to deal directly with Israel. The Arabs demanded that Israel readmit the Palestinian refugees. Israel wanted first to establish a permanent peace settlement. The Arabs rejected this plan and would not let the refugees stay in their lands.

Palestinian Arabs were placed in camps. Conditions in the camps fostered poverty, disease, and hopelessness. The refugees depended on help from the Arab states and UN charities. Some camps in Egypt, Jordan, and Lebanon became training centers for terrorism against Israel and its supporters. Chief among the guerrilla groups was the Palestine Liberation Organization (PLO), headed by Yasir Arafat.

In the meantime, Israel welcomed Jewish settlers from around the world. With support from the United States, it became a strong democratic force in the Middle East. Leaders such as David Ben-Gurion, Golda Meir, and Menachem Begin gained worldwide fame and respect.

   c.   *Three more wars.*   Israel again fought wars to maintain its existence in 1956, 1967, and 1973. Each time, it defeated Arab forces. Since 1948, Israel has suffered terrorist attacks along its borders and within its cities. On the West Bank of the Jordan River, one of the areas conquered by the Israelis in 1967, the large Palestinian Arab population refused to accept Israeli rule. Led by the PLO, many Palestinians demonstrated to call attention to their demands for the creation of a Palestinian state and an end to Israeli occupation.

   d.   *More recent developments.*   In the 1990's, some Muslim fundamentalist groups in the Middle East and North Africa made violent attempts to replace nonreligious governments with ones under Islamic religious rule. In the Israeli-controlled West Bank and Gaza territories, the fundamentalist Hamas organization challenged the leadership of the PLO. Faced with this new threat, many Arabs and Israelis made stronger demands for peace. In 1993, Prime Minister Yitzhak Rabin of Israel and PLO chairman Yasir Arafat reached a historic agreement. It provided for Palestinian self-government in Gaza and the West Bank city of Jericho.

Many Israelis feared that Palestinian control of Jericho and Gaza would leave Israeli settlers living in and around those areas exposed to Palestinian violence. Many Palestinians felt that the agreement did not provide for an end to Israeli occupation of most of the West Bank.

In October 1994, Israel and Jordan signed an agreement ending nearly 50 years of war. Unfortunately, some Israeli and Palestinian groups continued to undermine the peace process. In February 1994, an Israeli settler killed several Palestinians praying

Israel After the 1967 War

Select each correct response.

1. The names of three Israeli cities are (*a*) Cairo, Damascus, Amman (*b*) Cairo, Aqaba, Beirut (*c*) Elath, Tel Aviv, Haifa (*d*) Jerusalem, Port Said, Beirut.

2. The Gaza Strip, West Bank, and Golan Heights were (*a*) territories seized by Arab nations in 1967 (*b*) Arab territories occupied by Israel (*c*) both of the above (*d*) neither of the above.

3. Israel has ports on the (*a*) Mediterranean Sea and the Gulf of Aqaba (*b*) Mediterranean Sea and the Suez Canal (*c*) Mediterranean Sea and the Gulf of Suez (*d*) none of the above.

---

in a mosque. Palestinian militants retaliated by bombing Israeli civilians. In 1995, an Israeli who opposed peace with the Palestinians assassinated Prime Minister Rabin. In the May 1996 elections, voters chose a prime minister, Benjamin Netanyahu, who took an uncompromising stance toward the Palestinians. He

A Palestinian youth uses a sling to throw stones at Israeli troops during a clash in Ramallah, West Bank, in 2000.

insisted that Arafat put a stop to terrorist attacks, but he continued to allow Israelis to build new settlements in the West Bank.

The demand for an end to violence against Israelis had little effect. In 2000, Palestinians, frustrated at continued Israeli presence in the West Bank, resorted to street fighting. Militants also stepped up suicide bombings in Israel. Israeli leaders responded by launching attacks on Hamas and other Palestinian leaders whom they suspected of ordering the bombings.

In January 2004, Israel began building a concrete barrier around Jerusalem, separating the city from Palestinian villages in the West Bank. This wall will be linked to a longer barrier that Israel is building along its border with the West Bank as protection from Palestinian suicide bombers. Following Yasir Arafat's death in November 2004, Mahmoud Abbas, a veteran peace negotiator, was elected chairman of the Palestine Liberation Organization and, later, president of the Palestinian Authority. Abbas has been a critic of the armed Palestinian uprising.

Israeli Prime Minister Ariel Sharon surprised many in May 2004 with a plan to withdraw Israeli settlers from Gaza and portions of the West Bank. In 2005, President Abbas persuaded the leaders of Hamas to join the political process. In January 2006, a Hamas victory in Palestinian elections created doubts about the future of the search for peace. Hamas does not recognize Israel's right to exist.

Fighters for Peace

Anwar Sadat, Jimmy Carter, and Menachem Begin (*left to right*) after signing agreements in 1978 that led to the 1979 peace treaty between Egypt and Israel.

In November 1977, two Middle Eastern leaders met in Jerusalem, the capital of Israel. Anwar Sadat (1918–1981), president of Egypt, and Menachem Begin (1913–1992), prime minister of Israel, were determined to end the series of wars that had been fought by their nations since 1948. At the time of their meeting, Israel and Egypt were still officially at war. Sadat's decision to go to Jerusalem was courageous. His Arab allies were outraged at his visit and thought him a traitor to the Arab cause against Israel. Begin welcomed Sadat and expressed his willingness to talk about peace.

Both men had similar backgrounds. Begin had come to British-ruled Palestine from Poland during World War II. He believed strongly in the Zionist dream of an independent Jewish nation. After the British closed Palestine to further Jewish immigration, Begin acted to end Britain's control of Palestine. He became a leader of Irgun, a Jewish organization that used terrorism to fight the British and the Palestinian Arabs.

In 1948, the state of Israel was created. Irgun was disbanded. Many of its members joined the new Israel Defense Force. Others formed Likud, a political party proud of its strong nationalism. Begin became the leader of Likud. The Likud Party's victory in the Knesset (parliamentary) election of 1977 brought Menachem Begin to the post of prime minister of Israel.

Anwar Sadat was also a revolutionary. As a young officer in the Egyptian army, Sadat was a member of an underground organization formed to end British control in Egypt. During World War II, Sadat was put into prison for several years for his revolutionary activities. In 1952, British-supported King Farouk was deposed by Colonel Gamal Abdel Nasser, Sadat, and other military officers. Under President Nasser, Sadat held a series of high government positions, including vice president. On Nasser's death in 1970, Anwar Sadat became president of Egypt.

In September 1978, a meeting between Begin and Sadat was arranged by President Jimmy Carter at Camp David, Maryland. The discussions led to the creation of a peace treaty between Egypt and Israel. The treaty was signed in 1979. Both Begin and Sadat received the Nobel Peace Prize for their efforts to bring peace to the Middle East.

Throughout the Arab world, Sadat was denounced as a traitor to the Arab cause. In October 1981, Anwar Sadat was assassinated.

What did Prime Minister Begin and President Sadat accomplish through their efforts?

CHRONOLOGY

For each of the following dates (or set of dates) state an important development in the history of the Middle East.

a. 1917
b. 1948
c. 1956, 1967, and 1973

d. 1993
e. 1994
f. 2005

CRITICAL THINKING

PROVE or DISPROVE: Conflicts between Jews and Muslims shaped the history of the Middle East in the 20th and 21st centuries.

4. The Muslim States. Most countries in North Africa and the Middle East are Muslim—that is, Islam is the chief religion. They are peopled mainly by Arabs. (Major exceptions are Iran and Turkey, which are not Arab.) In most Muslim countries, religious leaders have a powerful influence on government and society.

a. *Independence movements.* For many years, the British and French controlled or dominated the governments of the Islamic countries. Between the 1920's and the late 1960's, this influence declined. Today, the Islamic states are independent. Most of them are ruled by monarchs or military leaders.

b. *Oil wealth.* Many Middle Eastern countries are rich in oil. To a great extent, much of the rest of the world depends on this oil for fuel in homes, factories, and automobiles. In 1960, several oil-producing countries formed the Organization of Petroleum Exporting Countries (OPEC). Their aim was to coordinate production so that they could get a good return for their oil. By the year 2000, there were 11 members of OPEC—six in the Middle East, three in Africa, and one each in Asia and South America.

The importance of Middle Eastern oil to the world was made clear in 1973. During a war with Israel, the Arab members of OPEC raised the price of oil. They also reduced or cut off shipments of oil to countries supporting Israel. This action caused a severe shortage of oil in Europe, Japan, and the United States. The higher prices also brought on economic problems for oil-consuming countries.

Rising global energy demands drove up the price of oil to $68 a barrel in 2005. In response, OPEC agreed to encourage its members to increase oil production. However, the capacity of oil refineries worldwide could not keep pace with the demand.

c. *Foreign relations.* Western nations do not want an unfriendly power to gain control of the Middle East. The United States in particular gives military aid to help some Middle Eastern nations defend themselves. Some countries also receive economic aid. Few of the Muslim states have well-developed industries. Most of their oil is shipped to other places to be refined.

Between 1948 and 1973, Egypt lost many soldiers and spent great sums of money in four wars with Israel. In 1977, President Anwar Sadat of Egypt decided it was time to improve relations with Israel. He made a dramatic visit to Jerusalem to meet with Israeli Prime Minister Menachem Begin and Israel's parliament. Sadat publicly acknowledged Israel's existence as a state. As a result, the other Arab states broke off relations with Egypt.

In 1978, Sadat and Begin met with President Jimmy Carter at Camp David in the United States. The three men created a "Framework for Peace in the Middle East." A peace treaty between Israel and Egypt was signed the following year.

Since the 1990's, radical Islamic fundamentalist groups have attempted to overthrow the governments of Egypt, Algeria, and other Arab nations. Faced with the need to defend themselves from this internal threat, the leaders of these nations became more willing to negotiate with Israel. In response, terrorists staged bloody campaigns against innocent civilians.

5. Revolution in Iran. Iran is a Muslim country. Monarchs known as shahs ruled the country beginning in 1925. For years, the British and Russians strongly influenced Iran. Then, after World War II, the United States took a greater interest in the country as an ally against the Soviet Union. The United States supplied the shah with the latest military equipment.

a. *Islamic revolution.* In the late 1970's, opposition to the Shah's efforts to modernize Iran gained strength. Islamic revolutionaries forced the shah to flee the country in 1979. Ayatollah Ruholla Khomeini, a Muslim religious leader, became the new ruler. He opposed the United States because it had aided the shah. In November 1979, Iranians invaded the American embassy in Teheran, the capital of Iran. They seized 52 Americans as hostages. In spite of strong international pressure, it took 444 days to negotiate their release.

Khomeini, like most Iranians, was a Shiite Muslim. Shiites, one of the two main branches of Islam, make up about 15 percent of the world's Muslims. The other branch, Sunnis, form a majority in most other Muslim countries.

b. *Iran-Iraq War.* Neighboring Iraq attacked Iran in 1980 in the hope of overthrowing Khomeini. The Iraqi government feared that Khomeini would convince the Shiite Muslims in Iraq to rebel. Shiites make up the majority of the population of Iraq. Many Iraqi Shiites revered Khomeini. Also, Iraq wanted to take control of the Shatt-al-Arab, a waterway used by both Iran and Iraq for shipping oil into the Persian Gulf.

By 1987, the war had reached a stalemate. Both sides had lost thousands of lives, yet neither one had gained anything. The war finally ended in 1988 when Iraq and Iran accepted a UN resolution calling for a cease-fire.

c. *More recent developments.* Iran has been accused of harboring terrorists and encouraging revolutionary activities in many nations. Leaders of other countries are concerned that Iran might be developing nuclear weapons. The election of a moderate Iranian, Mohammed Khatami, as president in 1997 indicated to some that the nation was moving toward less militant policies. Then in 2005, however, a more conservative president named Mahmoud Ahmadinejad was elected. Despite international protests, he declared Iran's intention to continue developing its nuclear capabilities. In early 2006, the United States and the EU referred the dispute to the UN Security Council.

6. The Persian Gulf War. In August 1990, Iraq invaded its tiny neighbor Kuwait and annexed it. The Iraqi dictator, Saddam Hussein, wanted Kuwait for its rich oil fields and a valuable seaport on the Persian Gulf. Hussein then moved his military forces to the border of Saudi Arabia.

U.S. President George H. Bush led worldwide opposition to the Iraqi aggression. He sent military forces to Saudi Arabia to protect it. The United Nations also took action. It condemned Iraq and demanded its withdrawal from Kuwait. The UN authorized the

The Middle East

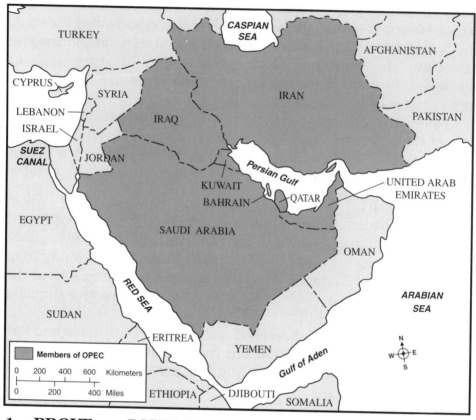

1. **PROVE or DISPROVE:** The influence of OPEC extends throughout much of the Middle East.

2. **PROVE or DISPROVE:** Saudi Arabia and Iran are major oil producers.

---

use of military force if Iraq did not meet a withdrawal deadline of January 15, 1991.

Iraq did not withdraw, so Operation Desert Storm began on January 17. A UN coalition of 28 nations used overwhelming military power (mostly U.S.) to drive Iraq out of Kuwait. The coalition victory, however, did not end Saddam Hussein's control over Iraq. Nor did it bring peace to the region. UN forces had to protect the Kurds, a minority group within Iraq that had rebelled against Hussein's harsh rule. And UN inspection teams had to comb Iraq to ensure that Iraq was dismantling its nuclear, chemical, and biological weapons factories. In the late 1990's, Saddam forced the UN teams out. Experts believed that Iraq still contained many weapons factories.

7. Invasion of Iraq. In March 2003, U.S. and British forces invaded Iraq to end the dictatorship of Saddam Hussein. American President George W. Bush had warned that Saddam Hussein was developing weapons of mass destruction (WMDs). However, none were found. A 15-month investigation by the American-led Iraq Survey Group concluded in 2004 that Saddam Hussein had destroyed his WMDs in 1991, following the Persian Gulf War.

By early 2005, a temporary Iraqi government, empowered to write a constitution, had been elected. However, a violent insurgency, or revolt, aimed at toppling the government and driving the Americans and their allies out of Iraq, raged with no end in sight. Supporters of Saddam Hussein and his Baath (Nationalist) Party joined with Islamic fundamentalists and militants from other countries to launch suicide bombings, kidnappings, beheadings of captives, ambushes of convoys, and attacks on military and police personnel. As the numbers of those killed or maimed rose, opposition to the war in Iraq increased in the United States and around the world. In December 2005, Iraqi voters participated in an historic election for a four-year government.

CRITICAL THINKING

1. Evaluate the Persian Gulf War. Was it a complete or incomplete victory for the United States and the United Nations?

2. Write a letter to President George W. Bush telling him why you support or oppose the 2003 invasion of Iraq.

8. Latin America. Most Latin American nations gained their independence from European countries in the 19th century. Since then, they have struggled to create modern economies and stable governments.

Often the United States has become involved in these two struggles. It has given a great deal of economic and military aid to Latin American countries. It has worked to keep communism out of the area. It has tried to eradicate the drug trade. Moreover, many U.S. businesses have invested in Central and South America and in the Caribbean.

a. Cuba. Cuba provides a vivid example of U.S. involvement in the affairs of a Latin American nation. During the first half of the 20th century, U.S. interests owned many businesses in Cuba. They controlled the sugar industry, which still provides Cuba's

Fidel Castro in 1959.

main export crop. Then in 1959, Fidel Castro and his followers overthrew the Cuban government and came to power. Under Castro, a Marxist, the government took over U.S.-owned businesses. He sought economic help from the Soviet Union. Soviet aid enabled the Soviets to dominate Cuba.

In 1961, the United States backed an invasion of Cuba by a group of anti-Communist Cubans. They hoped to overthrow Castro, who had established himself as a dictator. This "Bay of Pigs" invasion failed because the people of Cuba did not support the U.S.-trained invaders.

The following year, the United States and the Soviet Union nearly went to war over Cuba. The Soviets had placed in Cuba missiles capable of carrying nuclear warheads to the United States. President John F. Kennedy demanded that Premier Nikita Khrushchev remove the missiles. After the United States ordered a naval blockade of the island nation, the Soviets finally agreed to Kennedy's demand. Soviet economic aid to Cuba continued until the breakup of the Soviet Union in 1991. The end of Soviet aid brought hardship to the Cuban people.

b. *Nicaragua.* Revolutions broke out in other Latin American countries as well. One place was Nicaragua. In 1979, the Sandinista National Liberation Front overthrew the U.S.-supported military dictatorship that had ruled the country for 50 years. The United States and some countries in Latin America opposed the Sandinistas because they were Marxists. The Sandinistas received aid from Cuba and sent arms to revolutionary groups in neighboring countries. In the 1980's, the United States aided anti-Sandinista groups. The *contras*, as they were called, fought to overthrow the Nicaraguan government, using weapons provided by the United States. Sandinista rule ended peacefully in 1990 with the election of Violeta Barrios de Chamorro, an opponent of the Sandinistas, as president of the country.

c. *Drug trafficking*. Drug trafficking is a major problem for several Latin American countries. Farmers in Colombia, Bolivia, and Peru grow coca because it yields high profits. The leaves from coca plants are made into cocaine, which is shipped through Colombia and Panama to the United States and elsewhere. The United States has tried to get the Colombian, Bolivian, and Peruvian governments to wipe out their coca crops, but has achieved only limited success. It has aided the government of Colombia, which has engaged in a violent struggle with brutal drug-producing organizations (narcoterrorists) and rebel groups. Right-wing paramilitary groups, originally formed to combat Marxist guerrillas, control much of Colombia's cocaine trade. They have killed thousands of civilians. Elected in 2002, President Álvaro Uribe has sought ways to end the violence. In mid-2005, Uribe's Justice and Peace Law created a framework for the voluntary disarming of both paramilitary groups and left-wing guerrillas.

d. *Haiti and elsewhere*. In the past, many people criticized the United States for supporting military dictatorships in Latin America. Recently, the United States has been opposing dictators in the area and working for democracy. In 1993, for example, the United States helped the exiled president of Haiti, Jean-Bertrand Aristide, negotiate an agreement for his return to Haiti. Although he had been democratically elected, Aristide was overthrown by the Haitian army. To ensure Aristide's return to office, and to maintain order, U.S. troops occupied Haiti in 1994. Aristide's successor, René Préval, was elected and took office without incident in 1996. Aristide was reelected in 2000 but was forced to resign and go into exile in 2004. Many Haitians blamed Aristide for allowing crushing poverty, corruption, and violence to continue. Haiti's vast economic and social problems have remained. While a small number of UN troops (which arrived in 2004) have tried to restore order, much of the country is controlled by private armed militias.

Other Latin American countries also had political and economic problems. An attempted military takeover in Venezuela failed in 1992. Labor strikes and rumors of a military coup troubled Bolivia. Peruvians suffered from terrorism, drug trafficking, and widespread poverty. Thousands of Peruvians were killed by a terrorist organization—the Shining Path.

Central America

1. Match each nation in Column A with its capital city in Column B.

Column A   **Column B**

1. Belize   *a.* Managua
2. Guatemala   *b.* Panama City
3. El Salvador   *c.* San José
4. Honduras   *d.* Belmopan
5. Nicaragua   *e.* San Salvador
6. Costa Rica   *f.* Guatemala City
7. Panama   *g.* Tegucigalpa

2. **EXPLAIN:** For reasons based on geography, the possible spread of communism in Central America was of concern to the United States during the Cold War.

From 1992 to 1993, Peru's President Alberto Fujimori, with military support, closed down Peru's congress and courts. Following a political scandal in 2000, Fujimori resigned. In 2001, Peruvians elected Alejandro Toledo as his successor. A business professor of Indian parentage, he had little political experience.

His efforts to sell government-owned businesses to private investors set off a popular revolt in 2002. More protests by civil service workers led to the resignation of Toledo's entire cabinet in 2003. The revival of the Shining Path movement further damaged Toledo's popularity, as did accusations of government corruption. By 2004, Toledo's approval rating had sunk to 10 percent.

e. *Mexico.* Elected president of Mexico in 2000, Vicente Fox faced many problems. Political assassinations and revolts by poor farmers had made the country extremely unstable. In 1995, a U.S. loan averted a fiscal crisis. High-ranking Mexican politicians had been accused of taking graft and aiding drug smuggling into the United States. Long-standing abuses of the Mexican justice system have been criticized by the UN high commissioner for human rights. These abuses include the torture of criminal suspects and the failure to protect vulnerable populations from discrimination and violent crime. A dramatic example of this has been the unsolved murders of hundreds of young women and girls in the past decade in Ciudad Juárez, a city on the U.S. border.

To assist Mexican immigrants, both legal and illegal, in 2004 Fox began to work with community leaders in the American Midwest. The Chicago-based Institute for Mexicans Abroad, which Fox established in 2004, has furthered the integration of a growing Mexican population into American businesses and schools.

Less successful was Fox's Puebla to Panama Plan, an economic development plan designed to benefit people in Mexico's poor southern states. Little has been accomplished to improve the lives of the poor there.

f. *Argentina.* Once-prosperous Argentina was hit by severe economic problems in the early 21st century. During most of the 1990's, Argentina's economy had grown rapidly. Much foreign investment took place. However, a recession began in 1998. By December 2001, however, inefficient industries, too much government spending, and a poor tax system had caused the collapse of Argentina's economy. Unemployment rose sharply. Thousands of people withdrew their money from banks until there was little money in circulation. To prevent further withdrawals, the government froze savings bank deposits for nine months. Finally, the government was forced to default on (declare it could not pay back) its public debt of $155 billion. By mid-2002, half of Argentina's 37 million people were living in poverty. In desperation, the government of President Eduardo Duhalde appealed for aid to the International Monetary Fund (IMF), the World Bank, and the Inter-American Bank. Meanwhile, millions of

Argentineans expressed their anger in strikes and street protests.

Elected president in 2003, Néstor Kirchner has led Argentina's economic recovery. Aided by rising prices for farm exports, the economic growth rate had reached 11 percent by mid-2004. This boosted tax revenues and made possible a fiscal surplus. In December 2005, Kirchner announced that Argentina had paid its debt to the IMF—$9.8 billion. Although unemployment has declined, more than half of all Argentineans remain below the poverty line.

ESSAY QUESTIONS

1. Why have U.S. leaders been concerned about events in Haiti and Peru?

2. Identify and explain *two* problems faced by President Vicente Fox of Mexico.

3. Explain why the government of Argentina appealed for aid to the International Monetary Fund and other agencies from 2001 to 2004.

9. Europe.   Although most of Europe was peaceful in the late 20th century, armed conflicts erupted in several places.

   a. *Northern Ireland.* Long-lasting differences disturbed Northern Ireland, a part of Great Britain located on the same island as the Republic of Ireland. Its inhabitants were divided into two main religious groups, Roman Catholics and Protestants. While many Roman Catholics wanted Northern Ireland to become part of the Republic of Ireland, many Protestants wanted it to remain part of Britain. Both sides sometimes turned to violence. The largest and most prominent terrorist organization has been the Irish Republican Army (IRA). Claiming to act in defense of Catholics and to be fighting for a united Ireland, the IRA has a long record of violent acts in Northern Ireland and England. Protestant groups such as the Ulster Defense Association (UDA) have bombed Catholic targets and carried out assassinations.

   In 1998, in the Good Friday peace accord, all sides agreed to determine Northern Ireland's future by democratic and peaceful means. But the newly elected Northern Ireland Assembly was suspended in February 2000 as Protestants pressed the IRA to surrender its weapons and Catholics demanded a new police service staffed by both Catholics and Protestants.

The peace process has suffered further setbacks. In Assembly elections of November 2003, the Democratic Unionist Party, led by Ian Paisley, won the largest number of seats. Paisley and his party have been bitter opponents of the Good Friday Accord. The situation worsened when the police accused the IRA of a $50 million bank robbery committed in Northern Ireland in December 2004. The IRA responded by announcing its withdrawal from peace negotiations in early 2005. Later that year, the IRA renounced violence.

b. _Russia._ Russia struggled to hold on to its territories. The most troublesome has been Chechnya, a small region in southern Russia. Here the mostly Muslim inhabitants declared their independence in 1994. Warfare broke out when Russian troops poured in. In 2000, Russia declared victory after destroying the Chechen capital of Grozny, but the rebels fought on. Chechen rebels were believed to be responsible for terrorist acts in Russia, including the February 2004 bombing of the Moscow subway and a September 2004 attack on a school.

Russian President Vladimir Putin's leadership has become increasingly authoritarian. One of his opponents, Mikhail Khodorkovsky, the billionaire head of the Yukos oil company, had funded political parties opposed to Putin. In May 2005, Khodorkovsky was sentenced to prison for fraud and tax evasion. This sentence has been regarded as Putin's message to Russian business leaders not to interfere in politics. President Putin also stopped the election of provincial governors. Instead, Putin appointed governors answerable to him.

Despite all the authoritarian methods of the government, Russia's market economy has continued to grow, partly because Russia's oil is in such demand.

c. _Balkan conflicts._ No area was more troubled than the Balkans, in southeastern Europe. The fall of communism in Eastern Europe led to a crisis in Yugoslavia, a union of six republics. The Communist Party ended its leading role there in 1990. The next year, the country was shaken when two republics, Croatia and Slovenia, declared their independence. Serbia, the largest of the republics, objected. Fighting between Serbs and Croats and among other ethnic groups exploded into a bloody civil war. In 1992, Bosnia and Herzegovina and Macedonia also declared their independence. Yugoslavia then consisted of just Serbia and Montenegro.

While the Croats and Serbs fought each other, both inflicted terrible damage on the Muslim population in Bosnia. The Serb

Kosovo rebel brigade, 1999.

policy of *ethnic cleansing* was especially brutal. Thousands of Muslims were killed, and thousands more became refugees. In 1995, under pressure from the United States and the United Nations, a peace agreement (the Dayton Accords) was reached by the warring factions. Bosnia was partitioned among the ethnic groups. Soldiers from NATO nations were dispatched to keep the peace and oversee free elections. They met considerable resistance from hard-core Serbian and Croatian nationalists. But elections were held, and a fragile peace prevailed.

Violence next broke out in Serbia itself. The southern province of Kosovo is inhabited mainly by ethnic Albanians—Muslims who speak Albanian. The Kosovars had some self-government until the late 1980's, when Serbia canceled it. Kosovar guerrillas, who had formed the Kosovar Liberation Army (KLA), then began a campaign for full independence.

In the late 1990's, the Serbian government launched an attack on the KLA, which soon turned into another program of ethnic cleansing. In a few months, as many as 1 million Kosovars were forced out of their homes, and villages were burned. Early in 1999, NATO launched air strikes against Belgrade, the Yugoslav capital. The Yugoslav government agreed to pull its troops out of Kosovo, and UN and NATO troops moved in to restore order. Although most refugees returned home, tensions have remained high in the region.

Early in 2001, ethnic violence spread to Macedonia, which borders Kosovo and the rest of Serbia on the south. Macedonia has a majority Serb population with an Albanian minority that has demanded more freedoms and limited self rule. Ethnic Albanian guerrillas launched attacks against government troops. NATO helped arrange a cease-fire in August 2001.

Serbian President Slobodan Milosevic was blamed for the ethnic cleansing tactics of Serbia's military forces. In the elections of September 2000, Vojislav Kostunica replaced him as president. In 2001, Milosevic was arrested and turned over to UN authorities for trial as a war criminal.

By 2005, the former Yugoslavia had been overrun by gangsters. This was especially true in Serbia, where security services allied with gangsters limited the powers of government. The U.S. and other Western governments have pressured the Serbian government to arrest mafia leaders.

POLITICAL CARTOON INTERPRETATION

Study the cartoon below and then answer the questions that follow.

Peace Process

1. Why do you think the cartoonist is in favor of the Multi-Party Agreement?

2. List the causes of violence in Northern Ireland.

3. Describe efforts to bring peace to the province.

SENTENCE COMPLETION

Complete each of the following sentences:

1. The peace process in Northern Ireland has been disrupted by —.

2. Acts of terrorism in Russia have resulted from that nation's war against —.

3. Violence in the Balkans has been caused by —.

GLOBAL ISSUES

In the late 20th and early 21st centuries, the world became interconnected as never before—a condition known as *globalization*. The popularity of hamburgers sold by American fast-food chains led to the expansion of cattle ranches in South America. Sneakers stitched in Indonesia were worn by Russians, and cars made in Mexico cruised the streets of Toronto. With globalization, national economies became more interdependent. Major issues that became global concerns included environmental destruction, population growth, use of natural resources, and human rights.

1. Population. The world's population has increased rapidly in the last 60 years. It has risen from 2.5 billion in 1950 to 6.5 billion today. Will it be possible to feed all these people? There are two main responses to this question. One is to increase the supply of food. The other is to slow down the growth of population.

  a. *Green revolution.* An important innovation was the "green revolution," which began in the 1950's. This was a combination of techniques aimed at making farmland more productive. The techniques included the development of new, high-yielding seeds for rice, wheat, and corn; greater use of fertilizers and pesticides; and improved irrigation. One result of the green revolution was an increase in the world's output of grain. It grew by 40 percent between 1950 and 1984.

  b. *Famines.* Despite improvements in farming technology, famine has remained one of the world's most persistent problems. From the 1970's to the 2000's, famines have swept through several African nations. In Ethiopia, Sudan, and Somalia, lack of rain-

Drought in North and Central Africa often causes famine. Here, Ethiopian refugees are fed and cared for.

fall, poor soil, poor means of transportation, and primitive technology have caused the deaths of thousands.

   c. *Population control.* Slowing population growth is a big issue in countries where women have many children. Most countries with high birthrates are less developed economically than the industrialized, or developed, countries. One reason for high birthrates has been that so many children died in infancy. As a country develops, however, health care improves and more children live. So some families may then turn to *birth control*—limiting reproduction by one means or another. One country that has promoted birth control is China, whose population reached 1.3 billion in 2005. To prevent increased growth, the Chinese government adopted a "one-couple, one-child" policy. It rewards couples that have only one child and punishes those that have more. Population growth in the developing countries slowed in the late 20th and the early 21st centuries. In Bangladesh, for example, the birthrate fell from 6.2 children per woman to 3.4 in the 1990s. Despite this, the world's population continues to grow.

   A major aim of people who worry about excess population is *zero population growth*, or ZPG. It occurs when the birthrate and death rate are equal.

   In the industrialized countries, declining birthrates are offset by longer life spans. This is due to improved medical services and economic conditions. Europeans live longer but are no longer having enough children to replace themselves when they die. As Europeans age, increased immigration may prove to be the only means of keeping their societies economically functional (by maintaining a balance of different age groups). Young people from Asia, Africa, and Latin America will be needed to offset the shrinkage of European populations. In the United States, a large pool of new immigrants already keeps the birthrate high—higher than in any other industrial country.

2. Natural Resources.   Most of the world's goods and services are produced in the industrial nations—mainly the United States, the countries of Europe, and Japan. Much of the world's raw materials —oil, copper, tin, rubber, and timber—are found in developing countries (those that do not yet have much heavy industry). A big problem faced by world leaders is bringing about a fair distribution of raw materials and finished goods among all the world's peoples.

Another problem is the depletion of those natural resources that are *nonrenewable*—ones that cannot be replaced once they are used up. Such resources include coal, oil, and copper. Oil shortages in the 1970's forced automobile companies to make cars that used less gasoline. Although oil became more plentiful in the 1980's, the world must still be concerned about the gradual reduction of the world's oil reserves. Someday there will be no more oil.

b.   *Alternative sources of energy.* Scientists continue to search for other sources of energy. *Solar energy* (the power of the sun) and *nuclear energy* (the power of the split atom) are strong

An oil rig in the Pacific Ocean off the Mexican coast.

alternatives. However, there are problems with each. Large-scale use of solar energy is not yet practical. And many people fear that nuclear energy is too dangerous. For example, an explosion at the Soviet nuclear power plant at Chernobyl in 1986 spread radiation over much of Europe.

c. *Pollution.* Non-nuclear pollution of the environment by factories, power plants, and motor vehicles has also become a major problem in both developed and developing nations. By the 1990's, atmospheric pollution had caused a annual thinning of the ozone layer over Antarctica and elsewhere. Scientists have warned that this loss of ozone allows more ultraviolet radiation to penetrate our atmosphere. This could cause increases in skin cancer and other illnesses.

Scientists have also warned of *global warming*, an increase in the temperature of the Earth's surface. As it continues, it causes changes in climate, the size of oceans, and the shape of the world's coastlines. In 2005, scientists noted the gradual melting of the polar ice cap. In recent years, many governments have begun to take steps to decrease air and water pollution. Experts also hope to reduce land pollution by finding new ways to dispose of garbage and chemical wastes.

The Kyoto Protocol of 1997 is the first international treaty to set binding limits on nations' emissions of carbon dioxide and five

Polluted air over Novokuznetsk, Russia. This Siberian city had a large steel plant. In 2004, Russia ratified the Kyoto Protocol.

other greenhouse gases. It calls upon industrialized nations to reduce emissions by 6 to 8 percent below 1990 levels by the year 2012. In March 2001, President George W. Bush rejected the Kyoto Protocol, but over 150 other nations have approved it.

MATCHING EXERCISE

Match each term in Column A with a description in Column B.

Column A	Column B
1. industrial nations	*a.* controlled power of split atoms
2. nonrenewable resources	
3. solar energy	*b.* increased heat on the Earth's surface
4. nuclear energy	
5. global warming	*c.* oil, copper, and coal
	d. the power of sunlight
	e. United States and Japan

3. Human Rights.   Beginning in the late 20th century, increased attention has been paid to such human rights as equality before the law, religious liberty, and freedom of expression. In some countries, repressive dictatorships have limited the rights of all citizens.

a. *Zimbabwe.*   The African country of Zimbabwe, for example, has had a dictatorship since 1987. Ruled by President Robert Mugabe and his ZANU-PF Party, its government has been condemned by the international community for human rights abuses. Political opponents have been repressed, often with violence. Journalists critical of Mugabe's government have been imprisoned and tortured. Farmlands have been expropriated and given to military and political officials.

b. *Cuba.*   Fidel Castro's Cuba is a dictatorship too, but a Communist one. Only the Communist Party and Communist newspapers are allowed. The government has imprisoned thousands of opponents.

c. *South Africa and Russia.*   Sometimes a powerful minority may discriminate against a weak majority. This happened in South Africa under the system of apartheid. More commonly, a majority discriminates against one or more minorities. This was the case for decades in the Soviet Union. Jews were prevented from practicing their religion freely and were barred from high-level jobs in government and industry. After the collapse of the

Soviet Union in the early 1990's, the various republics granted Jews full human rights.

d. ***Kurds.*** In the Middle East, a minority group known as the Kurds have demanded more political power. In fact, many Kurds would like to have their own country. They live in adjacent areas of five nations: Iraq, Iran, Armenia, Syria, and Turkey. In each country, a Kurdish separatist movement has been suppressed by the respective government. The American and British invasion of Iraq in March 2003 gave the Kurds of that country an opportunity to be represented in a new, more democratically elected government.

e. ***Palestinians.*** Palestinian Arabs in Israel, Jordan, and Kuwait have also demanded more political power. For example, the Palestinian citizens of the West Bank, under Israeli military control since 1967, have tried to halt further Israeli settlements in the area. They have also demanded an end to the Israeli occupation of the West Bank. In 2005, the Israeli government agreed to withdraw its settlements from Gaza and some West Bank areas. It was hoped this decision would further peace negotiations with the Palestinian Authority.

f. ***Women.*** As a group, women have been discriminated against in most societies—frequently unable to vote, to own property, or to take full advantage of economic and educational opportunities. In the late 20th century, women in the developed countries—and in some developing countries as well—gained a wide range of human rights. They served as prime minister (Margaret Thatcher of Britain, Indira Gandhi of India), as president (Kumaratunga of Sri Lanka), and as cabinet officials (Secretary of State Condoleezza Rice of the United States). But in most Muslim countries, women generally are forbidden to vote, hold public office, inherit property, or travel alone.

g. ***Terrorism.*** A special issue affecting human rights is *terrorism*—the use of violence, or the threat of violence, to achieve political or social goals. Both Roman Catholics and Protestants in Northern Ireland have set off bombs that killed innocent civilians. So have Palestinian Arabs protesting Israeli rule in the Middle East. Other terrorist acts have included the bombing of Pan Am Flight 103 over Scotland in 1988, the bombing of the World Trade Center in New York City in 1993, the destruction of a federal office building in Oklahoma City in 1995, and the bombing of U.S. embassies in Kenya and Tanzania in 1998.

The most devastating terrorist attacks on the United States took place on September 11, 2001. Terrorists hijacked four

Prime Minister Margaret Thatcher

Margaret Thatcher with her successor as prime minister, John Major.

In 1979, Margaret Hilda Thatcher (b. 1925) became Great Britain's first woman prime minister. The leader of the Conservative Party, Thatcher became prime minister after the Conservatives defeated the Labour Party in the 1979 general elections. She retained her position for a long time—until 1990.

Thatcher, a graduate of Oxford University, was trained as a chemist. In 1953, however, she became a lawyer specializing in taxes. Elected to the House of Commons in 1959, Thatcher was secretary of state for education and science from 1970 to 1974. In 1975, she became the first woman to head a major British political party when the Conservatives elected her as their leader.

Prime Minister Thatcher worked to solve Britain's worst economic problems—inflation and unemployment. To slow the high rate of inflation, she reduced government spending. As a result, the rate of inflation slowed, but unemployment rose. The problems continued.

Another great challenge was the violence between Catholics and Protestants in Northern Ireland (part of the United Kingdom). Britain and Ireland worked together to try to solve the problem. In 1986, an agreement was signed by the two governments. It provided for consultation between Britain and Ireland in the making of policies for Northern Ireland.

In the area of foreign policy, Thatcher was committed to strengthening the British role in NATO and the Common Market. In 1982, Great Britain became involved in a brief war with Argentina. Argentina had seized the British-ruled Falkland Islands located 300 miles off Argentina's shore. In the conflict that followed, Britain recovered the Falklands. President Ronald Reagan of the United States supported the British prime minister during that war.

In turn, Thatcher supported many of the foreign policies of the United States. For example, both nations denounced terrorism. Her decision to allow U.S. bombers to raid Libya from

British bases in 1986 drew much praise from her American allies.

Economic problems ultimately led to Thatcher's resignation, in 1990. John Major, another Conservative Party leader, succeeded her. Many Britons regard Thatcher to have been an effective and courageous prime minister.

Why do many people consider Margaret Thatcher to be a remarkable person?

commercial airliners. They flew two planes into the twin towers of the World Trade Center in New York City, destroying the buildings. A third plane damaged the Pentagon near Washington, D.C. The fourth plane crashed in Pennsylvania. It is estimated that more than 2,800 people died in these events.

American leaders linked Osama bin Laden to the attacks. The Islamic extremist bin Laden leads Al Qaeda, an organization that recruits and trains anti-Western terrorists. Bin Laden had been suspected of organizing the 1998 attacks on U.S. embassies in Africa. Since Al Qaeda's base of operations was in Afghanistan in 2001, President George W. Bush asked that nation's Taliban rulers to give up bin Laden. When they refused to do so, Bush declared war. Aided by countries near Afghanistan, U.S. troops ousted the Taliban rulers but did not capture bin Laden. The Afghan people then elected a more democratic regime. Nevertheless, rival Afghan warlords and the Afghans' extreme poverty have made difficult that country's transition to a working democracy.

Besides the large number of victims, the attacks on the United States seriously damaged the economy and shook Americans' confidence in their security. President Bush set up a new Cabinet-level Office of Homeland Security. Congress gave existing agencies, such as the FBI, greater freedom to investigate people and organizations suspected of terrorist links.

ESSAY QUESTIONS

1. Provide *two* examples of human rights being abused.

2. Describe the impact of terrorism on the United States in the 1990's and early 2000's.

4. Technological Transformations. By the 21st century, advances in technology had transformed both transportation and communication. People, goods, and news could travel around the world in far less time than had been possible just a few decades earlier.

a. *Transportation.* Transportation has come to rely to a great extent on motor vehicles, especially cars and trucks. In developed countries, almost every family has at least one car, and many have two or more. Automobile travel has resulted in networks of highways and the growth of suburbs. It has also led to the decline of central cities and an increase in air pollution.

Air travel, especially jet planes, has made it possible to go thousands of miles in just a few hours. People routinely take planes where they used to rely on trains or ships.

b. *Communication.* In the second half of the 20th century, developments in the field of electronics were so important that they were called a communication revolution. Beginning in the 1950's, television sets entered millions of homes—first broadcasting in black and white and then in color. Later, television viewing was supplemented by recording devices such as videocassette recorders and DVDs. Even more innovative was the computer, which can store huge amounts of data and process it in seconds. By the 1970's, computers were being used for everything from booking airline seats to pouring steel. The next development was the Internet, an international network that linked computers (whether commercial, institutional, or personal) by telephone or cable on the World Wide Web. The explosive growth of the Internet is indicated by this statistic: In 1992, there were 50 Web sites (addresses) on the Internet; by 2004,

Computers are used in all types of businesses.

there were more than 63 million of them. One of the most convenient uses of the Internet has been e-mail, by which people can communicate around the world in seconds for the price of a local phone call.

Another new communication device is the cellular telephone. Since these phones transmit calls by radio waves, people can carry them wherever they go. By 2005, the number of cell-phone users had risen to more than 140 million. In addition, cell phones have been given a variety of new designs and innovative features. Cell phones now often have color screens and built-in cameras. Voice calls have been supplemented with text messaging, music, and games. The BlackBerry e-mail hand-held device, to which telephone functions have been added, is a popular example.

CRITICAL THINKING

PROVE or DISPROVE: Computers control every aspect of modern economic, political, and social life.

5. Space Exploration.   In 1957, the Soviet Union startled the world by launching the first artificial satellite. Called *Sputnik I*, it orbited the Earth. The United States responded by speeding up its own space exploration program. The first U.S. satellite, *Explorer I*, was launched in 1958.

U.S. astronaut Edwin Aldrin walks on the moon in 1969 (*left*). *Pathfinder* photograph of its land rover exploring the Martian landscape in 1997 (*right*).

a. ***Manned space flight.*** The Soviets put the first person into space. In 1961, cosmonaut Yuri Gagarin orbited the Earth. The following year, astronaut John Glenn became the first American to orbit the Earth. In 1969, the United States landed two men on the moon.

b. ***Unmanned satellites.*** Human travel has not been the main advantage of space exploration. Unmanned satellites have brought the greatest benefits. Orbiting satellites transmit television, telephone, and radio signals around the earth. This has greatly improved communications. Orbiting cameras have made weather forecasting more accurate.

Since 1986, space stations have continuously orbited the Earth. Astronauts in space stations have enough room and time to conduct experiments in the gravity-free environment of space. In 1997, American astronauts aided Russian astronauts in repairing their damaged space station *Mir.* Eventually, *Mir* was abandoned. The *International Space Station* (ISS) has been under construction since 1998. It is designed to house rotating teams of up to seven researchers from the United States and other nations. In June 2004, an American and a Russian astronaut conducted repairs to the exterior of the ISS while maneuvering in space suits. Space shuttles travel between the ISS and Earth.

The United States introduced the reusable space shuttle in the 1980's. A combination space capsule and airplane, the space shuttle *Columbia* completed its first mission in 1981. In 1999, *Columbia* deployed the Chandra X-Ray Observatory. This is a telescope designed to study the far-distant universe. In March 2002, the crew of another shuttle flight made several improvements to the Hubble Space Telescope. Among these was the installation of a new camera that takes sharper, more detailed pictures of the universe than the one it replaced. Following the explosion of the *Columbia* in 2003, shuttle flights were suspended. Another shuttle, *Discovery,* resumed flights to the ISS in 2005.

c. ***Unmanned probes to other planets.*** Exploration missions to other planets have provided important information. The spacecraft *Galileo*, launched in 1989, studied the planet Jupiter and its moons. In 1997, the *Pathfinder* landed on Mars and sent back detailed photographs of the planet's surface. In mid-2004, the *Cassini* spacecraft completed a 2.2-billion-mile journey to Saturn of nearly seven years. Orbiting the planet, it transmitted striking pictures of the planet's ice and rock rings.

IDENTIFICATIONS

Identify each of the following:

a. *Sputnik I*   e. *Columbia*
b. *Explorer I*   f. *Galileo*
c. *Mir*   g. *Pathfinder*
d. ISS   h. *Cassini*

6. Science.   Many scientific researchers worked to combat diseases.

   a. *Antibiotics.*   An important new weapon of the 20th century, the group of drugs known as *antibiotics*, began with the 1928 discovery of penicillin by British scientist Alexander Fleming. Penicillin and other antibiotics stop the growth of bacteria and thus cure such illnesses as tuberculosis. Antibiotics have also saved lives by preventing infections after surgery.

   b. *AIDS research.*   A new challenge to medical science was AIDS, which first became widely recognized in the 1980's. Spread mainly by sexual contact and infected needles, it apparently originated in Africa and then spread throughout the world. By 2004, some 20 million people had died from AIDS, and approximately 40 million worldwide were infected with the disease. Many of these were doomed as well, since the drugs known to halt progress of the disease are too expensive for most people in developing countries. In 2001, drug companies began to lower prices of AIDS drugs sold to some of these countries. In that same year, clinics that were able to treat AIDS patients inexpensively began to open in remote places throughout the world.

   c. *Lasers.*   Another scientific tool that became widely used in the late 20th century is the *laser*, invented in 1960. Laser beams store energy and release it in an intense beam of light. The beam remains straight, narrow, and very concentrated, even after it has traveled millions of miles. Lasers have many uses. They are used in surgery to repair damaged tissue and remove growths. They measure distances, such as the distance from Earth to the moon. They help engineers on construction projects. They make possible precision cutting of hard substances, such as diamonds. Lasers also send radio, television, and telephone signals through space.

   d. *DNA research.*   In the 1950's, American and British scientists discovered the structure of DNA (deoxyribonucleic acid). DNA is a basic part of *genes*, the small biological units that carry physical traits, such as height and eye color, from parents to children. Understanding DNA helps us to understand how genes are put together. Scientists called this "genetic coding."

In the 1980's, DNA experimenters came closer to explaining how different life-forms are created. This made possible new research into viruses, bacteria, human cells, and diseases such as cancer. DNA experiments may lead to major advances in treating illness. By the 1990's, "genetic engineers" were designing improved food crops and livestock.

One of the most exciting breakthroughs occurred in 1996, when British scientists succeeded in *cloning* a living creature—that is, growing a complete organism from genetic material of another. Using DNA from a sheep, they created in a laboratory a second animal that was genetically the same as the first. Despite some objections on religious grounds, experimentation with cloning has continued. Creating new colonies of stem cells that match the DNA of their donors is necessary to achieve the goal of growing replacement tissues for conditions like spinal cord injuries and juvenile diabetes and congenital immune deficiencies.

In 2005, U.S. President George W. Bush announced that he would veto legislation that allowed public financing for research on stem cells created with newly harvested human eggs. President Bush also expressed his opposition to human cloning. Both the controversy over stem cell research and the development of new medical technologies continues.

A breakthrough in the field of genetics occurred in 2001. Two different scientific teams—the International Human Genome Sequencing Consortium and Celera Genomics—succeeded in mapping the human genome (the code of all human DNA). Mapping the human genome will help doctors identify people susceptible to hereditary diseases. They can then teach those people how to reduce their chances of developing the diseases. Also, chemists can use the new knowledge to make drugs suited to the genetic makeup of specific individuals.

Chapter Review

MULTIPLE-CHOICE

Choose the item that best completes each sentence.

1. To stimulate its economy, China encouraged (*a*) government-owned businesses (*b*) foreign investment and private enterprise (*c*) greater democracy (*d*) higher consumer prices.

2. An African nation ruled by a white minority until 1994 was (*a*) Kenya (*b*) Tanzania (*c*) Ethiopia (*d*) South Africa.

3. The movement to set up a Jewish homeland, or state, is called (*a*) Zionism (*b*) Socialism (*c*) Marxism (*d*) Communism.

4. The Arab nations of the Middle East have fought repeated wars against (*a*) the United States (*b*) the Soviet Union (*c*) Israel (*d*) Iran.

5. OPEC is powerful because it controls (*a*) Arab military forces (*b*) the quantities and prices of oil produced and sold (*c*) transportation and communication in the Middle East (*d*) the foreign policies of Middle Eastern nations.

6. Countries that had civil wars in the 1990's were (*a*) Japan and Taiwan (*b*) Norway and Sweden (*c*) Congo and Sudan (*d*) Zambia and South Africa.

7. A nation accused of attempting to spread communism throughout Latin America was (*a*) Paraguay (*b*) Argentina (*c*) Brazil (*d*) Cuba.

8. A nation criticized for giving support to military dictators in Latin America was (*a*) Canada (*b*) the United States (*c*) the United Kingdom (*d*) France.

9. Two Latin American nations beset by major political troubles in the 1990's and the 2000's are (*a*) Brazil and Chile (*b*) Haiti and Peru (*c*) Costa Rica and Argentina (*d*) Paraguay and Uruguay.

10. During the late 20th and 21st centuries, two world problems that concern many people have been (*a*) the environment and human rights (*b*) declining population and temperatures (*c*) colonialism and civil wars (*d*) entangling alliances and imperialism.

CHART INTERPRETATION

Study the table on page 547 and then explain the following statement: "One of the major tasks of the 21st century is to bring the standards of education, health, and general welfare that are enjoyed by people in the industrialized nations to the rest of the world."

 ## MATCHING EXERCISE

Match the person in Column A with the correct description in Column B.

Column A	Column B
1. Alexander Fleming	a. first person in space
2. Anwar Sadat	b. first American to orbit earth
3. Ayatollah Khomeini	c. Iranian religious leader
4. Margaret Thatcher	d. discoverer of penicillin
5. Theodor Herzl	e. British prime minister, 1979–1990
6. John Glenn	f. founder of Zionism
7. Yuri Gagarin	g. president of Mexico, 2000–2006
8. Vicente Fox	h. president of Egypt, 1970–1981

CRITICAL THINKING

1. Reread "3. Human Rights," on pages 536–537, 539. Then explain why you AGREE or DISAGREE with the following statement: "Violence is not a good way to increase human rights."

2. Reread "5. Space Exploration," on pages 541–542. Then explain why you AGREE or DISAGREE with the following statement: "Sending astronauts into space is more helpful to scientific research than are unmanned space flights."

3. Reread "6. Science," on pages 543–544. Then explain why you AGREE or DISAGREE with the following statement: "Regardless of the medical benefits, stem cell research is morally wrong and should be stopped."

More Developed and Less Developed Countries: Measuring the Differences

Region or Country	Per Capita GDP (U.S. Dollars)	Infant Mortality (per 1,000)	Life Expectancy (years)	Literacy Rate (percent)	Energy Consumption Per Capita (kilowatt-hrs.)	2001 Population (millions)	Annual Population Growth Rate (percent)	Projected Population 2050 (millions)	Percent of GDP Devoted to Agriculture
More Developed Countries	$26,283	5.8	74.9	n.a.	8,038.0	995.0	0.2	1,014.0	2.3
Less Developed Countries	440	93.3	50.5	45.0	68.5	4,865.0	1.1	8,141.0	30.8
Bangladesh	$2000	62.6	62.08	43.1	142.8	144.3	2.09	254.6	20.5
Brazil	8,100	29.6	71.6	86.4	1,091.0	186.1	1.06	233.2	5.2
China	5,600	24.1	72.2	90.9	903.0	1,306.0	0.5	1,395.2	15.0
Egypt	4,200	32.5	71.0	57.7	728.0	77.5	1.78	127.4	15.0
Ethiopia	800	95.3	48.8	42.7	291.0	73.0	2.3	170.9	46.1
Germany	28,700	4.2	78.6	94.0	4,178.0	82.4	0.0	79.1	1.0
India	3,100	56.2	64.3	59.5	508.0	1,080.0	1.4	1,531.4	22.0
Indonesia	3,500	35.6	69.5	87.9	692.0	241.9	1.4	280.0	35.0
Japan	29,400	3.3	81.1	99.0	4111.5	127.4	0.05	109.7	3.4
Kenya	1,100	61.4	47.9	85.1	514.0	33.8	2.56	6.5	37.0
Malaysia	9,700	17.7	72.2	88.7	2080.0	23.9	1.8	33.3	34.0
Mexico	9,600	20.9	75.1	92.2	1537.0	106.2	1.17	130.0	4.0
South Korea	14,200	7.6	75.0	97.9	4968.0	48.4	0.3	50.7	7.0
Russia	9,800	15.0	67.0	99.0	4218.0	143.3	-.37	144.4	9.0
Switzeralnd	33,800	4.3	80.0	99.0	3688.0	7.4	.49	6.3	1.0
United States	40,100	6.5	77.0	97.0	12,399.0	295.7	.92	331.0	2.0

Sources: CIA World Fact Book, 2005, World Development Report, 2005.

WORD GROUPS

Rearrange each of the following word groups into complete sentences:

1. The population 20th late the in century increased rapidly world's

2. decreases Governments and water begun to air take pollution steps in to require have

3. dictatorships some In limit all repressive the of citizens' countries rights

4. reusable the introduced United space 1980's shuttle The States in the

DOCUMENT-BASED QUESTION

This question is based on the accompanying documents (1–5). It will improve your ability to work with historical documents.

Historical Context:

Since the end of the Cold War, the world has become interconnected as never before in history. It has been transformed by the spread of democracy, advances in technology, the growth of a global economy, and the rise of international terrorism.

Task:

Using information from the documents and your knowledge of world history, answer the questions that follow each document. Your answers to each question will help you write the document-based essay.

Document 1. Excerpt from *Silent Spring* (1962) by Rachel Carson, a marine biologist who was one of the first Americans to speak about environmental issues:

> [N]ew chemicals come from our laboratories in an endless stream; almost five hundred annually find their way into actual use in the United States alone. . . . 500 new chemicals to which the bodies of men and animals are required somehow

to adapt each year, chemicals totally outside the limits of biologic experience.

Along with the possibility of the extinction of mankind by nuclear war, the central problem of our age has therefore become the contamination of man's total environment with such substances of incredible potential for harm.

> **Source**: Rachel Carson, *Silent Spring*. Boston: Houghton Mifflin, 1962, pp. 7–8.

According to this document, why was Carson concerned for the future of humankind?

Document 2.   Excerpt from "Message to the Pilgrims," a speech by Ayatollah Ruhollah Khomeini of Iran, on September 13, 1980:

Muslims the world over who believe in the truth of Islam, arise and gather beneath the banner of tauhid [divine unity] and the teachings of Islam! Repel the treacherous superpowers from your countries and your abundant resources. Restore the glory of Islam, and abandon your selfish disputes and differences, for you possess everything! Rely on the culture of Islam, resist Western imitation, and stand on your own feet. Attack those intellectuals who are infatuated with the West and the East, and recover your true identity.

> **Source**: Khomeini, Imam. *Islam and Revolution*, translated and annotated by Hamid Algar. Berkeley, CA: Mizan Press, 1981, p. 304.

According to this document, what did Khomeini want Muslims to do?

Document 3.   Excerpt from "Inaugural Address of President Nelson Mandela," May 10, 1994, following South Africa's first multiracial election:

Out of the experience of an extraordinary human disaster [apartheid] that lasted too long, must be born a society of which all humanity will be proud. Our daily deeds as ordinary South Africans must produce an actual South African reality that will reinforce humanity's belief in justice, strengthen its confidence in the nobility of the human soul and sustain all our hopes for a glorious life for all.

We must, therefore, act together as a united people, for national reconciliation, for nation building, for the birth of a new world. Let there be justice for all. Let there be peace for all. Let there be work, bread, water and salt for all. Let each know that for each the body, the mind and the soul have been freed to fulfill themselves. . . . Let freedom reign.

Source: "Inaugural Address of Nelson Mandela," May 10, 1994. Found at: http://www.sa-venues.com/nelson_mandela.htm.

According to this document, what was Mandela calling upon all South Africans, black and white, to accomplish?

Document 4. Excerpt from *The Crisis of Global Capitalism* (1998) by international financier George Soros, discussing the world's economy:

> The development of a global economy has not been matched by the development of a global society. The basic unit for political and social life remains the nation-state. International law and international institutions, insofar as they exist, are not strong enough to prevent war or the large-scale abuse of human rights in individual countries. Ecological threats are not adequately dealt with.
>
> To put the matter simply, market forces, if given complete authority . . . produce chaos and could ultimately lead to the downfall of the global capitalist system. . . .
>
> The world has entered a period of profound imbalance in which no individual state can resist the power of global financial markets and there are practically no institutions for rule making on an international scale. Collective decision-making mechanisms for the global economy simply do not exist.

Source: Soros, George, *The Crisis of Global Capitalism*. NY: Public Affairs, 1998, pp. xix–xx, xxvii–xxviii.

According to this document, what did Soros suggest is needed to bring order to the global economy?

Document 5. Look at the chart on page 547.

What does it indicate are major differences between the more developed nations and the less developed nations?

DOCUMENT-BASED ESSAY

Using information from the above documents and your knowledge of world history, write an essay in which you:

- Discuss how the world has been transformed since the end of the Cold War.
- Assess the extent to which the global community has adapted to political, social, and scientific changes.

REFERENCE SECTION

REGIONAL MAPS

Europe

BARENTS SEA

NORWEGIAN SEA

ICELAND
⊛ Reykjavik

ATLANTIC OCEAN

SWEDEN

FINLAND

RUSSIA

NORWAY

Helsinki ⊛

ESTONIA

Oslo ⊛   Stockholm ⊛

⊛ Tallinn

Moscow ⊛

LATVIA

LITHUANIA

⊛ Riga

SCOTLAND

DENMARK

NORTH SEA

N. IRELAND

Copenhagen ⊛

BALTIC SEA

Vilnius ⊛

⊛ Minsk

Dublin ⊛   GREAT BRITAIN

IRELAND

NETH.

Berlin ⊛

Warsaw ⊛

BELARUS

ENGLAND

WALES

London ⊛

⊛ Amsterdam
The Hague

Kiev ⊛

POLAND

UKRAINE

English Channel

Brussels ⊛

GERMANY

BELGIUM

THE
CZECH
REPUBLIC

⊛ Prague

SLOVAKIA

MOLDOVA

Chisinau ⊛

Paris ⊛

LUX.

Bratislava ⊛

SWITZ.

Vienna ⊛

Budapest ⊛

Bern ⊛

AUSTRIA HUNGARY

RUMANIA

Bay of Biscay

FRANCE

Ljubljana ⊛

SLOVENIA

⊛ Zagreb

Bucharest ⊛

BLACK SEA

Sarajevo ⊛

⊛ Belgrade

CROATIA

BULGARIA

⊛ Sofia

PORTUGAL

Madrid ⊛

ITALY

CORSICA

⊛ Rome

Tirana ⊛

⊛ Skopje
MACEDONIA

TURKEY

Lisbon ⊛

SPAIN

SARDINIA

ALBANIA

GREECE

BALEARIC IS.

BOSNIA
AND
HERZEGOVINA

SERBIA
AND
MONTENEGRO

⊛ Athens

SICILY

CRETE

AFRICA

MALTA

MEDITERRANEAN SEA

N
W E
S

⊛ Capital City

| 0 | 200 | 400 | 600 | Kilometers |

| 0 | | 200 | | 400 | Miles |

553

Africa

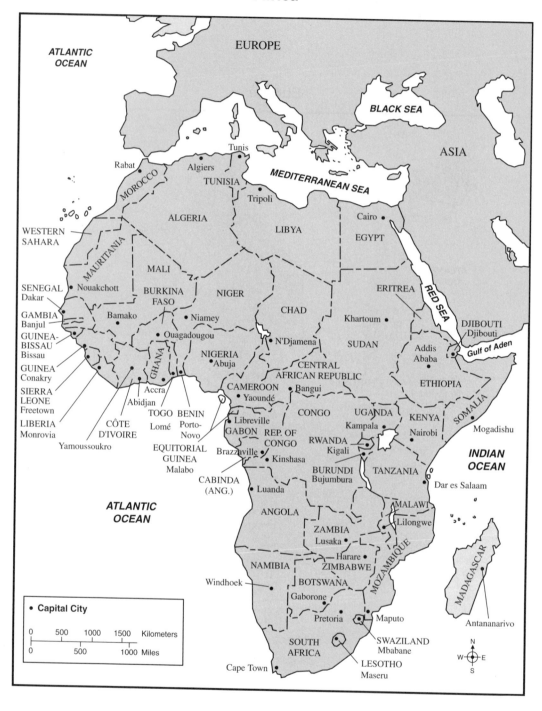

North and South America

Asia and Australia

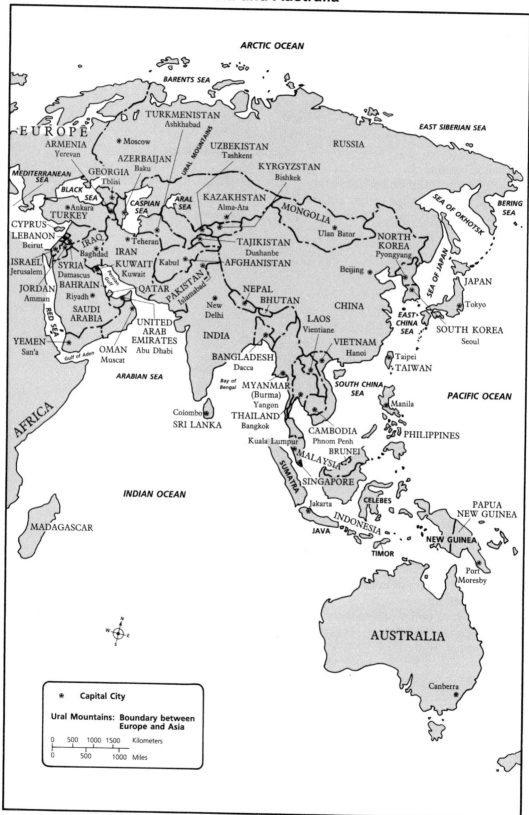

GLOSSARY

abacus   early Chinese adding machine

abolitionist   a person acting to end slavery

absolute monarch   a hereditary ruler with nearly unlimited power who claimed to derive his or her authority from God

adobe   sun-dried bricks used to build houses

aediles   Roman mayors

Age of Metals   a period of history, beginning about 5,000 years ago, in which human beings learned to make wide use of metal for tools and weapons

alphabet   the letters used in writing a language

anarchy   a state of lawlessness, confusion, or disorder

anesthetic   a drug causing temporary loss of sensation

Anschluss   a political union between Nazi Germany and Austria in 1938

anthropologist   a scientist who studies human beings—their physical characteristics, origins, cultures, and artifacts

antibiotic   a substance used to kill or prevent the growth of harmful bacteria

antiseptic   a substance that checks the growth or action of microorganisms in a living tissue

apartheid   a policy of racial segregation practiced in the Republic of South Africa

apostle   one of the 12 men chosen by Jesus Christ to spread his ideas

appeasement   giving in to someone in order to avoid conflict

archbishop   a bishop of highest rank

archdiocese   the area in which an archbishop is in charge

archeologist   a scientist who deals with past human life and activities as shown by the monuments and relics left by ancient peoples

archipelago   a group of islands

aristocracy   a state ruled by nobles

artifact   an object made by human beings, especially a simply, primitive object

assembly line   a grouping of machines and workers so arranged that work passes from one to another in direct line until the finished product has been made

astrologer   a person who studies the stars to predict future events

astronomer   a scientist who studies the heavenly bodies

atheism   the belief that there is no God

balance of power   an equal amount of power between two nations or groups of nations sufficient to prevent any one from becoming strong enough to make war or impose its will upon another

banknote   paper money

bard   a Celtic person especially trained to memorize and recite poems about great events and the deeds of heroes

bill of exchange   a written document ordering the paying of money to someone

Bill of Rights, English   a declaration that Parliament has more power than the monarchs of England and that individuals have certain rights

Bill of Rights, U.S.   a summary of fundamental rights and privileges for the people against violation by the state

bipedalism   using or having two feet

birth control   method(s) to limit reproduction

bishop   a church official who oversees many religions denominations

blacklisting making a list of workers branded as troublemakers or undesirables to be circulated among other employers

blitzkrieg a violent and lightning-like military offensive

bourgeoisie middle class

bronze a metal produced by mixing copper and tin

Bushido the Japanese code of feudal chivalry emphasizing loyalty and valuing honor above life

caliph a title used by Muslim rulers

calligraphy a writing system to represent words or ideas

canon law the body of laws governing the Roman Catholic Church

capitalism a system under which the ownership of land and wealth is for the most part in the hands of private individuals

cardinal a high official in the Roman Catholic Church

caste system the division of Aryan society into four major groups, each with special work assigned to it

cavalry soldiers mounted on horseback

checks and balances the ways in which one branch of government influences and limits the actions of other branches

city-state an independent city governing itself and the territory surrounding it

civilization a way of life that has reached an advanced stage of social development

civil service a process of hiring and promoting government employees based on competitive tests

Classical Age the period in history, from about 500 to 323 B.C., when Greek civilization reached its highest point of development

cloning making an identical copy of an organism

collective bargaining negotiations between an employer and union representatives, usually on wages, hours, and working conditions

collective farm in Communist countries, a large, government-run farm populated by many families

command economy one in which decisions to allocate resources are made by the government

common law the body of law developed in England primarily from judicial decisions based on custom and precedent

Commonwealth the republic of England from the death of Charles I in 1649 to 1653

communism a system of social organization that provides for common ownership of the means of production and strives for an equal distribution of the products of industry

congress a formal meeting of delegates for discussion and action

conscription forcing people into armed forces

conservative a person opposed to sudden or radical changes in government policies; supports traditional order

consul one of the two officials at the head of the government of ancient republican Rome

containment the policy of preventing the expansion of a hostile power or ideology

convent an area where nuns live

Counter-Reformation the reform movement in the Roman Catholic Church following the Reformation

Critical Period the years 1781–1789 in U.S. history between the Revolution and adoption of the Constitution

Cro-Magnon a presapien closer in physical appearance and mental ability to people today than was any other early ancestor

crusade one of the military expeditions undertaken by Christian countries in the 11th, 12th, and 13th centuries to recover the Holy Land from Muslims

cultural diffusion the spread of ideas, customs, values, and beliefs among different cultures

cuneiform a system of writing that used wedge-shaped characters

czar   the title used by the male rulers of Russia, 1547–1917

daimyo   a class of powerful landowner in Japan in the feudal period

democracy   a system of government in which the people rule

détente   a relaxation of strained relations or tensions

dialogue   a conversation between two or more persons

dictator   in ancient Rome a man chosen by the consuls to rule in times of emergency

Diet   the lawmaking body of Japan

dike   a bank of earth keeping a river from overflowing

direct democracy   a system of government in which the citizens themselves, not their representatives, participate in making major decisions

dividend   a share of profits distributed to stockholders

Dollar Diplomacy   diplomacy used by a country to promote its financial or commercial interests abroad

domestic system   manufacturing by workers in their homes using raw materials supplied by their employers

druid   a Celtic priest or learned man

dynamo   electric generator

dynasty   a series of rulers of the same family or line of descent

economics   the study of the production, distribution, and consumption of goods and services

emir   a Muslim prince

empire   a group of territories or peoples under one ruler

enclosure movement   the practice among large landowners in Britain during the 1700's of fencing off common lands for their own use

Enlightenment (Age of Reason)   the period of the 1700's in Europe when philosophers emphasized the use of reason as the best way to learn truths

environment   the physical surroundings in which human beings and other creatures live

ephor   one of five officials who exercised the greatest power in the government of ancient Sparta

equestrian   a middle class businessperson in ancient Rome

Estates General   a legislative assembly of clergy, nobility, and commoners in France

ethnic cleansing   the removal of an ethnic group from an area by force and terror

evolution   the theory that the various kinds of animals and plants now existing have developed from previously existing kinds and that all animals and plants are descended from simple forms

excommunication   exclusion from communion with or membership in the Church

exploit   to make use of people or objects for one's own advantage, sometimes unfairly

extraterritorial rights   those exempting foreigners from the jurisdiction of local laws or tribunals

factory system   the production of goods in factories instead of in workers' homes

fasces   a bundle of rods surrounding an ax, used as a symbol of authority by the ancient Romans as well as by the Fascist party in Italy in the 20th century

Fertile Crescent   a large arc of land that starts at the eastern end of the Mediterranean Sea and curves northeastward and then southeastward, ending at the Persian Gulf

fief (or feud)   the land granted to a vassal for his own use by a feudal lord

flint   a very hard stone used by early human beings to make tools and weapons

friar   a member of a religious order

Führer   leader; the title used by Adolf Hitler

gene   a specialized structure in a cell nucleus that carries hereditary characteristics from parent to offspring

genocide the deliberate extermination of a whole racial, religious, or cultural group

glacier a large body of ice moving slowly down a slope or over a wide area of land

glasnost the policy of opening up Soviet society and political process by granting greater freedoms

globalization increased movement of goods, people, and funds among countries all over the world

global warming a theory that world-wide temperatures are gradually increasing

Glorious Revolution the series of events that ended the reign of King James II of England and brought William and Mary to the throne

Greco-Roman formed by the blending of ancient Greek and Roman cultural elements

guillotine a machine used to cut off a person's head

habeas corpus a writ obtained for the purpose of bringing a person before a court

Hellenistic Age the period in ancient Greek history between 336 and 30 B.C.

helot a slave in ancient Sparta

hegira Muhammad's departure from Mecca to Medina

heresy a religious opinion or teaching contrary to the accepted beliefs of the Church

hieroglyph a picture or symbol used by the ancient Egyptians to represent a sound, a word, or an idea

historic period the extent of time since the invention of writing

Holocaust the deliberate murder of more than 6 million Jews before and during World War II by the Nazis

humanist a Renaissance scholar devoted to classical letters who emphasized reason and worldly concerns

humanitarian a person who promotes human welfare and social reform

Ice Age the period of time, from about 1,500,000 to about 10,000 years ago, during which much of the northern part of the Earth was covered with ice

ideograph a written symbol representing an idea, a date, a number, or a sound

imam a Muslim who leads the faithful in prayer in mosques

imperialism the policy of extending authority and control over another territory or country

Impressionism 1. a movement in modern art in which the artist tries to record momentary impressions of nature, especially the effects of light; 2. a style of musical composition designed to create moods through rich and varied harmonies

indulgence the entire or partial remission of punishment for ones sins, either in this world or in purgatory

Industrial Revolution the historical process of changing from making goods by hand to making goods by machine

interchangeable parts a system in which individual pieces of a product are made exactly the same way and can be exchanged with one another

interdict an order by the Church banning religious services in an area

Intolerable Acts a series of laws passed by the British Parliament to punish colonists in Massachusetts

invest to put money into property or into a business enterprise for income or profit

joint-stock company a type of business that raised money from a group of investors, each of whom would contribute a share of the total and then receive that share of any profits

ka the word meaning "soul" in ancient Egypt

kachina an ancestral spirit of the Pueblo Indians

karma in Hinduism, the belief that a person's actions influence the future life of the soul

kayak an Inuit canoe made of a frame entirely covered with skins except for a small opening for its paddler(s)

kiva a round, underground Pueblo ceremonial structure

knight in feudal times, a mounted warrior serving a noble

Koran the holy book of the Muslims

labyrinth a place with passageways and blind alleys so constructed as to make it difficult for a person to find the way out; a maze

laissez-faire a doctrine preventing government interference in economic affairs

laser a device that produces an intense beam of light of a very pure single color

latifundia in ancient Rome, the estates owned by patricians and worked by slaves

legend a story coming down from the past that may be at least partly true but cannot be proved

legitimacy the view that the royal families have a right to be in power

liberal a person who is willing to break with tradition and welcomes governmental activism

limited monarchy a government in which the powers of a hereditary ruler are kept within certain limits, usually by a constitution or a lawmaking body

lord in feudal times, a noble landowner

lunar based on the phases of the moon

magistrate an official who assisted consuls in the republic of Rome

Magna Carta the charter of civil liberties to which English barons asked King John to give his assent in 1215

manor the large house and surrounding lands in which a feudal lord lived

Marxism the political and economic doctrines developed by Karl Marx and Friedrich Engels

mass production the production of goods in large quantities by machines

matriarchal having to do with female leaders of families, groups, or the state

megalith a huge stone used in prehistoric monuments

mercantilism an economic system developed during the 17th and 18th centuries to increase the power and wealth of a nation by strict governmental regulation of its economy

mesa a flat-topped hill or small plateau with steep sides

messiah the person expected by the Jews to be their deliverer

microchip a tiny complex of electronic components and their connections that is produced in or on a small slice of material (i.e., silicon); a necessary component of a computer

microlith a small, triangular-shaped blade of stone used by early humans for knives and spears

migration the movement of people from one area to another with the intention of settling in the new area

militarism a policy of maintaining large military forces in a high degree of readiness for action

militia a small, often private, army

missionary a person sent to spread religious faith among unbelievers

moat a deep, wide ditch, usually filled with water, around the walls of a castle

modern humans people who are human in every way; the human race

monarchy an area, such as a country or a city-state, ruled over by a king or queen

monastery a building or group of buildings in which religious persons live and carry on their work

monotheism belief in one God

Monroe Doctrine a U.S. foreign policy that opposed the extension of European control or influence in the Western Hemisphere

mummification the art by which ancient Egyptian priests preserved dead bodies

nationalism loyalty and devotion to one's country

natural rights ones assumed to belong to every person

Navigation Acts a series of British laws restricting foreign shipping in the 18th century with its colonies

Neanderthal a presapien who lived in parts of Europe, Asia, and Africa from about 250,000 years ago to about 28,000 years ago

Neolithic Revolution changes brought about by many new ideas and inventions during the New Stone Age (8,000 to 5,000 years ago)

nepotism favoritism shown to a relative (as by giving an appointive job) on the basis of their relationship

nirvana a condition in which the soul enjoys perfect peace

nomad a person who has no fixed home but wanders from place to place in search of food and other necessities of life

nonrenewable resource one incapable of being replaced or renewed

No play a classic Japanese dance-drama having a heroic theme

nuclear energy that produced by the splitting of an atom

pariah a person, also called an untouchable, excluded from the caste system of India

Parliament the assembly that makes up the lawmaking branch of the British government

pasteurization the heating of food (most commonly milk) to preserve it

patriarch a bishop in the Orthodox Church

patrician a member of one of the original citizen families of ancient Rome

patron a wealthy or influential supporter of the arts

Pax Romana a period of peace in the Roman Empire, beginning in 27 B.C. and lasting 200 years

peaceful coexistence living together in peace rather than in constant hostility

peasant a small farmer or farm laborer

peninsulare a Latin-American colonist who had been born in Spain or Portugal

Petition of Right a document created by the British Parliament declaring the fundamental rights of the people

perestroika attempts at restructuring the Soviet economy under Gorbachev to allow free enterprise

phalanx in ancient warfare, a body of heavily armed foot soldiers carrying lances and fighting in close ranks

pharaoh a ruler of ancient Egypt

philosopher a person who seeks truth and wisdom

pilgrimage a journey to a holy place made as an act of devotion

plantation a large farm worked by resident labor

plebeian a working-class citizen in ancient Rome

polis an ancient Greek city-state

polytheism a belief in many gods

pope top leader in the Roman Catholic Church

potlatch a ceremonial feast of Northwest Coast Indians in which the host and guests distribute gifts lavishly

praetor a magistrate in ancient Rome who presided over trials in the courts

prehistoric period the extent of time before the invention of writing

presapien a creature, now extinct, similar to but essentially different from a modern person

priest a man who has the authority to conduct religious rituals

priestess a woman who has the authority to conduct religious rituals

primary source written information or artifacts created by a person who witnessed an event firsthand

profit the gain after all the expenses are subtracted from the total amount received

prophet a person who brings messages from God to other people

Protestant during the Reformation, a person who challenged or rejected the authority of the Roman Catholic Church

pueblo   a Spanish word for town

purgatory   in the teachings of the Roman Catholic Church, an intermediate state after death in which the souls of those who die in God's grace are purified by suffering

quaestor   a magistrate in ancient Rome who handled such matters as censuses and property tax assessments

ratification   to approve something in a formal manner

Realism   in literature and art, the representation of things as they are in life

Reformation   the movement for certain changes in the Roman Catholic Church that began in Europe and led to the formation of the various Protestant churches

reincarnation   rebirth of the soul in another person or in an animal

Renaissance   the great rebirth of interest in learning and the arts in Europe at the end of the Middle Ages

reparations   money paid in compensation for war damages

republic   a government in which supreme power is held by its citizens and is exercised by representatives elected by and responsible to the voters

reservation   a tract of land set aside by the U.S. government for use by Native Americans

Restoration   the period of English history (1660–1685) during which Charles II ruled

resurrection   the act of rising to life from the dead

revolution   the overthrow of one government and the substitution with another

Romantic   an artistic style characterized chiefly by an emphasis on the imagination and emotions and an appreciation of nature

sachem   one of 50 men who governed the Iroquois League of Six Nations

saga   a story of heroic deeds

samurai   the warrior aristocracy of Japan during the feudal period

satellite nation   a country dominated by another, more powerful country

satrap   the governor of a province in ancient Persia

scapegoat   a person bearing the blame for others

scientific method   a way of studying nature that uses experiments, observations, and mathematics to prove scientific theories

secede   to withdraw formally from an organized body

secondary source   information and texts used by historians to interpret, analyze, and understand the past

sectionalism   extreme devotion to the interests of one part or region of the country

separation of powers   the division of a government into three branches: legislative, executive, and judicial

sepoy   a native of India employed there as a soldier by a European power

seppuku   a type of suicide sometimes practiced by the Japanese samurai

serf   in feudal times, a peasant laborer bound to the land and subject to the will of the landowner

shaman   an Inuit priest who uses magic to cure the sick and control events

shogun   one of a line of military governors ruling Japan beginning in 1192

socialism   a political and economic system of social organization based on government ownership, management, and control of the essential means of production and distribution

sociology   the study of society, social institutions, or social relationships

solar energy   that obtained from the sun's rays

solar system   the sun and the planets, comets, and meteors that revolve around it

strike   the act of a body of workers in quitting work together in order to force concessions from their employer

sultan   a leader of the Ottoman Turks

superpower   one of the most powerful nations in the world

swastika   a cross with the ends of the arms extended clockwise at right angles, used as the emblem of the Nazi party

tariff   a tax on imported goods

terrorism   use of violence or threat of violence to instill fear for political purposes

totalitarian   a political system by which the government has total control over all institutions in society, including the press and religions

tournament   a contest of skill and courage between armored knights with blunted lances or swords

traditional economy   an economy in which ways of producing goods are continued without change for generations

tribune   a Roman official with the function of protecting the plebeians from arbitrary action by patrician magistrates

typhoon   a tropical cyclone occurring in the Pacific Ocean

Upanishads   a collection of writings on the nature of the universe and the meaning of life composed by the Aryans

utopian   a person proposing ideal social and political communities

vaccination   taking a vaccine as a protection against diseases

vassal   in feudal times, a person who placed himself under the protection of another to whom he swore allegiance as his lord

Vedas   books in which the Aryans in India set down their prayers, songs, and religious formulas

vernacular   spoken

veto   to refuse approval and so prevent enactment

zero population growth (ZPG)   the situation that occurs when the birth rate is equal to the death rate

ziggurat   multilevel tower that served as a temple

INTERNET SOURCES IN WORLD HISTORY

The Internet offers a wealth of information on the topics covered in this book. On the following two pages, you will find a guide to search engines, sites that link you to sources of information, primary sources, and visuals, and suggested sites in which to research selected topics from each unit of *Essential World History*.

Search Engines

www.google.com
www.teoma.com
www.dogpile.com
www.refdesk.com/newsrch.html

World/Global History Sites

Readings About the World: A Reader for the Study of World Civilizations
http://www.wsu.edu:8080/~wldciv/world_civ_reader/

The Internet Medieval Sourcebook
http://www.fordham.edu/halsall/sbook.html

The Stanford Program on International and Cross-Cultural Education
http://spice.stanford.edu/

World Religions
http://www.beliefnet.com/

Women in World History
http://www.womeninworldhistory.com/

Several Online Encyclopedias

Wikipedia
http://en.wikipedia.org/wiki/Main_Page

Encyclopaedia Britannica Online
http://www.eb.com/

MSN Encarta
http://encarta.msn.com/

Columbia Encyclopedia
http://www.bartleby.com/65/

Suggested Web Sites for Researching Topics Found in Essential World History

Unit I

Anthropology: Site gives articles on basic topics in physical and cultural anthropology.
http://anthro.palomar.edu/tutorials/physical.htm

Sociology: Site offers a menu of links to sources dealing with sociology—institutions, directories of resources, research centers, databases, and archives.
http://socserv2.mcmaster.ca/w3virtsoclib/

Geography: Site offers links to such useful things as world atlas and maps (including blank maps), geography terms, population country information, etc.
http://geography.about.com/

Economics: Site offers links to a variety of topics and services.
http://economics.about.com/

Political Science: Site offers links to a variety of topics and services.
http://www.lib.umich.edu/govdocs/polisci.html

Presapiens: Site gives discussion of presapiens with links to related subjects.
http://www.mnh.si.edu/anthro/humanorigins/ha/primate.html

Neanderthals: Site gives a variety of information on Neanderthals. Good visuals.
http://www.d.umn.edu/cla/faculty/troufs/anth1602/pcneand.html

Stone Age: Site gives a variety of information on Stone Age.
http://www.creswell-crags.org.uk/virtuallytheiceage/Stone%20Age%20People/index.html

Unit II

Ancient Civilizations: *Archaeology Magazine*: Site covers a variety of topics, including new archaeological findings.
http://www.archaeology.org/

Christianity: Site gives comprehensive history of early Christianity.
http://www.wsu.edu:8080/~dee/CHRIST/CHRIST.HTM

Unit III

Middle Ages: Site gives information about life and social conditions in the middle ages. Good visuals.
http://www.mnsu.edu/emuseum/history/middleages/

Islam: Site gives a categorized listing of links to aspects of the history of Islam; also includes translations of source texts and articles.
http://www.fordham.edu/halsall/islam/islamsbook.html

Unit IV

African Civilizations: Site gives comprehensive history of early African civilizations.
http://www.wsu.edu:8080/~dee/CIVAFRCA/IRONAGE.HTM

Pre-Columbian American Civilizations: Site gives information on early American civilizations.
http://home.cfl.rr.com/crossland/AncientCivilizations/Civilizations_of_the_Americas/civilizations_of_the_americas.html

European Renaissance: Site gives information on exploration and trade.
http://www.learner.org/exhibits/renaissance/

The Reformation: Site is a guide to Internet information on the Reformation.
http://www.educ.msu.edu/homepages/laurence/reformation/

Unit V
The American Revolution: Site gives links to time lines and primary sources.
http://www.historyplace.com/unitedstates/revolution/

French Revolution: Site gives links to time lines, documents, images, etc.
http://chnm.gmu.edu/revolution/

Industrial Revolution: Gives links to information on the industrial revolution and to protest movements of the time.
http://www.schoolshistory.org.uk/IndustrialRevolution/

Imperialism: Site discusses European and American imperialism.
http://www.smplanet.com/imperialism/toc.html

Unit VI
World War I: Site gives links to information on various aspects of WWI.
http://www.firstworldwar.com/

World War II: Site gives links to documents concerning WWII in Europe and Asia.
http://www.fordham.edu/halsall/mod/modsbook45.html

Unit VII
Cold War and Aftermath (through the Clinton administration): Site gives time line with links to visuals and text.
http://history.acusd.edu/gen/20th/coldwar0.html

Human Rights: Site gives explanatory text, and links to documents, organizations and resources.
http://www.hrweb.org/resource.html

INDEX

ACKNOWLEDGMENTS

We gratefully acknowledge the permission of the following persons and organizations to reproduce the prints, photographs, and literary excerpts in this book. Each bold number refers to the page number where the image appears in this book.

PHOTO CREDITS

6: Univ. of Pennsylvania Museum of Art and Archaeology/AP Photo **8:** Tim Sloan/AFP/Getty Images **12:** Perry Morse **16:** Rob Crandall/The Image Works **19:** American Museum of Natural History **32:** The Granger Collection **37:** Corbis/Bettmann **40:** North Wind Picture Archives **44:** Corbis/Bettmann **45:** Corbis/Bettmann **49:** Laurie Platt Winfrey/Orleans Musée Historique et Archéologique **53:** Macduff Everton/The Image Works **58:** Bridgeman-Giraudon/Art Resource **60:** Corbis/Bettmann **67:** Laurie Platt Winfrey/The Avery Brundage Collection/Asian Art Museum of San Francisco **71:** North Wind **73:** North Wind **74:** Photo Researchers/Omikron **83:** Leonard Von Matt/ Photo Researchers **85:** Corbis/Bettmann **86:** Metropolitan Museum of Art, Louisa Eldridge McBurny Gift Fund, 1953 **90:** The British Museum **91:** North Wind **93:** The Granger Collection **97:** Corbis/Bettmann **98:** The Granger Collection **101:** Corbis/Bettmann **105:** Corbis/Bettmann **112:** Corbis/Bettmann **115:** Corbis/Bettmann **119:** Corbis/ Bettmann **121:** Ray Gardner/The British Museum **125:** Metropolitan Museum of Art, Bequest of Mary Clark Thompson, 1926 **126:** The Granger Collection **141:** Corbis/ Bettmann **145:** Corbis/Bettmann **146 (both):** Museum of Cultural History/University of Oslo, Norway **147:** Corbis/Bettmann **152:** New College, Oxford University, England **155:** David Frazier/The Image Works **160:** Corbis/Bettmann **163:** The Granger Collection **164:** Library of Congress **168:** The Granger Collection **171:** The British Museum **174:** Marcel & Eva Malherbe/The Image Works **175:** Corbis/Bettmann **178:** Ann Ronan Picture Library/HIP/The Image Works **182:** The Granger Collection **185:** Corbis/Bettmann **188:** The Metropolitan Museum of Art, The Cora Timken Burnett collection of Persian miniatures and other Persian art objects. Bequest of Cora Timken Burnett, 1957 **194:** The Granger Collection **195:** Library of Congress **199:** The Granger Collection **205:** The Granger Collection **215:** Werner Forman Archive/The Image Works **220:** North Wind **221:** American Museum of Natural History **223:** Lawrence Ausburn **227:** The Granger Collection **228:** North Wind **231:** North Wind **235:** Corbis/Bettmann **239:** North Wind **245:** Library of Congress **247:** Paolo Koch/Photo Researchers **249:** Culver Pictures **252:** The Granger Collection **255:** Corbis/Bettmann **257:** Ben Mangor/SuperStock **259:** Corbis/Bettmann **261:** Victoria and Albert Museum/Art Resource **266:** Corbis/Bettmann **267:** Zoriah/The Image Works **276:** The Granger Collection **280 (both):** Corbis Bettmann **281:** The Granger Collection **283:** The Granger Collection **284:** North Wind **287:** Corbis/Bettmann **288:** Corbis/Bettmann **298:** Corbis/Bettmann **301:** North Wind **303:** Corbis/Bettmann **305:** Corbis/Bettmann **308 (both):** Corbis/Bettmann **309:** Corbis/Bettmann **310:** Corbis/Bettmann **314:** Charles Marden Fitch/FPG International/ Getty Images **321:** Corbis/Bettmann **323:** Mary Evans Picture Library/The Image Works **327:** Library of Congress **333:** Corbis/Bettmann **334:** Library of Congress **336:** Topham/ The Image Works **339:** Roger-Viollet/Topham/The Image Works **343:** Corbis/Bettmann **346:** Corbis/Bettmann **349:** Roger-Viollet/Topham/The Image Works **359:** The Granger Collection **360:** Library of Congress **361:** Corbis/Bettmann **362:** Corbis/Bettmann **363:** Corbis/Bettmann **364:** The Granger Collection **367:** Corbis/Bettmann **369:** Corbis/ Bettmann **371:** Corbis/Bettmann **374:** Corbis/Bettmann **375:** Corbis/Bettmann **377:** Corbis/Bettmann **378 (left):** Library of Congress **378 (right):** Corbis/Bettmann **380 (top, left):** The Granger Collection **380 (top, right and both on bottom):** Corbis/Bettmann **390:** Corbis/Bettmann **395:** Corbis/Bettmann **399:** North Wind **403:** Corbis/Bettmann

LITERARY SOURCES